UNITY AND DIVERSITY
IN THE GOSPELS AND PAUL

Society of Biblical Literature

Early Christianity and Its Literature

Gail R. O'Day, General Editor

Editorial Board

Number 7

UNITY AND DIVERSITY IN THE GOSPELS AND PAUL
Essays in Honor of Frank J. Matera

UNITY AND DIVERSITY
IN THE GOSPELS AND PAUL

ESSAYS IN HONOR OF FRANK J. MATERA

Edited by

Christopher W. Skinner

and

Kelly R. Iverson

Society of Biblical Literature
Atlanta

UNITY AND DIVERSITY IN THE GOSPELS AND PAUL
Essays in Honor of Frank J. Matera

Copyright © 2012 by the Society of Biblical Literature

Library of Congress Cataloging-in-Publication Data

Unity and diversity in the Gospels and Paul : essays in honor of Frank J. Matera / edited by Christopher W. Skinner and Kelly R. Iverson.
    p. cm. — (Early Christianity and its literature ; number 7)
    ISBN 978-1-58983-681-5 (paper binding : alk. paper) — ISBN 978-1-58983-683-9 (electronic format) (print)
    1. Bible. N.T. Gospels—Criticism, interpretation, etc. 2. Bible. N.T. Epistles—Criticism, interpretation, etc. I. Skinner, Christopher W. II. Iverson, Kelly R. III. Matera, Frank J. IV. Series: Early Christianity and its literature ; no. 7.
    BS2555.52.U558 2012
    225.6—dc23   2012024839

Printed on acid-free, recycled paper conforming to
ANSI/NISO Z39.48-1992 (R1997) and ISO 9706:1994
standards for paper permanence.

∞

Contents

Foreword

It takes a tremendous amount of cooperation, enthusiasm, and, most importantly, secrecy, to bring a project like this to fruition. We would like to express our appreciation to a number of individuals who displayed all three on the way to helping us produce this volume in honor of Frank Matera. First, of course, had it not been for an outstanding group of contributors, there would be no book. Everyone worked with a sensitivity to the looming deadline and with an excitement that is not common to the production of an academic monograph. To each of our contributors, we owe a debt of gratitude. Second, we must thank Msgr. Kevin Irwin, former dean of the School of Theology and Religious Studies at the Catholic University of America, as well as his successor, Rev. Mark Morozowich, for their invaluable assistance in helping us procure information necessary for the completion of the volume. Third, we want to express our appreciation to Dr. Gail O'Day and the editorial board of the Society of Biblical Literature Early Christianity and Its Literature series for enthusiastically accepting our proposal to include this book in the series. A special thanks goes to Susan Ryberg, the references and extended services librarian at Mount Olive College (North Carolina) for her help in tracking down numerous obscure monographs and other bibliographic information useful for the completion of the book. As always, we owe a tremendous debt of gratitude to our families, particularly our wives, Tara and Kim, for their patience as we spent extra time in libraries, offices, and in front of computer screens.

Chris and Kelly

Preface

In a career that spans nearly forty-five years as a professor, scholar, and priest, Frank Matera has demonstrated a unique ability to interpret and communicate the diverse voices at work within the writings of the New Testament. In addition to serving as an acknowledgment of his seventieth birthday, this volume is a celebration of his work and a tribute to his impact as both a professor with keen pastoral sensitivities, and a scholar with an admirable breadth of expertise. During his productive career, Frank has published major commentaries on the writings of Paul (Galatians, 2 Corinthians, Romans), three volumes devoted to the Synoptic Gospels, and significant works on New Testament theology, ethics, and homiletics. In all of these endeavors Frank has displayed a range of scholarly proficiency and has become an acknowledged authority.

The unifying theme of this volume—the diverse unity of New Testament theology—has been a particularly important emphasis in Frank's teaching and writing. We have chosen this theme as a launching point for the essays in this book. In the introduction to his massive *New Testament Theology*, Frank makes this underlying assumption in his thinking explicit to the reader: "there is a rich diversity in the way the New Testament writers express the experience of salvation the first believers enjoyed because of God's salvific work in Christ," while there is also "an underlying unity in the diverse theologies of the New Testament."[1] The contributors to this volume—Frank Matera's colleagues, former students, and friends—have come together to reflect on and interact with this important theme in his scholarly writings, as well as other prominent foci that emerge from his academic publications.

After a series of reflections from Francis T. Gignac, Frank's longtime colleague at Catholic University, the essays that follow are divided into

---

1. Frank J. Matera, *New Testament Theology: Exploring Diversity and Unity* (Louisville: Westminster John Knox, 2007), xxviii.

two areas: studies in the New Testament narratives and studies in the Letters of Paul. Admittedly, this division is somewhat artificial, as many of the essays attempt to draw connections between both groups of writings. These essays attempt to interact in detail with contemporary scholarship vis-à-vis the scholarly publications of Frank Matera.

The first section of this book contains seven essays. In the first essay, Kelly R. Iverson engages the current debate over the supposed anti-Paulinisms in Matthew's Gospel, with a view to evaluating the various arguments set forward by David Sim. In the next essay, Francis J. Moloney analyzes the Matthean use of δικαιοσύνη, a term otherwise known for its prominence in the Pauline corpus. The next three studies focus on the Gospel of Mark; Jack Dean Kingsbury, John R. Donahue, and Paul J. Achtemeier explore Markan Christology, social ethics, and soteriology, respectively. Then, in an essay devoted to Luke-Acts, William J. Kurz asks how the mission of God's servant in Isaiah influences the portrayal of Paul in Acts, specifically Paul's witness to the one living God. In the final essay of the first section, John Paul Meier examines the so-called parable of the Wicked Tenants in order to shed light on the potential relationship between the Synoptic Gospels and the extracanonical Gospel of Thomas.

The second section of the book also consists of seven essays. Matthew G. Whitlock begins the section by attempting to construct a bridge from Acts to Paul, with an emphasis on how modern literary studies help to illuminate the use of different nonauthorial voices in each text. Michael J. Gorman follows by locating elements of cruciform teaching in the Synoptic tradition—chiefly represented by the Gospel of Mark—and compares them to the Pauline understanding of cruciform spirituality. The next four essays are devoted to theological themes in Paul's Letters. A. Andrew Das raises questions about the legitimacy of foisting the law upon the Gentiles, filtering his discussion through the grid of Gal 3:10. Luke Timothy Johnson offers a fresh examination of the σῶμα concept in Paul, with special attention to the Corinthian correspondence. Sherri Brown visits the notoriously difficult issue of the πίστις Χριστοῦ formulation in the context of Paul's understanding of salvation history. Raymond F. Collins explores the transformation of a Pauline motif—the early expectation of Jesus' παρουσία ("coming" or "presence") alongside Paul's later emphasis on Jesus' ἐπιφάνεια ("appearance"). In the book's final essay, Christopher W. Skinner compares Pauline and Johannine views on virtue as a means to the end of illuminating foundational elements of their ethical teachings.

Finally, we want to offer a special word to Frank: It is our hope that this volume will communicate to you the depth of our appreciation for what you have imparted to so many. We also hope that it will, in some small measure, return to you some of the benefits we have gained from hearing your lectures, reading your books, and sharing in different kinds of enlightening and challenging conversations with you over the years. Congratulations on your stellar career and forthcoming retirement.

Chris and Kelly (on behalf of all the contributors)
October 2011

Cursus Vitae of the Reverend Doctor
Frank J. Matera

1942	Born in New Britain, Connecticut
1960	Graduated from St. Thomas Aquinas High School (New Britain, Connecticut)
1964	Earned BA from St. Bernard Seminary (Rochester, New York)
1968	Earned MA in Theology from the University of Louvain (Louvain, Belgium)
1968	Ordained in Louvain to the Archdiocese of Hartford, Connecticut
1968	Appointed Temporary Assistant Pastor at St. Vincent DePaul Parish (East Haven, Connecticut)
1968–1970	Taught Theology at the Diocesan Sisters College (Madison, Connecticut)
1968–1972	Served as Assistant Pastor of St. Margaret Parish (Madison, Connecticut)
1971–1972	Taught Christian Ethics at St. Joseph College (Hartford, Connecticut)
1972–1978	Served as Copastor of St. Rose Parish (Meriden, Connecticut)
1981	Earned PhD from Union Theological Seminary (Richmond, Virginia)
1981	Appointed Assistant Pastor of St. Joseph Parish (New Haven, Connecticut)
1982	Appointed to the full-time faculty of St. John's Seminary (Brighton, Massachusetts)
1987	Appointed Assistant Pastor of St. Thomas Parish (Southington, Connecticut)
1987–1993	Served as Associate Editor of *Catholic Biblical Quarterly*

1988	Appointed Assistant Professor of New Testament Studies at Catholic University of America (Washington, D.C.)
1990–Present	Served as Weekend Assistant at Holy Family Parish (Davidsonville, Maryland)
1990	Promoted to Associate Professor of New Testament at Catholic University of America (Washington, D.C.)
1994	Served as Delegate of the Roman Catholic Church to the Meeting of Faith and Order (Santiago, Spain)
1994	Promoted to Ordinary Professor of New Testament at Catholic University of America (Washington, D.C.)
1994–1996	Served as Consulter for the Catholic Biblical Association of America
1994–2000	Served as Member of the Plenary Commission of Faith and Order
1995–1998	Served as Associate Chair of the Department of Theology at Catholic University of America (Washington, D.C.)
1998–2001	Served as Chair of the Department of Theology at Catholic University of America (Washington, D.C.)
2003	Served as Vice-President of the Catholic Biblical Association of America
2003–2004	Served as President of the Catholic Biblical Association of America
2004	Appointed the Andrews-Kelly-Ryan Professor of Biblical Studies at Catholic University of America (Washington, D.C.)
2009	Awarded Doctor of Divinity *honoris causa* from St. Mary's Seminary and University (Baltimore, Maryland)
2011	Received the Catholic University of America Award for Overall Teaching Excellence
2012	Retirement from Catholic University of America

Publications
Compiled by Christopher W. Skinner and Kelly R. Iverson

Listed below are the publications of Frank Matera that have appeared in print as of December 2011. The list includes 12 books (three of which have been translated into Portuguese, Spanish, or Italian); 65 articles, essays, or chapters; and 75 book reviews. This list is a testament to the breadth of Fr. Matera's research interests and expertise.

1968

"Interpreting Mark—Some Recent Theories of Redaction Criticism." *LS* 2 (1968): 113–31.

1982

The Kingship of Jesus: Composition Theology in Mark 15. SBLDS 66. Chico, Calif.: Scholars Press, 1982.

Review of Louis Marin, *The Semiotics of the Passion Narrative: Topics and Figures. CBQ* 44 (1982): 516–17.

Review of John Riches, *Jesus and the Transformation of Judaism. Int* 36 (1982): 91–92.

1983

Review of Josef Ernst, *Das Evangelium nach Markus. CBQ* 45 (1983): 686–87.

Review of August Strobel, *Die Stunde der Wahrheit: Untersuchungen zum Strafverfahren gegen Jesus. JBL* 102 (1983): 336–38.

1984

"Matthew 27:11–24." *Int* 38 (1984): 55–59.

Review of Ernest Best, *Following Jesus: Discipleship in the Gospel of Mark. Int* 38 (1984): 93–94.

Review of Klyne Snodgrass, *The Parable of the Wicked Tenants. CBQ* 46 (1984): 592–93.

1985

"Gospel." Pages 354–55 in *HBD.*

"Incarnation." Page 420 in *HBD.*

"Reconciliation." Page 856 in *HBD.*

"Repentance." Pages 861–62 in *HBD.*

"Servant." Pages 929–30 in *HBD.*

"The Death of Jesus According to Luke: A Question of Sources." *CBQ* 47 (1985): 469–85.

"Preaching Paul." *Chicago Studies* 24 (1985): 323–38.

Review of Cilliers Breytenbach, *Nachfolge und Zukunftserwartung nach Markus: Eine methodenkritische Studie. CBQ* 47 (1985): 343–44.

Review of Barnbas Lindars, *Jesus Son of Man: A Fresh Examination of the Son of Man Sayings in the Gospels. CBQ* 47 (1985): 732–33.

Review of Douglas J. Moo, *The Old Testament in the Gospel Passion Narratives. JBL* 104 (1985): 542–44.

Review of Christopher Tuckett, ed., *The Messianic Secret*; Paul D. Hanson, ed., *Visionaries and Their Apocalypses*; Graham Stanton, ed., *The Interpretation of Matthew*; and James L. Crenshaw, ed., *Theodicy in the Old Testament. Int* 39 (1985): 314–16.

1986

Passion Narratives and Gospel Theologies: Interpreting the Synoptics through Their Passion Stories. New York: Paulist Press, 1986. Repr., Eugene, Ore.: Wipf & Stock, 2001.

Review of Walter Schmithals, *Einleitung in die drei ersten Evangelien. CBQ* 48 (1986): 758–59.

1987

What Are They Saying about Mark? New York: Paulist Press, 1987. Repr., Eugene, Ore.: Wipf & Stock, 2002.

"Acts 10:34–43." *Int* 41 (1987): 62–66.

"The Passion According to Matthew, Part One: Jesus Unleashes the Passion." *Clergy Review* 62 (1987): 93–97.

"The Passion According to Matthew, Part Two: Jesus Suffers the Passion." *Priests and People* [formerly *Clergy Review*] 1 (1987): 13–17.

"The Plot of Matthew's Gospel." *CBQ* 49 (1987): 233–53.

Review of Hans F. Bayer, *Jesus' Predictions of Vindication and Resurrection. CBQ* 49 (1987): 661–62.

Review of Xavier Leon-Dufour, *Life and Death in the New Testament: The Teachings of Jesus and Paul. Cross Currents* 37 (1987): 328–30.

Review of Donald Senior, C.P., *The Passion of Jesus in the Gospel of Matthew. JBL* 106 (1987): 543–44.

Review of Walter Wink, *Unmasking the Powers: The Invisible Forces that Determine Human Existence. Int* 41 (1987): 210–11.

1988

"The Culmination of Paul's Argument to the Galatians: Gal. 5.1–6.17."
JSNT 32 (1988): 79–91.

"'On Behalf of Others,' 'Cleansing,' and 'Return': Johannine Images for
Jesus' Death." *LS* 13 (1988): 161–78.

"The Prologue as the Interpretative Key to Mark's Gospel." *JSNT* 34
(1988): 3–20.

"II Peter, Jude." Pages 353–57 in *The Books of the Bible: The Apocrypha
and the New Testament*. Edited by Bernard W. Anderson. Vol. 2 of *The
Books of the Bible*. New York: Scribner's, 1988.

Review of Reinhard Feldmeier, *Die Krisis des Gottessohnes: Die Gethsema-
neerzählung als Schlüssel der Markuspassion*. *CBQ* 50 (1988): 315–16.

Review of C. S. Mann, *Mark: A New Translation with Introduction and
Commentary*. *Int* 42 (1988): 193–96.

Review of Bernard Orchard, *The Order of the Synoptics: Why Three Synoptic Gospels? CBQ* 50 (1988): 539–40.

1989

"The Ethics of the Kingdom in the Gospel of Matthew." *Listening: Journal
of Religion and Culture* 24 (1989): 241–50.

"His Blood Be on Us and Our Children." *The Bible Today* 27 (1989): 345–
50.

"The Incomprehension of the Disciples and Peter's Confession (Mark
6,14–8,30)." *Bib* 70 (1989): 153–72.

"Luke 22,66–71: Jesus before the *Presbyterion*." *ETL* 65 (1989): 43–59.
Repr. pages 517–33 in *L'Évangile de Luc/The Gospel of Luke*. Edited by
F. Neirynck. BETL 32. Leuven: Peeters, 1989.

"Luke 23,1–25: Jesus before Pilate, Herod, and Israel." Pages 535–51 in
L'Évangile de Luc/The Gospel of Luke. Edited by F. Neirynck. BETL
32. Leuven: Peeters, 1989.

"Mystery and Humanity: The Jesus of Mark." *Church* 5 (1989): 20–24.

"Something to Say: John 20:1–18." *Int* 43 (1989): 402–6.

Review of John Dominic Crossan, *The Cross That Spoke: The Origins of the
Passion Narrative*. *Worship* 63 (1989): 269–70.

Review of James Luther Mays, ed., *Harper's Bible Commentary*. *ThTo* 46
(1989): 212–14.

Review of Ched Myers, *Binding the Strong Man: A Political Reading of Mark's Story of Jesus. ThTo* 46 (1989): 354.

Review of Jerome H. Neyrey, *An Ideology of Revolt: John's Christology in Social-Science Perspective*; and David Rensberger, *Johannine Faith and Liberating Community. TS* 50 (1989): 791–93.

Review of Gerard Rosse, *The Cry of Jesus on the Cross: A Biblical and Theological Study. CBQ* 51 (1989): 381–82.

1990

"Jesus before Annas: John 18, 13–14.19–24." *ETL* 66 (1990): 38–55.

"Jesus in the Gospel according to Mark: The Crucified Messiah." *Priests and People* 4 (1990): 87–90.

"Responsibility for the Death of Jesus according to the Acts of the Apostles." *JSNT* 39 (1990): 77–93.

Review of William A. Beardslee et al., eds., *Biblical Preaching on the Death of Jesus. ThTo* 47 (1990): 226.

Review of Joel B. Green, *The Death of Jesus: Tradition and Interpretation in the Passion Narrative. Int* 44 (1990): 206–7.

Review of Bertram L. Melbourne, *Slow to Understand: The Disciples in Synoptic Perspective. CBQ* 52 (1990): 759–60.

1991

"The Trial of Jesus: Problems and Proposals." *Int* 45 (1991): 5–16.

Review of William S. Babcock, ed., *Paul and the Legacies of Paul. Catholic Historical Review* 77 (1991): 492–93.

Review of Donald Senior, ed., *The Catholic Study Bible. National Catholic Reporter* (1990): 27.

Review of Mary Ann Tolbert, *Sowing the Gospel: Mark's World in Literary-Historical Perspective. Int* 45 (1991): 186–87.

1992

Galatians. SP 9. Collegeville, Minn.: Glazier, 1992. Repr. in paperback with an updated bibliography in 2007.

"Christ, Death of." *ABD* 1:923–25.

Review of John S. Kloppenborg, *Q-Thomas Reader. CBQ* 54 (1992): 394–95.

Review of Gerd Theissen, *The Gospels in Context: Social and Political History in the Synoptic Tradition*. *TS* 53 (1992): 548–50.

1993

"The Death of Jesus and the Cross in Paul's Letter to the Galatians." *LS* 18 (1993): 283–96.

"'He Saved Others: He Cannot Save Himself': A Literary-Critical Perspective on the Markan Miracles." *Int* 47 (1993): 15–26.

"Jesus' Journey to Jerusalem (Luke 9.51–19.46): A Conflict with Israel." *JSNT* 51 (1993): 57–77.

"Jesus through the Gospels." *The Living Light* 30 (1993): 51–60.

Review of Robert W. Herron Jr., *Mark's Account of Peter's Denial of Jesus: A History of Its Interpretation*. *CBQ* 55 (1993): 370–71.

Review of Richard N. Longenecker, *Galatians*. *JBL* 112 (1993): 730–32.

Review of Joel Marcus, *The Way of the Lord: Christological Exegesis of the Old Testament in the Gospel of Mark*. *ThTo* 50 (1993): 490–91.

1994

"Moral Exhortation: The Relation between Moral Exhortation and Doctrinal Exposition in the Letter to the Hebrews." *Toronto Journal of Theology* 10 (1994): 169–84.

Review of Raymond E. Brown, *The Death of the Messiah: From Gethsemane to the Grave*. *TS* 55 (1994): 739–41.

Review of John Paul Heil, *The Gospel of Mark as a Model for Action: A Reader-Response Commentary*. *CBQ* 56 (1994): 139–40.

1995

"The Crucified Son of God: Introducing the Gospel according to Mark." *Chicago Studies* 34 (1995): 6–16.

"Ethics for the Kingdom of God: The Gospel according to Mark." *LS* 20 (1995): 187–200.

Review of James D. G. Dunn, *The Epistle to the Galatians*. *CBQ* 57 (1995): 175–76.

Review of Jan Lambrecht, ed., *The Truth of the Gospel (Galatians 1:1–4:11.)* *LS* 20 (1995): 426–27.

Review of Wayne A. Meeks, *The Origins of Christian Morality: The First Two Centuries*. *Bible Review* 11 (1995): 13–14.

Review of Darrell J. Pursiful, *The Cultic Motif in the Spirituality of the Book of Hebrews*. *Toronto Journal of Theology* 11 (1995): 252–53.

1996

New Testament Ethics: The Legacies of Jesus and Paul. Louisville: Westminster John Knox, 1996.

"Jesus among Gentiles and Jews." *The Bible Today* 34 (1996): 148–52.

Review of Morna D. Hooker, *Not Ashamed of the Gospel: New Testament Interpretations of the Death of Christ*. LS 21 (1996): 289.

Review of Howard Clark Kee, *Who Are the People of God? Early Christian Models of Community*. TS 57 (1996): 523–25.

Review of Rudolf Schnackenburg, *Jesus in the Gospels: A Biblical Christology*. CBQ 58 (1996): 773–74.

1997

Review of Richard B. Hays, *The Moral Vision of the New Testament: Community, Cross, New Creation: A Contemporary Introduction to New Testament Ethics*. TS 58 (1997): 537–39.

Review of James M. Scott, *Paul and the Nations: The Old Testament and Jewish Background of Paul's Mission to the Nations with Special Reference to the Destination of Galatians*. CBQ 59 (1997): 398–99.

Review of Sondra Ely Wheeler, *Wealth as Peril and Obligation: The New Testament on Possessions*. Int 51 (1997): 206–8.

1998

"Preaching the Spirit in the Year of Luke." *Church* 14 (1998): 29–32.

Review of M. John Farrelly, *Faith in God through Jesus Christ: Foundational Theology II*. ThTo 55 (1998): 144.

Review of Jeffrey S. Siker, *Scripture and Ethics: Twentieth-Century Portraits*. Int 52 (1998): 106–7.

1999

Etica do Novo Testamento: os legados de Jesus e de Paulo. São Paulo: Paulus, 1999. (Portuguese translation of *New Testament Ethics.*)

New Testament Christology. Louisville: Westminster John Knox, 1999.

Review of J. Louis Martyn, *Galatians: A New Translation with Introduction and Commentary. CBQ* 61 (1999): 367–68.

Review of William C. Spohn, *Go and Do Likewise: Jesus and Ethics. TS* 60 (1999): 542–43.

2000

"Galatians and the Development of Paul's Teaching on Justification." *WW* 20 (2000): 239–48.

"Galatians in Perspective: Cutting a New Path through Old Territory." *Int* 54 (2000): 233–45.

"Galatians, Letter to the." Pages 476–78 in *Eerdmans Dictionary of the Bible.* Edited by David Noel Freedman. Grand Rapids: Eerdmans, 2000.

"Theologies of the Church in the New Testament." Pages 3–21 in *The Gift of the Church: A Textbook on Ecclesiology in Honor of Patrick Granfield, O.S.B.* Edited by Peter Phan. Collegeville, Minn.: Liturgical Press, 2000.

Review of Charles K. Barrett, Martin Hengel, and Donald Hagner, eds., *Conflicts and Challenges in Early Christianity. CBQ* 62 (2000): 586–87.

Review of Darrell L. Bock, *Blasphemy and Exaltation in Judaism and the Final Examination of Jesus: A Philological-Historical Study of the Key Jewish Themes Impacting Mark 14:61–64. CBQ* 62 (2000): 137–39.

Review of Gerd Theissen, *The Religion of the Earliest Churches: Creating a Symbolic World. TS* 61 (2000): 558–59.

2001

Strategies for Preaching Paul. Collegeville, Minn.: Liturgical Press, 2001.

"Christ Will Come Again." *The Living Light* 37 (2001): 47–55.

"Jesus and the Law according to Matthew: Fulfilling the Law through a Greater Righteousness." *The Bible Today* 39 (2001): 271–76.

2002

Coedited with A. Andrew Das. *The Forgotten God: Perspectives in Biblical Theology: Essays in Honor of Paul J. Achtemeier on the Occasion of His Seventy-Fifth Birthday*. Louisville: Westminster John Knox, 2002.

"Apostolic Suffering and Resurrection Faith: Distinguishing between Appearance and Reality (2 Cor 4,7–5,10)." Pages 387–406 in *Resurrection in the New Testament: Festschrift for Jan Lambrecht*. Edited by R. Bieringer, V. Koperski, and B. Lataire. BETL 165. Leuven: Leuven University Press, 2002.

"Don't Forget Paul: What Preachers and Teachers Should Know." *Church* 18 (2002): 11–13.

"Imitating Paul in Order to Follow Christ." *The Living Light* 38 (2002): 35–43.

And A. Andrew Das. "Introducing the Forgotten God." Pages 1–10 in *The Forgotten God: Perspectives in Biblical Theology: Essays in Honor of Paul J. Achtemeier on the Occasion of His Seventy-Fifth Birthday*. Edited by Frank J. Matera and A. Andrew Das. Louisville: Westminster John Knox, 2002.

"Preaching Romans: This Summer's Once-Every-Three-Year Opportunity." *Church* 18 (2002): 50–53.

Review of Markus N. Bockmuehl, *Jewish Law in Gentile Churches: Halakhah and the Beginning of Christian Public Ethics*. CBQ 64 (2002): 369–71.

Review of Seyoon Kim, *Paul and the New Perspective: Second Thoughts on the Origin of Paul's Gospel*. Princeton Seminary Bulletin 23 (2002): 247–48.

Review of Margaret M. Mitchell, *The Heavenly Trumpet: John Chrysostom and the Art of Pauline Interpretation*. CBQ 64 (2002): 585–87.

2003

Christologia Narrativa do Novo Testamento. Petró, Brazil: Vozes, 2003. (Portuguese translation of *New Testament Christology*.)

II Corinthians: A Commentary. NTL. Louisville: Westminster John Knox, 2003.

Strategie per Predicare Paolo: Le Letture paoline nelle domeniche del tempo ordinario Anni A—B—C. Milan: San Paolo, 2003. (Italian translation of *Strategies for Preaching Paul*.)

"The Letter of Paul to the Galatians." Pages 2079–88 in *The New Interpreter's Study Bible*. Edited by W. J. Harrelson. Nashville: Abingdon, 2003.

"Mark, Gospel According to." Pages 183–87 in vol. 9 of *New Catholic Encyclopedia*. Edited by Berard L. Marthaler. 14 vols. 2nd ed. Detroit: Gale, 2003.

"To Preach as Paul Preached." *New Theology Review* 16 (2003): 37–47.

Review of Pheme Perkins, *Abraham's Divided Children: Galatians and the Politics of Faith*. *CBQ* 65 (2003): 134–35.

2004

"Joseph Jensen, O.S.B.: A Tribute to His Life and Work on the Occasion of His Eightieth Birthday." *CBQ* 66 (2004): 513–18.

Review of William Baird, *From Jonathan Edwards to Rudolf Bultmann: History of New Testament Research*. *TS* 65 (2004): 401–2.

Review of Elliot C. Maloney, O.S.B., *Jesus' Urgent Message for Today: The Kingdom of God in Mark's Gospel*. *CBQ* 66 (2004): 660–61.

2005

Estratégias para a pregação de Paulo. São Paulo: Edições Loyala, 2005. (Portuguese translation of *Strategies for Preaching Paul*.)

"New Testament Foundations for Christian Ethics." Pages 23–39 in *Scripture as the Soul of Theology*. Edited by Edward J. Mahoney. Collegeville, Minn.: Liturgical Press, 2005.

"New Testament Theology: History, Method, and Identity." *CBQ* 67 (2005): 1–21.

"Paul and the Renewal of the Ministerial Priesthood: A Reflection on 2 Cor 2:14–7:4." *LS* 30 (2005): 49–69.

"Preaching in a Different Key: Preaching the Gospel according to Paul." *New Theology Review* 18 (2005): 52–65.

"Transcending Messianic Expectations: Mark and John." Pages 201–16 in *Transcending Boundaries: Contemporary Readings of the New Testament*. Edited by R. M. Chennattu and M. L. Coloe. Rome: LAS, 2005.

Review of Daniel J. Harrington, S.J., *The Church According to the New Testament: What the Wisdom and Witness of Early Christianity Teach Us Today*. *New Theology Review* 154 (2005): 81–82.

Review of Thomas P. Rausch, *Who Is Jesus? An Introduction to Christology*. *Int* 59 (2005): 324–25.

2006

"Christ in the Theologies of Paul and John: A Study in the Diverse Unity of New Testament Theology." *TS* 67 (2006): 237–56.

"The Future of Catholic Biblical Scholarship: Balance and Proportion." *Nova et Vetera* 4 (2006): 120–32.

Review of I. Howard Marshall, *New Testament Theology: Many Witnesses, One Gospel. Int* 60 (2006): 84–86.

Review of Jan G. van der Watt, ed., *Salvation in the New Testament: Perspectives on Soteriology. RBL.* Online: http://www.bookreviews.org/pdf/5171_5446.pdf.

2007

New Testament Theology: Exploring Diversity and Unity. Louisville: Westminster John Knox, 2007.

"Biblical Authority and the Scandal of the Incarnation." Pages 98–105 in *Engaging Biblical Authority: Perspectives on the Bible as Scripture.* Edited by William P. Brown. Louisville: Westminster John Knox, 2007.

"Ethics in the New Testament." Pages 328–38 in vol. 2 of *The New Interpreter's Dictionary of the Bible.* Edited by Katharine Doob Sakenfeld. 5 vols. Nashville: Abingdon, 2007.

Review of David E. Aune, ed., *Rereading Paul Together: Protestant and Catholic Perspectives on Justification. Catholic Historical Review* 93 (2007): 871–72.

Review of William S. Campbell, *Paul and the Creation of Christian Identity. CBQ* 69 (2007): 812–13.

Review of James H. Charlesworth, ed., *Resurrection: The Origin and Future of a Biblical Doctrine. CBQ* 69 (2007): 185–86.

Review of Simon Gathercole, *The Pre-existent Son: Recovering the Christologies of Matthew, Mark, and Luke. RBL.* Online: http://www.bookreviews.org/pdf/5607_5904.pdf.

2008

Estrategias para predicar a Pablo: Las lecturas de san Pablo en los domingos del tiempo ordinario Circlos A- B- C. Riobamba, Argentina: San Pablo, 2008. (Spanish translation of *Strategies for Preaching Paul*).

"Preaching Paul's Story." *The Priest* 64 (8) (2008): 10–13.

"The Jesus of Testimony: A Convergence of History and Theology." *Nova et Vetera* 6 (2008): 491–500.

Review of Gordon D. Fee, *Pauline Christology: An Exegetical-Theological Study*. *TS* 69 (2008): 192–93.

2009

Review of Stephen Andrew Cooper, *Marius Victorinus' Commentary on Galatians: Introduction, Translation, and Notes*. *SJT* 62 (2009): 370–72.

Review of Larry R. Helyer, *The Witness of Jesus, Paul, and John: An Exploration in Biblical Theology*. *CBQ* 71 (2009): 647–48.

Review of Russell Pregeant, *Knowing Truth, Doing Good: Engaging New Testament Ethics*. *Int* 63 (2009): 206–7.

Review of Stephen H. Travis, *Christ and the Judgement of God: The Limits of Divine Retribution in New Testament Thought*. *CBQ* 71 (2009): 911–13.

Review of Calvin Roetzel, *2 Corinthians*. *RBL* 11 (2009): 412–14. Online: http://www.bookreviews.org/pdf/6204_6643.pdf .

2010

Preaching Romans: Proclaiming God's Saving Grace. Collegeville, Minn.: Liturgical Press, 2010.

Romans. Paideia. Grand Rapids: Baker Academic, 2010.

Review of Kieran J. O'Mahony, O.S.A., *Do We Still Need St. Paul? A Contemporary Reading of The Apostle*; and Geoffrey Harris, *Paul*. *Irish Theological Quarterly* 75 (2010): 326–27.

Review of Udo Schnelle, *Theology of the New Testament*. *CBQ* 72 (2010): 841–43.

2011

"Living in Newness of Life: Paul's Understanding of the Moral Life." Pages 152–68 in *Celebrating Paul: Festschrift in Honor of Jerome Murphy-O'Connor, O.P., and Joseph A. Fitzmyer, S.J.* Edited by Peter Spitaler. CBQMS 48; Washington, D.C.: Catholic Biblical Association of America, 2011.

"The Theology of the Epistle to the Hebrews." Pages 189–208 in *Reading the Epistle to the Hebrews: A Resource for Students.* Edited by Eric F. Mason and Kevin B. McCruden. SBLRBS 66. Atlanta: Society of Biblical Literature, 2011.

Review of Ben Witherington III, *The Individual Witnesses.* Vol. 1 of *The Indelible Image: The Theological and Ethical Thought World of the New Testament. Int* 65 (2011): 102.

MEDIA:

"Romans." Now You Know Media, 2009. Letters of Saint Paul. 150 minutes. Audio CD.

PROFESSIONAL LECTURES, PAPERS, AND PRESENTATIONS (1988–2011)

1. "The Prologue of Mark's Gospel." Regional Meeting of the Catholic Biblical Association of America. Corpus Christi Church. New York. October 21, 1988.
2. "Jesus before Herod." Annual Meeting of the Catholic Biblical Association of America. Syracuse. August 16, 1989.
3. "Steps on the Journey: A Biblical Basis for Covenanting." Lutheran–Anglican–Roman Catholic Conference. Annandale, Va. November 10–11, 1989.
4. "Jesus and Annas." Union Theological Seminary. Richmond, Va. February 20, 1989.
5. "The Trial of Jesus of Nazareth—Historical Problems and Theological Questions." Holy Cross Parish. Dover, Del. April 4, 1990.
6. "The Gospel Passion Narratives." Six talks. United States Air Force Chaplains. Phoenix. October 8–10, 1990.
7. "The Gospel of Mark." Holy Family Parish. Davidsonville, Md. November 14, 1990.
8. "The Gospel Passion Narratives." Six talks. United States Air Force Chaplains. Lantana, Fla. January 28–29, 1991.
9. "The Two Faces of Death: The Passion according to Mark and John." St. Rose Parish. Meriden, Conn. March 6, 1991.
10. "Reading the Gospel of Luke." Holy Family Parish. Davidsonville, Md. November 18, 1991.
11. "Our Journey with Jesus: Discipleship in Luke 9:51–19:46." Two talks to the priests of the Archdiocese of Hartford. March 23, 1992.
12. "Jesus' Journey to Jerusalem (Luke: 9:51–19:46): A Narrative Read-

ing." Annual Meeting of the Catholic Biblical Association of America. Washington, D.C. August 17, 1992.

13. "Reading the Gospel of Matthew." Holy Family Parish. Davidsonville, Md. November 16, 1992.

14. "The Ethics of Mark's Gospel." The Christian Ethics Roundtable. Wesley Theological Seminary. Washington, D.C. May 17, 1993.

15. "The Death of Christ and the Cross in Paul's Letter to the Galatians." Annual Meeting of the Society of Biblical Literature. Washington, D.C. November 22, 1993.

16. "On the Way to Santiago: A Report on the Fifth World Conference on Faith and Order." The Lutheran–Roman Catholic Lay Dialogue of Washington. Washington, D.C. December 7, 1993.

17. "The Passion and Death of Christ: Our Passover from Death to Life." Holy Family Church. Davidsonville, Md. March 6 and 23, 1994.

18. "Christ Will Come Again." Holy Family Parish. Davidsonville, Md. November 14, 1994.

19. "The Two Faces of Death." St. Margaret Parish. Madison, Conn. March 13, 1995.

20. "The Gospel of Mark." Six talks. St. Joseph College. West Hartford, Conn. June 28–29, 1995.

21. "Confessing the Faith." Four talks on the Creed. Holy Family Parish. Davidsonville, Md. October 15, 22, 29, and November 5, 1995.

22. Disclosing the Mystery: Preaching the Christmas Cycle." Priests of the Archdiocese of Hartford. St. Thomas Seminary. Bloomfield, Conn. December 11, 1995.

23. "Biblical Foundations for Ethics." Annual Alumni Meeting of the North American College. Hartford, Conn. June 25, 1996.

24. "Gospel Christology Today." Catholic Biblical School. St. Mary's Church. Newington, Conn. September 14, 1996.

25. "The Ten Commandments in the New Testament." Serra Club International. Washington, D.C. September 19, 1996.

26. "The Moral Vision of the New Testament." St. Bartholomew Parish. Bethesda, Md. October 1, 1996.

27. "Preaching a Crucified Messiah." Priests of the Archdiocese of Washington. Theological College. Washington D.C. October 21, 1996.

28. "Ethics in the New Testament." A workshop of seven talks to the Clergy of Amarillo. Amarillo, Tex. November 4–5, 1996.

29. "The Priest as Prophet." Theological College. Washington, D.C. March 17, 1997.

30. "Reading the Gospel of Mark." The Catholic Biblical School of the Archdiocese of Hartford. St. Mary's Church. Newington, Conn. September 13, 1997.
31. "The Cross and the Spirit: Reflections on the Spirit in the Theology of St. Paul." Blessed Sacrament Parish. Washington, D.C. March 15, 1998.
32. "Christ Yesterday, Today, and Tomorrow: Reflections on New Testament Christology." Theological College Alumni Association. Theological College. Washington, D.C. October 8, 1998.
33. "Narrative Christology in the Speeches of the Acts of the Apostles." Annual Meeting of the Catholic Biblical Association of America. University of Scranton. Scranton, Pa. August 8–11, 1998.
34. "The Spirit in the Theology of St. Paul." A workshop of four talks to the priests of the Archdiocese of Hartford. Holy Family Monastery. West Hartford, Conn. May 19–20, 1998.
35. "The Gospel of Mark." A one-day workshop for the Catholic Biblical School of the Archdiocese of Hartford. St. Mary's Church. Newington, Conn. September 12, 1998.
36. "New Testament Spirituality." Theological College. Washington, D.C. March 22, 1999.
37. "Justified by Grace through Faith." Martin Luther Colloquium. Lutheran Theological Seminary. Gettysburg, Pa. October 27, 1999.
38. "Christ Will Come Again: Interpreting the Second Coming." St. Bartholomew Parish. Bethesda, Md. October 17, 2000.
39. "Imitating Paul as the Imitation of Christ." Catholic University of America. Washington, D.C. June 21, 2001.
40. "To Preach as Paul Preached." St. Mary's College and Seminary. Emitsburg, Pa. October 17, 2001.
41. "Preaching Paul: Overcoming the Silence from the Pulpit." Saint Mary's Seminary and University. Baltimore. November 14, 2001.
42. "A Pauline Spirituality." St. Bartholomew Parish. Bethesda, Md. March 19, 2002.
43. "New Testament Foundations for Christian Ethics." St. Michael's College. Colchester, Vt. July 12, 2002.
44. "Second Corinthians: One or Many Letters?" Regional Meeting of the Catholic Biblical Association of America. Dominican House of Studies. Washington, D.C. January 29, 2003.
45. "Second Corinthians: One or Many Letters?" Annual Meeting of the Catholic Biblical Association of America. University of San Francisco, Calif. August 3, 2003.

46. "The Death of Christ and Our Salvation: The Letter to the Galatians and the Epistle to the Hebrews." Six lectures. Annual Scripture Seminar sponsored by the Texas Catholic Conference. Austin, Tex. October 15–16, 2003.
47. "New Testament Theology: History, Method, Identity." The Presidential Address at the Annual Meeting of the Catholic Biblical Association of America. Halifax, Nova Scotia. August 7, 2004.
48. "Christ in the Theologies of Paul and John: A Study in the Diverse Unity of New Testament Theology." Andrews-Kelly-Ryan Professorship Inaugural Lecture. Catholic University of America. Washington, D.C. November 17, 2004.
49. "Preaching in a Different Key: Preaching the Gospel according to Paul." The Marten Homiletics Lecture. St. Meinrad Seminary. St. Meinrad, Ind. October 5, 2004.
50. "Preaching Romans." A one-day workshop on preaching Romans. St. Meinrad Seminary. St. Meinrad, Ind. October 6, 2004.
51. "St. Paul and the Renewal of Our Ministry." A workshop of three lectures delivered to the priests and deacons of the Diocese of Springfield, Mass. May 18, 2004.
52. "Jerusalem: The City of the Great King." A talk sponsored by the School of Architecture. Catholic University of America. Washington, D.C. January 27, 2005.
53. "The Word of the Cross." The Paulist House of Studies. Washington, D.C. January 29, 2005.
54. "Paul and the Moral Life." The Msgr. George Denzer Lecture. Seminary of the Immaculate Conception. Huntington, N.Y. March 13, 2005.
55. "Ethics in the New Testament." A series of four talks at the Castelot Summer Scripture Institute. Plymouth, Mich. June 19–20, 2005.
56. "Preaching Paul." Four talks to the permanent deacons of the Archdiocese of Philadelphia on preaching from the Letters of St. Paul. St. Charles Seminary. Philadelphia, Pa. September 5, 2007.
57. "Paul: Theologian and Pastor." Annual Meeting of the Alumni of Theological College. Theological College. Washington, D.C. October 8, 2008.
58. "Paul's Letter to the Romans." Five lectures. University of Maynooth. Maynooth, Ireland. March 3–7, 2008.
59. "Preaching the Gospel according to Paul." Clergy Study Days for the Archdiocese of Oklahoma City. Oklahoma City, June 9–11, 2008.

60. "A Response to Stephen Westerholm." Center for Law, Philosophy and Culture. Catholic University of America. Washington, D.C. March 30, 2008.
61. "Baptism in Romans 6." Annual Meeting of the Catholic Biblical Association of America. Fordham University. New York. August 3, 2008.
62. "Reflections on Writing a New Testament Theology." Annual Meeting of the Catholic Biblical Association of America. Fordham University. New York. August 3, 2008.
63. "Reflections on Writing a New Testament Theology." Washington Theological Consortium Meeting. Virginia Theological Seminary. Alexandria, Va. October 24, 2008.
64. "Death Swallowed up in Victory: Paul's Understanding of the Resurrection of the Dead." Saints Cyril and Methodius Seminary. Orchard Lake, Mich. November 2, 2008.
65. "The Conversion of St. Paul." The Archdiocese of Harford. St. Thomas Seminary. Bloomfield, Conn. January 24, 2009.
66. "Christ in the Theology of Saint Paul." University of St. Thomas. Miami. February 20, 2009.
67. "Living in Newness of Life: Paul's Understanding of the Moral Life." Villanova University. Philadelphia. March 18, 2009.
68. "Introducing Paul the Theologian." School of Theology and Religious Studies Conference on the Year of Paul. Catholic University of America. Washington, D.C. March 20, 2009.
69. "Paul's Understanding of the Resurrection of the Dead." The Archdiocese of Baltimore. Basilica of the Assumption. Baltimore. May 18, 2009.
70. "Renewing New Testament Theology." Annual Meeting of the Society of Biblical Literature." New Orleans. November 21, 2009.
71. "Christ in the Theology of Saint Paul." Marie Joseph Lagrange Biblical Conference. Fulton Sheen House of Formation. Chillum, Md. February 4, 2010.
72. "Paul's Letter to the Galatians." A series of five talks. Georgetown Scriptural Institute. Georgetown University. Washington, D.C. June 2010.
73. "Paul's Experience of God's Saving Grace." Annual Meeting of the Catholic Biblical Association of America. Loyola Marymount University. Los Angeles. August 1, 2010.
74. "A Response to Michael Gorman on Justification by Faith." Washington Adventist University. Takoma Park, Md. March 18, 2011.

75. "Paul's Letter to the Romans." A workshop of four talks on Romans to the Clergy of Richmond, Newport News, and Roanoke, Va. May 10–12, 2011.
76. "The Passion and Death of Jesus." Two talks. Holy Family Parish. Davidsonville, Md. March 22 and 29, 2011.
77. "A Pauline Theology of God's Saving Grace." Annual Meeting of the Catholic Biblical Association of America. Assumption College. Worcester, Mass. August 7, 2011.
78. "The Use of Scripture in the New Evangelization: Reclaiming the Narratives." Conference on the New Evangelization sponsored by the USCC and the School of Religious Studies. Washington Court Hotel. Washington, D.C. September 17, 2011.
79. "The Gospel of Matthew: Its Meaning for Our Lives." A four-part series given at Holy Family Parish. Davidsonville, Md. September 12, 26; October 17; November 14, 2011.

DOCTORAL STUDENTS

Juraj Fenik, "Enthroned with Christ: An Exegetical and Theological Study of Ephesians 1:20–23 and 2:5–6."

Matthew G. Whitlock, "Unity in Conflict: A Study of Acts 4:23–31."

Peggy Vining, "Galatians and First-Century Ethical Theory."

Tyrell J. Alles, OSB, "The Narrative Meaning and Function of the Parable of the Prodigal Son (Luke 15:11–32)."

Gilbert Soo Hoo, "The Pedagogy of the Johannine Jesus: A Comparative Study of Jesus' Pedagogy to the World and to His Own."

Robert P. Miller, "*Ti emoi kai soi*: John 2:4—Rebuke or Expression of Mutual Concern."

Diana Jill Kirby, "Repetition in the Book of Revelation."

Roberto Martinez, "The Question of John the Baptist and the Testimony of Jesus: A Narrative-Critical Analysis of Luke 7:18–35."

Wenxi Zhang, "Paul among Jews: A Study of the Meaning and Significance of Paul's Inaugural Sermon in the Synagogue of Antioch in Pisidia (Acts 13:16–41) for His Missionary Work among Jews."

John Szukalski, "Tormented in Hades: A Socio-Narratological Approach to the Parable of the Rich Man and Lazarus (Luke 16:19–31)."

Marianus Pele Here, "Christology and Discipleship in John 17."

Piotr Bajer, "The Parable of the Good Samaritan (Luke 10:25–37): Its Function and Purpose within the Lukan Journey Section."

Jason Weaver, "Paul's Call to Imitation: The Rhetorical Function of the Theme of Imitation in Its Epistolary Context."

Brent Kruger, "If God Is for Us: A Study of Pauline Theodicy in Rom 18:18–39."

Abbreviations

AB	Anchor Bible
ABD	*Anchor Bible Dictionary*. Edited by D. N. Freedman. 6 vols. New York: Doubleday, 1992.
ABRL	Anchor Bible Reference Library
AcBib	Academia biblica
AGJU	Arbeiten zur Geschichte des antiken Judentums und des Urchristentums
AJT	*Asia Journal of Theology*
AnBib	Analecta biblica
ANTC	Abingdon New Testament Commentaries
AT	*Annales theologici*
ATANT	Abhandlungen zur Theologie des Alten und Neuen Testaments
AThR	*Anglican Theological Review*
BBR	*Bulletin of Biblical Research*
BDAG	W. Bauer, F. W. Danker, W. F. Arndt, and F. W. Gingrich. *Greek-English Lexicon of the New Testament and Other Early Christian Literature.* 3rd ed. Chicago: University of Chicago Press, 1999.
BDB	F. Brown, S. R. Driver, and C. A. Briggs. *A Hebrew and English Lexicon of the Old Testament.* Oxford: Oxford University Press, 1907.
BDF	F. Blass, A. Debrunner, and R. W. Funk. *A Greek Grammar of the New Testament and Other Early Christian Literature.* Chicago: University of Chicago Press, 1961.
BETL	Bibliotheca ephemeridum theologicarum lovaniensium
Bib	*Biblica*
BJRL	*Bulletin of the John Rylands Library*
BNTC	Black's New Testament Commentaries
BSac	*Bibliotheca sacra*

BZNW	Beihefte zur Zeitschrift für die neutestamentliche Wissenschaft
CBQ	*Catholic Biblical Quarterly*
CBQMS	Catholic Biblical Quarterly Monograph Series
CBR	*Currents in Biblical Research*
CNT	Commentaire du Nouveau Testament
CTJ	*Calvin Theological Journal*
CurBS	*Currents in Research: Biblical Studies*
EBib	Études bibliques
ETL	*Ephemerides theologicae lovanienses*
EvQ	*Evangelical Quarterly*
ExpTim	*Expository Times*
FCB	Feminist Companion to the Bible
FRLANT	Forschungen zur Religion und Literatur des Alten und Neuen Testaments
GNS	Good News Studies
HBD	*Harper's Bible Dictionary.* Edited by Paul J. Achtemeier. San Francisco: HarperSanFrancisco, 1985.
HBT	*Horizons in Biblical Theology*
HNT	Handbuch zum Neuen Testament
HTKNT	Herders theologischer Kommentar zum Neuen Testament
HTR	*Harvard Theological Review*
HUCA	*Hebrew Union College Annual*
HvTSt	*Hervormde teologiese studies*
IBC	Interpretation: A Bible Commentary for Teaching and Preaching
ICC	International Critical Commentary
Int	*Interpretation*
IVPNTC	InterVarsity Press New Testament Commentary
JBL	*Journal of Biblical Literature*
JECS	*Journal of Early Christian Studies*
JETS	*Journal of the Evangelical Theological Society*
JRE	*Journal of Religious Ethics*
JSJ	*Journal for the Study of Judaism*
JSNT	*Journal for the Study of the New Testament*
JSNTSup	Journal for the Study of the New Testament Supplement Series
JSOT	*Journal for the Study of the Old Testament*
JSOTSup	Journal for the Study of the Old Testament Supplement Series
KJV	King James Version

LHBOTS	Library of Hebrew Bible/Old Testament Studies
LNTS	Library of New Testament Studies
LS	*Louvain Studies*
LSJ	H. G. Liddell, R. Scott, and H. S. Jones. *A Greek-English Lexicon.* 9th ed. with revised supplement. Oxford: Oxford University Press, 1996.
LXX	Septuagint
MT	Masoretic text
NAB	New American Bible
NAC	New American Commentary
NCBC	New Cambridge Bible Commentary
NCCS	New Covenant Commentary Series
Neot	*Neotestamentica*
NET	New English Translation of the Bible
NETS	*A New English Translation of the Septuagint.* Edited by Albert Pietersma and Benjamin G. Wright. New York: Oxford University Press, 2007.
NIB	*The New Interpreter's Bible.* Edited by Leander E. Keck. 12 vols. Nashville: Abingdon, 1994–2004.
NICNT	New International Commentary on the New Testament
NIGTC	New International Greek Testament Commentary Series
NIV	New International Version
NovT	*Novum Testamentum*
NovTSup	Novum Testamentum Supplements
NRSV	New Revised Standard Version
NTAbh	Neutestamentliche Abhandlungen
NTL	New Testament Library
NTS	*New Testament Studies*
OBT	Overtures to Biblical Theology
OGIS	*Orientis graeci inscriptions selectae.* Edited by W. Dittenberger. 2 vols. Leipzig: Hirzel, 1903–1905.
OTP	*Old Testament Pseudepigrapha.* Edited by James H. Charlesworth. 2 vols. New York: Doubleday, 1983–1985.
R&T	*Religion and Theology*
RAC	*Reallexikon für Antike und Christentum.* Edited by T. Kluser et al. Stuttgart: Hiersemann, 1950–.
RBL	*Review of Biblical Literature*
RevistB	*Revista biblica*
RSPT	*Revue des sciences philosophiques et théologiques*

RSV	Revised Standard Version
SBL	Society of Biblical Literature
SBLDS	Society of Biblical Literature Dissertation Series
SBLSP	Society of Biblical Literature Seminar Papers
SBLSymS	Society of Biblical Literature Symposium Series
SBLWGRW	Society of Biblical Literature Writings from the Greco-Roman World
SIG	*Sylloge inscriptionum graecarum.* Edited by W. Dittenberger. 4 vols. 3rd ed. Leipzig: Hirzel, 1915–1924.
SJT	*Scottish Journal of Theology*
SNT	Studien zum Neuen Testament
SNTIW	Studies of the New Testament and Its World
SNTSMS	Society for New Testament Studies Monograph Series
SNTSU	*Studien zum Neuen Testament und seiner Umwelt*
SP	Sacra Pagina
TCGNT	*Textual Commentary on the Greek New Testament.* Edited by Bruce M. Metzger. 2nd ed. Stuttgart: Deutsche Bibelgesellschaft, 1994.
TDNT	*Theological Dictionary of the New Testament.* Edited by G. Kittel and G. Friedrich. Translated by G. W. Bromiley. 10 vols. Grand Rapids: Eerdmans, 1964–1976.
THKNT	Theologischer Handkommentar zum Neuen Testament
ThTo	*Theology Today*
TLZ	*Theologische Literaturzeitung*
TrinJ	*Trinity Journal*
TS	*Theological Studies*
TynBul	*Tyndale Bulletin*
TZ	*Theologische Zeitschrift*
VT	*Vetus Testamentum*
WBC	Word Biblical Commentary
WTJ	*Westminster Theological Journal*
WUNT	Wissenschaftliche Untersuchungen zum Neuen Testament
WW	*Word and World*
ZBK	Zürcher Bibelkommentare
ZNW	*Zeitschrift für die neutestamentliche Wissenschaft und die Kunde der älteren Kirche*
ZST	*Zeitschrift für systematische Theologie*
ZTK	*Zeitschrift für Theologie und Kirche*

INTRODUCTION

Francis T. Gignac, S.J.

I am very grateful to be invited to write an introduction to the Festschrift on the occasion of Frank Matera's seventieth birthday and retirement from the Catholic University of America. I am honored and enthusiastic to do so. The Reverend Doctor Frank J. Matera, the Andrews-Kelly-Ryan Professor of Biblical Studies, has been an outstanding teacher here at CUA since 1988.

Among his twelve published books that nicely serve the needs of both the academy and the church, several are magnificent syntheses that show both the unity and the diversity of New Testament writings. His *New Testament Christology* (1999) has insightful analyses of the Christology of each individual writer and concludes with a chapter on the diverse unity of New Testament Christology.

New Testament Theology: Exploring Diversity and Unity (2007) is even more impressive. After an introduction to New Testament theology, he examines the theologies of the Synoptic Gospels: the kingdom of God in Mark, the righteousness of the kingdom in Matthew, and the salvation that the kingdom brings about in Luke–Acts. Then he focuses on the Pauline tradition, distinguishing among a theology of election in the Thessalonian correspondence, a theology of the cross and resurrection in the Corinthian correspondence, a theology of righteousness in Galatians and Romans, a theology from prison in Philippians, Philemon, Colossians, and Ephesians, and a theology of the Pauline tradition in the Pastoral Epistles. Then he analyzes the Johannine tradition, including a theology of revelation in the Gospel of John and a theology of communion with God in 1 John. He concludes the analytical part by treating a theology of priesthood and sacrifice in Hebrews, a theology of wisdom and perfection in James, a theology for a time of affliction and disorder in 1 and 2 Peter and Jude, and a theology of God's final victory over evil in Revelation. The final chapter is a brilliant synthesis of the diverse unity of New Testament theology.

Besides these syntheses, he has also written commentaries on individual New Testament books, including 2 Corinthians for the New Testament Library, Galatians for Sacra Pagina, and most recently Romans for the Paideia series (2010). This is a chapter-by-chapter and verse-by-verse commentary in which he discusses the text type, the Greek language used, and the cultural, literary, and theological settings in which the text took form. Over the years he has also written sixty-five articles for various periodicals, books, dictionaries, encyclopedias, and Festschriften.

He was the primary organizer and keynote presenter in our Year of Paul symposium, which was extremely successful. He has presented almost eighty lectures on Paul in various universities and dioceses, and his *New Testament Ethics: The Legacies of Jesus and Paul* (1999) and his *Strategies of Preaching Paul* (2001) are very popular.

He has taught doctoral-level seminars in the Gospel of Luke, the Acts of the Apostles, 2 Corinthians, Romans, Galatians, and Philippians, as well as courses in New Testament Christology and New Testament ethics, courses in the Pauline Letters and the Synoptic Gospels, and undergraduate courses in the Letters of Paul and New Testament introduction. He has also supervised the development of our curriculum. His contributions to the biblical studies area and to the School of Theology and Religious Studies are outstanding and have brought great honor to STRS and to CUA.

For the past ten years he has directed more dissertations than any other professor in our academic area. In doing so, he is very attentive to the needs and interests of his directees and meets with them regularly to help and encourage them in their work. He is by far the most sought-after dissertation director in our academic area.

Even in his final year he has devoted himself to the needs of our school, serving on the search committee for a new dean, taking care to see the rest of his directees through their dissertations and defenses, and providing alternate directors for those unable to complete their work under him.

He and I have been working closely together for the last ten years now and he has also been so good to me in other ways. There is no one comparable to him at the Catholic University of America.

He is also very devoted to pastoral work. For many years he has served as assistant to the pastor at Holy Family Catholic Church, Davidsonville, Maryland, where he not only celebrates masses every weekend but also conducts Bible study classes on weekday evenings.

He has personal interests that have benefited us residents of Curley Hall. For years he has maintained a vegetable garden in our backyard, planting tomatoes and cucumbers in the spring, tending and watering the garden all summer, picking the ripe fruit for us to eat, and closing down the garden in the fall.

In addition, he is personally generous and shows the greatest concern for those of us with whom he lives. He offers to drive us wherever we have to go and is especially attentive to our physical health, assisting us personally in any way he can. He is truly one of the best people with whom I have been privileged to live.

Unity and Diversity in the Gospels

An Enemy of the Gospel? Anti-Paulinisms and Intertextuality in the Gospel of Matthew[*]

Kelly R. Iverson

For more than a decade, David Sim has advanced the argument that Matthew's Gospel evidences a specific and directed attack on Pauline Christianity.[1] Reminiscent of F. C. Baur and the Tübingen school,[2] as well as the work of S. G. F. Brandon,[3] Sim contends that the majority of scholars have ignored the inherent tension between Matthew and Paul.[4] What is more,

---

[*] In appreciation of his unfailing support and numerous contributions to the field, it is a pleasure to offer this essay in honor of Frank Matera.

1. David C. Sim, *Apocalyptic Eschatology in the Gospel of Matthew* (SNTSMS 88; Cambridge: Cambridge University Press, 1996); idem, "Christianity and Ethnicity in the Gospel of Matthew," in *Ethnicity and the Bible* (ed. Mark G. Brett; Leiden: Brill, 1996), 171–95; idem, *The Gospel of Matthew and Christian Judaism: The History and Social Setting of the Matthean Community* (SNTIW; Edinburgh: T&T Clark, 1998); idem, "Matthew's Anti-Paulinism: A Neglected Feature of Matthean Studies," *HvTSt* 58 (2002): 767–83; idem, "Matthew 7.21–23: Further Evidence of Its Anti-Pauline Perspective," *NTS* 53 (2007): 325–43; idem, "Matthew, Paul and the Origin and Nature of the Gentile Mission: The Great Commission in Matthew 28:16–20 as an Anti-Pauline Tradition," *HvTSt* 64 (2008): 377–92; idem, "Matthew and the Pauline Corpus: A Preliminary Intertextual Study," *JSNT* 31 (2009): 401–22.

2. F. C. Baur, *Paulus, der Apostel Jesu Christi. Sein Leben und Wirken, seine Briefe und seine Lehre* (Stuttgart: Becher & Müller, 1845). For a recent reprint and English translation, see idem, *Paul the Apostle of Jesus Christ: His Life and Works, His Epistles and Teachings* (Peabody, Mass.: Hendrickson, 2003).

3. S. G. F. Brandon, *The Fall of Jerusalem and the Christian Church: A Study of the Effects of the Jewish Overthrow of A.D. 70 on Christianity* (London: SPCK, 1951), 242. Sim acknowledges that Brandon's argument is not overly persuasive and that "it is quite understandable that his hypothesis found no support in later scholarship" (Sim, "Matthew's Anti-Paulinism," 769).

4. See, e.g., Daniel Marguerat, *Le jugement dans l'Evangile de Matthieu* (Geneva:

when their writings are compared (usually in relation to the use of Torah), the tendency is to downplay or harmonize the perspectives. The unfortunate consequence, Sim maintains, is that scholars have failed to address an elemental question: What would the law-observant Matthew have thought of the law-free Paul?

Based upon his analysis, Sim concludes that Matthew and Paul might have "agreed on many important issues" (e.g., the significance of Christ's death), but they would have been "bitter enemies" due to their radically divergent perspectives concerning the role of the law.[5] Matthew's Jewish proclivities and strict Torah observance would have necessitated a sharp counterresponse to Paul's unscrupulous gospel. As such, Matthew was deliberately written as a polemic against those advocating a law-free gospel and evidences a deep-seated struggle in the early church:

> The conflict between Paul and the Jerusalem church was never resolved while the major participants were living. The dispute between Christian Judaism and Gentile Christianity over the role of the law in the Christian movement was still very much alive in the decades and centuries following the Jewish war and the destruction of the Jerusalem church. In general terms the law-observant Matthean community can be firmly placed in the tradition of and chronologically between the circumcision party which openly opposed Paul and the later Christian Jewish sects which so vilified him. Specifically, this Christian Jewish church of Antioch was aligned with the tradition of the Jerusalem church through its connection with Peter. In promoting the primacy of Peter, Matthew openly and savagely attacks Paul and his law-free gospel. *This version of the gospel is not simply wrong, but those who choose this easy option are earmarked for severe eschatological punishment.*[6]

Sim's bold conclusion is based upon various arguments, including the continued use of Torah in the Matthean community, the depiction of the disciples, family of Jesus, and Peter, the congruence between Matthean theology and Paul's Galatian opponents, and the polemic inferred from Matthew's redactional activities. Perhaps most interesting and surprising

---

Labor et Fides, 1981); Roger Mohrlang, *Matthew and Paul: A Comparison of Ethical Perspectives* (SNTSMS 48; Cambridge: Cambridge University Press, 1984); R. T. France, *Matthew: Evangelist and Teacher* (Exeter: Paternoster, 1989), 110–11.

5. Sim, "Matthew's Anti-Paulinism," 771, 774.
6. Sim, *Matthew and Christian Judaism*, 213 (emphasis added).

in the unfolding of Sim's many-faceted argument is that only recently has he attempted to address one of the key methodological planks to the discussion. Crucial to Sim's argument, though largely assumed in previous works, is the role of intertextuality and the methodological criteria that undergird his study. If Matthew genuinely believed that "Paul and similar Christians would be utterly rejected by Jesus at the time of the judgment," how is such a perspective to be deduced from a narrative that never mentions Paul by name?[7] Since, as Sim acknowledges, "any such textual comparison of Matthew's Gospel and the letters of Paul inevitably raises the general question of method and the specific issue of intertextuality," an evaluation of Sim's hermeneutical argument has important implications for assessing the overall thesis.[8] Thus the objective of this essay is to explore Sim's intertextual method, articulated in a recent article entitled "Matthew and the Pauline Corpus: A Preliminary Intertextual Study."[9] As well as providing an assessment of Sim's work, the essay reflects upon what one scholar has deemed "trendy intertextuality."[10]

INTERTEXTUAL ANTI-PAULINISMS

Intertextual studies have become increasingly common in New Testament research, and Sim's recent work joins an already lively conversation.[11]

---

7. Sim, "Matthew 7:21–23," 327.

8. Sim, "Matthew and the Pauline Corpus," 402. Other scholars have evaluated different aspects of Sim's thesis. See, e.g., the helpful essays by Joel Willitts, "Paul and Matthew: A Descriptive Approach from a Post–New Perspective Interpretive Framework," in *Paul and the Gospels: Christologies, Conflicts and Convergences* (ed. Michael F. Bird and Joel Willitts; LNTS 411; London: T&T Clark, 2011), 62–85; and Paul Foster, "Paul and Matthew—Two Strands of the Early Jesus Movement with Little Sign of Connection," in Bird and Willitts, *Paul and the Gospels*, 86–114.

9. Sim, "Matthew and the Pauline Corpus."

10. Ellen van Wolde, "Trendy Intertextuality?" in *Intertextuality in Biblical Writings: Essays in Honour of Bas van Iersel* (ed. Sipke Draisma; Kampen: Kok, 1989), 43–49.

11. Reflecting on the widespread adoption of intertextuality in the field of biblical studies, Richard Hays observes ("Foreword to the English Edition," in *Reading the Bible Intertextually* [ed. Richard B. Hays, Stefan Alkier, and Leroy A. Huizenga; Waco, Tex.: Baylor University Press, 2009], xi): "Biblical critics are sometimes a little slow on the uptake with regard to such cultural fashions, but once we get wind of a new 'method,' we are sure to pursue it relentlessly for all it is worth—and maybe then some."

Despite the widespread reference to "intertextuality"—both in biblical studies and beyond—the term is not easily defined, and numerous scholars have lamented the myriad of "controversial definitions and contradictory usages."[12] Much of this conversation, which engages issues pertaining to the essence of "texts," how traditions are related to one another, and the nature of interpretation, is beyond the scope of this essay.[13] Nonetheless, it is important to note that while the concept of intertextuality as pioneered by Julia Kristeva is "less a name for a work's relation to particular texts than a designation of its participation in the discursive space of a culture,"[14] the theory has been adapted to describe the development of texts and their subsequent influence upon biblical traditions.[15] Sim makes no attempt to define the term but employs *intertextuality* to describe the relationships that exist between *written* artifacts, a perspective that adopts a rather limited view of "texts" and is, no doubt, determined by his aim to establish a causal link between Matthew and Paul.[16]

---

12. Frank Schulze-Engler, "Cross-Cultural Criticism and the Limits of Intertextuality," in *Across the Lines: Intertextuality and the Transcultural Communication in the New Literatures in English* (ed. Wolfgang Klooss; Amsterdam: Rodopi, 1998), 3.

13. For a helpful introduction to the subject, see Graham Allen, *Intertextuality* (London: Routledge, 2000); Mary Orr, *Intertextuality: Debates and Contexts* (Cambridge: Polity, 2003).

14. Jonathan D. Culler, *The Pursuit of Signs: Semiotics, Literature, Deconstruction* (London: Routledge & Kegan Paul, 1981), 103.

15. Kristeva, who was the first to introduce the concept of "intertextuality" in 1966, ultimately abandoned the term in 1974. Due to what she regarded as a misuse of the theory for the "banal" practice of traditional source criticism, Kristeva instead opted for the term *transposition*. See Julia Kristeva, *Revolution in Poetic Language* (trans. Margaret Waller; New York: Columbia University Press, 1984), 59–60.

16. This use of *intertextuality* has been sharply criticized. In what van Wolde describes as "trendy intertextuality," she observes that many scholars "use intertextuality as a modern literary theoretical coat of veneer over the old comparative approach" ("Trendy Intertextuality," 43). Others are even more trenchant in their critique. George Aichele and Gary A. Phillips ("Introduction: Exegesis, Eisegesis, Intergesis," *Semeia* 69/70 [1995]: 9–10) argue that "[i]ntertextuality is not some neutral literary mechanism but is rather at root a means of ideological and cultural expression and of social transformation. This makes the narrow, conservative use of the term by certain biblical critics all the more ironic and ideologically contradictory." This response is grounded in the assumption that texts are "so thoroughly and deeply interwoven that tracing lines among them becomes as meaningless as distinguishing among water drops in the ocean" (Patricia Tull, "Intertextuality and the Hebrew Scriptures," *CurBS* 8 [2000]: 59–90).

Aside from this theoretical shortcoming, Sim's analysis is based on the broad but accurate assumption that texts are not autonomous literary creations but part of a dialogical process, whereby precursor texts are incorporated into the creation of successive textual expressions. As Roland Barthes helpfully observes, "any text is a new tissue of past citations," and no text exists on a proverbial island, impervious from the literary influences of the surrounding cultural matrix.[17] While Sim does not develop the significance of this theoretical grounding, and his essay might have been strengthened by further discussion of the matter, the assumption has important hermeneutical and interpretive implications. Because all texts are a "mosaic of quotations" and therefore participate in a web of communicative activity, readers must develop the interpretive agility to navigate between textual expressions.[18] Graham Allen, for instance, suggests that an intertextual perspective encourages a different kind of reading experience:

> The idea that when we read a work of literature we are seeking to find a meaning which lies inside that work seems completely common-sensical.... The act of reading ... plunges us into a network of textual relations. To interpret a text, to discover its meaning, or meanings, is to trace those relations. Reading thus becomes a process of moving between texts. Meaning becomes something which exists between a text and all the other texts to which it refers and relates, moving out from the independent text into a network of textual relations.[19]

Thus from a purely methodological perspective, Sim's thesis is conceivable. It is *possible* that a relationship does exist between Matthew and Paul. Likewise, though intertextual discussions often fixate on the use of the Jewish Scriptures in the New Testament, it is *possible* that a more contemporaneous dialogue is at work in Matthew—a point that is tacitly affirmed by the majority of scholars who recognize this type of intertextual activity

---

17. Roland Barthes, "Theory of the Text," in *Untying the Text: A Post-structuralist Reader* (ed. Robert Young; Boston: Routledge & Kegan Paul, 1981), 39. Barthes (ibid.) goes on to state that "bits of codes, formulae, rhythmic models, fragments of social languages, etc. pass into the text and are redistributed within it, for there is always language before and around the text."

18. Julia Kristeva, *Semeiotike: Recherches pour une sémanalyse* (Paris: Seuil, 1969), 146.

19. Allen, *Intertextuality*, 1.

in Matthew's use of Mark and Q. Furthermore, Sim is right to argue that scholars should not assume that the presence of an intertext necessarily implies conceptual agreement with its successor text.[20]

The question that naturally follows is how the interpreter is to identify intertextual relationships. Following Hays, Sim argues that the use of intertexts varies considerably with the level of explicit or implicit signals falling along a continuum.[21] In some texts citations are overtly marked (e.g., fulfillment citations), while in other instances antecedents are more ambiguous and indirect, eliciting what scholars refer to as allusions or echoes.[22] Hays proposes seven criteria for the identification of echoes, including availability, volume, recurrence, thematic coherence, historical plausibility, history of interpretation, and satisfaction.[23] Of these, Sim adopts the position of Brawley and suggests that only two criteria (availability and volume) are necessary.[24] Beginning with availability, Sim contends that it is "highly probable" that the First Evangelist had access to the writings of Paul.[25] Though Sim concedes that "there can be no definitive answer" regarding Matthew's use of Paul and that there is no "clear and decisive evidence in the Gospel itself," he nonetheless argues that (1) the chronological relationship between Matthew and Paul establishes a conceivable window of opportunity; (2) the Pauline corpus was collected and distributed—perhaps with Paul's own assistance—at a very early date and possibly during or shortly after the apostle's lifetime; and (3) the evidence suggests that by the late first/early second century Ignatius was already familiar with most of the Pauline corpus—an observation that is highly significant since Ignatius was the bishop of Antioch, the same geographic locale that many

20. Sim, "Matthew and the Pauline Corpus," 403.

21. Richard B. Hays (*Echoes of Scripture in the Letters of Paul* [New Haven: Yale University Press, 1989]) is widely regarded as a pioneer of intertextuality in the field of biblical studies. Also published in the same year was another volume on the subject: Draisma, *Intertextuality in Biblical Writing*.

22. The distinction between *allusions* and *echoes* is difficult to classify. Hays suggests that an allusion is an "obvious" intertextual reference, while an echo is "subtler" (*Echoes of Scripture*, 29). In the end, although Hays posits some differentiation, he utilizes the terms in an interchangeable fashion. This essay follows a similar convention.

23. For a description of all seven criteria, see ibid., 29–32.

24. On the rationale for the two selected criteria, see Robert L. Brawley, *Text to Text Pours Forth Speech: Voices of Scripture in Luke–Acts* (Bloomington: Indiana University Press, 1995), 13–14.

25. Sim, "Matthew and the Pauline Corpus," 405.

postulate as the provenance for the First Gospel.[26] Therefore, if Matthew was written decades after the Pauline corpus, which began circulating at an early date and was already known in the city where the First Gospel was composed, then perhaps Matthew possessed the means and opportunity to engage in intertextual dialogue with Paul.

Sim next turns to the criteria of volume, attempting to evaluate the relative "loudness" of the echoes based upon the repetition of lexical terms or syntactical patterns. He argues that Matthean scholars have ignored Pauline echoes because they have mistakenly assumed that Matthew was either un-Pauline or pro-Pauline.[27] Sim suggests that "rather than listening for verbal and thematic echoes on the assumption that Matthew would have looked to Paul as an authoritative and doctrinal source for his narrative about Jesus, our attention should be attuned to possible Matthean *responses to and corrections of* Pauline themes and doctrines."[28] According to Sim, once perceptions have been recalibrated, "the whole enterprise radically changes," resulting in the discovery of "loud" echoes that demonstrate Matthew's anti-Pauline perspective.[29]

Sim goes on to describe the "clearest example" of this intertextual phenomenon by examining the lexical and thematic parallels between Matt 16:17–18, Gal 1:12, 16–17, and 1 Cor 10:4.[30] Sim notes that both writers use ἀποκαλύπτω (Matt 16:17; Gal 1:16; or its cognate ἀποκάλυψις, Gal 1:12) and the phrase σὰρξ καὶ αἷμα (Matt 16:17; Gal 1:16) within the context of a divine commission. Since the confluence of these terms is not found elsewhere in early Christian literature, Sim argues that there is "no reason" to suggest that the Evangelist was working with a pre-Matthean tradition. Instead it appears that Matthew adopted the material directly from the writings of Paul.[31] Sim detects further parallels between Matt 16:18 and 1 Cor 10:4. In particular, he argues that Matthew has effectively

---

26. Ibid., 405–8.

27. Graham Stanton (*A Gospel for a New People: Studies in Matthew* [Louisville: Westminster John Knox, 1993], 314) is often cited as a proponent of the un-Pauline view: "Matthew's gospel as a whole is neither anti-Pauline, nor has it been strongly influenced by Paul's writings; it is simply un-Pauline." For a pro-Pauline perspective, see W. D. Davies, *The Setting of the Sermon on the Mount* (Cambridge: Cambridge University Press, 1963), 325–66.

28. Sim, "Matthew and the Pauline Corpus," 410 (emphasis original).

29. Ibid., 411.

30. Ibid.

31. Ibid., 413.

misunderstood the thrust of Paul's thought in 1 Cor 10:4. Although the latter passage depicts the seemingly benign event of Israel's wilderness wanderings, the Evangelist has misconstrued the text as a Pauline response intended to delegitimize the status of Peter, the "rock" (Matt 16:18). That the Messiah is identified as the "rock" from which Israel drank (ἡ πέτρα δὲ ἦν ὁ Χριστός, 1 Cor 10:4) is interpreted as a direct blow against Petrine authority. The same thought is accentuated in 1 Cor 3:11—a passage that describes Jesus, not Peter, as the foundation of the church. Sim reasons that the polemic inferred from the text was likely not intentional but was misconstrued by Matthew as an affront to Petrine authority. As Sim observes, "since Christ is the foundation of the church (1 Cor. 3.11), and Paul has gone on the record as describing Christ as the rock (1 Cor. 10.4c), there is an implicit denial of Peter's foundational role in the establishment of the Christian church and, more importantly, his authority over the whole Christian movement."[32]

In response to the perceived attack, Matthew launches a counternarrative to defend the authority of Peter. According to Matthew, it is *Peter*—not Paul—who receives a divine commission that is not from "flesh and blood" (Matt 16:17), and it is *Peter* who is the "rock" upon which the church is to be built (16:18). Though brief, these narrative features represent Matthew's intertextual rebuttal and express "a direct refutation of Paul's belief that Peter was not the foundation rock for the whole church."[33]

---

32. Ibid., 415–16. This is one of the weaker arguments in Sim's essay. Are we to assume that Matthew is so opposed to Paul that he cannot appreciate a text that identifies *Jesus* as the foundation of the church? If this is the case, one wonders what "agreement" (Sim, "Matthew's Anti-Paulinism," 771) actually exists between Matthew and Paul. It would seem that Matthew has already acknowledged that the teachings of Jesus are the "rock" upon which anything enduring must be constructed (cf. 7:24–25). See W. D. Davies and Dale C. Allison, *A Critical and Exegetical Commentary on the Gospel According to Saint Matthew* (3 vols.; ICC; Edinburgh: T&T Clark, 1988–1997), 1:721.

33. Sim, "Matthew and the Pauline Corpus," 416. Sim's depiction of Paul's anti-Petrine rhetoric differs at various junctures in the article. In reference to the discussion of 1 Cor 3:11, he suggests that the language "may well be a ploy on Paul's part to deride the reputation of Peter" (ibid., 414). Elsewhere the discussion is more nuanced: "what is important in this regard is not Paul's actual intention in this passage, *which in all likelihood had nothing to do with Peter*, but Matthew's understanding of the apostle's intention" (ibid., 415 [emphasis added]). In the quotation above, however, Sim appears to suggest that Paul had a genuine disdain for Petrine authority.

Matthew destabilizes the Pauline tradition by legitimating the authority of Peter through Jesus himself. By advancing pro-Petrine rhetoric that implicitly usurps the chronological priority of the Pauline tradition, Sim argues that the concomitant effect is to undercut the authority of Paul via direct interaction with his writings.

INTERTEXTUAL INTENSITY IN MATTHEW 16:17–18

The identification of allusions and echoes is a challenging and potentially subjective enterprise. Indeed, before intertextuality became a fashionable term, Samuel Sandmel had already warned of its potential abuses. In his 1962 article "Parallelomania," Sandmel decried the often extravagant and dubious association of texts, enjoining scholars to "recognize parallelomania for the disease that it is."[34] Yet despite the rhetoric, Sandmel was not opposed to the identification of literary sources or what is now termed *intertextuality*. Instead he recognized that the identification of intertexts is a delicate task that requires methodological rigor. Though at times the subtle undertones are readily discernible and influential beyond "the loudest instruments in the orchestra," often they require the listener to nudge forward with rapt and disciplined attention.[35] Considering the inherent obstacles associated with the task, Adele Berlin rightly cautions scholars to think "through the criteria more carefully … both in the interest of developing sound exegetical principles and in the interest of untangling the literary history of the Bible."[36] For this reason, an evaluation of Sim's intertextual methodology—the infrastructure upon which his argument is constructed—is all the more crucial to the present discussion.

Initially, Sim appears to follow a course of study that is similar to many intertextual projects, but ultimately he adopts a methodological approach that is problematic for two reasons. First, Sim dismisses five of the seven criteria developed by Hays without explanation (other than to concur

---

34. Samuel Sandmel, "Parallelomania," *JBL* 81 (1962): 13.

35. Steve Moyise, "Intertextuality and the Study of the Old Testament in the New," in *The Old Testament in the New: Essays in Honour of J. L. North* (ed. Steve Moyise; JSNTSup 189; Sheffield: Sheffield Academic Press, 2000), 17.

36. Adele Berlin, "Literary Exegesis of Biblical Narrative: Between Poetics and Hermeneutics," in *Not in Heaven: Coherence and Complexity in Biblical Narrative* (ed. Jason P. Rosenblatt and Joseph C. Sitterson; Bloomington: Indiana University Press, 1991), 128.

with Brawley). The unfortunate result is that by adopting a minimalist approach, the ability to assess the overall strength of the echo is limited. Because of the uncertainties associated with intertextuality and because "precision ... is [often] unattainable," additional criteria provide an array of tests to assess the data and to avoid distortion. By unnecessarily restricting the criteria, it is even possible to create the false impression that an echo exists (when it does not) or is louder than may actually be the case.[37] Though several of the criteria might be secondary (i.e., historical plausibility, history of interpretation, satisfaction), the probative value of the criteria should not be underestimated, particularly as a means to further substantiate possible intertextual activity.

Second, not only does Sim uncritically dismiss several criteria, but his use of Brawley reflects an uncritical reading that has a similar effect. To his credit, Brawley argues that Hays does not go far enough in describing the broad and diverse phenomena associated with intertextuality. In particular, Hays's only criteria for evaluating the localized features of an intertext is "volume"—which he defines as the verbal correspondence between a text and its pre-text.[38] As Brawley notes, Hays "measures volume only on the phraseological plane and overlooks reiteration on other levels," such as form, genre, setting, plot, and ungrammaticalities.[39] What is striking about this observation is that although Brawley provides additional criteria for assessing volume, Sim ignores these identifiers just as he does with Hays. The result is that Sim defaults to an overly reductive approach that lacks methodological reflection. Because Sim provides no justification for

---

37. Hays, *Echoes of Scripture*, 29. Conversely, it is also possible to underplay intertextual references by failing to recognize clues flagged by the criteria.

38. In a more recent work, Hays attempts to clarify the criteria. He observes that volume is also impacted by the "rhetorical stress placed upon the phrase(s) in question." Although largely undefined, Hays seems to acknowledge that verbal correspondence is not the only characteristic of volume. See Richard B. Hays, *The Conversion of the Imagination: Paul as Interpreter of Israel's Scripture* (Grand Rapids: Eerdmans, 2005), 34–37.

39. Brawley, *Text to Text*, 13. For additional reflections on Hays's *Echoes of Scripture*, see Craig A. Evans and James A. Sanders, eds., *Paul and the Scriptures of Israel* (JSNTSup 83; Sheffield: JSOT Press, 1993); Stanley E. Porter, "The Use of the Old Testament in the New Testament: A Brief Comment on Method and Terminology," in *Early Christian Interpretation of the Scriptures of Israel* (ed. Stanley E. Porter and James A. Sanders; JSNTSup 148; Sheffield: Sheffield Academic Press, 1997), 79–97.

his approach, one gets the impression that not only is the model underdeveloped, but that it has possibly been adopted for a particular end.

In light of these methodological issues associated with Sim's approach, in this section I will assess Matt 16:17–18 utilizing the work of Manfred Pfister, whose intertextual model has been adapted by an array of scholars in fields such as biblical studies, literature, poetry, fairy tales, and parody.[40] Rather than attempting to measure the volume or "intensity" of an intertextual reference with a single criteria (cf. Sim and Hays), Pfister proposes a "bundle of criteria" that offers a more comprehensive approach to the rich and complex ways in which intertexts are embedded. The model can be visually described as a series of concentric circles emanating out from a single point, which Pfister calls the "hard core." This center demarcates the highest grade of intertextual intensity and suggests a conscious and marked association between text and pre-text. The greater the distance from the foci, the more difficult, if not impossible, it becomes to discern authorial-derived intentionality.[41] Pfister argues that the evaluation of intertextual intensity is primarily determined by qualitative measures, which can be delineated as six criteria: referentiality, communicativity,

---

40. Manfred Pfister, "Konzepte der Intertextualität," in *Intertextualität: Formen, Funktionen, anglistische Fallstudien* (ed. Ulrich Broich and Manfred Pfister; Tübingen: Niemeyer, 1985), 1–30. On the use of Pfister's model in biblical studies and other academic fields, see, e.g., Claudia Rakel, " 'I Will Sing a New Song to My God': Some Remarks on the Intertextuality of Judith 16.1–17," in *Judges* (ed. Athalya Brenner; FCB 2/4; Sheffield: Sheffield Academic Press, 1999), 27–47; Mathew Palachuvattil, *"The One Who Does the Will of the Father": Distinguishing Character of Disciples according to Matthew: An Exegetical Theological Study* (Tesi Gregoriana 154; Rome: Gregorian University Press, 2007); Lars Eckstein, *Re-membering the Black Atlantic: On the Poetics and Politics of Literary Memory* (Amsterdam: Rodopi, 2006); Vanessa Joosen, *Critical and Creative Perspectives on Fairy Tales: An Intertextual Dialogue between Fairy-Tale Scholarship and Postmodern Retellings* (Detroit: Wayne State University Press, 2011); Beate Müller, *Parody: Dimensions and Perspectives* (Rodopi Perspectives on Modern Literature; Amsterdam: Rodopi, 1997); Valerie Robillard, "In Pursuit of Ekphrasis (An Intertextual Approach)," in *Pictures into Words: Theoretical and Descriptive Approaches to Ekphrasis* (ed. Valerie Robillard and Else Jongeneel; Amsterdam: VU University Press, 1998), 53–72.

41. The genius of Pfister's model is that it charts a mediating position between two divergent conceptions of intertextuality as advanced by structuralists and post-structuralists. The former assumes that intertextuality is finite and determinable, while the latter adopts a broader perspective such that "jeder Text als Teil eines universalen Intertexts erscheint." See Pfister, "Konzepte der Intertextualität," 25.

autoreflexivity, structurality, selectivity, and dialogibility.[42] While the criteria are expressed as individual parameters, they are not mutually exclusive but overlap and interweave one another. The characterization of an intertextual reference and its corresponding intensity can only be assessed when the range of criteria are considered.

1. *Referentiality* denotes the qualitative manner by which an intertext is incorporated into its metatext. The more seamlessly a pre-text is woven into its intertextual context—that is, without explicit citation or means of calling attention to itself—the lower the pre-text's intertextual intensity. On the other hand, intertexts that are overtly identified and exploited for their content (or theme) have a high degree of referentiality. At issue is the notion of integration and whether a text is merely used or mentioned, as opposed to the intricate referencing that typifies developed, intertextual dialogue.

2. *Communicativity* corresponds to the "communicative relevance" of a proposed intertext. A higher degree of communicativity is achieved if the intertext suggests a conscious and intentional engagement with the pre-text. In addition, not only will an intense reference indicate the author's deliberate use of a pre-text (as opposed to the use of stock, idiomatic expressions and allusions), it should also indicate that an audience is expected to recognize the intertextual reference.[43]

3. *Autoreflexivity* is an extension of the first two criteria. Whereas intense occurrences of referentiality and communicativity assume that the text is clearly and consciously marked—or is obvious enough that signposting is unnecessary—the criteria of autoreflexivity observes a certain kind of intertextual marking. When the author reflects upon the justification, problems, or presuppositions associated with an intertext, the tangential effect is to elevate intertextual awareness and the overall intensity of the reference.

---

42. For a discussion of Pfister's six criteria, see ibid., 26–29.

43. This latter point is best illustrated with the example of plagiarism. Although, in such instances, an intertext is deliberately and intentionally used, the author makes no attempt to refer the audience back to the pre-text. In this sense, while the writing may display signs of intertextual intensity (e.g., structurality), given the plagiarist's desire to shroud the source of his or her work, the overall communicativity is rather low and far removed from the "hard core." See ibid., 27.

4. *Structurality* refers to the "syntagmatic integration" between a pre-text and a metatext.[44] The extent to which a metatext is penetrated by the literary shape of a pre-text is a guide to structurality and intertextual intensity. Texts that allude to or paraphrase a pre-text but otherwise exhibit no deeper or underlying influence have a low intensity level. Conversely, intensity is highest in those texts whose literary framework has been impacted by the structural concerns of the pre-text.

5. *Selectivity* is a criterion that attempts to scale the conciseness or abstraction of the intertextual reference. Intensity is highest when an author references a specific unit of material rather than a generalized motif or topos within the pre-text. By drawing from a distinct segment of the pre-text, the author contributes to the intertextual density of the passage.

6. *Dialogicity* assesses the degree of tension between a pre-text and a metatext. Rather than evaluating the structural or literary relation between the two, dialogicity seeks to examine the ideological connection. Textual relations that exhibit conflict and conceptual divergence are particularly intense, whereas those that maintain a univocal perspective suggest a low degree of dialogicity.

When the proposed intertexts in Matt 16:17–18 are evaluated in light of Pfister's criteria, most surprising is the conspicuous lack of intertextual intensity. The low degree of referentiality, autoreflexivity, structurality, and selectivity all suggest relatively weak intertextual referencing. The proposed references are not marked through explicit citation or extended quotation, and neither the grammar nor style calls attention to intertextual traditions (referentiality). The Evangelist offers no reflective commentary on the use of Gal 1:12, 16–17, or 1 Cor 10:4 (autoreflexivity), and the broader contours of the narrative are not shaped by the underlying structure of Paul's agenda(s) but by the concern to tell the story of Jesus (structurality). At best, the Gospel of Matthew betrays a number of concepts that *might* intersect with Paul's writings, though the absence of distinctive features (selectivity) and the generally low scaling of the other criteria tacitly argue against Sim's thesis.[45]

---

44. Ibid., 28.

45. Sim argues that the proposed intertexts are demarcated through the use of specific terms; however, this should not be construed as an indicator or selectivity. While the catchwords are "concise," the proposed antecedents represent a swath of material that encompasses several different contexts.

In terms of Pfister's criteria, Sim would likely contend that the text displays a high level of referentiality (and possibly selectivity) because of the "close verbal parallels" with Paul's letters.[46] According to Sim, the parallels guide the reader to an appreciation of the intertextual references and draw attention to the underlying conflict. The question, however, is whether the agreements actually point in this direction. In total, the verbal similarities amount to one phrase (σὰρξ καὶ αἷμα, Matt 16:17; Gal 1:16) and two words (ἀποκαλύπτω, Matt 16:17; Gal 1:12, 16; πέτρα, Matt 16:18; 1 Cor 10:4; and possibly 1 Cor 3:11). Although biblical writers often evoke intertextual traditions through the use of compressed and elliptical language, Matt 16:17–18 lacks distinguishing features that might indicate an intertextual reference. If, for example, Matthew had used a *hapax legomenon* that was linked to a unique Pauline expression, the relative intensity and verbal correspondence would have been more discernible. The problem, however, is that all of the individual terms are found with some frequency elsewhere in the Gospel (and in the New Testament). Indeed, the only explicit connection between Matt 16:18 and 1 Cor 10:4 is the term πέτρα, which hardly qualifies as a unique lexeme in Matthew (7:24, 25; 16:18; 27:51, 60), particularly if one considers the conceptual evocation with each occurrence of Peter's name (Πέτρος, 4:18; 8:14; 10:2; 14:28, 29; 15:15; 16:16, 18, 22, 23; 17:1, 4, 24; 18:21; 19:27; 26:33, 35, 37, 40, 58, 69, 73, 75).[47]

Sim ignores these observations, instead focusing on the collocation σὰρξ καὶ αἷμα plus ἀποκαλύπτω. Because the constellation of ideas does not occur elsewhere in the New Testament, Sim argues that "there is little option but to conclude that there is a direct link between Matthew and Paul."[48] What is interesting, however, is that the verbal parallels are not as similar as Sim maintains. In Matthew the phrase σὰρξ καὶ αἷμα is directly linked to the verb ἀποκαλύπτω (Matt 16:17), while in Paul the expression is associated with the verb προσανατίθημι (Gal 1:16). This is no small distinction, for in Matthew the phrase occurs in reference to the revelatory experience that leads to Peter's confession, while in Paul the expression is used to describe the activities (or the lack thereof) that take place after his

---

46. Sim, "Matthew and the Pauline Corpus," 411.

47. For a discussion of the name Πέτρος, which "is otherwise virtually unknown as a personal name in the ancient world," as well as the obvious wordplay with πέτρα in v. 18, see R. T. France, *The Gospel of Matthew* (NICNT; Grand Rapids: Eerdmans, 2007), 620–23.

48. Sim, "Matthew and the Pauline Corpus," 412.

calling/conversion. Considering that none of the individual terms in question is distinguished in Matthew (σάρξ, 16:17; 19:5, 6; 24:22; 26:41); αἷμα, 16:17; 23:30, 35; 26:28; 27:4, 6, 8, 24, 25; ἀποκαλύπτω, 10:26; 11:25, 27; 16:17), that the phrase σὰρξ καὶ αἷμα (or αἷμα καὶ σάρξ) is used elsewhere in the New Testament (1 Cor 15:50; Eph 6:12; Heb 2:14), that the juxtaposition of "flesh and blood" predates the Gospels and Paul (Sir 14:18; 17:31), and that the expression ultimately became "a technical term in rabbinic texts,"[49] it is difficult to conclude with Sim that there are "rather loud intertextual echoes" in Matt 16:17–18.[50]

Moreover, in the pursuit to describe the intertextual relationship between Matthew and Paul, Sim unwittingly offers a counterargument to his own thesis and thus to the text's referentiality. Since many have argued that Matt 16:17–18 is pre-Matthean—some even suggesting that Paul is the respondent—Sim is compelled to argue that the tradition is a later reaction to Paul and his erroneous, law-free gospel.[51] In order to show that the verses are Matthean and not an early, independent tradition adopted by the Evangelist, Sim engages in a redactional discussion to highlight the Matthean contribution to the passage. Noting that the text contains "a number of Matthean themes and expressions" (e.g., ἀποκριθεὶς δὲ ὁ Ἰησοῦς εἶπεν αὐτῳ; μακάριος; Βαριωνᾶ; ὁ πατήρ μου ὁ ἐν τοῖς οὐρανοῖς; κἀγώ; σοι λέγω; σὺ εἶ Πέτρος; οἰκοδομέω; and ἐκκλησία), Sim argues that the heavily redacted passage is "more likely than not a creation of Mat-

---

49. Davies and Allison, *Matthew*, 2:623.

50. Sim, "Matthew and the Pauline Corpus," 412.

51. For those advocating that "flesh and blood" is pre-Matthean and reflects a tradition that is independent of Paul, see John Nolland, *The Gospel of Matthew: A Commentary on the Greek Text* (NIGTC; Grand Rapids: Eerdmans, 2005), 665–66. Bernard Robinson, however, argues that Matthew is not trying to justify the authority of Peter vis-à-vis Paul, but that Paul is staking "a claim comparable with that made for Peter" ("Peter and His Successors: Tradition and Redaction in Matthew 16.17–19," *JSNT* 21 [1984]: 85–104). As support for the notion that Matthew has adopted an early tradition in 16:7, Robinson argues that "in Matt. 11.25–27 Jesus' divine sonship is stated to have already been revealed to the disciples generally. Having written this, is it likely that Matthew would himself have made up, five chapters later, a logion conferring this privilege on Simon alone? Surely the fact that Matthew has allowed himself in ch. 16 to contradict what he had written earlier is most readily to be explained on the supposition that in ch. 16 he is allowing himself to be guided by tradition" (ibid.). For a similar interpretation, see David Wenham, *Paul: Follower of Jesus or Founder of Christianity?* (Grand Rapids: Eerdmans, 1995), 200–203.

thew himself."[52] However, while this assertion may address the question of whether verses 17–18 are a later tradition, it raises a more serious issue regarding intertextual intensity. If verses 17–18 are thoroughly Matthean, as Sim maintains, then it is all the more difficult to understand how the intertextual references are distinguished from the surrounding narrative. In other words, if the passage has been systematically redacted, what alerts the audience to the proposed intertexts? The problem is exacerbated by the "verbal parallels," which, as noted above, also display Matthean characteristics and are undifferentiated in the First Gospel. It would appear that the parallels blend seamlessly into Matthew's narrative and that there is little, if any, indication that the proposed allusions are marked for identification.

Sim might counter that the lack of intertextual intensity (across all the criteria but more specifically structurality, autoreflexivity, or selectivity) must be appreciated in view of the Evangelist's desire to narrate the Jesus story. More specifically, the concern manifests itself in the writer's reluctance to insert material that is blatantly incongruous with the primary story line. According to Sim, that Matthew "never refers overtly to Paul ... [and] never quotes his letters ... is hardly surprising. Given that the Evangelist wrote a story about Jesus of Nazareth, any such explicit mention of the apostle or his writing would have been anachronistic in the extreme."[53] In this sense, it might appear that Sim offers a plausible rationale for the dilemma; however, the argument is not as straightforward as he envisions. On the one hand, Sim is right to affirm that Matthew's primary objective was to narrate the Jesus story. But this observation does not alleviate the inherent tension in relation to the criteria of autoreflexivity, structurality, and selectivity (as well as referentiality). Indeed, it draws attention to the inherent problem since one could argue (1) that the subject of Greco-Roman βίος—not the Matthean community—is the governing focus and interpretive lens through which to understand the narrative, or (2) that adequate marking is all the more necessary in order to discern those places where contemporary events and discussions have intruded upon the story of Jesus.[54]

---

52. Sim, "Matthew and the Pauline Corpus," 412–14.

53. Ibid., 403–4.

54. On the centrality of the subject in Greco-Roman biography, see Richard A. Burridge, *What Are the Gospels? A Comparison with Graeco-Roman Biography* (SNTSMS 70; Cambridge: Cambridge University Press, 1992); Justin Marc Smith, "About Friends, by Friends, for Others: Author-Subject Relationships in Contempo-

Moreover, while it is true that an "explicit mention of the apostle ... would have been anachronistic," to assume that an explicit reference to *Paul's writings* would have had the same effect is a non sequitur.[55] Had the Evangelist intended to evoke an intertextual Paulinism, a creative and resourceful writer such as Matthew could have easily mirrored the language in Gal 1:12: "Blessed are you Simon son of Jonah, *for you did not receive this from a human source, nor were you taught it, but you received it through a revelation*." Of course, any number of reconstructions are possible, but this example illustrates how the Evangelist might have linked the text to Paul, while simultaneously adhering to the narrative and without falling prey to the jolting anachronism of which Sim warns. If handled in the proper fashion, a direct, or near direct, quotation from Paul is not disruptive to the primary story line of Matthew's gospel. Despite Sim's insistence to the contrary, anachronism is not a satisfying rebuttal to the underlying problem, namely, the lack or intertextual signposting. Perhaps most ironic about this line of argumentation is that Sim's thesis is dependent upon Matthean anachronism.

COMMUNICATIVITY AND INTERTEXTUAL RECEPTION

In the same way that referentiality, structurality, autoreflexivity, and selectivity suggest that the intensity in Matt 16:17–18 is *extremely low*, the criterion of communicativity exposes additional problems with Sim's thesis. For intertextual communication to be effective, both sender and receiver must be cognizant of the intertexts and informed participants in the exchange. Generally speaking, "a maximum level of communicativity is attained if the author is aware of the intertextual relationships with the pre-text, and if the text makes clear that the recipient is intended to recognize these references."[56] Sim's proposal is challenged on both sides of the communicative equation. On the authorial side, the thesis rests upon the assumption that Ignatius maintained a broad awareness of Paul (from which Sim deduces that Matthew possessed a similar knowledge of Paul). The prob-

---

rary Greco-Roman Biographies," in *The Audience of the Gosepls: The Origin and Function of the Gospels in Early Christianity* (ed. Edward W. Klink III; LNTS 353; London: T&T Clark, 2009), 49–67.

55. Sim, "Matthew and the Pauline Corpus," 403–4.
56. Rakel, "Intertextuality," 30.

lem, however, is that while "the figure of Paul looms large for Ignatius,"[57] scholars continue to debate the extent of his knowledge. At present, the consensus is that 1 Corinthians is the only "certain usage."[58] Indeed, many would argue that it is questionable, even "unlikely," that Ignatius knew Galatians, making it all the more problematic to assume that Matthew— written decades prior to the Ignatian correspondence—had access to this important text.[59] It is therefore speculative to assume that Matthew was fully conversant with the Pauline corpus and deliberately inserted a veiled reference to a Galatians.

Furthermore, even if we grant (1) that the Pauline corpus was available to Matthew and (2) that the proposed intertexts were deliberately used, a high level of communicativity should not be presumed. Sim focuses exclusively on the authorial component but makes no attempt to engage the intertextual reception of Matt 16:17–18. The assumption is that if an author makes reference to a pre-text, a communicative chain is established that inevitably leads to the audience's full understanding of the intertext. This general perspective is problematic as evidenced by Matthew's explicit quotations and the use of more subtle intertexts. Matthew often makes overt reference to the Hebrew Bible and therefore alerts the audience to intertextual citations, but it is not uncommon for the communicative stream to be disrupted by the ambiguous style of referencing (2:23) or, as some would suggest, false attribution (27:9). In these instances, it is not as though the audience is unable to discern the primary thrust of the references—to historicize Jesus in light of the past. Rather it is the style of referencing that challenges the hearer to identify the pretextual background in the manner suggested. As a case in point, Matt 27:9–10 explicitly identifies the citation as deriving from the prophet Jer-

---

57. Matthew W. Mitchell, "In the Footsteps of Paul: Scriptural and Apostolic Authority in Ignatius of Antioch," *JECS* 14 (2006): 27–45.

58. William R. Schoedel, *Ignatius of Antioch: A Commentary on the Letters of Ignatius of Antioch* (Hermeneia; Philadelphia: Fortress, 1985), 9. For a recent discussion of the issue, see Paul Foster, "The Epistles of Ignatius of Antioch and the Writings that Later Formed the New Testament," in *The Reception of the New Testament in the Apostolic Fathers* (ed. Andrew F. Gregory and Christopher M. Tuckett; Oxford: Oxford University Press, 2005), 159–86.

59. On the relationship between Ignatius and Galatians, see Andreas Lindemann, "Paul's Influence on 'Clement' and Ignatius," in *Trajectories through the New Testament and the Apostolic Fathers* (ed. Andrew F. Gregory and Christopher M. Tuckett; Oxford: Oxford University Press, 2005), 20–21.

emiah (τότε ἐπληρώθη τὸ ῥηθὲν διὰ Ἰερεμίου τοῦ προφήτου λέγοντος). What follows, however, is a passage based primarily on Zech 11:13. Though the quotation reflects a conflation of motifs (including Jeremiah; cf. Jer 18:1–11; 19:1–13; 32:6–15) and is perhaps explained by the fact that Jeremiah was the better-known figure, the scribal history demonstrates that the reception was adversely affected. Many manuscripts omit the name of the prophet altogether (Φ 33 157 1579 it^a, b vg^ms syr^s, p, pal cop^boms pers^P Diatessaron^a, l mss^acc. to Augustine), and others substitute Zechariah for Jeremiah (22 syr^hmg arm^mss).[60] While this is not intended to suggest that Matt 27:9–10 is indicative of all such formula citations in Matthew, it underscores that communicativity is not as straightforward as Sim envisions.[61] Even with consciously used and explicit intertexts, we should not presume unhindered communicativity.

The same is true when the author uses intertexts of a less overt nature. In an interesting study of Matthean intertextuality, Ulrich Luz offers some striking observations about the use of Mark—without question the most significant intertext in the First Gospel. Though it is certain that Matthew is aware of Mark, Luz considers the question of whether the audience was familiar with Mark:

> The Gospel of Matthew never mentions its hypotext [Mark]; it never thematizes or problematizes its relation to it.… There is no reason to reject the thesis that at least some of Matthew's first readers, or hearers, must have known it, not to mention those hearers and readers in other churches where the Gospel of Matthew became known very quickly. But it is surprising that the evidence within the text amounts to almost nothing. *It cannot be proved that the Gospel of Matthew presupposes the knowledge of the Gospel of Mark by its implicit reader.* Only in a very few cases has Matthew omitted stories narrated in Mark. But in no case, not even in the case of Matthew's omission of Mark 4:26–29 (the parable of the seed that grows without human aid), is it necessary to assume that

---

60. For a fuller discussion of the text-critical issues, see *TCGNT*, 55.

61. An important distinction exists between the use of explicit citations and echoes. To some degree, an explicit citation can be appreciated whether or not an intertextual background is recognized, but this is not the case for the alleged anti-Paulinisms. Sim's thesis depends upon the audience's correct and specific identification of the intertextual background.

the reader knows what Matthew has omitted in order to understand his text.[62]

Matthew's use of Mark may seem tangential to the present discussion, but Luz's assessment demonstrates the need to distinguish between authorial and audience perceptions of intertextuality. Although Sim is content to assume a direct link between the two, it is erroneous to accept this conclusion without further reflection. Matthew may be indebted to Mark, but there is no indication that Matthew's audience is dependent upon Mark in the same way. What can be affirmed from Matthew's use of Mark (or for that matter Q) is that *it is not always certain that the audience is intended to detect pre-textual backgrounds, even when they are clearly being used*. Of course, numerous examples might be cited as evidence of the communicativity that Sim envisions, but these texts are differentiated by their intertextual intensity.[63] In comparison, Matt 16:17–18 hardly registers on Pfister's intensity scale. The absence of distinguishing criteria suggests that, while Sim proposes an intriguing dialogical relationship between Matthew and Paul, the controlling narrative must be retrojected onto Matthew's story, rather than deriving from it.[64] In theory, Pfister's criteria should have aided Sim's intertextual thesis. Instead, the criteria provide no indication that the audience was expected to interpret Matthew as a defense of Petrine authority over and against Paul.

INTERTEXTUALITY, ORALITY, AND MEMORY

Implicit in Sim's conception of intertextuality is the assumption that Matthew's audience consisted primarily of "readers."[65] Although Sim utilizes the acoustic metaphor of the "echo" and makes reference to the intertextual "volume," his analysis is guided by a literary perspective that ignores developments in ancient media studies. Scholars are beginning to recog-

---

62. Ulrich Luz, "Intertexts in the Gospel of Matthew," *HTR* 97 (2004): 125–26 (emphasis added).

63. For an example of more explicit echoes in Matthew, see Dale C. Allison, *The New Moses: A Matthean Typology* (Minneapolis: Fortress, 1993).

64. I have included very little discussion of "dialogicity" because it must be entirely inferred from Sim's proposed reconstruction.

65. On various occasions Sim refers to "readers" of Matthew, but makes no mention of hearers, orality, or performance. See idem, "Matthew and the Pauline Corpus," 404–5.

nize that oral performance, though operating alongside the production of literary texts, was the primary means through which the Jesus story was communicated.[66] Given the reality of widespread illiteracy in the first century, those who came in contact with the Gospel are best described as "hearers," in lieu of the fact that the message was typically experienced as an aural event. The distinction between "readers" and "hearers" is not semantic equivocation since performance is crucial for understanding the rhetorical environment in which the Gospel was delivered, as well as the process of intertextual communication within the dynamics of oral discourse.

Despite a growing sensitivity to the oral context surrounding the Jesus tradition, discussions of intertextuality have yet to engage ancient media studies. Indeed, it is often assumed that intertextual techniques transcend media type and that the exchange between author and audience is not affected by the mode of delivery. However, in a recent article that explores the intersection between intertextuality and memory, Cynthia Edenburg develops a "theory for understanding the cognitive processes involved in encoding and decoding the various types of intertextual devices."[67] Significant for the present discussion is Edenburg's conclusion that *readers and hearers utilize different memory processes in order to interpret intertextual references.*

Edenburg begins her study with a broad overview of human memory "since intertextuality indicates the association evoked in one's mind between one text and another."[68] While much is still unknown about the brain, cognitive and neurophysiological research indicates that information is stored in either short- or long-term memory. Short-term memory, like computer RAM, functions as a clearinghouse for information received in real time, as well as the reactivation of previously stored data (short-term memory is also called "working memory"). Though short-term

---

66. See, e.g., the fine collection of essays in Richard A. Horsley, Jonathan A. Draper, and John Miles Foley, eds., *Performing the Gospel: Orality, Memory, and Mark* (Minneapolis: Fortress, 2006); Holly E. Hearon and Philip Ruge-Jones, eds., *The Bible in Ancient and Modern Media: Story and Performance* (Biblical Performance Criticism; Eugene, Ore.: Cascade, 2009); Annette Weissenrieder and Robert B. Coote, eds., *The Interface of Orality and Writing: Speaking, Seeing, Writing in the Shaping of New Genres* (Tübingen: Mohr Siebeck, 2010).

67. Cynthia Edenburg, "Intertextuality, Literary Competence and the Question of Readership: Some Preliminary Observations," *JSOT* 35 (2010): 131–48.

68. Ibid., 137.

memory is efficient at handling streams of incoming data, it has a limited capacity and can store information for only brief periods before discarding it (less than twenty seconds without the use of rehearsal techniques). By contrast, long-term memory involves the quasi-permanent storage of information and might be compared to the relationship between a hard drive and RAM. Like a computer's hard drive, long-term memory has an infinitely greater capacity than its short-term counterpart (RAM).

According to cognitive psychologists, the retrieval of data stored in human memory is accomplished through the process of *recall* or *recognition*. Accessing information from long-term memory, without the aid of external cuing, occurs through *recall*. In contrast, the activation of the memory through a form of prompting or assistance is termed *recognition*. As Robert Sternberg summarizes, "in recall you produce a fact, a word, or other item from memory," but "[i]n recognition, you select or otherwise identify an item as being one that you learned previously."[69] The distinction may be illustrated in the kinds of retrieval mechanisms utilized when taking an exam that contains multiple testing strategies. Fill-in-the-blank questions challenge students to *recall* specific pieces of information. Though contextual data provide some peripheral help, a specific memory must be evoked with minimal outside assistance. On the other hand, multiple choice, matching, and true/false questions involve a selection process whereby the student identifies or *recognizes* data (ostensibly) stored in long-term memory.

Intertextual studies often take for granted the intricate and dynamic processes involved with human memory. For both readers and hearers, memory has a pivotal role in the interpretive process. The reader has the advantage of possessing a memory tool (i.e., the written text) and may return to a passage over and over again, but the impulse to consider an intertextual reference typically stems from the memory of another text that is not physically present (before it is consulted in written form). This is true not only for echoes or allusions whose pre-textual connections are subtle, but with explicit citations that demand consideration of the greater intertextual context.[70] This same general principle applies to audiences that hear the Gospel as an oral performance. The only difference is that one's

---

69. Robert J. Sternberg, *Cognitive Psychology* (Belmont, Calif.: Wadsworth, 2009), 178.

70. It is important to note that the demands placed upon ancient and modern readers are significantly different. With limited access to documents, ancient readers

reliance upon memory is even greater in an aural environment. Whereas readers have access to written texts, an audience has recourse only to what can be retained in memory. As Edenburg explains, "In the case of oral and aural association, the role of memory is all the more critical since one must retain the memory of a text as it is performed, while searching through long term memory in order to retrieve the recollection of the other text evoked by the association."[71] For both readers and hearers intertextual association is a memory-rich process, but it is particularly demanding for audiences who must simultaneously access two contexts within the temporal flow of the performance and without recourse to written texts.

Edenburg goes on to analyze the various cognitive particularities associated with the interpretation of shared motifs, formulaic language, type scenes, genres, parallel accounts, inner-biblical interpretation, and quotations. Most relevant to the present essay is her discussion of allusion.[72] While Edenburg does not refer to intertextual "intensity," she emphasizes the importance of markers in the identification process:

> For allusion to fulfill its purpose as a signifying device, it must be accompanied by textual markers that alert the audience to an underlying significance. The marker is an element that is "borrowed" from another context where it is at home, and then planted in a new, foreign context. The foreignness of the marker hampers superficial comprehension of the text's overt significance, and intimates that full comprehension of the text will be attained only after identifying the function and significance of the marker in its original textual context.[73]

The problem with Sim's thesis is that Matt 16:17–18 lacks the "foreignness" or "intensity" that would suggest an intertextual reference. The terms and phrase that purportedly link the First Gospel to Paul all have a home in Matthew's narrative and thus lack the necessary signposting. Moreover, it would be extremely difficult for the audience to interpret the passage as Sim envisions due to the performative context and the cognitive demands placed upon the audience. Edenburg explains:

---

were far more reliant upon memory than their modern counterparts, who may typically default to pre-texts in written or electronic format.

71. Edenburg, "Intertextuality, Literary Competence," 137.

72. Ibid., 144–45.

73. Ibid., 144.

For an audience to decode allusion, they must first take heed of the ungrammatical application of the marker, then they must note or *recognize* the familiarity of the marker. Afterwards, they must identify or *recall* the marker's original context. Finally they must hold both the host and the alluded text in the working memory, compare them and extrapolate significance from the analogy that is then reapplied to the host text. The likelihood that an allusion is formulated or decoded in an oral/aural environment depends upon whether it can be comprehended in its entirety during live performance, since given the continuous flow of the performance there is no possibility to pause and reflect upon the nature of the marker and its significance.[74]

In essence, what Edenburg argues is that an audience of hearers is at a unique disadvantage in comparison to a reader of the same material. The ability to recognize the appropriate, narratival markers, while at the same time recalling a detailed intertextual background, is a challenging cognitive task that has certain limitations in a performance arena. The burden upon short-term memory to understand a primary story line, while attempting to assess, identify, and evaluate intertextual references in long-term memory, is significantly more difficult than often assumed. Due to the cognitive challenges inherent in an aural setting, Edenburg concludes that many allusions "would be difficult to formulate or comprehend without perusing a text fixed in writing."[75] This is not to deny the inclusion of authorially derived, allusionary material—whether conscious or unconscious—but it does suggest that an audience's ability to comprehend *certain types* of intertextual references is restricted in an oral environment.

---

74. Ibid., 145 (emphasis original). Because certain types of intertextuality are better suited for literary audiences (e.g., parallel accounts, allusion, and implicit citation), Edenburg argues that texts containing highly allusive material "point away from the oral-aural environment ... and presume a small circle of highly literate writers and readers" (ibid., 147). Though an insightful article, Edenburg's conclusion requires additional nuancing. Not only would this imply that the Gospels (or other New Testament documents for that matter) were written for a very limited and elite audience—which is problematic—it neglects a distinction between authorial and audience competencies. Allusions are often unconsciously embedded (by the author) and largely immaterial for interpretation (by the audience). When echoes are deliberately used that reflect a conscious decision by the author, an audience may be in the cognitive position to appreciate the intertexts due to adequate signposting or the recurrence of a particular motif.

75. Ibid.

With respect to Matt 16:17–18, one has to consider whether it was possible for an audience to identify the array of intertexts proposed by Sim. If Matthew genuinely "sought to challenge or deny Paul's claim that he was divinely commissioned to conduct a mission independently of the Jerusalem church," we should expect to find echoes that are readily discernible for a listening audience. However, not only does Matt 16:17–18 lack the necessary signposting, if Sim is correct, it utilizes intertextual techniques that would be extremely difficult for a listening audience to detect. In the span of two verses, Sim assumes that the audience was able to identify three (possibly four) intertextual citations, all the while attending to Matthew's narrative and appreciating the deeper, subversive message. Given the challenging cognitive hurdles for the hearer of Matthew's Gospel, it is hard to imagine that an audience could have appreciated the complex web of intertexts, delivered within the span of a few short seconds and without sufficient marking. Such an interpretation is far from obvious and runs contrary to Sim's assertion that the text "contains clear echoes of certain Pauline passages."[76] If the allusions were not evident to ancient readers—and Sim provides no evidence that they were—it is even less likely that an audience of listeners was able to appreciate the array of proposed intertexts.

Conclusion

Throughout this essay I have argued that Sim's analysis of Matt 16:17–18 suffers from an inadequate hermeneutical model that employs limited intertextual criteria and ignores the interpretive impact of the oral mileu in which the Gospel was transmitted and performed. If, as Sim implicity affirms, intertextuality denotes "only those texts which an author is consciously, intentionally, and pointedly alluding to [a pre-text], and which the reader is able to recognize as such," then there is very little to suggest that Matthew regarded Paul as an enemy of the Gospel. Moreover, although in this essay I have not sought to explore the many facets of Sim's wider argument, I must tentatively conclude that the interpretive matrix is also flawed since Matt 16:17–18 is hardly a "clear and distinct" example of the Evangelist's anti-Pauline bias. Sim is right to affirm that scholars must be willing to listen for potentially lost frequencies, but we must also be

---

76. Sim, "Matthew and the Pauline Corpus," 412.

sensitive to the inherent challenges associated with the enterprise. Interpreters must be cognizant that the biblical writers often employ pregnant expressions, but we tend—particularly when exploring potentially allusive texts—to find what we are looking for. As Hays cautions, when "we near the vanishing point of the echo, it inevitably becomes difficult to decide whether we are really hearing an echo at all, or whether we are only conjuring things out of the murmurings of our own imagination."[77] In this essay, beyond evaluating the alleged anti-Paulinisms in Matt 16:17–18, I have tried to expose the need for more robust intertextual analysis, along with greater sensitivity to the cognitive features that differentiate hearers and readers of the Gospel.

---

77. Hays, *Echoes of Scripture*, 23.

MATTHEW 5:17–18 AND THE
MATTHEAN USE OF ΔΙΚΑΙΟΣΥΝΗ

Francis J. Moloney, S.D.B.

One of the enigmas of the Gospel of Matthew is the apparent contradiction between Jesus' program not to abolish but to fulfill the law found at the beginning of the Gospel (5:17–18) and the risen Jesus' commission of the disciples to preach all that he has commanded to all nations (28:16–20). The closing scene in the Gospel appears to be a deliberate christological rereading of issues dear to the life and practice of the Judaism of the post-war period: all authority is given to Jesus (see Deut 6:4–9; Dan 7:14). He breaks through national and religious boundaries as he invites his disciples to preach to all nations, replacing circumcision with baptism.[1] He teaches the observance of what Jesus has commanded them (πάντα ὅσα ἐνετειλάμην

---

1. This is widely, but not universally, accepted. See, e.g., Michel-Joseph Lagrange, *Évangile selon Saint Matthieu* (EBib; Paris: Gabalda, 1927), 544–45: "On comprend très bien que la restriction au brébis d'Israel (Mt. X, 5s) ait été levée en ce moment." See also Wolfgang Trilling, *Das Wahre Israel. Studien zur Theologie des Matthäus-Evangelium* (3rd ed.; Munich: Kösel, 1964), 21–51. For David C. Sim (*The Gospel of Matthew and Christian Judaism: The History and Social Setting of the Matthean Community* [SNTIW; Edinburgh: T&T Clark, 1998], 252–55), every aspect of the law was still practiced in the post-Easter Matthean community, including circumcision. Ulrich Luz (*Matthew* [trans. James E. Crouch; 3 vols.; Hermeneia; Minneapolis: Fortress, 2001–2007], 3:631–32) says that we do not know whether the practice of circumcision continued. W. D. Davies and Dale C. Allison (*A Critical and Exegetical Commentary on the Gospel According to Saint Matthew* [3 vols.; ICC; Edinburgh: T&T Clark, 1988–1997], 3:685) argue, "That he expected Jewish Christians to circumcise their male children is plausible; but he evidently did not think such necessary for Gentiles." As Davies, Allison, and Luz all argue that 5:17–18 means that the law must be rigorously kept till the end of all time (see below), Sim (*Gospel of Matthew*, 252) is rightly critical of their lack of logic.

ὑμῖν) as the law (see Exod 29:35).[2] This puzzle is intensified by Jesus' sending of his disciples only "to the lost sheep of the house of Israel" (10:5–6),
and his explanation of his own mission as "only to the lost sheep of the
house of Israel" (15:24).[3] At the same time, Jesus is actively involved with
Gentiles in two miracles stories (8:5–13; 15:21–28), which are directed
toward Gentiles, but are instructive for Israel (see 8:10–12; 15:26–28).

In this essay, offered with respect and gratitude to Frank Matera,
scholar, colleague and dear friend, I argue that the contradiction should
not be regarded as an unresolvable tension in Matthew's narrative. It points
to the situation of the Matthean Jewish Christian community, struggling
with its own identity vis-à-vis the Judaism of its time, and initiating a
Gentile mission. This context determines the Evangelist's appreciation and
presentation of Jesus, his mission, and the mission of the church.[4]

TIME IN MATTHEW'S NARRATIVE

Focusing our attention on the temporal element in the passages that highlight the contradiction between the accepted ways of Judaism and the new
openness to "all the nations," we notice that the passages that limit Jesus'
and his disciples' activities to Israel are located at the beginning of Jesus'
ministry and then during his public ministry (5:17–18; 10:5–6; 15:24). The
mission to "all the nations" is the final scene of the Gospel (28:16–20).

---

2. This affirmation must be nuanced, as Matthew by no means regarded the
Mosaic law as abolished (see, e.g., 9:14–17; 13:52), but it is Jesus' teaching as the
interpretation of the law that must be taught (28:20). See the excellent comment by
Luz, *Matthew*, 3:633–34. For a detailed summary of this discussion and a balanced
response, see Roland Deines, "Not the Law but the Messiah: Law and Righteousness
in the Gospel of Matthew—An Ongoing Debate," in *Built upon the Rock: Studies in the
Gospel of Matthew* (ed. Daniel M. Gurtner and John Nolland; Grand Rapids: Eerdmans, 2008), 53–84. See the annotated discussion of 28:16–20 in John P. Meier, *Law
and History in Matthew's Gospel: A Redactional Study of Mt. 5:17–48* (AnBib 71; Rome:
Biblical Institute Press, 1976), 35–40.

3. Robert H. Gundry (*Matthew: A Commentary on His Literary and Theological Art* [Grand Rapids: Eerdmans, 1982], 8), eliminates the problem by claiming that
"in their numbers and in their following Jesus during his earthly ministry, the Jewish
crowds symbolize the international church, including the many Gentiles who were
later to become disciples (4:25–5:1 with 7:28–8:1; 21:8–9, 11)."

4. This perspective, and much of the study that follows, depends upon Meier,
Law and History; and Roland Deines, *Die Gerechtigkeit der Tora im Reich des Messias*
(WUNT 177; Tübingen: Mohr Siebeck, 2004). See also Deines, "Not the Law," 53–84.

The temporal element of Jesus' words in 5:17–18 calls for a closer examination. His words open the Matthean Jesus' interaction with the law in verses 21–48. They form part of one of Matthew's favorite themes: Jesus the teacher (see the summaries of 4:23; 9:35; and the discourses of 5:1–7:29; 10:1–11:1; 13:1–53; 18:1–35; 24:1–25:45). Although 5:17–18 comes early in Jesus' story, they contain words that look further into the narrative.

> Think not that I have come to abolish the law and the prophets; I have come not to abolish them but to fulfill them. For truly, I say to you, *till* [ἕως ἄν] *heaven and earth pass away*, not an iota, not a dot, will pass from the law *until* [ἕως ἄν] *all is accomplished.*

The two expressions of time in the passage refer to some future "time," using the same Greek words to point to the future: ἕως ἄν. There is the "now" of Jesus' preaching in his first discourse, but there is a time "yet to come" when the present order of things will be changed. These expressions refer to a time in the future when the perfection of the law will be completed: "till [ἕως ἄν] heaven and earth pass away … until [ἕως ἄν] all is accomplished."[5] In the light of our understanding of Jesus' eschatological teaching beginning in the Christian narrative tradition in Mark 13 and importantly present in Matt 24, most scholars continue to read Matt 5:17–18 as a reference to the traditional Jewish notion of the end of time.[6]

This understanding of the future events referred to in 5:17–18 strengthens Jesus' limitation of his disciples' and his own preaching to the lost sheep of Israel (10:5–6; 15:24), and his hesitation before working two miracles for Gentiles (8:5–13; 15:21–28). However, in 28:16–20 Matthew reports words of the risen Jesus that reach outside the narrated events of the Gospel. The disciples are sent on a mission to the ends of the earth, and Jesus promises that he will be with them till the close of the age. If the future time of 5:17–18 referred to the end of all time, the command of Jesus that the law be observed, without changing even the tiniest detail, would still be in force in the post-Easter Matthean community and in any subsequent Christian community using this document as Sacred Scripture, awaiting

---

5. See Meier, *Law and History*, 48: "It is important for the subsequent exegesis that 'until' is the *only* possible meaning. There are no solid grounds for changing the meaning to 'in order that'" (emphasis original).

6. See, e.g., the authoritative interpretation of Davies and Allison, *Matthew*, 1:482–503; and Luz, *Matthew*, 1:213–19.

Jesus' final coming.[7] But whatever one makes of Jesus' relationship to the law during his ministry, he abandons the perfect observance ("not an iota or a dot") of the law in 28:16–20 when he sends his disciples on a mission to all nations.[8]

For many exegetes these tensions reflect tensions already existing in pre-Matthean traditions. They remain within the narrative, once these traditions have been incorporated into Matthew's story of Jesus' life, teaching, death, and resurrection. In the end, we are left with ragged tensions that cannot or should not be resolved as they reflect the Matthean experience.[9] This study takes a different methodological approach. The Gospel must be read as a single utterance that made sense to an author. Matthew did not leave these contradictory understandings of his community's relationship to Torah and its mission to the Gentiles to stand unresolved in the Gospel.[10]

Between Jesus' insistence on the mission to Israel at the beginning and during the course of his public ministry (5:17–18; 10:5–6; 15:24), and his final commission as the risen Lord to the Matthean disciples to go out to the whole world (28:16–20), something happens that dramatically changes the future roles of both Jesus and his disciples. John Meier has drawn attention to the account of Jesus' death and resurrection. Two descriptions are found there—reported only in Matthew—of events that could be regarded as signs of "heaven and earth passing away" (see 5:17–18). The first of these moments is at the death of Jesus:

---

7. This is argued by Luz, *Matthew*, 1:218: "If the Matthean Jesus had temporarily limited the validity of the Torah, that would have been a completely surprising message for the Jewish Christian readers of the Gospel. It would not at all have been in keeping with the one who wants to keep the same Torah down to its last iota."

8. There is some ambiguity over the meaning of τὰ ἔθνη in 28:19. Jews and Gentiles are included in this expression. See, among many, the summary in Luz, *Matthew*, 3:628–31. For Deines (*Gerechtigkeit der Tora*, 183–256), Matt 5:13–16 is already a clear indication of Jesus' preparation of his disciples for a universal mission.

9. See the early study of Ulrich Luz, "The Fulfillment of the Law in Matthew (Matt 5:17–20)," in *Studies in Matthew* (trans. Rosemary Selle; Grand Rapids: Eerdmans, 2005), 185–218 (original German dates back to *ZTK* 75 [1978]: 398–435). Davies and Allison (*Matthew*, 3:707) give up on a theological synthesis: "He did not, however, explicitly reconcile 10:5 with 28:18–20. Perhaps exclusive attention to the accumulation of the implicit and explicit theological meanings of the text obfuscates the contradictory social realities behind Matthew."

10. See Meier, *Law and History*, 44; Deines, *Gerechtigkeit der Tora*, 28–30.

From the sixth hour there was darkness all over the land until the ninth
hour.... The veil of the temple was torn in two from top to bottom; the
earth quaked; the rocks were split; the tombs opened and the bodies of
many holy men rose from the dead. (27:45, 51–53)

The second of these moments is found in the Matthean description of the
events surrounding the resurrection of Jesus:

All at once there was a violent earthquake, for the angel of the Lord,
descending from heaven, came and rolled away the stone and sat upon
it. His face was like lightning, his robe white as snow. And for fear of him
the guards trembled and became like dead men. (28:2–4)

For Meier, *heaven and earth are passing away*. Matthew has taken
some of his imagery and language from the Christian tradition concerning Jesus' death. It is found in Mark's report of the tearing of the veil, the
darkness at the death of Jesus, and the whiteness of the robe of the figure
at the tomb, although he was a "young man," not an angel (Mark 15:38;
16:5).[11] However, it is obvious that Matthew has changed the Markan scenario considerably. He has drawn upon some traditionally "apocalyptic"
symbols from Jewish thought but has shifted their timing. The events
described—darkening of the skies, splitting of the rocks, earthquakes,
lightning, the rising of the dead, the appearance of angels, and men struck
down as if dead—are events that were expected at the end of all time when
YHWH would return as Lord and Judge (see Amos 8:9; Joel 2:10; Hag 2:6;
Zech 14:5; *1 En.* 1:3–9; 71:1–2; Jer 15:9; Ezek 37:7, 12–13; Isa 26:19; Dan
7:9; 10:7–9, 16; 12:2; *T. Levi* 4:1). Matthew indicates that these events will
take place not only at the end of history, as was held by Jewish traditions,
well represented in Matt 24. They have already happened at the death and
resurrection of Jesus.[12]

---

11. It is often easily assumed that Mark's young man is an angel. For a different
opinion, linking the young man in Mark 14:51–52 with the young man in 16:5, see
Francis J. Moloney, *The Gospel of Mark: A Commentary* (Peabody, Mass.: Hendrickson, 2002), 344–46. It is only the more apocalyptic Matthew who introduces an angel.
Luke (24:4) has two men.

12. See Meier, *Law and History*, 30–35. Donald Senior ("The Death of Jesus and
the Resurrection of the Holy Ones [Matthew 27:51–53]," *CBQ* 38 [1976]: 312–29)
argues that the addition of these eschatological events are part of the Matthean redaction. Dale C. Allison (*The End of the Age Has Come: An Early Interpretation of the Death*

Roland Deines agrees that the future time indicated in 5:17–20 is fulfilled in the death and resurrection of Jesus, but regards Meier's limitation of the fulfillment to the paschal events as too narrow. For Deines,
everything that is said about Jesus (Son of God, son of David, Messiah,
the fulfillment of the Scriptures) and the kingdom, from the beginning to
the end of the Gospel, must come into play when the theme of "righteousness" emerges in the narrative. Jesus' coming (5:17), his fulfillment of the
abiding validity of the Torah (v. 18), and his instruction to the teachers (v.
19) establish the righteousness that leads to heaven (v. 20). The disciples'
righteousness as God's righteousness establishes the kingdom of God (6:1,
33). Israel's traditional link between righteousness, the law, and Davidic
messianic expectation is maintained but transformed and "fulfilled" in the
life, teaching, ministry, and eschatological events of the death and resurrection of Jesus, son of David, Son of God, Messiah.[13]

Matthew shows that Jesus lived out the perfection of the Mosaic tradition not only in what he does but also in who he is. Before the story of
Jesus begins, in the incontrovertible information provided for the reader
in the Gospel's prologue (1:1–4:16), Jesus is portrayed as son of David and
son of Abraham (1:1, further spelled out in 1:2–17), Messiah (1:16), king
of Israel (2:1–6), and Son of God (2:15; 4:1–11). The events of the birth and

---

and Resurrection of Jesus [Philadelphia: Fortress, 1985], 40–50), against Senior, claims
that Matthew is incorporating a pre-Christian eschatological tradition. Jesus' death
and resurrection draw eschatological events into the human story. To use the language
of Meier, this marks the "turning point of the ages." It is not the end of human history.
The Matthean Christians were firmly located in a time and a place, living in the "in-
between time," awaiting the final end of history (see Matt 24; 28:20). See Allison, *End
of the Age*, 49–50. For a recent and very different reading of these apocalyptic elements
as a figurative presentation of Jesus as the firstborn from the dead, corresponding to
the birth of the believer, see Serge Wüthrich, "Naître de mourir: la mort de Jésus dans
l'Évangile de Matthieu (Mt 27.51–56)," *NTS* 56 (2010): 313–25.

13. One cannot do justice to this remarkable study in a few lines. For his closing summary, see Deines, *Gerechtigkeit der Tora*, 639–54. In terms of "the turning
point of the ages," see p. 449: "Matthäus beschreibt in seinem Evangelium die eine
heilsgeschichtliche Wende, in der die Offenbarungsgeschichte Israels in Gestalt von
Gesetz und Propheten in Jesus kulminiert und durch ihn einen neuen Anfang zu den
Völkern der Welt nimmt." One of the strengths of Meier's position is his location of
the death and resurrection of Jesus as the moment "when heaven and earth pass away."
See Deines acceptance of this in *Gerechtigkeit der Tora*, 359. For Deines's inclusion of
Meier's thesis as a culmination of Jesus' life, teaching, death and resurrection, see ibid.,
278–79, 355–57.

infancy of Jesus bridge the time between the former covenant and the days of Jesus. They are a fulfillment of the promises of the law and the prophets. Almost every scene in the Matthean prologue indicates that the events of Jesus' birth and infancy are "to fulfill what was said by the prophet" (see 1:22–23, 2:5–6, 15, 17–18, 23; 3:3; 4:6–7, 14–16).[14] The same theme also flows into the ministry of Jesus (see 8:17; 12:17; 13:35; 21:4; 26:54, 56).[15]

The members of Matthew's community are caught up (perhaps, for some, unwillingly?) in the Gentile mission (28:19). Nevertheless, Matthew makes clear that they are products of the perfection of the law and the prophets in the person and teaching of Jesus, and that they are summoned to follow his way till the end of the age. Then the Son of Man will come in final judgment (ch. 24). As this is the case, the Evangelist can claim that the followers of Jesus of Nazareth must still strive to live and teach what Jesus has taught them as they await, assured of the presence of their risen Lord, the end of this age (chs. 24–25; 28:20). For Matthew, the synagogue-centered religion of postwar Judaism, which rejected and expelled the followers of Jesus, had said a definitive no to Jesus' teaching of God's law.[16]

The breakdown between Jesus and the leaders of Israel that dominates 11:2–16:12 and the harshness of the Matthean presentation of Jesus' Jewish accusers during the final days in Jerusalem and his death and resurrection (21:1–28:15) are the major, but not the only, pointers to this truth. Only in Matthew's Gospel do we find the chilling words on the lips of "all the people" (πᾶς ὁ λαός): "His blood be upon us and on our children!" (27:25). Only in Matthew do the leaders of Israel pay those whom they set to guard the tomb, so that a lie could be spread abroad: Jesus was not raised; his disciples stole the body (27:62–66; 28:11–15). The Matthean church was living out God's saving history, from Abraham to Jesus (see 1:1–17) into the Gen-

---

14. On the formative role of the "prologues" in all four Gospels, see Francis J. Moloney, *Beginning the Good News: A Narrative Approach* (Homebush, Austral.: St. Paul Publications, 1992). On Matthew see pp. 73–100.

15. This is not the place to enter into an extended proof of this affirmation, but see Deines, *Gerechtigkeit der Tora*, 453–638, with extensive focus upon Jesus' fulfillment and transformation of Torah, righteousness, and Davidic messianic expectation (pp. 469–500), as found in the use of Torah and righteousness in the Prophets (pp. 501–74) and the Psalter as a Davidic Torah (574–638).

16. As Luz (*Matthew*, 1:55) succinctly and correctly points out: "The Gospel of Matthew is a response to the no of Israel's majority to Jesus. It is an attempt to come to terms with this no by defining the community's position and to contribute to forming and preserving its identity in a situation of crisis and transition."

tile mission (28:16–20).[17] I remain puzzled by the widespread rejection of any historical scheme behind Matthew's narrative.[18] It is generally coupled with a tortured attempt to understand how Matthew understood the role of the law, and the need for the Christian community to adhere to every detail until the end of all time. Every suggestion stumbles over several elements in Jesus' life and teaching that transcend the law. Outstanding, in this respect, is the almost total neglect of the extreme tension that exists between (at least) 5:17–20, 21–48; 10:5–6; 15:24 and 28:16–20.[19]

The Matthean Use of ΔΙΚΑΙΟΣΥΝΗ

I was initially drawn to consider Matthean use of δικαιοσύνη by the encounter between John the Baptist and Jesus in 3:14–15: "John would have prevented him, saying, 'I need to be baptized by you, and do you come to me?' But Jesus answered him, 'Let it be so now [ἄφες ἄρτι]; for thus it is fitting for us to fulfill all righteousness [πληρῶσαι πᾶσαν δικαιοσύνην].' Then he consented." This is the first time that the word δικαιοσύνη appears in the Gospel. These are *the very first words Jesus utters in the Gospel of Matthew*. They do not depend upon the Markan version of this encounter (as does Luke 3:21–22), there is no evidence that it may have come to Matthew from Q, and the passage thus represents a Matthean use of a time scheme of "now ... later."

---

17. For a recent tracing of a saving history through Matthew, see Marvyn Eloff, "Ἀπό ... ἕως and Salvation History in Matthew's Gospel," in *Built upon the Rock: Studies in the Gospel of Matthew* (ed. Daniel M. Gurtner and John Nolland; Grand Rapids: Eerdmans, 2008), 85–107.

18. See the unconvincing appendix of Davies and Allison on theology and salvation history in Matthew (*Matthew*, 3:704–7). I take for granted that Matthew is *not* interested in the "stages of salvation history," so often identified in Luke. I suspect much of the rejection of a Matthean salvation history comes from a correct rejection of any attempt to impose a Lukan scheme upon Matthew.

19. See, e.g., the two important works of David C. Sim, *Apocalyptic Eschatology in the Gospel of Matthew* (SNTSMS 88; Cambridge: Cambridge University Press, 1996); and *Gospel of Matthew*. Sim argues passionately for a Christian Jewish community unconditionally committed to the observance of Torah, bitterly opposed to a Gentile mission, living in a context of an imminent apocalyptic eschatology. No matter what 28:16–20 might suggest (e.g., baptism replaced circumcision), Sim claims that this was not happening in a community where "all parts of the law, both weighty and less weighty, are to be obeyed in full (cf. 23:23)" (*Gospel of Matthew*, 253). See also idem, *Apocalyptic Eschatology*, 208–9.

Matthew uses the expression δικαιοσύνη seven times (3:15; 5:6, 10, 20; 6:1, 33; 21:32), and it is universally accepted that every usage reflects the Matthean redaction. The expression is chosen and used by Matthew.[20] The discussion of this usage is clouded by two issues. Matthew is the most Jewish of the Gospels, and the interpreter leans naturally toward an interpretation of δικαιοσύνη within the broad semantic range of "law-righteousness." This interpretation is supported by Matthew's many uses of the adjective δίκαιος, all of which, with different nuances, describe law-abiding characters (sometimes unfavorably) within the narrative (1:19; 5:45; 9:13; 10:41; 13:17, 43, 49; 20:4; 23:28, 29, 35; 25:37, 46; 27:19).

The shadow of the Pauline use of the expression δικαιοσύνη looms large. Current scholarship supports a blanket understanding of Matthew's use of δικαιοσύνη or "righteousness" as "moral conduct."[21] One of the driving principles of this interpretation is a distinction between Paul and Matthew. God's action (Paul) must be eschewed in favor of human action (Matthew). "Hence 'righteousness' does not refer, even implicitly, to God's gift. The Pauline (forensic, eschatological) connotation is absent."[22] What follows attempts to show that this blanket exclusion of the action of God has narrowed interpretation too severely.

The temporal and spatial location of Matthew's use of δικαιοσύνη deserves attention. Five of the seven sayings appear in Jesus' first discourse and are associated with the instruction of his disciples on the perfect living of the law (5:6, 10, 20; 6:1, 33). They are flanked by the remaining two sayings, both of which are associated with John the Baptist (3:15; 21:31). Jesus' *first words* are marked by the use of δικαιοσύνη in his discussion with John the Baptist, his *first discourse* is studded with its use, and his *final reference* to John the Baptist returns to the expression. The first two of these

---

20. See, among many, Luz, *Matthew*, 1:142.

21. My analysis will refer especially to the outstanding commentaries of Davies and Allison and Luz.

22. Davies and Allison, *Matthew*, 1:499. See also, among many, Gundry, *Matthew*, 70: "No evidence leads us to think that in a Pauline manner he means a sentence of justification when he uses the term. Ordinarily in his Gospel 'righteousness' refers to right conduct on the human side." As Georg Strecker (*The Sermon on the Mount: An Exegetical Commentary* [trans. O. C. Dean Jr.; Edinburgh: T&T Clark, 1988], 98) comments, "the integrity of Jesus' disciples is expressly characterized as human doing (ποιεῖν) and not as divine gift." For the discussion, see Benno Przbylski, *Righteousness in Matthew and His World of Thought* (SNTSMS 41; Cambridge: Cambridge University Press, 1980), 1–8; Deines, *Gerechtigkeit der Tora*, 152–54.

sayings (3:15; 5:6) are future oriented, while the remaining five address a "present" challenge or reality.[23]

MATTHEW 3:15 AND 5:6

Jesus' command to the Baptist: ἄφες ἄρτι, well translated by the RSV as "let it be for now," indicates to the reader (as well as to John the Baptist) that for "now" unexpected events must take place, and that the Baptist must be associated with God's design for Jesus in his response to this "now": "it is fitting for *us*" (πρέπον ἐστὶν ἡμῖν). However, there will be a later time when all righteousness (πᾶσαν δικαιοσύνην) will be fulfilled (πληρῶσαι). Commentators are unwilling to read this passage as a reflection of Matthew's view of salvation history.[24] But it is a time "now" when the Baptist must associate himself with Jesus as that is part of God's *present* design. There will be a later time, when God's intervention in the human story by means of his Son, Jesus, when such actions will no longer be needed. "John no longer simply points to the fulfiller, as did the Law and the prophets. Now, along with the fulfiller, John is also fulfilling God's prophesied plan for salvation."[25] A time will come when all righteousness will be fulfilled.

---

23. For an introduction to the principles guiding literary readings of narrative passages, see Moloney, *Beginning the Good News*, 19–42.

24. See, e.g., Davies and Allison, *Matthew*, 1:325–27. The crux of the issue lies in their following prejudice: "Because with the possible exception of 5.6, δικαιοσύνη seems in Matthew to be uniform in meaning—moral conduct in accord with God's will— we are inclined to define the 'righteousness' of 3.15 as moral conduct." See also Luz, *Matthew*, 1:142–43; Strecker, *Sermon*, 36–38; Pierre Bonnard, *L'Évangile de Matthieu* (CNT 1; Neuchâtel: Delachaux & Niestlé, 1963), 40: "soumission fidèle à la volonté de Dieu." This monochromatic interpretation of δικαιοσύνη in Matthew has its roots in the authoritative work of Georg Strecker, *Der Weg der Gerechtigkeit* (3rd ed.; Göttingen: Vandenhoeck & Ruprecht, 1971), 149–58; and Jacques Dupont, *Les Béatitudes* (3 vols.; EBib; Paris: Gabalda, 1969–1973), 3:211–384, esp. 383–84 (conclusions). It has been recently confirmed by Przybylski, *Righteousness*. For a Pauline reading of "righteousness" in 3:14–15, see John Nolland, *The Gospel of Matthew: A Commentary on the Greek Text* (NIGTC; Grand Rapids: Eerdmans, 2005), 153–54 ("that state of affairs which is all right between God and his world" [p. 154]). Donald A. Hagner (*Matthew* [2 vols.; WBC 33–33A; Dallas: Word Books, 1993–1995], 1:993–95, 55–57) sees the importance of the notion of fulfilling God's will, but argues that at least in 3:15 the salvation-historical perspective of how that happens applies (esp. p. 56).

25. John P. Meier, "John the Baptist in Matthew's Gospel," *JBL* 99 (1980): 392. See also Joachim Gnilka, *Das Matthäusevangelium* (2 vols.; HTKNT I.1–2; Freiburg:

This passage comes *before* 5:17–18 and thus guides the reader better to understand the references to the "now" of the perfect living of the law and the prophets, and the "later" when the law and the prophets will be fulfilled (v. 17) and heaven and earth will pass away (v. 18). In the context of a discussion between Jesus and the Baptist, present practices are to continue—for now. When all righteousness is fulfilled, this will no longer be the case. The same promise will be made later in the story when Jesus instructs his disciples, "This generation will not pass away till all these things take place [ἕως ἂν πάντα ταῦτα γένηται]" (24:34). Jesus' first words immediately alert the reader that there will be a time when all righteousness will be fulfilled (πληρῶσαι πᾶσαν δικαιοσύνην, 3:15), when the law and the prophets have reached their eschatological fulfillment (πληρῶσαι, 5:17).[26] The reader is led by these words of Jesus, his first δικαιοσύνη saying, to recognize on arrival at 5:17–18 that Jesus is pointing forward not to the final end of all time, but to the moment in the story of Jesus when all righteousness will be fulfilled.

This interpretation is strengthened by asking *when* of some crucial Matthean texts. On three occasions during his ministry Jesus threatens Israel that the kingdom will be taken away from them and given to others (8:11–12; 21:42–43; 22:1–10)—when? The prologue to the Gospel (1:1–4:16) is framed by a reference to Abraham, the father of all nations (1:1), and Galilee of the Gentiles (4:16). Hope, nourishment, and forgiveness of sins are offered universally (3:13–19; 12:15–21; 14:13–21; 15:32–39; 26:28), and Jesus teaches that the gospel will be preached to ἐν ὅλῃ τῇ οἰκουμένῃ εἰς μαρτύριον πᾶσιν τοῖς ἔθνεσιν (24:14) before the coming of the end of time. *When will all these things happen?* All these things (πάντα, 5:18; 24:34) will be experienced in the life, teaching, death, and resurrection of Jesus. For the *readers of the story* the fulfillment of all these things has already taken place.[27] They do not have to wait until the end of all time for the fulfillment of "divine expectation." For those living in the presence of the risen Christ

---

Herder, 1986–1988), 1:77; Deines, *Gerechtigkeit der Tora*, 127–32. Warren Carter (*Matthew and the Margins: A Sociopolitical and Religious Reading* [Maryknoll, N.Y.: Orbis, 2000], 102) remarks, "God's saving action, previously stated by the scriptures, is being enacted in Jesus' and John's actions." Contrast David E. Garland (*Reading Matthew: A Literary and Theological Commentary* [Macon, Ga.: Smyth & Helwys, 2001], 37): "It is simply the right thing to do."

26. See Meier, *Law and History*, 41–89; Deines, *Gerechtigkeit der Tora*, 257–87.

27. On 5:18 and 24:34, see Meier, *Law and History*, 57–65.

(28:20), it has already taken place in the life, teaching, death, and resurrection of Jesus.[28] This "temporal" aspect in the reading process is central to an understanding of the shift from Jesus speaking of the fulfillment of righteousness in the future (3:6 and 5:6) to the present experience of the disciples (5:10, 20; 6:1, 33; 21:32), living in the period *after* that fulfillment.

This interpretation of 5:6 must be influenced by the meaning of δικαιοσύνη in 3:15. The beatitudes as a group, the fourth beatitude (5:6) among them, promise a future blessedness dependent upon a way of life. Within that context Jesus points to a future time when God *will satisfy* those who *now* hunger and thirst for righteousness. The "now" of those who hunger and thirst for righteousness who will be blessed with a "future" satisfaction (χορτασθήσονται). As we will see, this "now and after" scheme is not found in the eighth beatitude (v. 10), where righteousness is attained in the "now" ("theirs *is* the kingdom of heaven") by enduring persecution (see also vv. 10–11). As Jesus asked John the Baptist to join him (πρέπον ἐστὶν ἡμῖν, 3:15) in God's design "to fulfill all righteousness," the disciples are invited to a restless yearning and search (hunger and thirst) for righteousness that they may be eschatologically satisfied.

The first words that Jesus speaks in the Gospel of Matthew (3:15) generate a narrative tension that leads the reader to look beyond the immediate context for the meaning of δικαιοσύνη, toward some future time in the story. Those who seek this eschatological gift of δικαιοσύνη are blessed (5:6) because their result of hungering and thirsting "now" for the righteousness that only Jesus can offer in its fullness (3:15) will eventually experience satisfaction.[29] At this stage in the story, the search for true righteousness marks the present experience of the listeners, while their satisfaction lies in the future. Those who hunger and thirst will come to final satiation in their search for the righteousness that God offers in and through Jesus. "The disciple, in effect, is to live now the life that is to be realized fully at the end of time, yet, through Jesus, is already breaking into the world."[30] From now on, however, as the disciples are drawn more deeply into the

---

28. See also ibid., 77–80.

29. See Donald Senior, *Matthew* (ANTC; Nashville: Abingdon, 1998), 71; Carter, *Matthew and the Margins*, 133–34.

30. Senior, *Matthew*, 73. See also Deines, *Gerechtigkeit der Tora*, 137–54, esp. 152: "Aber das 'gesättigt werden,' d.h. das reichliche und ausreichende Empfangen dieser Gerechtigkeit ist denen verheißen, die danach hungern und dürsten. Wie das möglich ist? Weil Jesus gekommen ist, um 'alle Gerechtigkeit zu erfüllen' (3:15)." Craig

kingdom by means of their association with Jesus, all the "righteousness" sayings point to a present challenge or situation.

MATTHEW 5:10

Continuing to read the narrative in the light of the first use of δικαιοσύνη in 3:15, now reinforced by the promise of eschatological satisfaction in the immediate context of 5:6, one can see that this text hints at commitment to righteousness that will lead to persecution. For most interpreters, hamstrung with their limited understanding of the Matthean use of δικαιοσύνη, moral achievement is again at stake: "'Righteousness' here can only be something people have, namely their obedient, righteous conduct."[31] But the immediate and broader context suggests that Christology is involved. The fullness of righteousness is yet to be achieved in the story (see 5:17–48; 27:45, 51–53; 28:2–4, 16–20), but the Matthean disciples are promised that persecution for the sake of righteousness (ἕνεκεν δικαιοσύνης) brings (present tense: ἐστιν) the kingdom of heaven. A christological reading of ἕνεκεν δικαιοσύνης is demanded by the expansion of what is meant by verse 10 in verses 11–12. "Blessed are you when people revile you and persecute you … because of me [ἕνεκεν ἐμοῦ]" (v. 11). The parallel between ἕνεκεν δικαιοσύνης (v. 10) and ἕνεκεν ἐμοῦ (v. 11) must be respected, since verses 10–11 are a Matthean addition to the tradition in order to relate verse 10 to the experience of the community.[32]

The theme is repeated in Jesus' instructions to his community in 10:22: "You will be hated by all for my name's sake [διὰ τὸ ὄνομά μου]." The suffering experience of the Matthean community was not primarily caused by their "obedient, righteous conduct." If persecution is the result of the Matthean disciples' living obediently, what distinguished them from their Jewish contemporaries? Were they also persecuted for their

---

L. Blomberg (*Matthew* [NAC 22; Nashville: Broadman, 1992], 95) speaks of "inaugurated eschatology."

31. Davies and Allison, *Matthew*, 1:459–60. See also Luz, *Matthew*, 1:195. Both take a close relationship between v. 6 and v. 10 as indicating moral performance.

32. As Luz (*Matthew*, 1:199) puts it: "The persecution for the sake of righteousness in v. 10 and the equally redactionally formulated persecution for 'my sake' in v. 11 mutually interpret one another." But he does not draw the christological consequences, concluding: "Confessing Christ manifests itself in deeds (7:21–23; 25:31–46)." This, of course, is correct, but does not do full justice to the christological possibilities of δικαιοσύνη. In response to Luz, see Deines, *Gerechtigkeit der Tora*, 179–80.

"obedient, righteous conduct"?[33] The immediate context spells out that Matthean disciples are reviled and persecuted because their commitment to Jesus renders the kingdom present "now" (5:11–12). In the next discourse (10:1–11:1, the community's mission) this is further reinforced. Disciples are instructed that they will be hated for the sake of Jesus' name (10:22).[34]

Persecution for righteousness' sake (5:10) is the consequence of a commitment to God's design for the fulfillment of all righteousness (see 3:15), the yearning for the perfection of God's will and design (5:6), in imitation of Jesus, who came to fulfill the law (see 5:17) and who called his disciples to follow him into a perfection of love that matches the perfection of God (5:48).[35] Rightly has David Garland commented on 5:10:

> It is one thing to pronounce blessed those who are persecuted because of righteousness or devotion to the law (2 Macc 7:9, 11, 23, 37; 4 Macc 6:24–30); it is something else to pronounce blessed those who are persecuted because of their relationship to Jesus, "for my sake" (see also 10:18, 39; 16:25; 19:29). This beatitude reflects the high christology of the Gospel.[36]

MATTHEW 5:20

Matthew 5:17–20 is generally regarded as an introduction to verses 21–48. But it is a continuation of what has been said since 5:3, an argument that is not completed until 5:48.[37] The exhortation of the disciples in the Beatitudes, and especially in the parables of 5:13–16, continues to determine

---

33. See the effort of Strecker, *Sermon*, 42–43, to respond to this question. Some suggest 1 Pet 3:14a ("But even if you suffer for righteousness' sake, you will be blessed") as a parallel to Matt 3:10. See Eduard Schweizer, *The Good News according to Matthew* (trans. David E. Green; London: SPCK, 1976), 95–96. This is helpful, as long as the whole context is taken into account: "Have no fear of them nor be troubled, but in your hearts reverence Christ as Lord" (1 Pet 3:14b–15).

34. See Gnilka, *Matthäusevangelium*, 1:127–29.

35. Rightly, Deines, *Gerechtigkeit der Tora*, 155–81. Meier argues for a variety of meanings for δικαιοσύνη in Matthew (*Law and History*, 76–77), but he accepts that in 5:10 "the meaning of Christian moral practice is clear" (77).

36. Garland, *Reading Matthew*, 59. Nolland (*Matthew*, 206), on the other hand, suggests that Matthew's inspiration was the martyr tradition of the Maccabean period.

37. See Deines, *Gerechtigkeit der Tora*, 429–34.

the argument. They are to be salt and light. God's righteousness must be manifested in them.

Meier has shown that verses 17–18 are the result of Matthew's rewriting of the tradition, and that verse 19 probably came to Matthew from a prior reworking of Q. The association of the Matthean verses 17–18 with the traditional verse 19 "resembles an undigested morsel in our text."[38] If everything in verses 17–19 was meant by Matthew to indicate that each commandment (v. 19) of the law and the prophets (v. 17) was binding until the end of all time (v. 18), *as that event is described in Matt 24*, and if anyone who dared to relax even the minutiae in life and teaching was to be least in the kingdom, then Jesus stands among the least in the kingdom of heaven (v. 19). Obviously, Matthew did not want to say that!

While verse 19 continues the argument of verses 17–18 by indicating the penalty ("least") or blessing ("great") flowing from one's observance of the various commandments that make up the law and the prophets, it looks forward to the series of reinterpretations of individual commandments (ἐντολαί) that Jesus puts in place in the antitheses of verses 21–48. And it leads into verse 20. In the light of 3:15 and 5:6, the warning that compares the believers' righteousness with the righteousness of the scribes and the Pharisees (v. 20) cannot *only* be a plea that the disciples be more moral than their Jewish contemporaries.[39] It has to do with the fulfillment of God's design, intimately associated with Jesus' understanding of the law, and his request that his disciples join him (5:3–13). The theme of righteousness that has appeared in this early section of the discourse has called followers of Jesus to a qualitatively "different righteousness" (3:15; 5:6). The believer's righteousness "exceeds [περισσεύσῃ] that of the scribes and Pharisees" because its measure is the person of Jesus Christ. The disciple is to "exceed" the righteousness of the scribes and the Pharisees, and exceed it πλεῖον. The comparison is a "qualitative" exceeding of the righteousness of the scribes and the Pharisees, as it is to reflect the eschatological righteousness of God.[40]

Jesus' authoritative reinterpretation of Torah across verses 21–48, stated categorically with the rhythmic repetition of ἐγὼ δὲ λέγω ὑμῖν (vv.

---

38. Meier, *Law and History*, 104.

39. Major commentators point to the comparison with the scribes and the Pharisees as an indication that v. 20 is about better moral performance. See Davies and Allison, *Matthew*, 1:499; Luz, *Matthew*, 1:221–22.

40. See Deines, *Gerechtigkeit der Tora*, 425–28.

22, 28, 32, 34, 39, 44), maps out what it means to fulfill (πληρῶσαι) the law and the prophets. At the end of his reinterpretation of Torah, he turns to his disciples and informs them that they are to parallel his life and ministry in their performance of reinterpreted Torah. He commands them: "Be perfect, as your heavenly Father is perfect" (v. 48). Jesus claims that he has come to "fulfill" (πληρῶσαι) the law and the prophets. The "perfection" (τέλειοι) of the disciples, matching that of their heavenly Father, is the way in which they are to greatly exceed the righteousness of the Pharisees. It is this "perfect righteousness" that leads to the eschatological gift of the kingdom of heaven. The association of the disciples with a christological principle is prepared in 5:3–16 and established in verses 17–20. In Jesus' teaching on the practice of disciples, outlined in verses 21–48, the accent is upon the eschatological style of their living, determined by the fact that they are disciples of Jesus who do not abrogate the Mosaic law but perfect it (v. 17).[41] "Despite appearances, despite all the eschatological sharpening and rescinding of the Law that goes on in the antitheses, Jesus' eschatological mission is not to do away with the Law and the prophets, but to give them their eschatological fullness."[42] Jesus' request that the righteousness of his disciples (v. 20) reflects the perfection of God (v. 48) draws them into this eschatological fullness.[43] In 6:1 and 6:33 the reader will learn that the disciples' righteousness is God's righteousness, and as such establishes the kingdom of God.

MATTHEW 6:1

A new section in the discourse opens with 6:1.[44] The theme of authentic religious practice, over against the falsity of the "hypocrites," dominates 6:2–6 (ὑποκριταί, v. 5) and its parallel in 6:16–18 (ὑποκριταί, v. 16). The identity of the hypocrites who parade their virtue is not specified, but their

---

41. See Meier, *Law and History*, 168: "The rule of life for the Christian is thus an 'umbrella concept': 'all things whatsoever I commanded you'—be that *secundum*, *praeter*, or *contra* the Mosaic Law."

42. Ibid., 69.

43. For a detailed analysis of vv. 17–20, set within its broader Matthean context, that supports this view, see Deines, *Gerechtigkeit der Tora*, 257–434.

44. There is some doubt about the originality of the first δέ in 6:1. The textual evidence is evenly balanced. It makes no difference to the interpretation of δικαιοσύνη. See further Deines, *Gerechtigkeit der Tora*, 435–46.

association with the synagogue (see vv. 2, 5) links Jesus' instruction in 6:1 with his parallel instruction in 5:20.[45] The exhortation to δικαιοσύνη in 6:1 acts as a "hinge passage" between 5:21–48 and 6:2–28.[46] The formal link with 5:20, in the light of 3:15, 5:6, 10, warns against making light of this Matthean expression, used consistently to speak of the fulfillment of divine expectation. The "doing" (ποιεῖν) of "righteousness" looks to the future reward (μισθόν) from the Father in heaven. This is contrasted with those whose public parading of accepted practices "already" (vv. 2, 5, 16) have their reward. The Matthean Christology demands that the disciples being instructed must live as Jesus lived, "doing" the righteousness that he has already "fulfilled" (3:15; 5:6, 10, 17–20).[47] Although the expression "kingdom of heaven" is not explicit, the reward from the Father who is in heaven is not lost or gained only from right religious practice *before God* (5:20; 6:1); it is a participation in the life that is available to Jesus' disciples by means of their participation in the eschatological gift of a righteousness that comes *from God* (3:15).[48]

MATTHEW 6:33

As 5:21–48 was introduced by describing its relationship to the fulfillment of the law and the prophets (5:17–20), 6:19–7:11 closes with a description of the relationship that exists between right living and the law and the prophets (7:12).[49] Many regard 6:33 as an "end point" or a summary of the Sermon on the Mount (5:1–7:28).[50] The search for righteousness is intimately linked with the kingdom of God. The joining of τὴν βασιλείαν

---

45. See Lagrange, *Matthieu*, 119: "Il est clair que la justice des disciples est celle de v. 20." See also Deines, *Gerechtigkeit der Tora*, 437–38.

46. Most commentators see 6:1 as "thematic" for 6:1–18. The presence of δικαιοσύνη in 5:6, 10, 20; 6:1, 33, leads Davies and Allison to claim that the term "expresses the essence of the sermon on the mount" (*Matthew*, 1:499).

47. Deines, *Gerechtigkeit der Tora*, 439: "Sie 'erfüllen' die Gerechtigkeit nicht, sondern 'tun' bzw. 'verwirklichen' die durch Jesus erfüllte (und ihnen auf seinen Jüngern aufgetragene) Gerechtigkeit."

48. Ibid., 440: "'Eure Gerechtigkeit' is darum keine andere als die, die Jesus erfüllt hat, es ist die Gerechtigkeit, die ihr Leben *von* Gott und *vor* Gott bestimmt. In 5,20 und 6,1 ist lediglich die Perspective eine jeweils andere, indem der Blick vom Jünger aus auf sein Tun geht."

49. For this structure see Luz, *Matthew*, 1:173.

50. For detail see Deines, *Gerechtigkeit der Tora*, 441.

τοῦ θεοῦ and τὴν δικαιοσύνην αὐτοῦ with καί can generate a hendiadys,[51] "the co-ordination of two ideas, one of which is dependent upon the other."[52] It is impossible to equate the kingdom with moral performance. As Meier rightly observes, "*dikaiosunēn* appears next to *basileia* as the co-equal object of the seeking."[53] Disciples are to seek, before everything else (ζητεῖτε δὲ πρῶτον), the righteousness that is the kingdom of God (τὴν βασιλείαν τοῦ θεοῦ) in their lives. The kingdom is further described as *his* (i.e., God's) righteousness (τὴν δικαιοσύνην αὐτοῦ). If "righteousness" in Matthew has "to be uniform in meaning—moral conduct according to God's will,"[54] how can this be said of God?[55] "No exegete would claim that the kingdom in Mt. is simply to be equated with Christian moral effort or the end result of that effort."[56]

This final use of the expression in the Sermon on the Mount reinforces what Matthew has taught to this point: the imperative to search for the kingdom of God and his righteousness indicates that "the righteousness of God" describes the fulfillment of God's design in and through the life, teaching, and especially the death and resurrection of Jesus that has fulfilled all righteousness (see 3:15). Disciples are not to seek "entry" into the kingdom, but to devote themselves assiduously to the spread and the strengthening of the kingdom in the world. It is an exhortation that they take seriously their universal mission as followers of Jesus.[57] The eschatological, beyond (but not excluding) the moral, aspect of the δικαιοσύνη

---

51. There is some doubt about the presence of τοῦ θεοῦ in 6:33. A stronger textual tradition supports it and is a reading that would not have been easily omitted. However, Matthew almost always uses βασιλεία without a modifier. I am retaining it also because of the textual evidence, and the literary and grammatical balance that exists between the τοῦ θεοῦ (after "kingdom") and αὐτοῦ (after "righteousness"). There is no textual doubt about the latter, which would have no antecedent noun if the former were omitted.

52. BDF, §442 (16). If this is not a hendiadys, recourse can be had to the use of the epexegetical καί where the second noun is an explanation of the first (§442 [9]).

53. Meier, *Law and History*, 78. See also Hagner, *Matthew*, 1:166.

54. Davies and Allison, *Matthew*, 1:327.

55. This problem is well discussed in Nolland, *Matthew*, 314–15; Strecker, *Sermon*, 139–40.

56. Meier, *Law and History*, 78. However, exegetes do make this claim for 6:33.

57. Deines, *Gerechtigkeit der Tora*, 446: "*Zusammenfassend* ergibt sich für 6,33, dass der Imperativ ζητεῖτε nicht im Sinne von eingehen in die Basileia zu interpretieren ist, sondern als *sich bemühen um die Ausbreitung und Geltung der Basileia in der Welt*, d.h. er ist Aufruf zu einer missionarischen Existenz" (emphasis original).

sayings in evidence throughout the discourse of 5:1–7:28 is summarized in 6:33.[58]

MATTHEW 21:32

The final use of δικαιοσύνη in Matthew is in 21:32. The first such saying appeared in a discussion with John the Baptist that asked the Baptist to accept the situation of Jesus' baptism and to look forward to a time of the fulfillment of righteousness (3:15). This final saying, coming after a series of such sayings in 5:1–7:28, returns to a context that involves John the Baptist and is Matthew's last reference to this figure.[59] It again associates him with righteousness. Located in the larger section of the story dedicated to the definitive breakdown between Jesus and Israel that leads to his death and resurrection (21:1–28:15), it is part of a bitter series of conflicts between Jesus and the leaders of Israel (21:12–23:39). As with 5:17–20 and 6:1, the expression δικαιοσύνη appears in a major introductory section of the narrative (21:12–33).

Following Jesus' action in the temple (21:12–17) and the cursing of the fig tree (vv. 18–22), Jesus' authority is questioned by the chief priests and the elders of the people (vv. 23–27). He addresses this situation of unbelief by means of the parable of the Two Sons (vv. 28–31). Interpreting the parable, he attacks the leaders of Israel as having given lip service to the commands of God, but doing what they want, while there are "outsiders"

---

58. Uncomfortably, Davies and Allison (*Matthew*, 1:661) recognize this. They conclude their analysis of 6:33 with the comment: "Righteousness is the law of the realm, the law of eschatological rule one must strive for, the better righteousness of 5:20." This contradicts their earlier blanket assessment of righteousness as "moral conduct," and makes nonsense of their interpretation of 5:17–20 as the abiding command to observe the letter of the law until the end of time. On the other hand, Luz (*Matthew*, 1:344) is more consistent (and consequently less satisfactory) as he comments: "'Righteousness' probably means, as in 3:15; 5:6, 10, 20; 6:1, the righteousness required of people, that is, the activity that God desires and that corresponds to his kingdom." His handling of the parallel between God's righteousness and God's kingdom is uncomfortable. He sees the parallel between this expression and the third and fourth petition of the Lord's Prayer, but must then comment, "here the person's task is in the foreground, while there it is God's asked-for acting for and through the person" (1:344–45). For a similar critique of Luz, see Deines, *Gerechtigkeit der Tora*, 443–45.

59. See Deines, *Gerechtigkeit der Tora*, 132–36. He refers to 3:15 and 21:32 as "der äuβere Rahmen" of Matthew's use of "righteousness."

who have responded. This was also the case in the time of John the Baptist, described as one who came to them "in the way of righteousness" (ἐν ὁδῷ δικαιοσύνης, v. 32). This phrase is regarded as a traditional expression used to indicate a good life.[60] Matthew's use of "the way" (see 3:3; 4:15; 5:25; 8:28; 10:10; 13:4, 19; 15:32; 20:17, 30; 21:8, 19; 22:16) is dependent upon Mark.[61]

The Baptist's coming "in the way of righteousness" brings Jesus' instruction to John the Baptist in 3:15 to closure. In their first encounter, the Baptist accepted his role as he waited for the fulfillment of righteousness. As with Jesus, so with the Baptist: both were rejected by a false Israel that claimed righteousness but did not live that way (see especially 15:10–20; 21:28–32, 33–41; 23:1–10, 11–36).[62] The consequence of this situation is that the "outsiders" (tax collectors and prostitutes) who join John and follow Jesus accept the fullness of righteousness present in Jesus (3:15). Israel will not repent and believe. This is already an initial fulfillment of Jesus' threats in 8:11–12, 21:42–43, and 22:1–10, and has been foreshadowed by Jesus' words on the reception of John the Baptist in 11:7–19. "Yet wisdom is justified [ἐδικαιώθη] by her deeds" (11:19). The situation will worsen from 21:33 through 28:16.

Given the complex of δικαιοσύνη sayings, their arrangement across the Gospel narrative, and the cumulative reading experience that leads to this final saying, understanding 21:32 as an indication that John the Baptist lived a morally upright life is unsatisfactory.[63] The Matthean uptake of the Markan theme of "the way" indicates that the dynamic sense of journey-

---

60. See the documentation in Davies and Allison, *Matthew*, 3:170 n. 42. It is never found in rabbinic sources. For a reading of these sources as the "Weg *zur* Gerechtigkeit," see Deines, *Gerechtigkeit der Tora*, 134–35.

61. There are a few uses in Matthean special material (2:12 [Magi]; 10:5 [the way of the Gentiles]; 22:9–10 [parable of the Marriage Feast]). We should not make too much of the remaining passages that come from Q (7:13–14 [see Luke 13:23–24: the narrow gate]; 11:10 [see Luke 5:27: citation of Mal 3:1, found in a different setting in Mark 1:2]). Matthew introduces ἡ ὁδός into the Q passage of the narrow gate (7:13–14; Luke 13:23–24).

62. See Hagner, *Matthew*, 2:614; Meier, "John the Baptist," 383–405; Carter, *Matthew and the Margins*, 425–26; Deines, *Gerechtigkeit der Tora*, 134.

63. Davies and Allison, *Matthew*, 3:170; Luz, *Matthew*, 3:31–32: "Life that corresponds to the will of God" (p. 31). Nolland (*Matthew*, 863–64) rightly looks back to 3:15, but repeats the Pauline interpretation offered there ("that state of affairs in which all is right between God and his world" [p. 364]).

ing, both physically and spiritually, is also congenial to Matthew.[64] John the Baptist, instructed by Jesus to attend to the fulfillment of righteousness (3:15), was ἐν ὁδῷ δικαιοσύνης; but the chief priests and the elders of the people (see v. 23) do not join him on this "way."

Israel's final rejection of the perfection of all righteousness that was first articulated during the Baptist's ministry (3:15) and further explained in Jesus' first discourse (5:6, 10, 20; 6:1, 33) is near at hand as Jesus turns toward the death and resurrection that will mark the turning point of the ages (21:32). Meier comments: "Both eschatological gift and man's moral effort may come together in 21:32."[65] The Matthean use of δικαιοσύνη marks both Jesus' first encounter with John the Baptist in 3:15 and his final comment on John's role in 21:32. This "location" of the sayings enhances the possibility that the theme of "eschatological gift," so prominent in 3:15, is also present in 21:32. This is further enhanced by the cumulative effect the sevenfold use of δικαιοσύνη has upon the reader. As Donald Hagner comments: "Probably this is to be understood as a reference to the process of the accomplishment of salvation in history through God's sending of John as the forerunner of Jesus."[66]

CONCLUSION

In this study I agree that the Matthean δικαιοσύνη is not Pauline.[67] But I attempt to indicate that mainstream scholarship has overreacted against possible Pauline interpretations of Matthew by insisting that *all* Matthean δικαιοσύνη sayings are to be associated with human action, and *never* with God's design. This appears to be a straitjacketing of the Matthean text.

---

64. See Deines, *Gerechtigkeit der Tora*, 135–36. On the Markan theme, see Ermenegildo Manicardi, *Il cammino de Gesù nel Vangelo di Marco: Schema narrativa e tema cristologico* (AnBib 96; Rome: Biblical Institute Press, 1986).

65. Meier, *Law and History*, 79. See also Meier, "John the Baptist," 401.

66. Hagner, *Matthew*, 2:615, with reference to 3:15. See also Gnilka, *Matthäusevangelium*, 2:222.

67. Contrast what follows with Frank Matera, *New Testament Theology: Exploring Diversity in Unity* (Louisville: Westminster John Knox, 2007), 35–36. Even more trenchant is Sim, *Gospel of Matthew*, 165–213: "Matthew openly and savagely attacks Paul and his law-free Gospel" (p. 213). These pages are reminiscent of Ferdinand Christian Baur's understanding of the factions that determined early Christianity, and the development of the NT. See William Baird, *History of New Testament Research* (2 vols.; Minneapolis: Fortress, 1992–2004), 1:258–69, esp. 263–69.

Jesus is the fulfillment of all the promises made to Israel, as he obediently responds to all that God asks of him (5:17–18). In his final act of obedience and God's response, death and resurrection, Matthew makes clear that a new era has dawned (27:45, 51–53; 28:2–4). Although, apart from δικαιοσύνη, Pauline language is not used (e.g., "in Christ," "grace," "sonship," "new creation," etc.), Matthew tells of the establishment of an eschatological people (28:16–20; see also 16:13–19; 18:15–20).[68]

As he opens his ministry, Jesus points to the future fulfillment of righteousness (3:15). A future (eschatological) orientation is maintained in 5:6. But, from that point on, there is a righteous way of living "now" that reflects the fulfillment of all righteousness (5:10, 20; 6:1, 33). This "now" of the life of Jesus closes as he returns to John the Baptist and shows that Israel has made its decision (21:32). From that point on in the story, Israel's no to the fullness of righteousness is played out. Jesus fulfills all righteousness. He is the perfection of the Davidic messianic promises, the Son of God, the perfection of Torah and the prophets. A final "turning point of the ages" is revealed when heaven and earth pass away (5:17–18; 27:45, 51–53; 28:2–4).

The search for righteousness, for Matthew, is not primarily commitment to required moral response. It is a discipleship transformed by Jesus' fulfillment of righteousness through his life and teaching as the son of David, son of Abraham, Messiah, and Son of God (1:1, 23; 4:1–11; 16:16–18), and climactically in and through his eschatological death and resurrection.

> In Matthew ... this age and the age to come seemingly overlap. Although the consummation lies ahead, although this age is still full of tribulation, and although the Christian casts his hope in the future coming of the Son of Man, saints have already been raised, the Son of Man has already been enthroned in the heavenly places, the resurrected Jesus is ever present with his followers (28:20). If we may so put it, Matthew's eschatology is, in some ways, more realized than that of Mark.[69]

---

68. Note the important closing comment of Deines, *Gerechtigkeit der Tora*, 654: "Das letzte Wort in dieser Sache haben aber weder Matthäus noch Paulus, sondern der auferstandene und wiederkommende Christus. Bis dahin wird die Christenheit gut daran tun, *beiden* Zeugen des Evangeliums mit ganzer Leidenschaft zuzuhören zu tun, was sie sagen" (emphasis original). See also Deines, "Not the Law," 80: "It is the eschatological, overflowing rich righteousness that Jesus fulfilled and made available to his disciples that from now on alone opens the way to the kingdom of God."

69. Allison, *End of the Age*, 49–50. See Meier, *Law and History*, 38: "There is much more 'realized eschatology' in Mt.'s theology than is usually admitted."

The Christology of Mark and the Son of Man

Jack Dean Kingsbury

The purpose of this article is to undertake a literary-critical survey of the Christology of Mark's Gospel with focus on the term *the Son of Man*. To set the stage, however, we need to review the corrective approach to Mark's Christology, based on the method of redaction criticism, and a narrative approach, based on the method of literary criticism. First, however, permit me to say that I write this article in honor of Frank Matera, who has been a prolific writer in the field of New Testament studies, a mentor of countless students, and a good friend to me and to many other scholarly colleagues.

The Corrective Approach to Mark's Christology

The method of redaction criticism focuses on the distinctiveness of each Gospel. Toward the end of the 1950s, redaction critics believed that they could best capture the distinctiveness of Mark's Christology by taking a corrective approach to it. This approach soon became dogma, and for twenty-five years it was the dominant way whereby Mark's Christology was interpreted. According to the corrective approach, Mark's Gospel was at home in a Hellenistic or Jewish Hellenistic environment. Within this environment, the so-called divine man, as sketched, for example, by Ludwig Bieler in 1935–1936, was thought to have been a familiar figure.[1] What Mark was about in his Gospel, therefore, was misdirection and correction. In the prologue and first half of his Gospel (1:1–13; 1:14–8:26), he invited the members of his Christian community to identify Jesus with the

---

1. Ludwig Bieler, *Theios Aner: Das Bild des "göttlichen Menschen" in Spätantike und Frühchristentum* (2 vols.; Vienna: Höfels, 1935; repr. in one volume, Darmstadt: Wissenschaftliche Buchgesellschaft, 1976).

Hellenistic divine man only to use the second half of his Gospel to correct this false image of Jesus.

It is in the episode of Jesus' baptism (1:9–11) that Mark was said to present Jesus as the Hellenistic divine man. In this episode, the heavens split apart, the Spirit descends "into Jesus," and the heavenly voice declares him to be God's Son. The declaration by the heavenly voice reveals that Mark's preferred title for Jesus as the Hellenistic divine man is that of "the Son of God." The Spirit's descent "into Jesus" shows that although he remains a human being, he is nevertheless transformed into the divine man and endowed with supernatural powers.[2] As he discharges his ministry to Israel in the first half of Mark's Gospel (1:14–8:26), these supernatural powers come to expression in the authoritative words he utters and the miraculous deeds he performs. As the Son of God, or the Hellenistic divine man, Jesus stands forth as a figure of power and glory.

In the second half of his Gospel (8:27–16:8), however, Mark corrects this image of Jesus as the Hellenistic divine man. He does so through the twin vehicles of Jesus' passion predictions (8:31; 9:31; 10:32–34) and the passion narrative (chs. 14–15). For Mark, Jesus is the Son of Man who must suffer and die. Through use of misdirection and correction, therefore, Mark weans the members of his community away from a false understanding of Jesus and leads them to adopt a true understanding of him. Decidedly, Mark's is a Son-of-Man Christology.

A NARRATIVE-CRITICAL APPROACH TO MARK'S CHRISTOLOGY

Come the early 1980s, the method of redaction criticism had gradually given way in Gospel research to literary criticism understood in the main as narrative criticism. As a narrative, a Gospel is made up of "story" and "discourse." The story each Gospel tells is that of Jesus. The discourse of each Gospel is "how" the story is told. A central feature of discourse is "point of view."[3] In exploring Mark's story, the most important aspect of point of

---

2. Ferdinand Hahn (*Christologische Hoheitstitel: Ihre Geschichte im frühen Christentum* [FRLANT 83; Göttingen: Vandenhoeck & Ruprecht, 1963], 342–45) charges that although Mark's Christology is "functional," the redaction critics who take the corrective approach interpret the phrase "into Jesus" in "ontic" terms: Jesus is transformed into the divine man.

3. See Boris Upsensky, *A Poetics of Composition: The Structure of the Artistic Text and Typology of a Compositional Form* (Berkeley: University of California Press, 1973).

view is the ideological or evaluative. This has to do with "worldview," with the perspective and values in terms of which an author or any character within a story views reality, looks at persons, things, or events, and evaluates them or makes sense of them.

In terms of point of view, a hierarchy of authority exists within the world of Mark's Gospel story. Although the story itself tells of Jesus, it nonetheless situates him within God's plan of salvation as it unfolds in the history of first Israel and then also of the nations (1:2–3; 8:31; 13:10). The upshot is that it is God's point of view that is made normative within this world. God is the one who is the supreme arbiter of truth, reality, and values: what is true or false, real or unreal, right or wrong. Truth is defined as "thinking the things of God," falsity as "thinking the things of human beings" (8:33), which is not only wrong but also satanic.

Because God twice calls Jesus "my Son" (i.e., the Son of God; 1:11; 9:7), Jesus' point of view in Mark's story is necessarily subordinate to, yet aligned with, that of God. Moreover, because Mark, as the voice that narrates the Gospel story, does not dissemble but speaks reliably to the readers, his viewpoint too is subordinate to, yet aligned with, that of God. As for all of the other characters or figures within the world of Mark's story, their viewpoints have validity only to the extent to which they agree with the viewpoints of God, Jesus, or Mark as narrator.

In 1983 narrative-critical method was first comprehensively applied to the Christology of Mark.[4] By demonstrating the crucial importance of point of view, by emphasizing the hierarchy of authority that exists in Mark's story, and by calling attention to the reliability of Mark as narrator, the effect such application had was to expose the untenability of redaction criticism's corrective approach. Narrative-critical method, indeed, brought about the sudden demise of the corrective approach. To illustrate, consider again the episode of Jesus' baptism. Because Mark as narrator speaks reliably, he is not to be seen as misdirecting the readers in telling of Jesus' baptism. Because God is the supreme arbiter of truth in Mark's story, it will not do to say that the heavenly voice, in calling Jesus "my Son," is conveying a false image of Jesus as the Hellenistic divine man. Nor will it do

---

4. Jack Dean Kingsbury, *The Christology of Mark's Gospel* (Philadelphia: Fortress, 1983). In the third chapter of his book, *Literary Criticism for New Testament Critics* (Philadelphia: Fortress, 1978), Norman Petersen had earlier used narrative criticism to analyze the plot of Mark's Gospel story but, in dealing with Mark's Christology, did not escape the corrective approach.

to claim that the title "the Son of God" is illegitimate and in need of correction through use of the expression "the Son of Man." On the contrary, because "the Son of God" is God's own designation for Jesus and because it attests to the unique filial relationship he has with God, the readers are given to know that it is the foremost title of majesty for Jesus.

The protagonist of Mark's story is "Jesus," who comes from Nazareth of Galilee (1:9, 24; 10:47; 14:67; 16:6). To ask who Jesus is is to ask how Mark makes use of point of view to reveal his identity. For Mark, the fundamental title of majesty for Jesus is "the Messiah," which is evident in that this title is the basis on which Mark creates a whole family of christological titles. In the opening verse of his story, which is the title to the whole story, Mark as narrator uses the name "Jesus Christ" to assert that "Jesus is the Messiah" (1:1). Throughout the rest of his story, Mark defines further the meaning of "Messiah" through use of such statements or expressions as "the Messiah, the king of Israel" (15:32), or "the Messiah is the son of David" (12:35), or "the Messiah, the Son of the Blessed One" (14:61). Through the creation of this messianic family of titles, Mark's firm reply to the question, "Who is Jesus?" is that he is the Messiah-king from the line of David, the royal Son of God.

Notice that just as Mark establishes a hierarchy of authority within his Gospel story, so he also establishes a hierarchy of importance among the titles of majesty that make up the messianic family. The framework for all of these titles is the purposes that God pursues in Jesus within the history of first Israel and then also the nations (e.g., 1:2–3; 8:31; 13:10). Within this framework, the titles that relate Jesus primarily to Israel are to be distinguished from the title that relates him to God. Suffice it to say that whereas "the Messiah," "the son of David," and "the king of the Jews/ Israel" all relate Jesus primarily to Israel, "the Son of God" relates Jesus to God. The title "the Son of God" thus embodies the deepest mystery of Jesus' identity.

I just stated that in Mark's story the identity of Jesus is that he is the Messiah-king from the line of David, the royal Son of God. To set forth Jesus' identity, Mark makes use of two literary devices, one of grammar and one of style. The grammatical device is that of apposition, as in the expression "the Messiah, the king of Israel" (15:32). As an appositive, the function of "the king of Israel" here is to specify who "the Messiah" is.

Overwhelmingly, however, it is the stylistic literary device that Mark uses to identify Jesus, namely, the formula of identification. This formula takes the form of some variation of a statement or question that asks or declares: "You are so and so!"; "Are you so and so?"; "This (man) is so and so!"; or "He is so and so!" For example, one finds such statements or questions with reference to Jesus as the following: "You are the Messiah!" (8:29); "Are you the king of the Jews?" (15:2); "The Messiah is the son of David!" (12:35); "This is my beloved Son!" (9:7). Sometimes Mark employs the formula of identification in abbreviated fashion, as when the bare name "John the Baptist" stands for the view that "he [Jesus] is John the Baptist" (6:14). The crucial thing to note in dealing with Mark's myriad use of the formula of identification is that the truth of any given question or statement does not depend on the character in the story who utters the formula but on whether what is said is true from the point of view of God, Jesus, or Mark as narrator. Thus the readers know that the notion of Herod Antipas that Jesus is John the Baptist raised from the dead is false because it does not square with the viewpoint of either God, Jesus, or Mark as narrator. Conversely, when the high priest asks Jesus whether he is the Messiah, the Son of the Blessed (14:61), the readers know that the high priest has rightly identified Jesus even though the high priest himself does not believe for a moment that Jesus is such.

More than a century ago, William Wrede advanced the thesis of the "messianic secret." The abiding kernel of truth in his thesis is that Mark deals with the identity of Jesus as with a secret. In narrative-critical terms, Mark distinguishes between readers and human characters. The readers are onlookers who stand outside the story, and they are privileged by Mark to know the identity of Jesus. In this respect, they know what God, Mark as narrator, such supernatural beings as demons, and also Jesus know. In contrast, Mark withholds knowledge of Jesus' identity from the human characters in the beginning and middle parts of his story and, in the end part, only gradually unveils it. Thus, in the beginning of his story (1:1–13), Mark presents Jesus to the readers as the Messiah and the Son of God but withholds such knowledge from human characters. In the middle of his story (1:14–8:26), although the demons know that Jesus is the Son of God (1:24, 34; 3:11; 5:7), the human characters either show themselves to be ignorant of Jesus' identity (4:41; 6:45–52) or they misperceive it (6:3, 14–16; also 8:27–28). Not until the end of his story (8:27–16:8) does Mark gradually unveil the identity of Jesus to human characters. For example, Jesus is confessed by Peter to be the Messiah, yet Jesus commands that Peter's confession be kept silent because Peter rejects the notion that the Messiah must suffer and die (8:29–33). Again, Bartimaeus, who is pointedly characterized as blind, nevertheless "sees" what the great crowd cannot, that Jesus is the son of David (10:46–52). Still, not until the culmination of his story does Mark depict a human character as finally attaining to God's viewpoint regarding Jesus' identity. At the baptism, God declared to Jesus, "You are my beloved Son!" (1:11). Now, in reaction to Jesus' death on the cross, the centurion exclaims, "Truly this man was the Son of God!" (15:39). The centurion says "was" and not "is" because he has just seen Jesus die and the event of the resurrection is yet to come (16:1–8). Regardless, the centurion's exclamation is the place where the two great motifs of Mark's story, that of Jesus' identity and that of his destiny, at last intersect. Through his death, Jesus fulfills his destiny by pouring out his blood for the salvation of the many (14:24). In seeing Jesus die, the centurion reacts by attesting to the deepest mystery of Jesus' identity, that he was the Son of God (15:39). Through his perfect obedience unto death, Jesus has demonstrated his unique filial relationship with God (14:36). Within Mark's story, the messianic secret has thus reached its goal.

INTERPRETING THE EXPRESSION "THE SON OF MAN"

Thus far I have highlighted the identity and significance of Jesus by dealing with the messianic titles of majesty that characterize him as the Messiah-king from the line of David, the royal Son of God. Conspicuously absent from the discussion, however, has been the expression "the Son of Man." For years now, Markan scholars have been preoccupied with this term. It has become commonplace to group "the Son of Man" with the other christological titles and to understand it to be a major title of majesty that is also messianic in nature. Markan scholars who so understand "the Son of Man" almost invariably base their understanding on external evidence, that is, on an outside trajectory that aims to explain how the nontitular Aramaic original that is thought to underlie "the Son of Man" (אנשא רב) became a title of majesty rendered in Greek by ὁ υἱὸς τοῦ ἀνθρώπου.

But outside trajectories are burdened by two insurmountable problems. The first is that because they are based on a paucity of hard evidence, they are inherently speculative. And the second is that they dictate how the internal evidence in Mark's story is to be understood. Before one has read even a single page of Mark's story, one will already have concluded that should Mark make use of "the Son of Man," the term will be both titular and messianic in nature.

Scrutiny of the internal evidence in Mark's story, however, shows that "the Son of Man" is not a major messianic title of majesty. We have already noted that to inform the readers of who Jesus is, Mark employs two literary devices to create a messianic family of titles. Decisive is that in Mark's use of these two devices, the expression "the Son of Man" never occurs. The one device, we recall, is stylistic in nature and is the formula of identification. Despite Mark's overwhelming use of this device, never is it asked or said with a view to Jesus: "You are the Son of Man!"; or "Are you the Son of Man?"; or "He is the Son of Man!"; or "This is the Son of Man!" The other device is grammatical in nature and is that of apposition. In this case, too, one never finds appositives such as "Jesus, the Son of Man" or "the Messiah, the Son of Man." The conclusion is compelling: in Mark's story, the expression "the Son of Man" stands apart from Mark's family of messianic titles, for it is neither a title that sets forth the identity of Jesus nor is it messianic in nature. So who is Jesus? He is, again, the Messiah-king from the line of David, the royal Son of God.

If "the Son of Man" is not a major messianic title, how does it function within Mark's story? It functions as a solemn self-reference: Jesus alone uses it, and he does so to refer exclusively to himself.[5] If one leaves open for a moment the synoptic question of how the first three Gospels are related to one another, indication of this self-referential nature of the expression "the Son of Man" can be found in parallel passages that Mark and Matthew on the one hand and Matthew and Luke on the other have in common. In these passages, "the Son of Man" is used interchangeably with the personal pronouns "I" or "he." Whereas in 8:27 Mark uses the personal pronoun "I" ("me") to refer to Jesus, in 16:12 Matthew refers to Jesus as "the Son of Man." Conversely, whereas in 8:31 Mark refers to Jesus as "the Son of Man," in 16:21 Matthew uses the personal pronoun "he" ("him") to refer to Jesus. Similarly, whereas in 10:32 Matthew refers to Jesus using the personal pronoun "I," in 12:8 Luke refers to Jesus as "the Son of Man." As these examples reveal, the Synoptic Evangelists were aware of the self-referential nature of the expression "the Son of Man." Still, such substitution of a personal pronoun for "the Son of Man" or "the Son of Man" for a personal pronoun should not be taken to mean that each time the expression "the Son of Man" occurs in the stories of Matthew, Mark, or Luke, it can simply

---

5. See Douglas R. A. Hare, *The Son of Man Tradition* (Minneapolis: Fortress, 1990), ch. 6.

be reduced to a personal pronoun. The reason is that whereas "the Son of Man" is indeed purely self-referential, it nevertheless lends a strong element of both solemnity and force to the sayings in which it appears.

The recognition that "the Son of Man" is not a messianic title of majesty but a term by means of which Jesus refers to himself creates a number of problems for all of those interpreters who regard "the Son of Man" as a major messianic title. One such problem is that Mark does not employ the expression "the Son of Man" in the beginning part of his story (1:1–13). In all four canonical Gospel stories, the beginning part is of special importance for two reasons. First, it is the place where each Evangelist introduces the readers to the protagonist of his story and tells them of who he is and what he will accomplish. In Mark's story, the narrator introduces the protagonist as "Jesus Christ" (1:1). Because "Christ" is not only a name but also a title, Jesus is introduced as the Messiah. In the episode of the baptism (1:9–11), Jesus is introduced by God himself as "my Son!" (1:11), that is, the Son of God.

The fact that Jesus is introduced by Mark as narrator and by God is of dual significance. For one thing, it means that "the Messiah" and "the Son of God" are the two most prominent titles of majesty in Mark's story. The prominence of "the Messiah" resides in that it is, as we have seen, the fundamental title around which Mark creates a family of titles that further define Jesus as being "the son of David" (e.g., 12:35), "the king of the Jews/ Israel" (e.g., 15:32), and "the Son of God" (e.g., 14:61). The prominence of "the Son of God" resides in that it is the title that harbors within it the deepest mystery of Jesus' identity, namely, that he is filially related to God in a unique way. It is by virtue of this unique filial relationship that God endows Jesus with the Spirit; and Jesus, by withstanding Satan, inaugurates the end-time age of salvation (1:9–13).

For another thing, Jesus' being introduced by Mark as narrator and by God means that Mark and God thus become the ones in Mark's story who authenticate, or validate, who Jesus is and what he will accomplish. Recall that the expression "the Son of Man" is used exclusively by Jesus to refer to himself. Should, therefore, the expression "the Son of Man" be messianic in nature and Jesus be described here in the beginning as introducing himself as such, then he would be authenticating himself, that is, he would himself be validating his identity and destiny. Such an act of self-authentication, however, is exactly what Mark and all the Evangelists go to all lengths to avoid. Their concern is to present Jesus as God's agent and not as one who is self-empowered; in their view those who are self-empowered are false messiahs (13:21–22). From this angle, too, it is apparent that the expression "the Son of Man" is not, and cannot be, a messianic title of majesty.

The second reason the beginning part of a Gospel story is of special importance goes hand in glove with the first: it is here that the principle of first impression is most forcefully at work. According to this principle, what is said in the beginning part of a story is of crucial significance for comprehending the middle and the end parts of the story. Because the expression "the Son of Man" is absent from the outset of Mark's story, it can make no powerful impression upon the readers. Instead, the two titles that do make such an impression are, as we have seen, "the Messiah" (1:1) and "the Son of God" (1:11). Indeed, the principle of first impression is doubly at work in the case of "the Messiah" because it is not only the first title for Jesus that the readers encounter but it also occurs in the opening words that serve as the title of the entire story, "The beginning of the gospel of Jesus Christ [Messiah]." In the case of the title "the Son of God," it is in the episode of Jesus' baptism (1:9–11) that the principle of first impression comes into play. Here Jesus sees the heavens split apart and the Spirit descend upon him, and God himself bursts into the world of Mark's story to declare to him, "You are my beloved Son!" The dramatic nature of the baptismal episode is matched only by that of the transfiguration (9:2–8), where God again enters the story world of Mark to declare Jesus to be "my Son!" Such drama impresses the title "the Son of God" indelibly upon the minds of the readers.

A second problem for those who would understand "the Son of Man" to be a major messianic title also has to do with the principle of first impression, but in a negative way: the manner in which Mark introduces the term into his story is prosaic and ordinary. Diverse factors account for this. Thus "the Son of Man" does not occur in Mark's story until the middle part, after Jesus has begun his public ministry to Israel. Also, it first surfaces in two sayings found in two debates (2:1–12, 23–28) that are situated within a cycle of five debates (2:1–3:6). When one considers the literary prominence or the high drama that are associated with Mark's introduction of Jesus as the Messiah (1:1) and the Son of God (1:9–11), one recognizes how poorly the two debates serve as an attention-grabbing setting for Jesus to introduce himself to the readers as the messianic Son of Man. Not only this, but the stress in the two sayings does not lie at all on the expression "the Son of Man." At 2:10 Jesus says, "But that you may know that the Son of Man has authority on earth to forgive sins...." At 2:28 Jesus asserts, "So that you may know that the Son of Man is lord even of the Sabbath." Notice that in neither saying does Jesus declare himself to be the Son of Man and that in both sayings the stress lies squarely on the divine authority he exercises. In Mark's story, however, Jesus does not exercise divine authority because of any reference to himself as the Son of Man but because God has anointed him with the Spirit at his baptism (1:10). For these various reasons, the potential of the expression "the Son of Man" to impress itself forcefully upon the readers in these two initial sayings is strictly limited. Indeed, from a literary perspective, the principle of first impression can only be said to apply to Jesus' use of "the Son of Man" in these sayings because the term has thus far not occurred in Mark's story.

A third problem for those who construe "the Son of Man" as being a major messianic title of majesty is that it plays no role in the motif of the messianic secret that Mark weaves so carefully throughout the length of his story. To safeguard the messianic identity of Jesus and to conceal his divine sonship from human characters until his death on the cross, Mark makes use of a host of literary techniques. These include, for example, commands to silence (1:24–25, 34; 3:11–12; 8:29–30; 9:9), fear and wonderment about who he is (4:41), a deserted location (5:7), misperception (6:3; also 3:20–21), speculation born of ignorance (6:14–16; 8:27–28), parabolic speech (12:6–7; see also 4:11–12; 8:17–18), obdurate understanding (12:12), a conundrum (12:35–37), an evasive answer (15:2), and especially irony, in which human characters unwittingly or obdurately speak the truth (11:8–10; 14:61; 15:3–32). Significantly, when one traces the trajectory of the expression "the Son of Man" in Mark's story, these techniques of concealment never accompany its use. The conspicuous absence of these techniques is yet another sign that the expression "the Son of Man" is nonmessianic in nature. Fourteen times Jesus refers to himself as "the Son of Man" in sayings he addresses to human characters. Consistently, Jesus' use of the term is open and straightforward. No command is given to the humans who hear him utter it that they tell it to no one. No suggestion is made that its meaning is hidden from its hearers or that they do not comprehend it. No indication accompanies its use to the effect that it is a codeword for the title "Messiah" or that it is a stand-in for the title "the Son of God." No hint is given that in its use prior to the Parousia sayings of Jesus, it nevertheless harbors within it a concealed reference to Jesus' second coming. No irony attaches itself to the fourteen sayings, and neither are they situated in parabolic speech or in a conundrum. In short, the use of "the Son of Man" betrays no level of ambiguity any greater than that otherwise associated with Mark's use of the personal name "Jesus" or of personal pronouns such as "I," or "me," or "he."

A fourth problem for those who would understand "the Son of Man" to be a major messianic title is that if it were such, Jesus' use of it in public would badly disturb, even distort, the narrative flow of Mark's story. In the first two sayings in which "the Son of Man" appears and in 8:38 as well, the publicness of the term is readily apparent. In claiming that the Son of Man has authority to forgive sins (2:10), Jesus utters the term in the full hearing of both the crowd and some of the scribes (2:2, 4, 6). In claiming that the Son of Man has authority to rule over the Sabbath (2:28), Jesus utters the term in the full hearing not only of the disciples but also of the Pharisees (2:23–24). And in declaring that whoever is ashamed of him, of that person will the Son of Man also be ashamed (8:38), Jesus utters the term in the full hearing of the crowd and the disciples (8:34). These hearers constitute three distinct groups of characters: the disciples; the crowd, or Jewish public; and the religious authorities. Should now "the Son of Man" be a major messianic title, then Jesus has divulged his identity as such to these three groups and shown that what he is about is exercising divine authority and coming again for judgment.

If, however, these groups know of Jesus' identity, authority, and second coming as the messianic Son of Man, then the narrative flow of Mark's story becomes discombobulated and confused. For example, why do the demons, even after Jesus has publicly referred to himself as "the Son of Man" (2:10, 28), never shout aloud to him, "You are the Son of Man!" but consistently, "You are the Son of God!" (3:11; 5:7)? Or why do the disciples, in whose presence Jesus has called himself "the Son of Man," nevertheless ask in perplexity after he has rescued them from the turbulent waters, "Who then is this that even the wind and the sea obey him?" (4:41)? Or why do the townspeople of Nazareth, who are aware of the mighty miracles Jesus performs, not wonder at all whether he is the Son of Man but instead ask more simply, "Is this not the carpenter, the son of Mary?" (6:3)? Or why does the Jewish public, who has heard Jesus designate himself as the Son of Man, not think of him as such but imagine that he is a prophet, whether it be John the Baptist, or Elijah, or another such figure (6:15; 8:27–28)? Or why does Herod Antipas, to whom Jesus' fame has become known, choose to regard him not as the Son of Man but as John the Baptist raised from the dead (6:14–16)? Or why does Peter, who with the disciples has heard Jesus refer to himself as "the Son of Man" but never as "the Messiah," not confess in view of Jesus, "You are the Son of

Man!" but confesses instead, "You are the Messiah!" (8:29). Or why does the high priest, despite the fact that Jesus has already referred to himself as "the Son of Man" in the presence of some scribes and the Pharisees, nevertheless ask him, "Are you the Messiah, the Son of the Blessed?" (14:61)? The point is this: the notion that Jesus, in referring to himself in public as "the Son of Man," utters a major messianic title that divulges his identity and significance results in a distortion of the narrative flow of Mark's story. "The Son of Man" is not a messianic title of majesty.

Yet a fifth problem for those who would understand "the Son of Man" to be a major messianic title of majesty is that this almost inevitably leads them to give pride of place to the story line of Mark's narrative as opposed to its plotline. In a narrative, the story line is temporal and sequential: all the events are arranged in chronological order so as to form a single time line. In contrast, the plotline charts the order within the narrative in which events actually occur. The crucial significance of the plotline lies in the fact that by tracking it, one discovers where the story reaches its denouement, where it culminates, and where the action gets resolved.

In Mark's narrative, the story line runs from references to events mentioned in the Old Testament all the way to the Parousia of Jesus. Scholars who give pride of place to the story line regard Jesus' Parousia as the culmination of Mark's story and treat "the Son of Man" in Jesus' self-references as a messianic title. The *locus classicus* for Jesus' Parousia is found in 13:24–27. The reference to it in 8:38b foreshadows 13:24–27, and the reference to it in 14:62 calls it to mind. Apropos of these three passages, three points indicate that Mark takes Jesus' Parousia to be of secondary significance as compared with his death and resurrection. The first has to do with the location of the chief passage, 13:24–27: it is situated not within the denouement of the story, which is the passion narrative (14:1–16:8), but outside it. The second is that whereas Jesus, in all three of the passion predictions that govern the flow of the entire second half of Mark's story (8:27–16:8), pointedly tells of his death and resurrection, he makes no mention whatsoever of his Parousia (8:31; 9:31; 10:32–34). And the third is that when Jesus answers, "I am!" in 14:62 to the question of the high priest concerning his identity, Jesus' acknowledgment is not that he is the Son of Man but that he is the Messiah, the Son of the Blessed/God! Later, we shall return to 8:38b.

Mark shows in key ways that his story of Jesus reaches its denouement, or fundamental outcome, in the passion narrative (14:1–16:8) and not in the passages that tell of his Parousia. Thus it is in the passion narrative that the three predictions Jesus has made of his suffering, death, and resurrection (8:31; 9:31; 10:32–34) find their fulfillment. As for the passion story itself, it culminates in the event of Jesus' death on the cross (15:24–39): the sufferings of Jesus lead up to his death, and the resurrection points back at it (16:6). The event of Jesus' death is the place in Mark's story where, as we said, two main motifs converge in climactic fashion: the motifs of the significance of Jesus' earthly ministry and of his identity. The ultimate significance of Jesus' ministry is that through his death, he pours out his blood on behalf of the many and thus accomplishes salvation (14:24). The deepest mystery of Jesus' identity is that he is the Son of God. This is why it is as the Son of God that Jesus is condemned to death, is confessed to be such upon his death, and is raised as such by God from death.

So as to condemn Jesus to death, the high priest asks him at his trial before the Sanhedrin, "Are you the Messiah, the Son of the Blessed?" (14:61). In reply, Jesus says, "I am!" (14:62), thus echoing the declarations God himself has made both at his baptism, "You are my beloved Son!" (1:11), and at his transfiguration, "This is my beloved Son!" (9:7). Upon Jesus' death, the centurion responds with the exclamatory confession, "Truly this man was the Son of God!" (15:39). Within Mark's story, this confession by the centurion is climactic because for the first time a human being other than Jesus himself (12:1–12) attains to God's understanding of Jesus (1:11; 9:7).

Finally, Jesus is also raised from death by God as "the Son of God." In his parable of the Wicked Tenant Farmers, Jesus foretold already that as the beloved Son of God, he would be both put to death and raised by God from death (12:6–8, 10). It is in the episode of the resurrection (16:1–8) that Jesus' prophecy about God's raising him comes to fulfillment. The angel says to the astonished women, "He has been raised [by God (divine passive)], he is not here!" (16:6). Attendant to God's raising of Jesus is the splendor alluded to both by Jesus in his parable of the Wicked Tenant Farmers (12:10–11) and by Mark in telling of Jesus' transfiguration (9:2–3). The point to observe is that in both cases the Jesus who is resplendent is the beloved Son of God (12:6, 10–11; 9:2–3, 7). In advance of the episode of the resurrection, therefore, one already knows that the Jesus whom God will raise in splendor from death is the Son of God.

The angel also declares to the astonished women, "You are seeking Jesus of Nazareth, the one who has been crucified and remains the crucified one [perfect passive participle]" (16:6). Recall that the climactic confession of the centurion was that the Jesus whom he saw die on the cross was the Son of God (15:39). Hence Jesus, both as the crucified one confessed by the centurion and the risen one for whom the women are searching, is the Son of God.

This brings us back at last to the Parousia passage of 8:38b. Here Jesus asserts to the Jewish crowd and the disciples, "For whoever is ashamed of me…, of him will the Son of Man also be ashamed, when he comes in the glory of his Father with the holy angels." The expression "his Father" captures one's attention because it raises a double question: is Jesus being identified in this passage as the Son of Man whose Father is God? Does, then, "the Son of Man" become a messianic title of majesty after all?

The answer is no, for three reasons. The first is that in the denouement, or fundamental outcome of his story, Mark goes to great lengths to present Jesus to his readers as the Son of God. This is true in both the episode of the crucifixion, in which the denouement reaches its culmination, and in the episode of Jesus' resurrection. It is as the crucified yet risen Son of God that the Markan Jesus comes again at the end of the age.

The second reason is that in those passages in Mark's story where Jesus stands opposite God as Son to Father, he is described as being the Son of God. This is the case whether it be at Jesus' baptism (1:11), at his transfiguration (9:7), in the parable he narrates of the wicked tenant farmers (12:6–7, 10–11), in his apocalyptic saying that not even the Son but only the Father knows when the end of the age will come (13:32), in his child-like appeal to God as Father in Gethsemane (14:36), and in his bold and open acknowledgment at his trial before the Sanhedrin that, yes, he is the Messiah, the Son of the Blessed (14:61–62ab).

And the third reason is that, as we have already seen, the internal literary evidence in Mark's story does not support the notion that "the Son of Man" is a messianic title of majesty. The only way, therefore, that one can justify the claim that the term is such in 8:38b is by presupposing it to be such. The problem with presupposing this, however, is that one then forces the internal evidence of Mark's story to comply with some form of external hypothesis.

Should it be, however, that, in the denouement of Mark's story, the crucified Jesus is raised by God to glory as the Son of God, that it is as the Son of God that Jesus stands opposite God at key points throughout Mark's story, and that the internal literary evidence in Mark's story does not support the popular presupposition that "the Son of Man" must necessarily be a messianic title of majesty, then the interpretation of Jesus'

Parousia saying in 8:38b ceases to be problematic. As with all the Son-of-Man references in Mark's story, Jesus in 8:38b is referring to himself. He is saying in effect, "Whoever is ashamed of me ..., of him will I, Jesus, also be ashamed, when I come in the glory of my Father with the holy angels." However much more meaning may legitimately be invested in the use of "the Son of Man" here, Mark himself does not make apparent. The point, however, is this: in all three Parousia passages, Jesus refers to himself as "the Son of Man" not to attribute to himself a messianic title of majesty, but solemnly and forcefully to claim for himself vindication in fulfillment of Old Testament prophecy.

SUMMARY

We have seen that the scholarly use of redaction criticism led to the corrective approach to Mark's Christology. The claim of this approach was that Mark employs a Son-of-Man Christology to correct a false divine-man, Son-of-God Christology. With the rise of narrative criticism, however, the corrective approach collapsed. The reason was that the application of the literary device of point of view did away with the divine-man theory and forced a reappraisal of especially the title "the Son of God" and the expression "the Son of Man." In a narrative-critical approach to Mark's Christology, Jesus stands forth as the Messiah-king from the line of David, the royal Son of God. Because the expression "the Son of Man" does not belong within the circle of these messianic titles of majesty, the question arises as to how it functions within Mark's Christology. The answer is that it is a solemn and forceful self-referential term that is used exclusively by Jesus to point to himself.

Refusing to settle for this understanding of the term, however, Markan scholars generally insist that "the Son of Man" is in fact a messianic title of majesty. To make their case, they assume or construct outside trajectories in speculative attempts to show how a nontitular Aramaic expression, "one like a son of man," became the Greek title, "the Son of Man." Still, what negates these outside attempts and demonstrates that "the Son of Man" is neither a title of majesty nor messianic in nature is the internal evidence of Mark's story.

To set forth the identity of Jesus, Mark employs two literary devices, the grammatical device of apposition and, overwhelmingly, the stylistic device of the formula of identification. Never, however, does Mark employ the expression "the Son of Man" in connection with either of these devices.

One never reads, "Jesus, the Son of Man," or "the Messiah, the Son of Man," or "Jesus is the Son of Man."

Moreover, for one to assume that "the Son of Man" is a messianic title of majesty is for one to encounter insurmountable obstacles in dealing with the story that Mark narrates. One must explain why Mark does not use the beginning part of his story to present Jesus as the Son of Man but does use it to present Jesus as the Messiah and the Son of God; why the principle of first impression applies so powerfully to Jesus as the Messiah and the Son of God but so prosaically to Jesus' first references to himself as the Son of Man; why Mark conceals the messianic identity of Jesus from the human characters in his story and only gradually reveals it to select individuals but is content that Jesus should, as early as Mark 2, refer to himself as the Son of Man in the full hearing of the disciples, the Jewish crowd, some of the scribes, and the Pharisees; why, if one understands "the Son of Man" to be a messianic title that reveals the identity and significance of Jesus, the effect this has on the story is to distort it and to discombobulate its flow; and why the denouement, or fundamental outcome, of the plot of Mark's narrative, which is found in the passion story, features Jesus not as the Son of Man but as the crucified and risen Son of God. No, on the basis of an investigation of the internal evidence of Mark's story, the expression "the Son of Man" proves itself not to be a messianic title of majesty but that solemn and forceful self-reference whereby Jesus points to himself.

THE LURE OF WEALTH:
DOES MARK HAVE A SOCIAL GOSPEL?

John R. Donahue, S.J.

In *New Testament Ethics: The Legacies of Jesus and Paul*, Frank J. Matera summarizes the scholarly consensus: "On first appearance the Gospel according to Mark, the oldest of the four Gospels, is an unlikely source for moral or ethical instruction."[1] Yet Matera presents a powerful exposition of how the kingdom proclamation of Jesus and his radical call to discipleship present a fundamental challenge to accept the values of God rather than the values that the world proposes.[2] He underscores three aspects of Jesus' life that are presuppositions to an ethics of discipleship: following the will of God, compassion, and faith and fidelity even in the face of rejection and suffering.[3] The ethics of Jesus are "necessarily bound up with the story of Jesus."[4] To know that story is to be shaped by a new ethical vision.

---

1. Frank Matera, *New Testament Ethics: The Legacies of Jesus and Paul* (Louisville: Westminster John Knox, 1996), 13. My title is intended to evoke memories of the Social Gospel movement in America, which arose in reaction to (among many causes) the impoverished living conditions and the gap between the rich and the poor. See Martin Marty, *Righteous Empire: The Protestant Experience in the United States* (New York: Dial, 1970), esp. 200–201; William McGuire King, "The Biblical Basis of the Social Gospel," in *The Bible and Social Reform* (ed. Ernest Sandeen; Philadelphia: Fortress, 1982), 59–84; and Christopher Lasch "Religious Contributions to Social Movements: Walter Rauschenbusch, the Social Gospel, and Its Critics," *JRE* 18 (1990): 7–25. As Mark Twain reputedly said, "history doesn't repeat itself, but it does rhyme."

2. Matera, *New Testament Ethics*, 22. Matera here calls attention to David Rhoads, "Losing Life for Others: Mark's Standard of Judgment," *Int* 47 (2004): 359–60.

3. Matera, *New Testament Ethics*, 32–34.

4. Ibid., 35.

Mark's story of Jesus relative to Matthew and Luke contains little explicit material that addresses a major concern of contemporary ethics: how the Bible can influence contemporary concerns for social justice. In a thought-provoking section of *Remembering Jesus: Christian Community, Scripture, and the Moral Life,* Allen Verhey, an ethicist and leader for over three decades in the dialogue between Scripture and ethics, when treating the questions of social justice, focuses mainly on Luke, as do most New Testament scholars.[5] In line with the statement attributed to Karl Barth that people should read the Bible with a copy of the daily newspaper at their side, in this essay I will explore one aspect of Mark's ethical vision, his statements on the "lure of wealth" and the "desire for other things" (4:18–19). As I compose this essay the daily papers note that from 1979 to 2009, "the income of the very rich, the top 100th of 1 percent of the income distribution, rose by 480 percent, and … in 2005 dollars, the average annual income of that group rose from $4.2 million to $24.3 million," at the same time when the percentage of people living in poverty and of children suffering hunger are at record high levels (veiled often by the euphemism, "food insecurity").[6]

Thorns, Cares of the World, the Lure of Wealth, and Desire for Other Things (Mark 4:19)

Jesus' teaching in parables (Mark 4:1–34) along with the apocalyptic discourse of Mark 13 constitute the longest body of teaching in the Gospel. It comes at a strategic position in the Gospel for two reasons noted by Joel Marcus: (1) the previous sections of Mark 2 and 3 heighten the opposition between Jesus and his opponents, culminating in a charge that he is under the power of Satan (3:22), and the first half (4:1–20) images division between good seed and bad seed, insiders and outsiders (4:11–12)—which is part of God's design; and (2) the second half (4:21–32) prepares for the expansion of Jesus' good news into Gentile territory by a collection of images: from darkness to light (4:21–22), the unpredictable growth of a seed (4:26–29), and the blossoming of a mustard seed into a mighty tree

---

5. Allen Verhey, *Remembering Jesus: Christian Community, Scripture, and the Moral Life* (Grand Rapids: Eerdmans, 2002). See esp. part 4, "Remembering Jesus in the World of Adam Smith," 243–305.

6. Paul Krugman, *New York Times,* Sept. 22, 2011. Data on hunger, domestic and abroad, can be found at the home page for Bread for the World: www.bread.org.

under which the birds of the air can find shelter (4:30–32).[7] Both of these subsections also end with a motif of revelation to insiders (4:11–12) and concealment or misunderstanding by outsiders (4:33–34).[8]

Our focus will be on the allegorical explanation of the parable of the Sower (4:13–20), which has long been recognized as an addition, either pre-Markan or by Mark himself, and provides privileged warnings to the disciples about the causes for the failure of Jesus' teaching. The initial statement, "Do you not understand this parable? Then how will you understand all the parables?" is ambiguous.[9] Given the broad use of "parable" in Mark, "this parable" (τὴν παραβολὴν ταύτην) could refer to the enigmatic saying of 4:11–12 or to the following explanation.[10] If the latter, then the fates of the various sowings are to be a key not only to other parabolic sayings of Jesus (e.g., 3:23–30; 7:14–23; 10:10–12, 23–27) but to the Gospel of Mark as a whole.[11]

The sower "sows the word," and the fates of the first two sowings are that Satan, like the birds of the air, snatches the seed along the path, and that those who accept it with joy but fall away amid persecution are like the seed on the rocky ground that never takes root. Jesus calls Peter "Satan" when he rejects the prediction that he will suffer and die (8:33). "Trouble or persecution on account of the word" (θλίψεως ἢ διωγμοῦ διὰ τὸν λόγον) foreshadow Jesus' warnings of defection in his final discourse to the disciples before his passion and death (13:9–13) and in the actual flight of

---

7. Joel Marcus, *Mark 1–8: A New Translation with Introduction and Commentary* (AB 27; New York: Doubleday, 2000), 288–89.

8. Ibid., 303–4.

9. All translations are from the NRSV, unless otherwise noted.

10. In the OT "parable" is used to describe a wide variety of literary forms, such as proverbs (1 Sam 10:12; Prov 1:1, 6; 10:1; 26:7–9), riddles (Judg 14:10–18), taunt songs (Mic 2:4; Hab 2:6), allegories (Isa 5:1–7; Ezek 17:3–24), and, in the intertestamental literature, long revelatory discourses such as the Similitudes of Enoch (1 En. 39–71). See Roy Stewart, "The Parable Form in the Old Testament and the Rabbinic Literature," *EvQ* 36 (1964): 133–47.

11. See Francis J. Moloney, *The Gospel of Mark: A Commentary* (Peabody, Mass.: Hendrickson, 2002), 98, "The parable of vv. 3–9 and its explanation in vv. 14–29 must be seen as the key to all the parables." For the parabolic nature of the Gospel of Mark, see John R. Donahue, S.J., "Jesus as the Parable of God in the Gospel of Mark," in *Interpreting the Gospels* (ed. James L. Mays; Philadelphia: Fortress, 1981), 148–67.

the disciples and in Peter's denial.[12] But the most elaborate failure is of the third sowing in Mark 4:18–19:

> And others are those sown among the thorns [οἱ εἰς τὰς ἀκάνθας σπειρόμενοι]: these are the ones who hear the word, but the cares of the world [αἱ μέριμναι τοῦ αἰῶνος], and the lure of wealth, and the desire for other things [καὶ ἡ ἀπάτη τοῦ πλούτου καὶ αἱ περὶ τὰ λοιπὰ ἐπιθυμίαι] come in and choke [συμπνίγουσιν τὸν λόγον] the word, and it yields nothing [or better, "becomes fruitless" (καὶ ἄκαρπος γίνεται)].

Because of its location in Mark, this failing "foreshadows" other events in the unfolding narrative. With the realization that Mark was proclaimed and heard, scholars such as Joanna Dewey and Elizabeth Struthers Malbon have noted that Mark has multiple characteristics of oral literature.[13] Among these are ways in which parts of a narrative foreshadow following sections or echo what has gone before. Subsequently Alberto de Mingo Kaminouchi has expanded these insight by describing an "echo principle" in the Gospel of Mark as "a formula or theme repeated as a motif through the text" and "echoes are not only a mnemonic resource for the speaker, but help the reader to follow the discourse.[14] My proposal is that the failed third sowing, because of the cares of the world, the lure of wealth, and the desire for other things, foreshadows the longest narrative on the failure of

---

12. See Mary Ann Tolbert, *Sowing the Gospel: Mark's World in Literary-Historical Perspective* (Minneapolis: Fortress, 1989), 175: "The parable of the Sower (or the parable of the Four Types of Earth) and its interpretational material following it in Mark 4:3–32 function as a plot synopsis or premium, a conventional feature of Greek literature, for the Gospel of Mark"; and "By Mark 4, or very soon thereafter, the authorial audience should not only understand the typology of hearing response, but also be able to identify the groups in the Gospel that illustrate each type" (159).

13. Very influential in understanding inner connections between sections of Mark are: Elizabeth Struthers Malbon, "Echoes and Foreshadowings in Mark 4–8: Reading and Rereading," *JBL* 112 (1993): 211–30; and Joanna Dewey, "Mark as Interwoven Tapestry: Forecasts and Echoes for a Listening Audience," *CBQ* 53 (1991): 221–36; idem, "Oral Methods of Structuring Narrative in Mark," *Int* 43 (1998): 32–44.

14. Alberto deMingo Kaminouchi, *"But It Is Not So among You": Echoes of Power in Mark 10.32–45* (JSNTSup 249; London: T&T Clark, 2003), 42–71, on "The Echo Principle," citation from p. 55. Also influential in my approach to Mark is Christopher Bryant, *A Preface to Mark: Notes on the Gospel in Its Literary and Cultural Setting* (New York: Oxford University Press, 1993), esp. 40–41, on "ordering references, both backward and forward," and 143–48, on the allusive use of Scripture.

the word in Mark, the refusal of the man with many possessions to accept Jesus' call to become a disciple (10:17–31), and echoes in other places in the Gospel.

More detail and vivid images describe this third failure than in the two previous sowings. Falling among "thorns" suggests entanglement, while "choking" (συμπνίγουσιν) describes a process where food and light are cut off from plants and ultimately they wither and die.[15] The failure thus develops inevitably over a longer period of time, and is due to three "entanglements." First are αἱ μέριμναι τοῦ αἰῶνος, translated variously as "worldly anxiety" (NAB) or "worries of this life" (NIV), which can either refer to concern over ordinary difficulties of life (e.g., 2 Cor 11:28), or have an eschatological sense where such concerns are the "preoccupations that arise out of and wed people to a dying eon."[16] Such concerns in Markan theology prevent people from responding to the proclamation of the kingdom and are specified in the final destructive attitudes of 4:19: lure of wealth and desire for other things. Here the original phraseology, καὶ ἡ ἀπάτη τοῦ πλούτου καὶ αἱ περὶ τὰ λοιπὰ ἐπιθυμίαι, is a condensed a-b-b'-a' structure, in which "lure" and "desire" bracket the seductive objects, "wealth" and "other things," so that the two attitudes or vices are virtually interchangeable and convey a fundamental distortion of values.[17]

The seduction of riches and "the desire for many things" reflect the tenth commandment of the Decalogue (Exod 20:17), which warns against "coveting" a neighbor's wife, family, or goods—which the LXX renders as "desiring" (ἐπιθυμήσεις). In his extensive treatment of this prohibition Patrick Miller notes that in many Old Testament texts the verb "signals an inordinate or ungoverned desire that leads to the taking of what is desired";[18] and as examples he cites Exod 34:24, Deut 7:25, Josh 7:21, and especially Mic 2:1–2, which proclaims: "Alas for those who devise wickedness and evil deeds on their beds! When the morning dawns, they perform

15. BDAG, 34, s.v. ἄκανθη; 959, s.v. συμπίγνω.

16. Marcus, *Mark 1–8*, 312.

17. "Lure" (ἀπάτη) has sexual overtones (Jdt 9:10, 16), and the verb ἀπατάω in both Classical and Koine Greek often implies cheating or fraud (LSJ, 181); the noun (ἐπιθυμία) and verb (ἐπιθυμέω, BDAG, 371–72) often suggest "forbidden desires," often with overtones of forbidden sexual desire since both involve excess and violating boundaries.

18. Patrick D. Miller, *The Ten Commandments* (IBC; Louisville: Westminster John Knox, 2000), 390.

it because it is in their power. They covet fields, and seize them; houses, and take them away."[19]

Dramatic narratives and harsh prophetic denunciations warn against the lure of wealth and desire for the goods of another.[20] Desire for possession dominates the story of Ahab's wish for Naboth's vineyard and his subsequent murder through Jezebel's machinations, which conclude with her directive to Ahab, "Go, take possession of the vineyard of Naboth the Jezreelite," which he promptly does (1 Kgs 21:1–16). The prophets emerge as defenders of the poor when others covet and claim their goods. Amos's harsh words against the prosperous must be set in this context. He laments the sins of Israel, "You who turn justice into bitterness and cast righteousness to the ground" (5:7), which are manifest when "they trample the head of the poor into the dust of the earth" (2:7), and through deceptive business practices, "buy the poor for silver and the needy for a pair of sandals" (8:5–6). Isaiah tells us that the elders and princes "devour" the poor and grind their faces in the dust (Isa 3:14–15); they turn aside the needy from injustice to rob the poor of their rights (10:2); wicked people "ruin" the poor with lying words (32:7).

In addition to the "seduction" of wealth, the failure of this third sowing due to a "desire" for possessions clearly reflects the strong prohibitions against greed in both the Jewish and Greco-Roman traditions, even though the text does not use the technical term πλεονεξία. In Luke Jesus

---

19. See also David L. Baker, *Tight Fists or Open Hands: Wealth and Poverty in the Old Testament* (Grand Rapids: Eerdmans, 2009), 35: "The particular concern of this commandment [the tenth] in relation to wealth and poverty is to discourage greed and exploitation."

20. Recent years have witnessed a renewed interest in the biblical concern for justice and critiques of abusive wealth and power. Cf., e.g., Joshua A. Berman, *Created Equal: How the Bible Broke with Ancient Political Thought* (New York: Oxford University Press, 2008); Walter Brueggemann, *Journey to the Common Good* (Louisville: Westminster John Knox, 2010); Walter J. Houston, *Contending for Justice: Ideologies and Theologies of Social Justice in the Old Testament* (LHBOTS 428; London: T&T Clark, 2006); Joseph Jensen, *The Ethics of the Prophets* (Collegeville, Minn.: Liturgical Press, 2006); Thomas Leclerc, *Yahweh Is Exalted in Justice: Solidarity and Conflict in Isaiah* (Minneapolis: Fortress, 2001); Stephen Mott, *Biblical Ethics and Social Change* (New York: Oxford University Press, 2011); J. David Pleins, *The Social Visions of the Hebrew Bible: A Theological Introduction* (Louisville: Westminster John Knox, 2001); Martin Sicker, *The Idea of Justice in Judaism* (Lincoln, Nebr.: iUniverse, 2006); Moshe Weinfeld, *Social Justice in Ancient Israel and in the Ancient Near East* (Minneapolis: Fortress, 1985).

tells a parable of a rich man who uses his surplus for aggrandizement, only to die alone with failed plans as a warning to avoid "all kinds of greed" (ἀπὸ πάσης πλεονεξίας, Luke 12:15). The rejection of greed is epitomized in the Letter to the Colossians (3:5), where the author warns the readers to be ready for the forthcoming judgment: "Put to death, therefore, whatever in you is earthly: fornication, impurity, passion, evil desire [ἐπιθυμίαν κακήν], and greed (which is idolatry) [τὴν πλεονεξίαν, ἥτις ἐστὶν εἰδωλολατρία]."

Greco-Roman authors also excoriate greed and a love of possessions. Plutarch, for example, states that the avaricious in general suffer hardships, lose sleep, engage in trade, chase after legacies, and truckle to others: "Thus the greedy rich kill and destroy people. ... What they pass on to their heirs is their avarice and meanness, a warped character and no formation in basic humanity"[21] Diodorus Siculus (fl. 60–30 B.C.E.) calls greed "the metropolis of all vices"; similarly, Dio Chrysostom (first century C.E.) calls it "the greatest cause of evil."[22]

"LET ANYONE WITH EARS TO HEAR LISTEN"

The failed sowing foreshadows and provides the hermeneutical key to Markan perspectives on wealth and its dangers, as we explore the link between Mark 4:18–19 and the failed call to discipleship of the man with many resources (10:17–22), which is the major section of Mark on the lure of wealth.[23] The narrative occurs during the journey of Jesus to Jerusalem

---

21. Plutarch, *On Love of Wealth*, 525–26, as cited in Bruce Malina, "Wealth and Poverty in the New Testament and Its World," *Int* 41 (1987): 365.

22. References in BDAG, 824, s.v. πλεονεξία. Brian S. Rosner (*Greed and Idolatry: The Origin and Meaning of a Pauline Metaphor* [Grand Rapids: Eerdmans, 2007], 149–71) presents a thorough discussion of the negative perspectives on greed; also, William Countryman, *Dirt, Greed, Sex: Sexual Ethics in the New Testament and Their Implications for Today* (Philadelphia: Fortress, 1988), 108: "In each of these letters [Colossians and Ephesians], references to uncleanliness always link up with references to greed. This greed (πλεονεξία) is not merely the private vice of lust, the desire to have something for oneself, but rather the social one of covetousness."

23. The traditional title "The Rich Young Man" can be deceptive since in Mark 10:17 and Matt 19:16 the questioner is simply "a man" (εἷς) and in Luke 18:18 "a certain ruler" (τις ... ἄρχων). The title comes from the editorial comment in Mark 10:22 and Matt 19:22 that he has many possessions and in Luke 18:23 that he was very rich. Only at the end of the narrative does the reader/hearer know that his many possessions are the reason that the man rejected the call to discipleship and went away sor-

and is punctuated by three predictions of his coming suffering and death to which the disciples react with misunderstanding or rejection (8:31–33; 9:30–32; 10:32–45), which then evokes further teaching by Jesus on the common life of the community of disciples. The largest collection of teaching occurs between the second and third passion predictions and is bracketed by two virtually identical sayings of Jesus: "Whoever wants to be first must be last of all and servant of all" (9:35), and "whoever wishes to be first among you must be slave of all" (10:44). In contrast to the desire of the disciples for power and prestige (9:34; 10:37, 41), Jesus presents a model of service in imitation of his self-offering (10:45).[24]

Within this larger section a major subdivision begins when Jesus leaves "that place" and goes "to the region of Judea and beyond the Jordan," where crowds gather, "and, as was his custom, he again taught them" (10:1). This rather ornate introduction prepares the reader for the most sustained ethical teaching of Jesus in Mark that addresses essential aspects of community life: divorce and remarriage (10:2–12), acceptance of children (10:13–16), and possessions (10:17–31).[25] Though only one section deals explicitly with riches, the close connection between wealth and power may explain the sequence. Each incident represents a challenge by Jesus to commonly accepted practices and values regarding possessions and power that prepare for the story of the man with possessions (10:1–22), its interpretation by Jesus (10:23–27), and his vision of the new community (10:28–31).

The Economics of Divorce (Mark 10:1–10)

The first challenge on accepted values arises from Jesus' radical teachings on marriage and divorce. The positive ideal set forth is that husband and wife become "one flesh," and the fulfillment of this ideal means no divorce. The main part of the passage takes the form of a controversy story in which

---

rowful or sad. See also Tolbert (*Sowing the Gospel*, 159), who argues that Mark 4:13–20 points to the "fatal flaw" of the rich man.

24. Joel Marcus (*Mark 8–16: A New Translation with Introduction and Commentary* [AB 27A; New Haven: Yale University Press, 2009], vii–viii) describes the fourth section of Mark as a collection of sayings on Christian living (9:33–50), followed by the third passion prediction (10:32–34), ending with the healing of another blind man (10:46–52).

25. On 10:1 as inaugurating a new subsection of Mark (10:1–45) see Craig A. Evans, *Mark 8:27–16:20* (WBC 34B; Nashville: Nelson, 2001), 76, who notes the change of direction in 10:1, and stresses that the material deals with relationships.

Pharisees (with hostile intent) seek to bring Jesus into conflict with what they regard as the clear teaching of the Torah. Pharisees pose their question to Jesus: "Is it lawful for a man to divorce his wife?" (10:2). When Jesus asks them what Moses said on this matter, they cite Deut 24:1–2, "Moses allowed a man to write a certificate of dismissal and to divorce her." Jesus then counters that this was a concession by Moses to "your hardness of heart." Jesus appeals in Mark 10:6–8 to two texts from Genesis (1:27 and 2:24) as expressing God's original plan for men and women ("no longer two but one flesh").[26]

This collection of texts by Jesus affirms that the possibility of easy divorce is counter to what marriage was intended to be. They attribute two essential aspects to marriage: unity—the two shall become one; and complementarity or mutual interdependence—neither man alone nor woman alone is the fullness of God's creative design, but man and woman in union mirror the mystery of God. The saying of Jesus means in effect that the Jewish divorce laws prevent such an imaging of God. From this divine ideal Jesus draws the conclusion in 10:9 that divorce is contrary to that ideal: "What God has joined together, let no one separate."[27]

Jesus' radical teachings on marriage and divorce in Mark 10:1–12 must be understood in the context of first-century Palestine and the Greco-Roman world, which was literally "patriarchal," under the rule of the father.[28] Marriage did not arise from the desire or love of a couple, but was primarily a joining of households with arrangements made between the fathers of the bride and groom, and involved the transfer of the woman from her father's house (and control) to that of the husband.

Divorce often involved wrangling over possessions. Apart from the rare instances where women could initiate divorce, she was the powerless partner.[29] Divorce also has socioeconomic implications, especially harsh for the woman, if her dowry was not returned, or if she did not

---

26. Adapted from John R. Donahue, S.J., and Daniel J. Harrington, S.J., *The Gospel of Mark* (SP 2; Collegeville, Minn.: Liturgical Press, 2002), 295–96.

27. See John R. Donahue, S.J., "Divorce: New Testament Perspectives," in *Marriage Studies: Reflections on Canon Law and Theology* (ed. Thomas P. Doyle, O.P.; Washington, D.C.: Canon Law Society of America, 1982), 1–19. John P. Meier offers an exhaustive treatment of Jesus' teaching on divorce in *Law and Love* (vol. 4 of *A Marginal Jew: Rethinking the Historical Jesus*; New Haven: Yale University Press, 2009), 74–181.

28. Donahue and Harrington, *Mark*, 296.

29. Many authors see Mark 10:12 (women divorcing their husbands) as a reflec-

bring a large one to the marriage.[30] Her status would be similar to that of a "widow" dependent on others (e.g., returning in disgrace to her father's home). Also, primarily in the Greco-Roman world, she would be separated from her children since minor children remained with the father, who retained *patria potestas.*

WHO SHALL ENTER GOD'S KINGDOM? (MARK 10:13–16)

Jesus' acceptance and praise of children follows naturally from the teaching on divorce since children were powerless and vulnerable during and after a divorce. This narrative concludes Jesus' earlier healing and exorcistic actions on behalf of children (5:22–34, 35–43; 7:24–30; 9:17–29), and is the third "child incident" in the journey to Jerusalem.[31] It echoes especially the first (9:35–36), where also Jesus embraces a child and says that one who receives "one such child in my name welcomes me, and ... the one who sent me." In the second, Jesus castigates those who would put a stumbling block in front of one of the little ones, and urges them to accept maiming and disfigurement rather than risk condemnation to the fires of hell over their evil to children (9:42–48).

Jesus now accepts children as models for receiving the kingdom of God (10:14–15), since "to such as these ... the kingdom of God belongs." The dual mention of "kingdom of God," and the reference to entering it, links this section closely to the following (10:23–24). The images and message of this brief narrative are powerful. The use of the imperfect ($\pi\rho o\sigma\acute{\epsilon}\phi\epsilon\rho o\nu$) in the initial verse implies that this may have been a frequent practice, which may explain the rebuke ($\acute{\epsilon}\pi\epsilon\tau\acute{\iota}\mu\eta\sigma\alpha\nu$) in the same way that Jesus "rebuked" a demon (1:29), the raging storm (4:39), Peter (called Satan 8:32), and an unclean spirit (9:25). Jesus' equally strong response ($\acute{\eta}\gamma\alpha\nu\acute{\alpha}\kappa\tau\eta\sigma\epsilon\nu$) and his command to welcome children underscores the significance of the narra-

---

tion of Roman law. Marcus (*Mark 8–16,* 706–7) treats this as well as the infrequent cases in a Jewish environment.

30. Tal Ilan (*Jewish Women in Greco-Roman Palestine* [Peabody, Mass: Hendrickson, 1996], 147–48) notes that divorce brings economic hardship on women. Still, the extensive secondary literature on divorce rarely discusses the economic impact of divorce (e.g., Meier, *Marginal Jew,* 4:146 n. 27; and Raymond F. Collins, *Divorce in the New Testament* [Collegeville, Minn.: Liturgical Press, 1992]).

31. Judith M. Gundry, "Children in the Gospel of Mark," in *The Child in the Bible* (ed. Marcia J. Bunge; Grand Rapids: Eerdmans, 2008), 149.

tive, which has two foci: the welcome of children into the kingdom of God, and children as models of discipleship.[32] This rebuke, according to Judith Gundry, manifests "Jesus' repudiation and defeat of any attempt to hijack his true mission: to bestow the blessings of God's kingdom on children and the childlike."[33]

The narrative also echoes the way in which participation in the kingdom of God unfolds in the Gospel as a whole. As Joel Marcus eloquently states: "The centerpiece of our passage uses this common image of children, but reverses it: precisely these deficient ones who have no intrinsic right to claim membership in the dominion of God, constitute its leading citizens (10:14c)"; and he links it with Jesus' favoring of the "disprized over the prized" and his call to "sinners rather than the righteous, the sick rather than the well, the last rather than the first (cf. 2:17; 9:35)."[34] This reversal of values by Jesus will prepare for the overturning of cultural values in the following narrative and for the denouement of this whole section: the one wishing to be great is to be a servant, and those aspiring to be first must be last (10:32–45).

Jesus' embrace of the children contains both proclamation that the kingdom of God belongs to children, and a warning that one must become like children to enter it. But Jesus gives no description of childlikeness, nor did he say *how* children receive the kingdom of God.[35] The acceptance, defense, and modeling of children is not because they are symbols of innocence, since prior to coming under the law they can do neither good nor evil, and are truly law-less. The fundamental characteristic of children is that they are powerless and need protection and care, and their

---

32. The verb ἀγανακτέω implies being "indignant against what is assumed to be wrong," BDAG, 5, s.v. ἀγανακτέω.

33. Gundry, "Children," 168. She also compares this to Mark 10:49, when the disciples rebuke (ἐπετίμων) the blind Bartimaeus, whom Jesus then summons and heals, where "Jesus succeeds in putting the young before the old, the disabled before the abled, and the poor before the rich." Adela Yarbro Collins (*Mark: A Commentary* [Hermeneia; Minneapolis: Fortress, 2007], 472) finds a parallel to this in the story of Elisha raising the son of the Shunammite woman (2 Kgs 8:37), where the servant Gehazi tries to push her away, but the prophet says, "Let her alone." She further notes that the rabbis debated whether children would be "raised from the dead and included in the age to come." By accepting them and saying that to such belong the kingdom of God, Jesus extends the reach of God's love.

34. Marcus, *Mark 8–16*, 718–19.

35. Gundry, "Children," 169.

state is "an echo of the Old Testament traditions in which Israel is depicted as the smallest, as an infant or child."[36] Children who are outside the law and powerless stand in stark contrast to the arrival of a rich man, who observed the law "from his youth" (ἐκ νεότητος) but who cannot give up those possessions that promise him power and security.[37]

A RICH MAN ENTANGLED BY THE THORNS: MARK 10:17–22 AND IMAGES OF THE HUNDREDFOLD (10:23–31)

The story of the rich man seeking to follow Jesus is ultimately an antik-ingdom narrative of one who refuses Jesus' call. It comprises two main sections: the narrative of the call by Jesus to "sell what you have and give to the poor," and the sad reluctance of the man to do this (10:17–22); and, as in other places in Mark, it is followed by private instruction to the disciples on the meaning of sayings or actions (10:23–31), with a warning that the community is also to be free of a love of possessions but countered by a promise of the hundredfold in possessions and ultimately "eternal life," which is precisely what the young man sought but did not claim because of his love of possessions (10:23–30). We will treat first the call and rejection and then turn to other passages on the danger of wealth, before return-ing to the promises given by Jesus to those who forsake possessions and family.

The details of the narrative are themselves the root of multiple expla-nations. As Jesus begins another phase of his journey, a man runs up and kneels before him to ask, "Good Teacher, what must I do to inherit eternal life?" In the other discipleship stories in Mark the initiative always comes from Jesus in the form of summons and response. The term *eternal life* appears only here and at the end of the narrative, where those disciples who leave everything to follow Jesus receive what the man sought (10:30). No one else addresses Jesus as "good," and Jesus rejects the greeting with the statement: "No one is good but God alone." Jesus then tells the man what he must "do" by quoting commands from the second table of the Decalogue. Both the order and content, however, differ from the Old Tes-

---

36. Ibid., 171, citing Deut 7:7–8; Hos 11:1–4.
37. David Rhoads, Joanna Dewey, and Donald Michie (*Mark as Story: An Intro-duction to the Narrative of a Gospel* [2nd ed.; Minneapolis: Fortress, 1999], 52): "two paired episodes often repeat a common theme, one illuminating the theme, by com-parison or contrast with the other."

tament and the LXX with prohibitions against murder, adultery, and stealing first in order and the addition of "do not defraud" (μὴ ἀποστερήσῃς).[38]

Reacting to his statement that he has observed all these from his youth (which suggests he is no longer a youth), Jesus, "looking at him, loved him," an action of Jesus found only here in Mark and omitted by Matthew and Luke, and that has itself generated multiple interpretations.[39] Then the mood shifts as Jesus points out a defect in his qualifications to inherit eternal life, by focusing on one thing he lacks (ὑστερεῖ, also translated as "fall short of" with connotations of "through one's own fault").[40] To complete his quest for eternal life, the man must then respond to a summons of Jesus, "go, sell what you own, and give the money to the poor," which will bring him treasure in heaven.[41] Only then does he hear the words of Jesus, "follow me"; at this point the reader realizes that all else depends on his response. The man who rushed up with enthusiasm and fell before Jesus "was shocked [στυγνάσας] and went away grieving, for he had many possessions [κτήματα πολλά]," and Jesus himself utters a virtual lament, "How hard it will be for those who have wealth [δυσκόλως οἱ τὰ χρήματα ἔχοντες] to enter the kingdom of God" (10:23). This is the hinge that opens the door to the next section, where the narrative then takes a completely new turn as the disciples are themselves "perplexed" (ἐθαμβοῦντο [v. 24], or better "amazed" or "astounded," as they were by the power of Jesus to cast out demons [1:27]). This then precipitates more extensive teaching of Jesus on the relation of family and possessions to discipleship.

---

38. James G. Crossley ("The Damned Rich [Mark 10:17–31]," *ExpTim* 116 [2005]: 397) cites here Sir 4:1, "do not cheat the poor of their living," and argues that the understanding of Mark 10:17–31 "comes close to absolutely condemning the rich."

39. Cf. Donahue and Harrington (*Gospel of Mark*, 303): "Jesus admires the sincerity and integrity of one who has observed the 10 commandments in his life;" Evans (*Mark 8:27–16:20*, 98) says that it describes simply Jesus taking him by the shoulders; Moloney (*Gospel of Mark*, 200) notes that the man asks what he "must" do but Jesus attempts "to wrest the initiative from the man and to call him to eternal life." Marcus (*Mark 8–16*, 722) offers what I feel is the most plausible view that Genesis frequently speaks of a father's love for a son (22:2; 25:28; 37:3; 44:20), but this love may involve the son in sacrifice (22:2).

40. BDAG, 1043–44, s.v. ὑστερέω.

41. The use of θησαυρόν here as a place where something is kept for safekeeping (BDAG, 456) is replete with irony since only by giving up those possessions will they promise "safety" for the future (eternal life).

Even a cursory account of this dense narrative merits calls for further exposition of its major challenge: why a person so dedicated to the law from his youth was unable to heed the call of Jesus. Particular details are equally perplexing: the man seeks "eternal life," but Jesus speaks of the obstacle that possessions pose for entry into the "kingdom of God"; the significance of the changed order and the addition of "do not defraud" to the commands of the Decalogue; the strong reaction of the man and the difference between "possessions" and "wealth." By attending to these we can hear the echo of Mark 4:19, where the proclamation of the kingdom can be choked by the seduction of wealth and the desire of possessions.

Joel Marcus opens the best path to interpretation and appropriation. The man's quest "to inherit eternal life" is grounded on the promise to Abraham and his descendants that they would possess the land, which promise evolved in Jewish history to an eschatological hope for participation in the life of the world to come.[42] Since, as noted, Jesus responds that only with difficulty can the rich enter the "kingdom of God," the man's question can be seen as a way of avoiding the often demanding conditions of entry into the kingdom proclaimed by Jesus (9:42–47; 10:15, 24). The citation of the second table of the Decalogue by Jesus is important since the prohibitions deal with situations that destroy communal life: murder, adultery, stealing, bearing false witness, followed by the reformulation of "do not covet" to "you shall not defraud" (μὴ ἀποστερήσῃς, omitted by Matthew and Luke), and concluding with honoring your father and mother.

While his rejection of the call of Jesus, despite his reverent approach to Jesus and his lifelong observance of the law, may evoke a certain admiration and even sympathy, the readers are left with the same great astonishment as the disciples (10:26). But lurking behind his self-affirmed virtues are the dangers of wealth. His first reaction to the call of Jesus (στυγνάσας ἐπὶ τῷ λόγῳ) is often translated as "he was shocked" (NRSV) or "his face fell" (NAB), but the phrase can also mean "be appalled," or as Marcus suggests, "be resentful."[43] If so, then there may be a certain arrogance in the man's response over Jesus' lack of appreciation of his virtue, followed by his grief, "for he had many possessions," which may reflect that strain of biblical thought that equated possessions as a sign of divine blessing or approval, so that he could not fathom the command to leave them.

---

42. Marcus, *Mark 8–16*, 720, 725.

43. Marcus (ibid., 723) notes that "*stygnazein* and cognate words come from a root meaning 'to hate'" and can suggest shocked resentment.

Other possibilities emerge. The term for "possessions" (κτήματα), which is derived from the verb κτάομαι (acquire or procure for oneself) rather than the more frequent and neutral τά ὑπάρχοντα (meaning "that which belongs to someone"), implies suspicious possession.[44] Coupled with the command by Jesus, "You shall not defraud," there are hints that the man's possessions were not simply gifts of God but may have been acquired through exploitation or appropriation, which also reflects the general suspicion of wealth mentioned below.[45] In effect he could not have left all to follow Jesus since he defined himself in terms of his possessions and to leave them would be an affront to his honor and self-identity. Also important is the command of Jesus not only to sell his possessions but to "give to the poor."[46] Earlier, though affirming that he has observed all the commandments from his youth, he seems never to have heard of the frequent commands throughout the Torah to care for the poor and other vulnerable people (Exod 22:25; 23:11; Lev 19:10; 23:22; Deut 15:6–15, esp. v. 11, "therefore I command you, 'Open your hand to the poor and needy neighbor in your land'"; and Deut 24:10–20). The cares of the world, the lure of wealth, and the desire for other things caused the word of Jesus, inviting him to be a disciple along the path to eternal life, to fall among thorns that choked the invitation (Mark 4:19).

A COUNTERVISION TO THE LURE OF WEALTH (MARK 10:23–31)

A new section of the narrative unfolds (10:23–27) after the man departs. Jesus looks around and directly addresses his disciples, "How hard it will be for those who have wealth to enter the kingdom of God," followed by a shocking hyperbolic image, "It is easier for a camel to go through

---

44. Marcus (ibid., 723) calls these "estates," with the suggestion that they were acquired by exploitation. Joseph Hellerman ("Wealth and Sacrifice in Early Christianity: Revisiting Mark's Presentation of Jesus' Encounter with the Rich Young Ruler," *TrinJ* 21 [2000]: 143–64) offers extensive evidence on practices of landownership in first-century Palestine that oppress the poor.

45. Marcus (*Mark 8–16*, 721) notes that the substitution of "do not defraud" for "do not covet" in the tenth commandment "is in line with certain Jewish traditions, in which it forbids not only craving for others' possessions but also usurping them."

46. The NRSV reads "give the money to the poor," but the Greek text has no word for "the money." In other Markan call narratives, people abandon family, possessions, and occupations (1:16–20; 2:14–15), but there is no subsequent command to give to the poor.

the eye of a needle than for someone who is rich to enter the kingdom of God." The two entry phrases link this passage to the previous saying about those who, like children, have no power or possessions but will enter the kingdom of God, while the man with possessions is shut out.[47] This so shocks the disciples that they wonder whether any rich man can be saved, only to hear another somewhat enigmatic response by Jesus that what seems impossible in human terms is "not for God; for God all things are possible" (see below).

Neglect of the use of hyperbole (absurdity to evoke strong emotion or reaction) has led to multiple interpretations, from the fanciful (e.g., a reference to a nonexistent city gate called "The Needle's Eye" too narrow for a camel loaded with baggage = possessions) to the allegorical (Christ as the camel and the gate is his sufferings).[48] Given the camel's reputation as a beast of burden and "the idea of riches as an encumbrance," the hyperbole is even more shocking when the camel (= rich man) is loaded with "many possessions" (10:23).[49] The switch from "many possessions" used initially by Jesus to the "rich man" ($\pi\lambda o\acute{u}\sigma\iota o\nu$) in the gnomic hyperbole can be seen in light of commonly held religious and cultural perspectives about the danger of riches.

In the Bible possessions and even wealth can be seen as a blessing and gift from God (Deut 28:1–14) and a blessing for the righteous: "Happy are those who fear the LORD, who greatly delight in his commandments.... Wealth and riches are in their houses, and their righteousness endures forever" (Ps 112:1, 3). But along with these blessings there is also a danger in wealth, especially in the wisdom traditions. It easily leads to pride (Prov 18:11) and false trust (Sir 11:19). One is tempted to use wicked means to attain it (Prov 28:6). It is impermanent (Eccl 5:10), carries disadvantages (5:11), and is only a relative good compared to, for example, health or a good name (cf. Sir 30:14–16). Also wealth is given by God for definite purposes. God abundantly bestows material blessings for the purpose of

---

47. Collins, *Mark*, 480.

48. Marcus, *Mark 8–16*, 731.

49. Ibid. Though the common interpretation of the camel saying is that it is a hyperbole, an equally apt description may be "riddle," understood as a saying "intentionally phrased to require ingenuity in ascertaining its answer or meaning" (*Oxford English Dictionary*), especially since Jesus then explains the meaning of the riddle. See also James L. Crenshaw, "Impossible Questions, Sayings, and Tasks," *Semeia* 17 (1980): 19–34.

meeting the needs of the poor and for powerless and suffering people heralded as "the widow, the orphan, and the stranger in the land" (Deut 15:10; 2 Cor 9:8–10). Job defended his integrity with the claim that he had given to the poor openhandedly (Job 31:16–20). Sodom was condemned for failing to do so (Ezek 16:49). As noted above, the lure of wealth and the desire for other things can lead to murder and exploitation of the poor, which brings down the wrath of God, spoken through the prophets.[50]

In a culture where there was a vast gap between rich and poor, and virtually no middle class, strong polemics exist against the wealthy. In a concise overview Bruce Malina writes that "in the eastern Mediterranean in New Testament times, 'rich' or 'wealthy' as a rule meant 'avaricious, greedy,' while 'poor' referred to persons scarcely able to maintain their honor or dignity."[51] Thus the rich became wealthy "as the result of their own covetousness, or greed, or that of their ancestors," and their wealth was often due to "defrauding or eliminating others."[52]

Jesus' dire view of the fate of the rich moves the disciples from being perplexed (ἐθαμβοῦντο, v. 24) to asking with complete astonishment (περισσῶς ἐξεπλήσσοντο, v. 26), "Then who can be saved?"[53] Jesus responds by stating that God's power can surpass human impossibility, which anticipates the paradox of the following verses that those who abandon everything will receive a hundredfold.[54]

---

50. Stephen C. Mott, "Wealth," HBD, 1122.

51. Malina, "Wealth and Poverty," 355.

52. Ibid., 357.

53. BDAG, 308, s.v ἐκπλήσσω. The verb suggests "amazement to the point of being overwhelmed." Collins (Mark, 481) calls the question of the disciples "nonsensical" since not everyone can be saved. "Saved" suggests "rescue" or "being made safe," but it is not immediately clear from what the man has been "saved." In Luke 19:9, after Zacchaeus gives half of his goods to the poor, Jesus says that "salvation" has come to this house. In Mark 10:26 salvation may suggest rescue from the entanglements of wealth.

54. Marcus (Mark 8–16, 731–32) notes that "impossible divine possibility" is often associated with creatio ex nihilo, and suggests that the closest parallel to Mark is Gen 18:14 LXX, where Sarah laughs in disbelief that she will bear a son, and exclaims, "Shall anything be impossible to God?" Sharyn Dowd (Reading Mark: A Literary and Theological Commentary on the Second Gospel [Macon, Ga.: Smyth & Helwys, 2000], 107–8) suggests that the answer is that the rich can be saved just as in his miracles. Jesus brings the possible out of the impossible, e.g., exorcism of legion (5:1–20), raising of Jairus's daughter, and the healing of the hemorrhaging woman (5:21–43).

This initial exchange then introduces the culmination of the narrative (10:28–31), where Peter in a truncated statement ("Peter began to say") seems to question the value of their choice to abandon everything and follow Jesus. In answering, Jesus summarizes the deepest meaning of a life of radical discipleship, and echoes the response of the seed falling on good soil describing those who hear the word, accept it, and bear fruit even to the hundredfold (Mark 4:20).

In response to the statement of Peter, "Look, we have left everything and followed you," Jesus says: "there is no one who has left house or brothers or sisters or mother or father or children or fields, for my sake and for the sake of the good news,[55] who will not receive a hundredfold now in this age—houses, brothers and sisters, mothers and children, and fields, with persecutions—and in the age to come eternal life" (10:29–30).[56] Leaving family and home to follow Jesus is a well-established part of the tradition of the sayings of Jesus. In Q it appears in a more radical form with the command to hate members of one's own family and to neglect familial duties such as the burial of a father.[57] Mark shows contact with such a tradition in the charge to the disciples in 6:7–13 to travel without bread or money and to move from place to place.

While all three Evangelists promise eternal life, only Mark states that the family that has been left behind will be replaced by a new family. The hundredfold that the Markan reader knows from 4:20 is the fruit of hearing and doing the word of God in a new family based not on natural kinship but on the power of God. Such language should not be considered merely as a metaphor, since in the early church the sense of community

---

55. Mark has "for the sake of the good news" (ἕνεκεν τοῦ εὐαγγελίου), while Matt 19:20 has "for my name's sake" and Luke 18:20, "for the sake of the kingdom of God." Mark's usage takes the reader back to the initial proclamation of Jesus in 1:14–15 with the call to place one's faith in the good news first announced by Jesus—which will subsequently unfold.

56. The New Testament often contrasts this age (τῷ αἰῶνι τούτῳ; Rom 12:2; 1 Cor 2:6) with the age to come (ἐν τῷ αἰῶνι τῷ ἐρχομένῳ, Mark 10:30), but here Mark uses ἐν τῷ καιρῷ, which has the overtone of an appropriate or favorable time (BDAG, 497, s.v. καιρός), which then echoes the initial proclamation of Jesus (1:15) that πεπλήρωται ὁ καιρός, "a special time has come to pass" (my trans.), and that in this time the values of the world will be reversed as people receive the benefits of the kingdom. See Marcus, *Mark 8–16*, 733.

57. Luke 14:25–26/Matt 10:37–38; Luke 12:49–53/Matt 10:34–35; Luke 9:57–62/Matt 8:19–22.

was expressed in familial language.[58] Paul speaks of Onesimus as his child (Phlm 10) and tells the Corinthians that he became their father through the Gospel (1 Cor 4:15). Paul compares his work among the Thessalonians to a nursing mother caring for children and a father encouraging them (1 Thess 2:7, 11), and calls the mother of Rufus his mother (Rom 16:13).

These new relationships promised by Jesus "in this time" for those who left everything come "with persecutions" (μετὰ διωγμῶν). The phrase breaks the rhythmic parallelism of the verse, and in content it relativizes the reward of the new family. Mark wants to convey that one who leaves family for Jesus' sake and for the sake of the gospel will necessarily be involved in following the way of the cross, which prepares for the expanded conclusion of the journey narrative (10:45–52). Here the disciples are not to seek dominating power over others, but to live in service of others in imitation of the Son of Man, who "came not to be served but to serve, and to give his life that people might be free [my trans. of λύτρον ἀντὶ πολλῶν]."

But through a careful inclusio, Jesus' final words in the story of the rich man are a promise to his followers that the very thing that the man sought but turned away from awaits those who leave everything: "eternal life" (10:17, 30).

ECHOES OF THE LURE OF WEALTH:
POSSESSIONS OVER PARENTS (MARK 7:1–13)

While the story of the man with many possessions in the context of Mark 10 may be the most dramatic echo of the lure of wealth and the desire for other things, some attention must be given to select other examples.

One of the anomalies of Jesus' quotation of the Decalogue to the rich man (10:19) was the location of the command, "Honor your father and mother," as the last command of the Decalogue, when in both the Hebrew

---

58. While the disciples will leave "house or brothers or sisters or mother or father or children or fields," all will be returned except "father." This could reflect that for early Christians the only father was the "God and Father of our Lord Jesus Christ" (Rom 15:6; 2 Cor 1:3; 11:31), or equally possible that the Markan version of the statement embodies an antipatriarchal stance, where Mark's new family is to be characterized by the renunciation of dominating power and by mutual service. See John R. Donahue, *The Theology and Setting of Discipleship in the Gospel of Mark* (Milwaukee: Marquette University Press, 1983), 43–44; also Elisabeth Schüssler Fiorenza, *In Memory of Her: A Feminist Theological Reconstruction of Christian Origins* (New York: Crossroad, 1983), 154: "the new family of Jesus has no room for father."

and Greek texts it is the fifth commandment (fourth in the traditional Catholic listing). The law of end stress indicates that this placement may be significant.[59] The only other place in Mark where this commandment is explicitly cited occurs in the complex dispute between Jesus and the Pharisees and scribes initially over clean, unclean, and ritual washing.

In the midst of the dispute, in order to counter the reliance of the Pharisees and scribes on "teaching human precepts as doctrines" (7:7), Jesus gives an example of how tradition can subvert the biblical commandment. A son can say, "'Whatever support you might have had from me is Corban' (that is, an offering to God)," which then dispenses him from doing anything for a father or mother, "thus making void the word of God" (7:11–13).

The practice involves use of resources in a way that Jesus rejects, again out of concern for the more vulnerable members of the community—parents, most likely of an adult male, who will depend on his support. The etymology and practice of Corban suggests not simply a gift to the temple, but one sealed by an oath.[60] Still, details remain obscure and are also connected with the binding power and nature of oaths. Especially absent are indications of the motive of the one making the vow. One scenario might be that the son, though giving up ownership of resources, could still benefit from their use, for example, by investment.[61] Another would be that he could seek a "dispensation" from the vow and the money or its equivalent would be returned.[62] Whatever the specific details of the practice, it echoes the failed sowing: strangled by entanglements (thorns) and the "lure of wealth" or "desire for other things" (4:18–19).

---

59. See Collins, *Mark*, 479.

60. Corban is a dedicatory formula under an oath or vow that sets aside something from human use. It is attested elsewhere in Jewish texts; see Marcus, *Mark 1–8*, 445–46; Collins, *Mark*, 352–53.

61. D. A. Carson (*Matthew* [vols. 1–2 of *The Expositor's Bible Commentary: With the New International Version*; ed. Frank E. Gaebelein; Grand Rapids: Zondervan, 1995], 2:349) argues that "greed" could keep the son from honoring his parents. Mark (7:22) lists this (πλεονεξίαι) among the vices that cause moral impurity.

62. Especially helpful is A. I. Baumgarten ("Korban and the Pharisaic *paradosis*," *Journal of the Ancient Near Eastern Society* 16–17 [1984–1985]: 5–17), who examines the institution in rabbinic texts, Philo, and Josephus, and finds evidence that the oath or vow could be broken so that the son may gain access to his resources.

CRAVING OTHER THINGS AND DEVOURING THE
HOUSES OF WIDOWS (MARK 12:38–44)

Throughout Mark there are foreshadowings of the lethal opposition to
Jesus (3:6, 21); for example, "scribes from Jerusalem" claim that his power
to exorcise comes from "the ruler of the demons" (3:22). Such opposition shifts dramatically when Jesus enters Jerusalem (predicted in 10:33).
After he drives the buyers and sellers out of the temple, priests and scribes
"kept looking for a way to kill him" (11:18). When he retells the story of
the failed vineyard from Isa 5:1–7, as the story of vineyard tenants who
commit murder to claim an inheritance (Mark 12:12), his hearers, real-
izing that the parable was directed against them, hatched a plot to arrest
him (12:13–14). The "lure of wealth" is a subtext both to Jesus' "cleansing"
the temple (i.e., rejection of mercantile activity in the temple) and to the
parable of Mark 12 (murder to gain an inheritance).[63]

The Jerusalem ministry of Jesus unfolds under an arch of lethal opposition to Jesus by chief priests and scribes (11:18) and his most acerbic
confrontation with temple authorities that comes at the close of his public
ministry. He launches a bitter attack on the scribes who not only flaunt
power and privilege (12:38–39) but "devour widows' houses and for the
sake of appearance say long prayers" (12:40). "Devouring" is an especially
vivid image since it suggests ravenous eating or "gobbling up" and is used
in many different contexts for "to destroy," or "to rob, " and echoes the
destruction of the first sowing of Mark 4:13, when the birds "eat up" (or
"devour," KJV) the seed.[64] Behind this charge is the vulnerable status of
widows and God's concern for them throughout the Old Testament since
"to violate them is an especially heinous crime" (Jer 7:6–7; Ezek 22:7; Zech
7:10–14; Mal 3:5),[65] made even worse under the pretense of devotion

---

63. For the differing interpretations of the action in the temple see Evans, *Mark
8:27–16:20*, esp. 176–89. Evans ("Jesus' Action in the Temple: Cleansing or Portent of
Destruction?" *CBQ* 51 [1989]: 237–69) interprets the scene as an "action against the
money changers and vendors." For the view that Jesus' actions are an "attack on com-
mercialism and exploitation by the temple authorities," see John R. Donahue, "From
Crucified Messiah to Risen Christ: The Trial of Jesus Revisited," in *Jews and Christians
Speak of Jesus* (ed. Arthur Zannoni; Minneapolis: Fortress, 1994), 93–121. E. P. Sanders (*Jesus and Judaism* [Philadelphia: Fortress, 1985], 61–76) argues that Mark envisions a "symbolic destruction."

64. BDAG, 531–32, s.v. κατεσθίω.

65. Marcus, *Mark 8–16*, 855; the irony here is biting since the scribes, experts in

(long prayers). The "greater condemnation" threatened by Jesus echoes the threat of Isaiah regarding the arrival of the day of punishment for those who "turn aside the needy from justice ... rob the poor of my people of their right,... that widows may be your spoil ... and orphans your prey" (Isa 10:1–4). Jesus' final confrontation with the temple aristocracy is a ringing recollection of "the lure of wealth and the desire for other things."

But just as the failure of the rich man is followed by the promise of eternal life to those who abandon all to follow him, Jesus offers an alternate vision to the previous failure of the scribes when a widow, as symbolic of the object of their greed (12:40), becomes the model of true religion. Sitting opposite the treasury, Jesus contrasts those offering gifts out of their abundance to a poor widow who gave "everything she had, all she had to live on" (lit. "her whole life," ὅλον τὸν βίον αὐτῆς).

Since the 1980s scholars have debated whether Jesus is praising the action of the woman as a model of discipleship or holding her up as an example of exploitation by the scribes (paraphrased as "look at what you have done, cajoling this poor widow into giving up her property").[66] Whatever the original intent of the story, in its present context the woman is praiseworthy not only because her gift is the radical opposite of the rich and powerful, but she is an icon of the action of Jesus, who soon will give his life to build a temple, an eschatological sanctuary not made with hands (14:58b) where his self-sacrifice "will confound human ways of knowing."[67] Such is the mystery of the kingdom of God revealed to Jesus' disciples (4:11).

A CONCLUDING REFLECTION

While social injustice is not the primary concern of Mark's Gospel, the text offers seeds that can grow into reflection on the seduction and dangers of the quest for wealth that are so much a part of our modern society. The

---

the law, violate the Torah, which stipulates that widows are among the groups to be most protected (Exod 22:22; Deut 10:18; 14:29; 24:17–20).

66. Example of exploitation: A. G. Wright, "The Widow's Mites: Praise or Lament," *CBQ* 44 (1982): 256–65; anticipation of Jesus who will give his life: Markus, *Mark 8–16*, 861–63. Elizabeth Struthers Malbon ("The Poor Widow in Mark, and Her Poor Rich Readers," *CBQ* 53 [1991]: 589–604) argues for a "both/and" solution: exploitation in the ministry of Jesus; model in the Markan redaction.

67. Marcus, *Mark 8–16*, 863.

Bible does not give direct solutions to rampant socioeconomic problems today, but tells us the kind of people Christians are to become if they are to confront such problems.[68] This involves hearing again the first words of Jesus in Mark, "change your way of thinking and place your faith in the gospel" (Mark 1:15, my trans.). As we hear the Gospel and read the signs of the times in 2012, this change of heart must confront "the lure of wealth and the desire for other things."

---

68. See James F. Gustafson, *Can Ethics Be Christian?* (Chicago: University of Chicago Press, 1975), 92–101.

Jesus and the Human Condition in Mark's Gospel: Divine Grace and the Shattering of Human Illusions

Paul J. Achtemeier

Mark's framing the story of Jesus under the rubric of his passion, death, and resurrection stands out as one of the signal accomplishments in the history of Christian reflection on the meaning of Jesus Christ. In addition to understanding Jesus as crucified and risen, however, there is also woven into Mark's narrative a running commentary on the futility of human goodness in the face of the divine righteousness to be found in Jesus. Now through the juxtaposition of traditions, now through telling irony, Mark crafts his deceptively simple narrative in such a way as to show that pretensions to goodness in all spheres of human endeavor are in the end simply shattered and discredited. In the face of the incarnate Son of God, Mark makes clear, human pretensions are unmasked, sin is shown for the destructive force it is, and the impossibility of any recourse but grace is made evident.

In the following pages, I want to show how this is worked out in three areas: the religious, the political, and finally the personal. In each instance, what on the face of it seem to be valid claims to goodness and justice are shown to be mere illusions.

The Shattering of Illusions in the Religious Sphere

First of all, then, let us examine the shattering of such human illusions in the religious sphere. In this area, Mark concentrates solely on Jewish religious practices and customs, which, since they grow out of the legitimate claim of the Jews to be God's chosen people, alone have any claim to validity in his eyes.

The gift to that people when it was chosen by God was its religious law. Given to a band of slaves who had floundered their way into the desert, the law gave them a chance to form themselves into, and act appropriately as, the chosen people God had named them to be. It is as though, to put it in modern parlance, Moses had come down from Mount Sinai and told the Israelites: "I have some good news and some bad news. The good news is, you are God's chosen people. The bad news is, God expects you to conduct your lives in a way appropriate to that designation, or you will face divine judgment." To a ragtag group of slaves, who had never been a people, let alone a chosen people, and who at that point were totally ignorant as to what a "chosen people" was, let alone how it was to act in a way befitting that role, the giving of the law was an act of divine grace. It enabled the Israelites not only to understand themselves as "chosen people," but also presented them with the chance to lead a life pleasing to the God who had chosen them. Here, if anywhere, it would seem, there could be a legitimate claim to human goodness as it strove to live by, and fulfill, God's law.

In a story of Jesus' healing a crippled hand on the Sabbath (3:1–6), Mark presents an example of what had happened to that striving. Here a bit of background is necessary to understand the situation more clearly.

A portion of the law God gave to Israel as an integral part of his covenant with them was the command to honor the Sabbath, and do no work on it, because God himself had rested on the Sabbath after completing creation. The Sabbath had become a great treasure of the law. Some rabbis named it the unique element of the Jewish religious law that set Israel apart from all other nations. Obedience to that Sabbath law therefore constituted one of Israel's basic religious responsibilities. To ensure that the Sabbath law was kept, the rabbis "built a fence around the law." That is, they laid down rules to be sure that the central command to rest, and not labor, would be observed. For example, one ought not to labor; if one could not carry tools, one could not labor, and so the rabbis said, "Do not carry anything on the Sabbath." Hence no labor could be done. If one had to go to one's field to labor, then if one could not go out to one's field, one could not labor; and if one could not go far from one's house, one could not get to one's field, so the rabbis said, "Do not go far from your house on the Sabbath." In this way the rabbis built their "fence around the law." As a fence around a lawn prevents people from walking on it, so a "fence around the law" would keep people from breaking the central command. This activity of building a fence around the law was so important that it constituted one

of the three central commands given to every rabbi as his main responsibility: be temperate in judgment, raise up many disciples, and build a
fence around the law. As in the case of the of the Sabbath laws, so in the
case of every law, the goal was clear: protect, at all costs, the law God gave
to Israel.

It was on such a Sabbath that Jesus was confronted in a synagogue
by a man with a crippled hand. Given Jesus' previous acts of healing, the
rabbis watched to see what he would do. It is not as though the Pharisees
knew nothing of mercy. The giving of the law to Israel was after all an act of
God's mercy to them. And in fact the rabbis (among whom the Pharisees
were numbered) had built mercy into their fence around the Sabbath law.
One could, in an emergency, labor on the Sabbath to save a life, even the
life of an animal. On that there was no question. But this man's deformity
did not represent an emergency; the healing could wait until sundown,
and the end of the Sabbath, without threatening the man's life. So the Pharisees watched, and waited.

Jesus, noting this, poses a question to them: "Is it lawful on the Sabbath to do good or to do harm, to save a life or to kill?" Hardly a difficult
question; the answer was obvious. Of course it is not lawful to do harm on
the Sabbath, or to kill. The whole thrust of the law is that one is to do good
and not evil, and not only on the Sabbath but every day. Yet Jesus got no
answer from the assembled Pharisees. Turning to the crippled man, Jesus
said, "Stretch out your hand." The man obeys, and the hand is healed.

Mark's story continues: "The Pharisees went out, and immediately held
counsel with the Herodians against him, how to kill him." What incred-
ible irony! The Pharisees, by their silence and their subsequent plotting,
demonstrate that they think Jesus' good deed to the cripple is illegal, while
they, on that same Sabbath, plot to kill, thus demonstrating they think it
legal to do harm and to plot to kill on the Sabbath. However obvious the
answer to Jesus' simple question may have been, and however simple the
answer in terms of the law, the actions of the very people charged with
upholding and defending that law show they are willing to approve and
do exactly what the law forbids. And in the name of that very law! By their
acts, they have shown that while they feel it illegal for Jesus to do good
on the Sabbath by an act of healing, it is not illegal for them to plot harm,
namely, how to kill him.

In this event, confronted with the Son of God, human pretensions to
do good in the religious sphere are laid bare, and the illusion of human
goodness is crushed. Could it be that what stands between God and his

creatures is not their evil, but their confidence in their own ability to determine goodness?

The account of Jesus cleansing the temple presents a further judgment on human activity in the religious sphere. Using a characteristic juxtaposing, a "sandwiching" of two traditions, Mark shows us how the two traditions aid us in interpreting that temple "cleansing," and therefore how we are to understand it. First, then, we need to look at the actual account of Jesus' activity in the temple (Mark 11:15–19).

The scene is not a gentle one. Activity in the outer court is brought to a halt. What those activities are provides our first clue to what Jesus is doing here. People who sold doves rendered a valuable, even necessary, service to faithful Jews who had traveled a distance in order to participate in temple worship. Only ritually unblemished animals were fit for sacrifice to almighty God. Any blemish, even one hardly noticeable to the untrained eye, rendered that animal unfit for sacrifice. Where then were travelers from distant lands to find unblemished animals fit to offer to almighty God, and so obey the commands of his law? It would have been all but impossible to bring them along on a long journey. And if they did, only to find in the end the animals brought bore a disqualifying blemish, what recourse would they have had? To make participation in temple worship possible for such people, the temple authorities had made arrangements so that such unblemished animals might be secured in the outer court of the temple. It is not a question here of commerce, or that those who sold such animals cheated the worshippers by charging too high a price. The point is that without such activity, participation in temple worship would be denied to many faithful Jews.

Every Jewish male also had to pay a tax to support the temple: one half-shekel per year. Yet this also posed a problem. Where could a Jew from the Dispersion find the necessary coin to pay that tax? Such coins were not widely accessible throughout the Roman Empire, and ancient cities did not have scattered here and there the kind of exchange services modern travelers are familiar with. How then could the pious Jew find the proper coin with which to pay the temple tax? It was to facilitate just such payments that tables were set up in the outer courtyard of the temple where travelers from foreign lands could find such coins. Without such money changers, the temple tax could not be paid—a severe inconvenience to payers. Without that tax, the temple could not survive as a viable institution.

Temple worship was largely sacrificial, and that required a large variety of pots and pans to carry off the blood of the sacrifices, the various parts of the animals, the fuels for the fire, and the like. Unless such vessels could move freely through the temple area, temple worship would come to an end.

Consider now what Jesus did: he stopped the sale of animals, he stopped the exchange of coins, and he stopped the carrying about of vessels. In short, he did not so much purify temple worship as bring it to a complete stop. The question here is this: Why did he do that? Had not God commanded such sacrifices? He had indeed, but he had also commanded that his temple be kept pure and undefiled. It could be entered only by persons who were ceremonially pure. Indeed, the temple in Jerusalem carried warnings apparently posted on its outside walls, stating that entry into the inner areas—entry into the Court of the Gentiles was permitted to all—meant death to the ceremonially impure. Zealous to keep God's law and thus to defend his honor, temple authorities intended to keep the temple areas pure and hence acceptable to God. No playing fast and loose with God's law. What God wanted was what temple authorities felt bound to do.

Why then did Jesus act as he did? He tells us in Mark: "Is it not written, 'My house shall be called a house of prayer for all the nations?' But you have made it a den of robbers." This last phrase has summoned forth considerable nonsense by various commentators, as though Jesus were condemning as dishonest the changing of money, or profiteering in the sale of animals—or just generally condemning the practice of commerce in the temple. Jesus called the temple a den of robbers—did he not thus refer to robbery being committed there? To suggest that shows a complete misunderstanding of the situation. The den is not where robbers commit their crimes. It is the place of refuge to which they retreat *after* they have committed their crimes. Jesus is here quoting Jeremiah, from Jeremiah's temple sermon:

> You steal, you murder, you commit adultery and perjury, you run after other gods whom you do not know; then you come and stand before me in this house which bears my name, and say, "We are safe"; safe, you think to indulge in all these abominations? Do you think this house, this house which bears my name, is a robber's cave? (Jer 7:9–11)

Here it is clear—the robbers' cave is the place of refuge to which they flee after they have committed their crimes. Jesus is here not condemning dishonest business practices; he is condemning a view of the temple that held that anything goes so long as the precincts of that temple are kept pure. Yet even more: Jesus, quoting Isaiah, says that the temple is to be a house of prayer for all nations. It is in Jesus' view not the preserve of cultically pure temple authorities and Jews. All nations are to come to its precincts and share in the worship of God. For these reasons, Jesus ends worship in the temple.

Yet the question remains: Does he end it? Perhaps he still intends merely to purge it, in a gesture of prophetic enactment, purging it so it can continue but in more acceptable form? No, in Mark's view he destroyed it. Mark makes that clear with the tradition that brackets the narrative of Jesus in the temple. The bracketing tradition is the story of the cursing of the fig tree (Mark 11:12–14, 20–25).

Because the fig tree was devoid of fruit, Jesus cursed it, and it died, withered to the roots. Clearly, by this device of bracketing tradition, often employed in Mark's Gospel, Mark wants us to understand that Jesus' activity in the temple amounts to a cursing of it, and as surely as the fig tree withered so will the temple. Jesus' act was in fact a prophetic enactment as Mark understood it, but it was a prophetic enactment of the temple's demise, not its cleansing.

One problem remains: Mark's tradition also notes "it was not the time for figs." Could Jesus really have cursed the tree when he found no fruit? Was it not out of character for Jesus, in a fit of hungry pique, to curse that fig tree for not having any fruit, even though it was not the time when such trees bore fruit? A great deal of ink has been spilled on this one, trying to justify the fig tree, or Jesus, or both. Yet when taken in the total context, this functions virtually as the key to understanding the passage. In God's plan, time had passed the temple by as the place where God's mercy was to be found. Such mercy is now to be found in God's Son, not in his temple. Using the analogy of the fig tree, we can see that the temple does not bear the fruit God seeks from it—Jesus' saying in the temple made that clear. Yet it in fact cannot bear fruit, since the fruit it could have borne is now to be found not in the temple but in Jesus. That is why the temple must come to an end: it no longer has a purpose. That purpose has been transferred to Jesus, who is now the locus, as it were, where access to God is to be found. Mark makes that clear by the final verses (22–25) he has added, which speak of prayer and faith. It is faith now that does the impossible: it allows us access to a holy God, and such prayer and faith are announced by the one who has taken the place of the temple, namely, Jesus himself.

Thus does temple worship come to an end. Thus is the pretension to goodness implied in temple worship unmasked for what it has become: a shield for human disobedience of God's holy laws. Yet the very time for the temple to be holy—to bear fruit before God, as it were—appears to have passed it by. Could it be that even such pretensions, such human failure, are included in the larger plan of God?

THE SHATTERING OF ILLUSIONS IN THE POLITICAL SPHERE

Yet Mark does not limit the exposure of human pretensions to goodness to the religious sphere. He also shows Jesus' confrontation with human goodness in the broader political sphere. That confrontation leads to the climax of Mark's portrayal of Jesus—the events surrounding his crucifixion.

While no one would want to present Pontius Pilate as a candidate for beatification, he did represent the Roman judicial system, which in turn relied on a system of law that was one of the great intellectual achievements of antiquity. If the Greeks had invented systems of philosophy, the Romans invented the concept of a civil law based on principles that could be applied justly to new situations as they arose. That was the expression of a noble idea, namely, a government based on law rather than on personal status, and the Romans took long steps toward achieving it. Roman citizenship was prized in the ancient world, and it put at the disposal of that citizen the entire structure of the Roman Empire. This was the legal structure Jesus confronted in his trial before Pilate (Mark 15:1–15).

The accusation by the Sanhedrin against Jesus that they brought before Pilate was clearly of a political nature. Jesus, they said, was fomenting sedition by claiming that he, not Caesar, ought to be given first political allegiance. The nature of their accusation is made clear by the first question Pilate addressed to Jesus: "Are you the King of the Jews?" A positive answer would demonstrate sedition, in which case Pilate could move against Jesus with a clear conscience. Pilate received no such answer. Yet Pilate's legal responsibility was to maintain peace in the province under his control, and when the leading citizens of a part of that province made accusations of sedition and insurrection, as the members of the Sanhedrin had done against Jesus, Pilate's responsibility was clear: he must avoid insurrection at all cost, lest the *Pax Romana* be breached, and many suffer. Yet Pilate wished, in the absence of a confession, nevertheless to appear evenhanded and just. Even without the confession, he wanted to make sure the charges were accurate, lest there be a miscarriage of justice that could, at some future time, return to haunt him.

Yet even justice alone is rarely sufficient in cases like this, and, as Mark explains, it was Pilate's custom publicly to temper justice with mercy. At such festal occasions as our text presents, Pilate, we are told, would release a prisoner to popular demand. So there is a choice: Jesus or Barabbas could be released. Pilate apparently knew that the call for Jesus' death was trumped up. It was religious envy, not political loyalty, that motivated those who had brought charges to Pilate against Jesus (v. 10). Yet the shouting of the crowd was sufficient to overcome Pilate's awareness of the injustice of the charge, and in the end expediency triumphed. Barabbas was released, and Jesus was put to death. So are human pretensions to evenhanded justice put to shame.

The irony goes deeper, however. Jesus, as we have seen, was brought before Pilate on charges of insurrection, and since that is the only charge that could have been effective with Pilate, that is quite apparently the charge on the basis of which Jesus was crucified. Yet the one released, Barabbas, had in fact been imprisoned precisely because of his role in an insurrection! What a cruel twist of irony: the one who had committed the capital crime of insurrection was set free, while the one innocent of insurrection was put to death for it. Thus is the impotence of human pretension to justice revealed: in the attempt to be just, even merciful, Pilate has enacted a travesty, and injustice has prevailed. In Mark's view, such is the inevitable result when human pretensions to goodness confront God himself: human pretensions to goodness are unveiled as the illusions they are. Roman "justice" had here accomplished the very purpose it had set out to avoid: release of the guilty and punishment of the innocent. If the impression here is that nothing could have saved Jesus from his death on the cross, one will have begun to understand Mark.

Yet it is not only the secular state whose evil is unmasked in the confrontation of humans with the Son of God. The history of the chosen people fares no better. That is made clear in the parable Jesus told about the unjust tenants in the vineyard (Mark 12:1–12).

This parable of a vineyard (in light of Isa 5, who could avoid the identification of the vineyard as Israel?) tells the story of God's relationship to his chosen people: continuing rejection. Servant after servant, sent to find fruit from the vineyard for its owner, is turned away emptyhanded. Some are abused, and some even killed. The owner's son fares no better: he too is killed. The religious authorities listening to this parable understand its point quite clearly, and irony of ironies, by their very objection to the one who tells this tale, they demonstrated its truth by bringing about the death of the Son! Thus is the zeal for the honor and religious purity of Israel turned into the very act of its ultimate rebellion and dishonor. Jewish religious history fares no better than the Roman legal structure: both, in the very practice of their craft, reveal their own inability to do good and avoid evil. In this way, Mark makes clear that the presence of the Son of God unmasks the illusion of goodness in the political sphere.

THE SHATTERING OF ILLUSIONS IN THE PERSONAL SPHERE

Yet the narrative that Mark composes betrays not only the illusory nature of human pretension to goodness in the religious and political spheres; the narrative shatters the illusion of goodness in the personal sphere as well. It is here that the story of the disciples plays out its theme within the larger narrative of the Gospel.

In Mark's Gospel, the story of the disciples is largely a matter of failure to follow or, in many instances, even to understand the Son of God. Their intentions are not open to question. The beginning of Mark's Gospel shows the unquestioning obedience the earliest disciples give to Jesus' command that they follow him. Without argument or persuasive invitation, indeed without prior acquaintance in the Gospel, they leave all and follow him. Simon and Andrew, James and John, Levi the son of Alphaeus, all follow Jesus immediately in response to his invitation. Yet despite it all, they are unable ever really to get it right. Peter, for example, can see who Jesus is: he is God's anointed, God's Christ. Yet his vision is blurred in such a way that Jesus perceives it as satanic. Indeed, Peter's understanding of Jesus would keep Jesus from the very path he must follow as the Christ: the path to suffering, the path to the cross.

In another instance, on a mountain, in the presence of the obvious divinity of Jesus, who is bright with divine glory and is seen conversing with Moses and Elijah, Peter, fearful and confused, blurts out a proposal that shows he did not really know what he ought to say. As Jesus comes down from that mountain, he confronts a tumult, and discovers that the disciples who remained behind had gotten in over their heads. Their attempt to heal a young lad had resulted only in anger and frustration. Later, along the way to Jerusalem, with the third passion prediction still fresh in their memories, James and John show, with their request for places of honor in the coming kingdom, just how badly they have misunderstood what following Jesus is all about.

Perhaps most ironic of all is their behavior during the last week in Jerusalem and its surroundings. Faced with Jesus' statement that one of the Twelve will not only fail him but indeed betray him, they all affirm with one accord that such a thing could simply not be true of them (14:17–21).

Once again, because the English translation could be confusing, a certain amount of nonsense has been attributed to this passage. The RSV reads: "They began to be sorrowful, and to say to him one after another, 'Is it I?'" Oh, the possibilities here for sermons on inner doubts and growing uncertainty at our own goodness, as reflected in this sorrowing question. What possibilities for introspective probing of the inner consciousness of the disciples. Sorrowing at Jesus' impending betrayal, they wonder if such depths of evil could, without their awareness, lurk in one of them. Hearing the prediction of the betrayal, they hesitantly ask the one with such power of foresight if that betrayal could come from one of them. Plagued with growing self-doubt, they fearfully ask the question, "Lord, is it I?"

While that is all very touching, even pious, it is moving in precisely the opposite direction Mark intends us to move in this narrative. That is shown by the very language of the narrative. In Greek it is possible to ask a question in a way that makes clear what, in the questioner's mind, the response must be, whether yes or no. The question in 14:19 is framed in such a way that the only possible answer the disciples expect Jesus to make to their question "Is it I?" is "Of course not, don't be silly." The disciples are not here plagued by introspection, with a dawning awareness of the depths of evil that may lurk in any human breast. On the contrary, they are asserting with absolute confidence that to think any of them could betray Jesus is utter foolishness. To be sure they are sorrowful, but not at their possible betrayal of Jesus, but at the fact that he could possibly imagine that any one of them could ever do such a thing. Far from introspective doubt, the form of their question shows supreme self-confidence that such a thing could never be done by one of them. That mood has not changed at all when, later on the Mount of Olives, Mark tells us, Peter "said vehemently, 'If I must die with you, I will not deny you,' and they all said the same" (14:31).

In light of such self-confident bravado, the disciples from that point on make a sorry scene. In the garden, asked to watch with Jesus while he prays, they drift off into sleep. While the Son of God sweats in agony for the sin of humankind, the disciples can do no better than catch a quick nap. Summoned to rise by Jesus, they confront his arrest, and despite all their brave words, they all flee. The story of Peter's denial is one of the most poignant and tragic in all of ancient literature. Once for each time Jesus had foretold he would suffer, Peter denied any association with him. Thus Peter moves from "If I must die with you, I will not deny you," to "I do not know of whom you speak," just as the other disciples have made the journey from "And immediately they left their nets and followed him" to "And they all forsook him and fled."

Thus in Mark's narrative is the illusion of human goodness, human faithfulness, in the personal sphere unmasked and shown to be without substance. The most resolute beginnings, the best intentions, the most attentive hearing and following, the strongest oaths right to the end, are shown to be sound and smoke, nothing more. Yet if his disciples who had known Jesus, who had followed him and heard him, who saw his mighty acts, and who had lived with him daily could not follow him, who can? If they could not summon the courage and resolution to do it, who can? Who indeed? What we have in Mark's narrative is little more than the story of complete human failure, collectively and individually. Clearly we have the shattering of illusions, but where is the grace? What in the end do these human failures have to tell us about the *grace* of God?

MARK'S GOOD NEWS: THE GOODNESS OF GOD

What these failures, these shatterings of human illusions, have to tell us is that Mark's Gospel is the story of the power of, and conquest by, God's grace and not the story of human goodness and faithfulness. It is in the face of total human failure that Christ followed God's mysterious way to become savior. Because of that fact, it is clear in Mark that Christ saves humanity not because of what individuals do or accomplish, but rather Christ saves humanity in spite of what they do and accomplish. The story of Jesus in the Gospel of Mark is not the story of the triumph of the human spirit, it is the story of the total defeat of human claims to justice and goodness. And it is precisely for that reason that it is a message of grace; indeed, that is why for Mark the good news of Christ is grace. It is grace because salvation is not due to what people do, but what God has done for humanity. It is God's faithfulness and grace that save, not one's ability to be faithful to him or to be just, or good, or righteous human beings. Mark's narrative, by its very shattering of human pretensions to be good, is in fact a story of grace, not so one can feel good about oneself or the accomplishments of one's fore-bears, whether Jew or Gentile. Rather, it is a story of grace because despite the worst that men or women could do, they could not thwart God's gracious plan to save them. It is grace because the very failure of human goodness was reckoned in God's plan and not allowed to thwart it.

The inability of anything human beings can do to thwart God's plan of gracious redemption is made clear in the supreme irony of the cross. There the final act of rejection by those who denied that Jesus was God's anointed, God's savior for humanity, that very act of rejection, the cross, became the instrument by which God's Son became the way of divine salvation. What Jews and Romans sought to thwart by the cross—the triumph of Jesus as the Son of God—they unwittingly accomplished. If one wishes to speak of predestination in relation to the divine plan for human redemption, here is the locus from which to start: that despite all human attempts to thwart that plan, indeed *through* those human attempts to thwart it, God accomplished his purposes of redemption. What the enemies meant as defeat—the cross—God used for victory. Thus are the plans of God immutable, and incapable of being turned aside.

It is precisely there that grace is to be found in the shattering of human illusions. The shattering of this final illusion comes through the realization that not only evil, but humanity's very goodness stands opposed to God—the Jews wanted Jesus killed to preserve the sanctity of God's law, a noble ideal; the Romans killed Jesus to preserve peace, a noble gesture. Yet even though goodness stands opposed to God, God is able nevertheless to allow his grace to be greater than sin. And it is precisely that which is demonstrated in the cross, where the victory of Jesus'—and God's—opponents becomes their defeat, and the intended defeat of the Son of God becomes his way to victory. Thus does Mark climax his story of grace and the shattering of human illusions.

CONCLUSION

What all of this has to do with how we understand Mark's presentation of the gospel is, one would hope, clear, and perhaps needs no further explication. But let us belabor the obvious, and underline a few points.

First, when one reads Mark, one must be aware of the subtlety of the narrative Mark has created. One ought not to assume one has understood all that is to be found there on a cursory reading of the text. Perhaps above all, one must be alert to the larger contexts within which Mark locates his material. Time and again, Mark intends the context to aid in interpreting the various stories. That is, Mark uses his traditions themselves to interpret one another, and the reader who wants to find the real power within the Markan narrative must be alert to the influences exerted on that narrative by the context within which he has placed his materials.

Second, when reading Mark, one must be alert to the ironies that abound in his narrative. We have examined some of them, but have by no means exhausted them. The whole of chapter 15, for example, is filled with instances of people expressing correct judgments about Jesus, even though they speak with the intention of making false statements about his significance. A telling example is the taunting of Jesus by the religious officials as Jesus hangs, dying, on the cross (15:31–32). A double irony is here on exhibit. People who shortly before this event misunderstood Jesus, and failed to identify him correctly, and on that basis condemned him (14:62–65), here, on the assumption that they are identifying him falsely, in fact identify him correctly by naming him the Son of God. So feeble is the good intention to speak truth in human beings. Seeking to find the truth, they earlier found lies; here, seeking to speak lies, they utter the truth. Once again, it is human goodness, in this case the desire to speak the truth, that stands between humanity and God.

Perhaps the supreme irony is to be found in the strange ending of Mark's Gospel in 16:8. The women, commissioned by the angel to tell the disciples the good news of Jesus' resurrection, and to remind them of his predicted meeting with them in Galilee, do not do so because of fear. Thus, in the end, all human beings prove unreliable. No one is finally able to master the situation. The women who remained faithful through Jesus' death now in the end also prove unfaithful. And here is the supreme irony. The disciples fled because they could not come to terms with Jesus' death. If they had been able to do that, perhaps they could also have come to terms with their own fear that caused them to flee in the face of Jesus' impending death. Here, however, we find the women at the tomb. They have come there precisely because they have come to terms with Jesus' death. And here is the irony: it is precisely because they have come to terms with it that they flee! If the disciples proved unfaithful in the face of Jesus' death because they had not come to terms with it, the women proved unfaithful at the tomb with the news of Jesus' resurrection precisely because they have come to terms with his death. It was his risen life that they could not come to terms with!

Now where does that leave them—us—in the ability to come to terms with Jesus' death? Dead or alive, Mark seems to say, Jesus remains the one who is finally beyond our ability to cope with or to understand. Yet he is our way to the Father. Therefore, we understand Jesus in faith, or we will not understand him at all. That, in the end, appears to be the key to Mark's understanding of Jesus.

It is thus precisely the ironies spread throughout the Gospel that help us to understand what we really are, and so open us to hear the message of God's grace, embodied in this Jesus of Nazareth.

Third, when we read Mark we must be alert to the power of God's grace that brings the career of Jesus to its intended triumph despite the opposition of well-intentioned people. It is a grace that has the power to overcome even that sin which poses as goodness and righteousness, a grace that brings itself to reality on the cross, thus turning intended defeat into victory. It is therefore a grace that will win in the end, and that is precisely the message of grace's power, a power that is capable of relieving us of the burden of sustaining the illusion of our own goodness. The repentance and confidence such grace brings makes the illusion of our own goodness no longer necessary and frees us to accept the gift of God's unmerited grace. It is that grace that the gospel message of Mark brought to its original readers, and still brings to us today.

Paul's Witness to Biblical Monotheism as Isaiah's Servant in Acts

William S. Kurz, S.J.

It is an honor to submit an essay for this Festschrift for Father Frank Matera, who contributes so much to our professional lives as scholar and colleague. Because of his solicitude for elaborating responsible theological approaches to Scripture based on scholarly historical and literary foundations, I dedicate to him these theological investigations into the significance of monotheism in Paul's Gentile mission in Acts. How does the mission of the Servant of God in Isaiah influence the portrayal in Acts of Paul's witness to the one living God and rejection of pagan idolatry and worship?

Introduction

The influence of the book of Isaiah on Luke and Acts has been widely discussed and generally admitted.[1] It has also become a consensus that Luke

---

1. See esp. Peter Mallen, *The Reading and Transformation of Isaiah in Luke-Acts* (LNTS 367; New York: T&T Clark, 2008); Kenneth Duncan Litwak, *Echoes of Scripture in Luke-Acts: Telling the Story of God's People Intertextually* (JSNTSup 282; London: T&T Clark, 2005); David W. Pao, *Acts and the Isaianic New Exodus* (Grand Rapids: Baker Academic, 2000); Luke Timothy Johnson, *Septuagintal Midrash in the Speeches of Acts* (Milwaukee: Marquette University Press, 2002); Mark L. Strauss, *The Davidic Messiah in Luke-Acts: The Promise and Its Fulfillment in Lukan Christology* (JSNTSup 110; Sheffield: Sheffield Academic Press, 1995); Darrell Bock, "Scripture and the Realization of God's Promises," in *Witness to the Gospel: The Theology of Acts* (ed. I. Howard Marshall and David Peterson; Grand Rapids: Eerdmans, 1998), 41–62, esp. 56–58; Andreas J. Köstenberger and Peter T. O'Brien, *Salvation to the Ends of the Earth: A Biblical Theology of Mission* (New Studies in Biblical Theology 11; Downers Grove, Ill.: InterVarsity Press, 2001), esp. ch. 2, "The Old Testament," 25–53; and ch.

used the Septuagint (LXX) Isaiah rather than pre-Masoretic Hebrew texts. The Greek translations of Luke's time had already applied and modified the theology of Hebrew Isaiah in usually small but sometimes significant ways.[2] It is also important to realize that the Lukan author was not aware that the especially influential section, "Second Isaiah," was a separate writing by a later author. Rather, Luke read the canonical Isaiah as a unified biblical book.[3]

Emphasis on Isaian influence on Luke-Acts does not discount the major effect of other Jewish Scriptures on Lukan narrative and theology. Commonly discussed are the Lukan theme of Jesus as the Deuteronomic "prophet like Moses" (Deut 18:15 in Acts 3:22–23; 7:37), and the messianic foreshadowing of Jesus in the Psalms, interpreted as authored by David and prophesying David's descendant Jesus (Pss 16:8–11; 110:1 in

---

6, "Luke-Acts," 111–59; Daniel Marguerat, *The First Christian Historian: Writing the "Acts of the Apostles"* (trans. Ken McKinney, Gregory J. Laughery, and Richard Bauckham; SNTSMS 121; Cambridge: Cambridge University Press, 2002), 224; Charles A. Kimball, *Jesus' Exposition of the Old Testament in Luke's Gospel* (JSNTSup 94; Sheffield: JSOT Press, 1994); R. E. Clements, "A Light to the Nations: A Central Theme of the Book of Isaiah," in *Forming Prophetic Literature: Essays on Isaiah and the Twelve in Honor of John D. W. Watts* (ed. James W. Watts and Paul R. House; JSOTSup 235; Sheffield: Sheffield Academic Press, 1996), 57–69, esp. 64–68; Robert F. O'Toole, "How Does Luke Portray Jesus as Servant of YHWH?" *Bib* 81 (2000): 328–46; Thomas S. Moore, "The Lukan Great Commission and the Isaianic Servant," *BSac* 154 (1997): 47–60; idem, "'To the End of the Earth': The Geographical and Ethnic Universalism of Acts 1:8 in Light of Isaianic Influence on Luke," *JETS* 40 (1997): 389–99; Steve Moyise, ed., *The Old Testament in the New Testament: Essays in Honour of J. L. North* (JSNTSup 189; Sheffield: Sheffield Academic Press, 2000); Robert L. Brawley, *Text to Text Pours Forth Speech: Voices of Scripture in Luke-Acts* (Indiana Studies in Biblical Literature; Bloomington: Indiana University Press, 1995); G. K. Beale, "Isaiah VI 9–13: A Retributive Taunt against Idolatry," *VT* 41 (1991): 257–78.

2. For the LXX see Joseph Ziegler, ed., *Isaias* (vol. 14 of *Septuaginta: Vetus Testamentum Graecum, Auctoritate Academiae Scientiarum Gottingensis editum*; 3rd ed.; Göttingen: Vandenhoeck & Ruprecht, 1983). Unless otherwise specified, English translations of the LXX are taken from *A New English Translation of the Septuagint and the Other Greek Translations Traditionally Included under That Title* (ed. Albert Pietersma and Benjamin G. Wright; New York: Oxford University Press, 2007). This translation (hereafter *NETS*) has some unusual literalistic spelling of names, such as Ierousalem.

3. See Mallen, *Reading and Transformation of Isaiah*, 204. Cf. Mark Walter Koehne, "The Septuagintal Isaian Use of ΝΟΜΟΣ in the Lukan Presentation Narrative" (PhD diss., Marquette University, 2010), 163–66.

Acts 2:24–36).[4] In fact, the only biblical book that Luke-Acts appeals to more than Isaiah is the book of Psalms.[5] Many have wondered which specific Scripture passages justify the repeated claims in Luke-Acts that Scripture prophesies that the Messiah must suffer (Luke 24:26, 46; Acts 3:18; 17:3; 26:23). Joshua Jipp argues that the Lukan author found the suffering and exalted Messiah primarily in the psalms and their depiction of King David's sufferings and vindications.[6]

Scholars have also discussed echoes from Isaiah's Suffering Servant in the Lukan passion account.[7] Less has been written about how in Acts and in Isaiah as understood during the Second Temple period, the Servant's focus on the nations is an organic development from Israel's promotion of monotheism and denunciation of pagan idolatry.

In this essay I will try to demonstrate how what at times appear to be digressions in Acts have an earnest theological purpose. They illustrate that Paul's servant mission to the Gentiles, from cultivated philosophers in Athens (Acts 17) to rustic "barbarians" at Lystra (Acts 14:8–18), had to combat ingrained cultures of polytheism and idolatry. In Acts, Paul grounded the Christian message to Gentiles in his monotheistic belief in the one living God who is both creator of everything and judge of all humans.

The explicit quotation of Isa 53:7–8 LXX in Acts 8:32–33 corroborates the Lukan application of Isaiah's Servant to Jesus in Acts. Clear allusions to other Isaian Servant passages (for Jesus in Luke 2:32 and Acts 26:23; for Paul and Barnabas in Acts 13:47) confirm this Isaianic influence on Luke-Acts. I hope that a closer look at the whole of septuagintal Isaiah may expose additional significant Isaian contexts and background for portraying the ministries of Jesus and of his followers. Already acknowledged Lukan applications of the Isaian Servant of the Lord to Jesus and his followers include being called by God from the womb (e.g., Isa 49:1), servant

---

4. See esp. Strauss, *Davidic Messiah in Luke-Acts*.

5. Mallen, *Reading and Transformation of Isaiah*, 3.

6. Joshua W. Jipp, "Luke's Scriptural Suffering Messiah: A Search for Precedent, a Search for Identity," *CBQ* 72 (2010): 255–74, esp. 257, where he cites David L. Tiede, *Prophecy and History in Luke-Acts* (Philadelphia: Fortress, 1980), 20. Cf. Mallen, *Reading and Transformation of Isaiah*, 20.

7. Cf. *Jesus and the Suffering Servant: Isaiah 53 and Christian Origins* (ed. William H. Bellinger Jr. and William R. Farmer; Harrisburg, Pa.: Trinity Press International, 1998); P. B. Decock, "The Understanding of Isaiah 53:7–8 in Acts 8:32–33," *Neot* 14 (1981): 111–33.

ministry to Jews and to all nations (49:6), and suffering as part of the Servant's calling (53:7–8).

MONOTHEISTIC MISSION TO THE NATIONS
OF THE SERVANT IN ISAIAH AND IN ACTS

Less frequently treated is how the Isaian servant outreach to the nations promotes Israel's monotheism and combats pagan idolatry. This is particularly evident in Paul's ministry to Gentiles in later parts of Acts.[8] To contextualize the portrayal of outreach to the nations in Acts, let us trace septuagintal Isaiah's themes of God's relationship not only to his chosen people Israel but to all the nations of the world that he created, and Israel's corresponding role in making God known to these nations.

Although Christians added christological developments to their proclamation of only one living God, they maintained the biblical tradition of God's universal care for all humans and nations he created, and his condemnation of human worship of other gods. Their preaching of biblical monotheism (in Christian form) to Gentiles jarred with their hostile pagan environment and culture of polytheism, magic, and occult public practices. This clash with pagan culture and religion brought intense resistance to Paul's servant testimony to God.[9]

In referring to the LXX of Isaiah, one must be careful not to identify the theology and focus of various sections of the Hebrew book of Isaiah with the linguistic reformulations and theological adaptations of Isaiah as a whole in the LXX. Neither Hebrew nor Greek texts of Isaiah fully accords with the emphases and theological adaptations of Isaiah in Luke and Acts. Questions calling for particular distinctions are the meaning and function of universalism in Isaiah.

---

8. In this essay I develop my earlier observations about the Isaian servant mission to the nations in "From the Servant in Isaiah to Jesus and the Apostles in Luke-Acts to Christians Today: Spirit-Filled Witness to the Ends of the Earth," in *Between Experience and Interpretation: Engaging the Writings of the New Testament* (ed. Mary F. Foskett and O. Wesley Allen Jr.; Nashville: Abingdon, 2008), 175–94.

9. Cf. C. Kavin Rowe, "The Book of Acts and the Cultural Explication of the Identity of God," in *The Word Leaps the Gap: Essays on Scripture and Theology in Honor of Richard B. Hays* (ed. J. Ross Wagner, C. Kavin Rowe, and A. Katherine Grieb; Grand Rapids: Eerdmans, 2008), 244–66.

Original meanings of Isaiah, especially the prophecies in Isa 40–55 (Second Isaiah) about Israel being and bringing light to the nations, have often been understood in light of their later interpretations, beginning already with the framework imposed by Isa 56–66 (Third Isaiah). Initially, Isa 40–55 was not as universalist about including Gentiles *as Gentiles* within the people of God as the New Testament would later interpret these chapters. Isaiah 40–55 generally presumed that Gentiles would either have to become Jews or be dependent on Jews. The book of Isaiah envisaged all nations coming *to Jerusalem* in a centripetal direction to be taught the law (e.g., Isa 2). Acts, on the contrary, presents believers going out *from Jerusalem* in a centrifugal movement to the ends of the earth to incorporate the Gentiles into the people of God, while letting them remain uncircumcised.[10]

Moreover, the later sections of Isaiah and Old Testament writings, as they are understood in Luke-Acts and the Pauline Letters, raise new questions about other gods when they insist that the gods of other nations are not gods (e.g., Acts 17:16–31; 1 Cor 8:4–7). There is only the one God worshiped by Israel, who created and will judge the world and all peoples in it. This belief in only one God challenged more primitive Israelite presuppositions about other nations and the reality of their gods (see Hos 8:6).

What the contemporary world calls monotheism seems to have developed gradually in ancient Israel.[11] At least by the time of both Paul and Luke-Acts, the Old Testament was interpreted as presenting the religion of Israel as monotheistic. Paul and Luke (and other Christians) explicitly contrasted Jewish religion to their neighbors' polytheism. Thus they denied that the gods of the Gentiles are genuine gods. Yet at least sometimes they admitted that gods worshiped by pagans had at least some reality, power, and influence on human events. Several Old Testament passages, when translated into Greek, refer to pagan gods as demons, which well before the New Testament had connotations of "evil spirits" (created by God, but not nothing).[12]

---

10. Joel Kaminsky and Anne Stewart, "God of All the World: Universalism and Developing Monotheism in Isaiah 40–66," *HTR* 99 (2006): 139–63.

11. See Mark S. Smith, *The Origins of Biblical Monotheism: Israel's Polytheistic Background and the Ugaritic Texts* (Oxford: Oxford University Press, 2001).

12. Examples include Deut 32:17 LXX, "They sacrificed to demons which were no gods" (RSV; δαιμόνιον, "minor divinity," later construed as "demonic spirit"); Ps 95:5 LXX, "For all the gods of the Gentiles are demons [δαιμόνια], but the Lord made the

Paul, for example, believed in angelic spirits and their influence on human life, as evidenced by his argument against eating food sacrificed to idols in 1 Cor 10:19–21. There, in question form, he challenges the widespread conviction among the Corinthians that idols to whom meat is sacrificed are "nothing" (v. 19). While admitting that idols and pagan gods are not gods, Paul still insists that they have some reality and power. Thus he counters, "No, I imply that what pagans sacrifice they offer to demons and not to God. I do not want you to be partners with demons. You cannot drink the cup of the Lord and the cup of demons. You cannot partake of the table of the Lord and the table of demons" (1 Cor 10:20–21 RSV).

Acts has both these ways of referring to pagan gods. It has some extreme denials that idols or the gods they represented were anything at all (e.g., Acts 17:29: "Being then God's offspring, we ought not to think that the Deity is like gold, or silver, or stone, a representation by the art and imagination of man," RSV). However, Acts also acknowledges the reality of demonic powers involved in magic and in pagan polytheistic beliefs. This is implied in exorcisms of evil spirits (Acts 5:16; 8:7; 19:11–16), burning of magic books (Acts 19:17–19), and expulsion of the spirit of divination from the slave girl in Philippi (Acts 16:16–19). The pagan spirits are real, but they are only creatures and are easily overcome by the power of God and his messianic servant Jesus.

LXX Isaiah as Context for Luke-Acts

Although most of the Isaian servant influences on Luke-Acts originate in the later chapters of Isaiah (esp. Isa 40–55), some early passages in Isaiah seem to have affected at least the setting and circumstances for describing some events, activities, and sayings of Jesus and the disciples in Luke and Acts. Without alluding, like Matthew, to Isa 7:14 LXX ("the virgin [vs. MT young woman] shall conceive"), Luke equally insists on Mary's virginity with respect to Jesus' conception. With Isa 9:6–7, Luke insists that this child is born to the throne of David. in Isa 11 messianic references to the root of Jesse in whom the nations will hope (11:10), as well as the call

---

heavens" (my trans.); Bar 4:7 LXX, "For you provoked the one who made you by sacrificing to demons [δαιμονίοις] and not to God." Cf. also Isa 65:11 LXX. Cf. Joel Marcus, "Idolatry in the New Testament," in Wagner et al., *Word Leaps the Gap*, 107–31, esp. 120–25.

to declare God's glorious deeds among the nations and in all the earth (12:4–5), seem relevant background for Luke-Acts.

Isaiah 37:16 quotes King Hezekiah's prayer to the Lord in the face of the Assyrian Sennacherib's threats, that "you alone are God of every kingdom of the world; you have made heaven and earth." In Isa 37:20 Hezekiah asks God to save Israel "so that every kingdom of the earth may know that you alone are God."

Isaiah 40 begins strong messages of consolation for Israel in her suffering for her sins after the destruction of Jerusalem by the Babylonians. His prophecy of the voice in the wilderness who will proclaim the way of the Lord is applied to John the Baptist at the beginning of Jesus' ministry in all four Gospels, and climaxes in the prophecy that "all flesh shall see the salvation of God" (Isa 40:5, quoted in Luke 3:6). Jesus' mission will benefit not only the chosen people but "all flesh."

Isaiah 41:8–10 addresses Israel as "my servant, Iakob, whom I have chosen, the offspring [σπέρμα] of Abraham, whom I have loved." The Lord has chosen as servant and will not forsake the people Israel (v. 9). Isaiah 42 continues to certify that the people Jacob is the Lord's (corporate) servant and Israel his chosen, on whom the Lord put his Spirit to bring forth judgment to the nations. He will not be overcome until he has established judgment on the earth and the nations hope in his name (42:1–4). The vocation of the servant is explicit in 42:6–7: "I have given you as a covenant to a race [εἰς διαθήκην γένους, "race" referring to Israel], as a light to the nations [εἰς φῶς ἐθνῶν]."

Although the context has continued to imply that the servant is the nation Israel, the servant who acts as covenant for the race of Israel in verse 6 has to be an individual servant ministering to the nation. As light to the nations, the servant Israel could be either the people Israel or the same individual servant commissioned to be a covenant for Israel. For the nations, the Lord's servant will "open the eyes of the blind," which is conversion imagery. Luke will take servant language that in Isaiah can have either corporate or individual referents and apply it to Jesus (and Paul and other followers of Jesus) as God's servant sent both to the chosen people and to the uncomprehending Gentiles.

Immediately following God's call to his servant in Isa 42:8 LXX, he declares his name as Lord God who will not give his glory "to another, nor my excellence to the graven [γλυπτοῖς, 'carved'] images." Isaiah 42:10–12 goes on to ask believing sailors and island dwellers to glorify God's name "to the end of the earth" (v. 10), to "declare his excellences [ἀρετάς] in the islands" (v. 12). After promising all the ways that God would bless and help his people, the prophecy complains that the unfaithful people "turned away backward," when they "trust in the graven images" and "say to the cast images, 'You are our gods'" (42:17). God's call to the servant is intimately related to his concern that his name be proclaimed everywhere and that idolatry and false worship by both his people and Gentiles be opposed.

Isaiah 43 then proclaims a gathering of all nations and rulers, before whom God insists that only he was able to predict what has come to pass. He asks God's people, "Be my witnesses," as God himself is a witness "and the servant [παῖς] whom I have chosen so that you may know and believe and understand that I am [ἐγώ εἰμι, the divine name]" (v. 10). Here not only the people are to be witnesses but also God himself and the individual who is called as God's servant to help the people comprehend God's divinity.

This servant is to help the people become witnesses that there was no other god before God, nor will there be any after (v. 10). Besides God, "there is none who saves" (v. 11). Regarding these truths about the only true and saving God, God says of the people after they have been instructed by the servant, "You are my witnesses; I too am a witness" (v. 12). God goes on to promise that he will again save his people from Babylon in a new exodus (vv. 13–21).

In Isa 44 the Lord again calls Jacob his servant whom he has chosen and formed from the womb. "I am first … besides me there is no god" (v. 6). God challenges other gods to duplicate God's ability to prophesy the future: "Who is like me? … let them declare to you the things that are coming before they come" (v. 7). To Israel he repeats, "You are witnesses whether there is a god besides me, and they were not formerly" (v. 8). If Israelites are God's witnesses, those to whom they witness seem logically to be or at least include Gentiles.

Isaiah 44:9–20 then mounts a vigorous polemic against idolatry and idol makers that mockingly describes the fashioning of idols especially from wood from the forest that the Lord had planted and his rain watered. With part of the wood, the artisan warms himself and cooks food. "But the rest they fashioned into gods, and they do obeisance to them. Half of it he burned up in the fire" and roasted and ate meat over it (vv. 15–16). "The rest he made into a graven god and does obeisance to it, and he prays, saying, 'Rescue me, for you are my god!'" (v. 17). This mocking picture of idolatry in Isaiah is probably a conscious exaggeration and caricature of actual pagan beliefs and practices, but this caricature of idolatry is a common Old Testament topos or theme that is also taken up in the New Testament, for example, by Paul and in Luke-Acts.[13]

Immediately following this anti-idolatry polemic is another address to Israel as "my servant" (παῖς). God urges Israel not to forget God, and assures him that his previous acts of lawlessness have been blotted out. However, Israel must return to the Lord, who will redeem him (Isa 44:21–22). The prophecy in 44:24–28 refers to God who both redeems Israel and also created the universe. As universal creator, God will undo the pagan practices of ventriloquists and divinations, making foolish the so-called wise practitioners of magic "and confirming the words of his servant" (v. 26). This, in effect, is what God did through Paul when in Jesus' name he expelled the fortune-telling demon from the slave in Acts 16:18–19.

Isaiah 44 introduces the Persian king Cyrus, who liberated the Jews from Babylon and had Jerusalem rebuilt. It proclaims that God is the one "who tells Cyrus to be wise" and says to Jerusalem, "You shall be built, and I will lay the foundations of my holy house" (v. 28). God has such dominion over even a Gentile ruler because he is the only God and Creator of the universe.

Isaiah 45 describes a servant calling made directly to the pagan Cyrus, whom God by his authority over all nations and peoples has made "my anointed" (χριστός) ruler, whose "right hand I have grasped so that nations will obey before him" (Isa 45:1 LXX). This use of "anointed" for a pagan ruler rather than for a Jewish king (usually a descendant of David) is a startling innovation in this prophecy. God will remove obstacles to Cyrus's rule and give Cyrus hidden treasures, "so that you may know that I am the Lord God, the God of Israel, who calls your name" (v. 3).

God will call Cyrus for the sake of his servant Jacob and chosen Israel, even though "you did not know me." To Cyrus God proclaims, "I am the Lord God, and there is no other god besides me, and you did not know me" (v. 5). Through Cyrus, all peoples "from the rising of the sun and from its going down may know that there is no one besides me. I am the Lord God, and there is no other" (v. 6). God proclaims that he has created everything and controls everything: "I am the Lord who does all these things" (v. 7).

This monotheistic prophecy to Cyrus goes on to say that God forms the clay like a potter, hence the clay cannot challenge the potter about what he is making (vv. 9–10). God repeats that he "made the earth and humankind

---

13. Cf. Marcus, "Idolatry in the New Testament," 107–31, esp. 108–11.

upon it," and he placed and commanded the stars. As creator of everything, he has raised Cyrus in righteousness, and Cyrus shall rebuild God's city "and turn back the captivity of my people, not with ransom or with gifts" but by his military power (v. 13). Nations "will do obeisance to you and pray in you, because God is in you" (v. 14). The Greek is less clear-cut than the Hebrew here about whether the nations perceive Cyrus himself as god or as having God present with him. However, the following verse, Isa 45:15 LXX, clearly refers to God, not Cyrus: "For you are God, and we did not know it, O God of Israel, Savior."

Isaiah 45:20–25 then rebukes Jews who were being thus saved from among the nations, and those who ignorantly lift up wooden graven images or idols "and pray as if to gods that do not save" (v. 20). The identity of this last group is not obvious, for its description could refer both to exiled Jews and to the nations among whom they lived. Thus the exhortation in 45:22, "Turn to me, and you shall be saved, you who are from the end of the earth! I am God and there is no other," could refer (or later be interpreted to refer) to both Diaspora Jews and Gentiles from afar. The prophecy, "to me every knee shall bow and every tongue acknowledge God" (v. 23), sounds like a universalist claim about God, and probably was so interpreted by Christians. However, the last verse directs these particular promises of God especially to Israel: "all the offspring of the sons of Israel shall be glorified in God" (v. 25).

Isaiah 46 then disaffirms the reality of the gods of Babylon and rebukes the people of Israel for heeding the so-called gods of their Babylonian conquerors instead of keeping their focus and hope on the only true and living God, the God of Israel. They should remember that it is God who has always rescued and saved them in their history. Not only can the Babylonian gods not save them, but the prophecy mocks them as gods who are fashioned by goldsmiths and have to be carried because they cannot move. Nor can such gods heed the people who cry out to them for help. The exiled Israelites are to remember God's many former deeds to save them, for he is the only God; he is the only one who prophesies the future and who fulfills his plan of salvation.

Isaiah 47 then prophesies the fall of Babylon, who had exiled Israel. God will deliver the Babylonians to defeat and shame, for they have defiled God's heritage (Israel). Though God had given his people over to the Babylonians, they had no mercy on the Israelites and oppressed them grievously. Babylon will suddenly become like a widow, and her impotent pagan enchantments and witchcraft and astrologers cannot help her. For Babylon there will be no salvation.

Therefore, Isa 48 exhorts the Israelite exiles to leave Babylon and reminds them that his prophecies of liberation have come true (v. 3). God rebukes the Israelite captives because of their stubborn and persistent attribution of their salvation not to God but to idols (v. 5). God reminds the exiles that he is now saving them as he had formerly saved his people (from Egypt). He emphasizes that he, who alone has created heaven and earth, has now worked his will against Babylon (vv. 6–14). He reminds the exiles that he alone is God who has shown them the way to go, but their disobedience has prevented the prosperity with which God wished to bless them (vv. 17–19). Now they are to flee Babylon and proclaim the joy of their deliverance "to the end of the earth," that the Lord has delivered his slave Jacob and will provide for their thirst from the rock in the desert (as in the exodus). But there is no rejoicing for the impious (vv. 20–22).

Isaiah 49 is frequently cited as especially influential in the structuring of the Luke-Acts narrative.

> Just as Isa 61.1–2 provides a concise summary of Jesus' messianic minis-
> try [in the Nazareth pericope in Luke 4], so Isa. 49.6 proves to be equally
> helpful for Luke in summarizing his narrative concerns. As David Tiede
> notes, "the allusion to Isa 49:6 [in Lk 2.32] ... might well be regarded as *a
> thematic statement of Luke's entire narrative*: the call of the servant (*pais*)
> to restore the diaspora of Israel and to be a light to the Gentiles to the
> end of the earth."[14]

In Isa 49 the servant's announcement of his vocation is surprisingly addressed not to the people Israel but to the islands and the nations. "Hear me, O islands; pay attention, O nations!" (v. 1). From its very first words, this direct address implies that God's call to his servant is projected more ultimately at proclaiming God to all nations, not only to Israel.

The servant's vocation by God even precedes his birth, as did the call-ings of Jesus and John the Baptist in Luke. "From my mother's womb he called my name" (v. 1). God equipped his servant to be his spokesperson: he "made my mouth like a sharp dagger" (v. 2). He protected him till he was old enough to begin his ministry ("he hid me" and "in his quiver he sheltered me," v. 2). Compare Jesus' hidden years at Nazareth under his

---

14. Quoted from Mallen, *Reading and Transformation of Isaiah*, 184, who cites with added italics Tiede, *Prophecy and History in Luke-Acts*, 31.

parents' authority (Luke 2:51–52), until his manifestation to Israel at the age of "about thirty" (Luke 3:23).

The servant's complaint that his labor has been in vain is answered by God, "who formed me from the womb to be his own slave [δοῦλος], to gather Iakob and Israel to him" (v. 5). Isa 49:6 LXX differs from the Hebrew, which calls the vocation to Israel "too light" or even "trivial" in comparison with being light to the nations (גוים). Instead, the LXX says, "It is a great thing [μέγα, the opposite of 'too light'] for you to be called my servant, so that you may set up the tribes of Iakob and turn back the dispersion of Israel." The LXX does, however, continue in closer approximation to the Hebrew: "See [an emphatic Greek ἰδού] I have made you a light to the nations, that you may be for salvation to the end of the earth" (v. 6). The LXX drops the negative comparison of the servant's ministry to Israel that is in the Hebrew, and instead characterizes as "great" his outreach to Israel. However, it actually places more emphasis than the Hebrew on the servant's ministry also to the nations by calling special attention ("see," "behold") to this additional mission.

Isaiah 49:7–12 LXX continues the motif of the servant's commission both as "a covenant to the nations" and "to establish the land" (of Israel), to call "those in bonds" and in darkness to be returned from exile by God to their land: "Lo, these come from far away, these from the sea, but others from the land of the Persians" (v. 12). God will summon the nations to bring back Israel's sons and daughters and compel them to do obeisance to Israel and to "lick the dust of your feet" (v. 23). The prophecy ends with this promise: "Then all flesh shall perceive that I am the Lord who rescued you" (v. 26).

In the LXX, Isa 50 is in the mouth of the servant: "the instruction of the Lord opens my ears, and I do not disobey nor contradict. I have given my back to scourges and my cheeks to blows" and face to spitting (vv. 4–6; cf. Luke 18:31–33). The servant willingly accepts suffering and humiliation that is occasioned by his preaching. He puts his trust in the Lord's help to keep him from being put to shame (vv. 7–9; cf. Luke 22:42). The servant and those to whom he speaks trust in the Lord, even though the Lord allows sorrow to come upon them (vv. 10–11).

Isaiah 51 LXX further exhorts the people to trust the Lord, who raised and multiplied a great number of descendants from the one man Abraham and his wife, Sarah. God will comfort his people in the most desolate situations. God promises that "a law will go out from me, and my judgment for a light to nations" (v. 4). God's "salvation will go out, and the nations will hope in my arm" (v. 5).

Isaiah 52:13–53:12 has been intensively investigated as the song of the suffering and triumphant servant of the Lord. Acts 8:32–33 explicitly quotes part of this song, Isa 53:7–8, and applies it to Jesus (Acts 8:35). Isaiah 53 LXX goes on to note that the servant had no glory or honor, and he was not esteemed by humans. But he is bearing our sins and is wounded because of our lawless acts, for on him was the punishment or discipline (παιδεία) that led to our peace, so that we were healed by his bruises.

Because we, like sheep, all went astray, the Lord handed him over (παραδίδωμι) for our sins (Isa 53:1–6). Luke repeats the term "hand over" in several passion prophecies by Jesus (e.g., Luke 9:44; 18:32; 20:20), in reference to Judas handing Jesus over (22:21–22; 23:48), and in prophecies that Jesus' disciples also will be handed over to persecution (21:12, 16). The Servant accepted this injustice without protest, in silence. His life was taken from this earth. He was put to death because of the lawlessness of God's people (vv. 7–8). The Greek reference to God giving the wicked for his burial is less clear than the Hebrew reference to the servant having a grave assigned among the wicked. In any case, the reason given is that the servant committed no lawlessness (ἀνομία, v. 9; cf. the centurion's declaration at the cross, "Certainly this man was innocent [δίκαιος]!" Luke 23:47 RSV).

The Lord will then vindicate his servant (Isa 53:10–12 LXX), to "cleanse him [καθαρίσαι, 'purify'] from his blow [πληγῆς]" (v. 10 LXX). This differs from the Hebrew text, in which the Lord crushes him. Isaiah 53:12 LXX, like the Hebrew, then promises reward for the servant because he bore the sins of many and was handed over for them.

Isaiah 55:3 has a *crux interpretum* in the LXX and its quotation in Acts 13:34: "I will make you an everlasting covenant, the sacred things of David that are sure" (v. 3; Greek τὰ ὅσια Δαυιδ τὰ πιστά, Hebrew "reliable mercies to David").[15] God's promises to David will be fulfilled in the servant (in Acts, particularly by the resurrection of the servant Jesus).

God has established David "as a testimony among the nations, a ruler and commander for the nations" (v. 4). "Nations that did not know you shall call upon you, and peoples that do not understand you shall flee to you for refuge, for the sake of your God" (v. 5). This reference to an indi-

---

15. See Mallen, *Reading and Transformation of Isaiah*, 110, 124; Joseph A. Fitzmyer, S.J., *The Acts of the Apostles: A New Translation with Introduction and Commentary* (AB 31; New York: Doubleday, 1998), 517; Luke Timothy Johnson, *The Acts of the Apostles* (SP 5; Collegeville, Minn.: Liturgical Press, 1992), 235.

vidual person who is in the Davidic tradition combines Davidic kingship with the servant's mission. This descendant of David who will be deliverer of nations is readily identified by Christians as the messianic savior, Jesus.

The prophecy in Isa 56 LXX proclaims that God's house (temple) welcomes any person who keeps God's Sabbaths. Neither should the foreigner (ἀλλογενής) say that God will separate him from his people, nor should the eunuch say he is a "dry tree" (v. 3) excluded from God's people and the temple. If even a eunuch keeps the Sabbaths, he will be welcome in the temple (as also in Wis 3:14 and Acts 8:34–39). God says to the eunuchs who hold fast his covenant that he will give them in his house (temple) "an esteemed place, better than sons and daughters; I will give them an everlasting name" (v. 5).

"And to the aliens who cling to the Lord ... so that they may be his male and female slaves ... I will bring them into my holy mountain and make them joyful in my house of prayer" (Isa 56:6–7). Their sacrifices will be accepted on God's altar, "for my house shall be called a house of prayer for all the nations" (v. 7). This prophecy welcomes all nations into God's temple, but in Isaiah it still seems to presuppose that the eunuchs and aliens become Jews subject to Jewish laws like the Sabbath. In Acts, however, the Ethiopian eunuch is baptized as a full member into the community and foreign converts are given equal standing with Israelites from birth, without eunuch or converts being circumcised.

In Isa 57:3–13 there follows a forceful condemnation of God's faithless people who turn to idolatry. They are blamed for calling on idols under trees, slaughtering children in ravines, and sacrificing and pouring out libations to pagan gods. "Shall I not therefore be angry for these things?" (v. 6). God further denounces his people for supposing that if they deserted their Lord they would obtain greater blessings from these foreign gods (v. 8). The people did not stop sinning or turn back to God to plead again for their needs. Although they feared other gods, they forgot their own God; therefore, let the other gods deliver them when they call for help. Those who cling to God, however, shall possess the earth and inherit Mount Zion (vv. 10–13).

Isaiah 61 LXX relates in the first person another calling by God and anointing by God's Spirit to minister to those in darkness and need. In the Lukan Gospel Jesus applies this calling to his own ministry (Luke 4:16–21), so that this Isaiah prophecy structures the individual stories about Jesus' ministry into a coherent narrative. "The spirit of the Lord is upon me, because he has anointed [ἔχρισέν] me" (v. 1). The one called is sent "to bring good news to the poor, to heal the brokenhearted, to proclaim release to the captives, and recovery of sight to the blind, to summon the acceptable year of the Lord and the day of retribution, to comfort all who mourn" (vv. 1–2). The prophecy goes on to promise that God "will make an everlasting covenant with them." And "their offspring and their descendants shall be known among the nations" (vv. 8–9), because they are blessed by God. All nations shall know of and admire Israel.

Isaiah 62 LXX portrays God's light shining forth from Jerusalem for all nations to see. God will make Jerusalem his bride, no longer known as Forsaken (vv. 1–5). God will post sentinels on Jerusalem's walls who will never cease talking about God. God will forever protect her (vv. 6–9). God says to "lift up a signal [σύσσημον] for the nations" (v. 10). The Lord makes the message heard to the end of the earth that God comes as the Israelites' savior and calls them a holy people redeemed by him (vv. 11–12). As Acts 26:26 expresses it, God's salvation of his people is widely known even among the nations, for "this was not done in a corner" (RSV).

Isaiah 65 LXX is another divine complaint against the chosen people. Its vehement denunciations of the Israelites' pagan sacrifices and idolatry sheds light on the importance of monotheism and indictment of idolatry in the Greek version of Isaiah that influenced the later narratives of Luke-Acts (vv. 1–3a). The divine charge against the idolatry of God's people includes this accusation, "they sacrifice in the gardens and burn incense on bricks to the demons [δαιμονίοις, inferior divinity or (evil) spirit], which do not exist" (v. 3b). The Hebrew lacks "to the demons, which do not exist," but states simply, "sacrificing in gardens and burning incense upon bricks" (Isa 65:3b RSV). By the time of the New Testament and already intimated in Greek Isaiah, the question about the existence of pagan gods was being answered by suggesting that the beings previously referred to as gods were actually demons, spirits created by God who rebelled against God. Therefore, they, like humans, were creatures, not other gods.

Isaiah 65:3b LXX seems somewhat ambivalent about even this mention of demons, as evidenced by its added qualification, "who do not exist." However, a similar later substitution of "demon" for a god in 65:11 LXX does not mention any doubt about its existence. The Hebrew says, "who set a table for Fortune, and fill cups of mixed wine for Destiny" (RSV), in which both Fortune and Destiny are generally understood as gods of Israel's neighbors. The Greek substitutes, "and prepare a table for the demon [δαίμων, in Hellenism, an inferior divinity; in the NT, an evil spirit], and fill a mixed drink for Fortune [τύχη, 'fortune, chance']."

Isaiah 65:4–5 LXX makes further accusations of idolatrous worship and practices: the people sleep in tombs to receive dreams and eat swine flesh and broth from sacrifices. Therefore, God's anger flared against their sins and those of their ancestors, burning incense on mountains and reviling God on hills (v. 6). But for the sake of a faithful minority, God will not destroy the whole people (v. 8; cf. Abraham and God concerning Sodom, Gen 18:23–32). Rather, God will bring the offspring of Jacob and Judah to inherit his holy mountain (Zion) and dwell there. And those who sought God shall have herds and flocks (vv. 9–10). But those who forsake God and "prepare a table for the demon and fill a mixed drink for Fortune," God will deliver to the slaughter because they did evil in his sight (vv. 11–12).

The book of Isaiah ends with a prophecy spelling out true and false worship of God. Isaiah 66:1–2 LXX is quoted verbatim in the climax of Stephen's speech (Acts 7:49–50). Stephen's speech had pointed out that God had rejected David's request when he asked to build God a house to replace the tent of God's presence in the wilderness. However, Solomon did build God a house (Acts 7:44–47). Stephen comments, "Yet the Most High does not dwell in houses made with hands" (Acts 7:48). The expression that houses are "made with hands" alludes to prophetic references to idols made with hands (Isa 31:7; Bel 5), and is here applied by Stephen to Solomon's building the temple. As God is not present in idols, neither does he live in houses made by human hands.

Compare Paul's argument to the philosophers of Athens in Acts 17:24–25: "The God who made the world and everything in it, being Lord of heaven and earth, does not live in shrines made by man, nor is he served by human hands, as though he needed anything, since he himself gives to all men life and breath and everything" (RSV). Stephen's speech then justifies this critical commentary on Solomon's building the temple by quoting Isa 66:1–2 LXX in Acts 7:49–50: "Heaven is my throne, and the earth is the footstool of my feet; what kind of house will you build for me, or what kind will be the place of my rest? For all these things my hands have made."

Isaiah 66:3–5 LXX goes on to reject several forms of sacrifice and worship, but it adds to the Hebrew a reference to "the lawless" (ἄνομος), in order to make the context and point clearer than the more cryptic and disturbing contrasts in the Hebrew. The Hebrew shockingly equates, "He who slaughters an ox is like him who kills a man, he who sacrifices a lamb, like him who breaks a dog's neck" (Isa 66:3 RSV). The LXX has instead, "But the lawless who sacrifices to me a calf is like one who kills a dog," providing a reason for the rejection of his sacrifice, because he is lawless and does not follow God's ways. Likewise those who offer fine flour are like those offering swine's blood. These rejections by God are also explained as due to the people choosing their own ways instead of God's (v. 4).

Isaiah 66:18–21 LXX is a prophecy of God gathering the nations that points to important context for the later ministry and events in Acts. "I am coming to gather all the nations and tongues, and they shall come and see my glory" (v. 18). "And I will leave signs [σημεῖα] upon them, and from them I will send forth those who are saved to the nations, to Tharsis and Phoud ... and to Greece and to the islands far away—those who have not heard my name nor seen my glory, and they shall declare my glory among the nations" (v. 19).

"They shall bring your kindred [ἀδελφούς] from all the nations as a gift to the Lord ... into the holy city Ierousalem" (Isa 66:20a). They will do this "as [ὡς ἄν] the sons of Israel bring to me their sacrifices with psalms into the house of the Lord" (v. 20b, my trans.). "And I will take for myself some of them as priests and as Leuites, said the Lord" (v. 21). Finally, month after month "all flesh shall come before me to do obeisance in Ierousalem, said the Lord" (v. 23).

There is some doubt about whether this refers to Diaspora Jews or Gentiles, but with my translation they can be understood to be Gentiles. Especially when read as an inclusio with Isa 56:1–8 about foreigners and eunuchs being accepted into God's people and invited to worship in the temple, the reference here seems to be to Gentiles. At least, that may well have been how Luke could have interpreted it.

Gentiles would thus be portrayed as coming in pilgrimage to Jerusalem, with some of them even being accepted in God's people as priests and Levites. It is not a strained construal for Acts to reinterpret and apply Isaiah's influx of Gentiles into God's people in Jerusalem as the influx of Gentiles into God's people when Paul and Jesus' disciples convert them in their native places, without their having to go to Jerusalem or to be circumcised and accept the law (cf. Acts 15), as Isaiah pictures them doing.

PAUL'S MISSION AS CONTINUING ISRAEL'S WITNESS TO THE ONE GOD AND OPPOSITION TO IDOLATRY

There remains space only for some brief examples from Paul's Gentile ministry that illustrate how it continues the mission of the Isaian servant of the Lord to witness to all nations about the sole living God and to combat Gentile idolatry and worship of pagan gods. Kavin Rowe treats the reaction to Paul and Barnabas after the healing of the lame man in Acts 14:12–19 and to Paul and Silas after the exorcism of the fortune-telling spirit from the slave girl in Acts 16:16–23.[16] At Lystra, Paul and Barnabas utterly reject the pagan interpretations of their healing of the lame man as the appearance of gods in human form, as well as their attempts to sacrifice to them as Hermes and Zeus. Because Paul's message about the one living God working through human instruments completely undermines their cultural worldview about gods and sacrifices, the crowd's sudden shift from worshiping to attempts to kill Paul and Barnabas is understandable.

Similarly, the vulnerability of the fortune-telling spirit in Philippi to expulsion by the greater power in the name of Jesus Christ destroys not only the source of income for the owners of the fortune-telling slave, but in principle is a threat to all in Philippi who profit from magic or spirits (Acts 16). Likewise, Paul's preaching against idolatry in Ephesus in Acts 19 leads to riots inspired by a silversmith whose living by making idols is threatened by Paul's message. Even in the more "philosophical" setting of Athens, Paul's speech pointedly attacks idolatry, polytheism, and the alleged need of the one living Creator God for houses or for anything humans could supply for him (Acts 17:16–32).

These are just some examples of what scholars have treated as merely humorous novelistic tales to enliven the narrative of Acts. But they illustrate how, throughout much of Paul's ministry to Gentiles in Acts, his preaching had to be rooted in the message of Jewish monotheism and attacks on pagan idolatry and religiosity. Before Paul could proclaim Christ, he had to first substitute for pagan cultures based on idolatry and polytheistic worldviews the biblical message and worldview of the sole living Creator God who created all things and will judge all humans (e.g., Acts 17:22–32). Because this biblical worldview so radically undermined the prevalent polytheistic cultures of their time, Paul and early Christians suffered intense persecution from many of the Gentiles whom they tried to evangelize as God's servants.

Epilogue

In this essay I have suggested that emphasis in the later chapters of Acts on the role of the servant of the Lord (especially but not exclusively from

---

16. Rowe, "Acts and Identity of God," 248–63.

Isaiah LXX) portrays the evangelistic mission of Paul and later Christians as an organic development from Israel's servant mission to witness to all nations about the sole living God and to combat Gentile idolatry and worship of pagan gods. If this is so, Christian accentuation of the one living God in evangelizing Gentiles seems to recommend increased attention by contemporary scholars to the central importance of monotheism in the earliest Christian message. This early Christian emphasis illustrates the importance of focusing interpretation of Luke-Acts on New Testament "theology" strictly speaking—that is, on study of (the one living) God.

THE PARABLE OF THE WICKED TENANTS
IN THE VINEYARD: IS THE GOSPEL OF
THOMAS INDEPENDENT OF THE SYNOPTICS?

John P. Meier

INTRODUCTION

From the time of his doctoral dissertation onward, Professor Frank Matera has focused a good deal of his work on the Synoptic Gospels. Over more than two decades, I have profited from his expertise in Synoptic studies, experienced not only in his books and articles but also in many personal conversations. Throughout the many years of writing *A Marginal Jew*, I have regularly sought his counsel, no more so than in my work on the Synoptic parables.

A major question in parable research today is the relationship between the Synoptic parables and the parallels found in the Coptic Gospel of Thomas. Proponents of Thomas's independence of or dependence on the Synoptics continue to debate the issue, with various scholars proposing a mediating position (some sayings are dependent, others independent), while still others profess agnosticism in some, if not all, cases.[1] In volume 1 of *A Marginal Jew*, I laid out various general considerations that placed me in the "dependence" camp.[2] Yet I am painfully aware that nothing short

---

1. For a brief historical survey of the debate, see Jörg Frey, "Die Lilien und das Gewand: *EvThom* 36 and 37 als Paradigma für das Verhältnis des *Thomasevangeliums* zur synoptischen Überlieferung," in *Das Thomasevangelium. Entstehung—Rezeption—Theologie* (ed. Jörg Frey, Edzard Popkes, and Jens Schröter; BZNW 157; Berlin: de Gruyter, 2008), 122–80.

2. See John P. Meier, *The Roots of the Problem and the Person* (vol. 1 of *A Marginal Jew: Rethinking the Historical Jesus*; 4 vols.; ABRL; New Haven: Yale University Press, 1991–2009), 123–39.

of the trench warfare of a saying-by-saying analysis of the entire Gospel of Thomas can create a fully satisfying argument.[3] The present essay that I offer in honor of Professor Matera is but one skirmish in this seemingly interminable war over Thomas.

Within the compass of this brief essay, it might seem foolhardy to choose as my battleground the parable of the Wicked Tenants of the Vineyard. After all, two distinguished scholars, Klyne R. Snodgrass and John S. Kloppenborg, have dedicated lengthy monographs to this parable, only to arrive at opposite conclusions about the Thomasine parallel (Snodgrass: dependent on the Synoptics; Kloppenborg: independent).[4] In addition, Charles L. Quarles has studied this parable as part of his critique of John Dominic Crossan's use of Thomas in the latter's research on the historical Jesus.[5] The depressingly predictable results (Crossan for Thomas's independence, Quarles against it) might lead the faint of heart to decide that the problem is insoluble. I would suggest instead that the question of the dependence or independence of the Synoptic-like logia in Thomas is not unlike philosophy's favorite chestnut, the epistemological question. One can learn a great deal from the pro-and-con arguments catalogued in the history of epistemology, as the problem has been debated by great minds down through the centuries. But in the end, a study of past positions does

---

3. For monographs that undertake this project, see, e.g., Wolfgang Schrage, *Das Verhältnis des Thomas-Evangeliums zur synoptischen Tradition und zu den koptischen Evangelienübersetzungen* (BZNW 29; Berlin: Töpelman, 1964); Michael Fieger, *Das Thomasevangelium. Einleitung, Kommentar und Systematik* (NTAbh 22; Münster: Aschendorff, 1991); Reinhard Nordsieck, *Das Thomas-Evangelium* (Neukirchen-Vluyn: Neukirchener, 2004); April D. DeConick, *The Original Gospel of Thomas in Translation* (LNTS 287; London: T&T Clark, 2007); Uwe-Karsten Plisch, *The Gospel of Thomas: Original Text with Commentary* (trans. Gesine Schenk Robinson; Stuttgart: Deutsche Bibelgesellschaft, 2008). Schrage and Fieger lean in the direction of Thomas's dependence, while the other authors generally favor the position of independence. However, almost all the authors admit that some cases remain uncertain and that a few examples may run counter to the general picture they see in Thomas.

4. Klyne R. Snodgrass, *The Parable of the Wicked Tenants: An Inquiry into Parable Interpretation* (WUNT 27; Tübingen: Mohr Siebeck, 1983); cf. the summary of his position in his *Stories with Intent* (Grand Rapids: Eerdmans, 2008), 280–81. For independence, see John S. Kloppenborg, *The Tenants in the Vineyard: Ideology, Economics, and Agrarian Conflict in Jewish Palestine* (WUNT 195; Tübingen: Mohr Siebeck, 2006).

5. Charles L. Quarles, "The Use of the *Gospel of Thomas* in the Research on the Historical Jesus of John Dominic Crossan," *CBQ* 69 (2007): 517–36.

not dispense the thoughtful individual from struggling personally with the question of whether and how we can know truth. Similarly, I am convinced that each scholar, after being duly instructed by learned predecessors, must fashion his or her own solution to the question of Thomas's dependence or independence by "getting one's hands dirty" with the text. It is in this spirit that I offer my own approach to the conundrum of the parable of the Wicked Tenants in the Synoptics and Thomas: Mark 12:1–11 || Matt 21:33–43 || Luke 20:9–18 || Gos. Thom. 65–66.[6]

The Test Case of the Wicked Tenants

Given the constraints of this essay, space does not allow a full verse-by-verse exegesis of each form of the parable. In what follows, I will simply take Mark, Matthew, Luke, and Thomas in turn, dividing each one's story into five stages of the narrative and noting each time the data relevant to the question of redactional activity and dependence.[7]

---

6. I enumerate the verses of the Synoptic versions so as to include only the text of the parable proper, without the reaction of the audience, which in each case is an addition by the Evangelist. Since Thomas has no audience or larger context, it naturally lacks any reaction. A complete treatment of the relationship of Thomas to the Synoptic parables would require careful scrutiny of all the presuppositions and postulates that are often not fully enunciated or examined by the exegetes who rely on them. Since I have already offered a critique of such presuppositions (*Roots of the Problem*, 131–38), I do not repeat it here. A critique of the postulates employed by Crossan in his analysis of the parable of the Wicked Tenants is offered by Quarles, "Use of the *Gospel of Thomas*," 524–34.

7. Helpful tables comparing and contrasting the subunits of each version of the parable can be found in Snodgrass (*Stories with Intent*, 282) and Arland J. Hultgren (*The Parables of Jesus: A Commentary* [Grand Rapids: Eerdmans, 2000], 358). As Hultgren points out (p. 356), there are many different source theories about this parable, even apart from Thomas's independence or dependence: e.g., besides Mark there was supposedly a Q version, or an M version, or an L version. Along with Hultgren (and contrary to Snodgrass), I think that the variations in Matthew and Luke (as well as the minor agreements between the two) can be adequately explained from the redactional tendencies of each. That Matthew and Luke are simply redacting Mark without any other source being used is argued at length by Kloppenborg, *Tenants in the Vineyard*, 173–218.

MARK 12:1–11

Mark's account may be divided as follows:

1. *Setup.* The planting of the vineyard clearly follows the LXX form of Isa 5:2. The new element vis-à-vis Isaiah is the letting out of the vineyard to the (tenant) farmers and the departure of the man who goes on a journey (ἄνθρωπος, the owner, who is *not* said to go abroad).[8]

2. *Sending Slaves to Collect the Fruit.* A slave is sent, beaten, and sent back empty-handed. A second slave is sent, and he is wounded in the head and dishonored. A third is sent and killed, "and many others," some of whom are beaten, while others are killed.

3. *Sending the Son.* It is important to note the order of the Greek text here: The owner "still had one person, [namely,] a beloved son. He [the owner, now obviously the father] sent him [as the] last one to them, saying [= thinking], 'They will respect my son.'"

4. *Killing the Son.* The tenants, knowing that the son is the heir, decide to kill him in order to obtain the inheritance. They kill him and then throw him out of the vineyard, thus denying him even decent burial.

5. *Double Conclusion.*

   a[1] Jesus asks rhetorically: What will "the lord [the owner/father] of the vineyard do?"

   a[2] Jesus answers his own question: "He will come and destroy the farmers and give the vineyard to others."

   b[1] Jesus asks rhetorically: "Or have you not read this scripture [text]?"

   b[2] Jesus quotes the scripture/text he has in mind, Ps 117:22–23 LXX ("The stone that the builders rejected, this became the cornerstone...").[9]

---

8. All the verb ἀποδημέω need signify is "to go on a journey," "to depart on a journey," or (metaphorically) "to be absent." Notice how Luke feels he must specify in the parable of the Prodigal Son (15:13) that the younger son journeys into a distant country (ἀπεδήμησεν εἰς χώραν μακράν); without that specification, a knowledgeable reader would be surprised or puzzled by the reference to raising pigs (15:15–16).

9. Various commentators speculate on the primitive parable supposedly lying behind Mark's version. Suggested Markan redactional elements include the allusion to Isa 5:2 in Mark 12:1, the superfluous sending of many other slaves in 12:5cde, the qualification of the son as "beloved" in v. 6, and the two-part conclusion, each part being introduced by a rhetorical question (v. 9 + vv. 10–11). Perhaps the best candidate is the presence of a double conclusion, which reflects perfectly Mark's well-

MATTHEW 21:33–43 (44?)

As Matthew often does with Mark's narratives, notably his miracle stories, here Matthew abbreviates the basic story. (Indeed, Matthew even manages to abbreviate Mark's version of the parable of the Mustard Seed, despite the fact the he combines the Markan with the Q form.) Matthew similarly abbreviates Mark's *basic story* of the Wicked Tenants, even though he lengthens certain individual phrases (notably in the sayings material).[10]

1. *Setup.* Matthew specifies that the man planting the vineyard is the head of a household (οἰκοδεσπότης).

2. *Sending Slaves to Collect the Fruit.* From the start, the man sends slaves (in the plural): one is beaten, another is killed, and another is stoned. The second sending involves more slaves than the first mission, with similar results.

3. *Sending the Son.* Omitting Mark's awkward third sending of a third servant plus "many others," Matthew says that "last [of all], he sent to them his son," omitting the adjective "beloved." At first glance, it seems strange that Matthew would omit "beloved," but the omission fits his general program of abbreviation.[11] In fact, it is not just the one word that is omitted; rather, the whole corresponding clause in Mark is slimmed down. Mark 12:6 reads: "He still had one person, [namely,] a beloved son. He sent him [as the] last one to them, saying...." Matthew collapses these two clauses into one: "Last [of all], he sent to them his son, saying...."[12]

---

known stylistic trait of duality. However, since our concern is with Thomas's version of the parable in relation to the three Synoptics, such speculation about a pre-Markan form may be waived.

10. To be precise: Matthew abbreviates the basic story within Mark's narrative proper by dropping whole incidents or statements. At the same time, he expands a phrase here or there as he sees fit. The result is that the overall word count of the core narrative of the parable is slightly less in Matthew (by "core narrative" I mean the plot stretching from the planting of the vineyard to the death of the son).

11. Hence I do not think that Snodgrass (*Stories with Intent*, 283) is correct in claiming that there is no convincing explanation for Matthew's omission of Mark's ἀγαπητόν; see also the considerations in the following note.

12. There may be other factors at work here: (1) Matthew's tendency to "cross-reference" key words and phrases in his Gospel to highlight corresponding scenes; (2) his concern with underlining the fulfillment of OT prophecies in the events of Jesus' public ministry; and (3) his love of threefold patterns and groupings. Thus it may not be simply by accident that there are precisely three occurrences of the adjective

4. *Killing the Son.* Intensifying the allegory, Matthew reverses the order of the crime in Mark: first the tenants cast the son out of the vineyard (now suddenly representing Jerusalem), then they killed him—mirroring more closely the succession of events in Jesus' passion and death.

5. *Double Conclusion.* Here Matthew lengthens the wording of Mark's double question and answer:

a[1]   Jesus asks rhetorically: "When then the lord of the vineyard comes, [borrowing the 'coming' from Mark's first answer], what will he do to those farmers?"

a[2]   The Jewish leaders answer (pronouncing judgment on themselves): "He will bring those evil men to an evil end, and will let out the vineyard to other farmers, who will render to him the fruits at their proper time."[13]

b[1]   Jesus' second rhetorical question, which leads into

b[2]   not only the citation of Ps 117:22–23 LXX (v. 42) but also Jesus' clear application of the whole parable to the Jewish leaders (v. 43): "The kingdom of God [= the vineyard] will be taken from you [the leaders] and will be given to a people [ἔθνος = the church made up of Jews and Gentiles] bearing its fruit."[14]

ἀγαπητός ("beloved") in Matthew, the three being found (1) in the two theophanies of the baptism and the transfiguration of Jesus, during which the voice of the Father from heaven announces, "This is my son, the beloved" (3:17; 17:5); and (2) in the fulfillment citation (12:18) that lies between these two theophanies, a citation that makes clear to the reader that the other two references to Jesus as "my beloved" fulfill the prophecy about the Servant of the Lord in Isa 42:1—according, that is, to Matthew's reading of the text (both the MT and the LXX read "my chosen" rather than "my beloved"). To have another reference to Jesus as ἀγαπητός in Matt 21:37 would spoil the pattern. For a list of other explanations for the omission of ἀγαπητός offered by various commentators, see Kloppenborg, *Tenants in the Vineyard*, 183–84.

13. Forcing the Jewish leaders to pronounce their own condemnation fits perfectly with Matthew's sustained polemic against the authorities. In particular, it coheres neatly with the other parables of judgment that Matthew adds just before (21:28–32) and after (22:1–14) this parable.

14. There is a difficult text-critical problem concerning whether Matt 21:44 (which alludes to Dan 2:34–35,44–45) is an original part of Matthew's text. A slightly different form of the verse certainly belongs in Luke 20:18. While the decision regarding Matt 21:44 could go either way, I think that it is more probable that the verse has been added to Matthew's Gospel by Christian scribes, one of whose tendencies is to harmonize the Synoptics. The 3rd edition of *The Greek New Testament* (ed. Kurt Aland et al.; New York: United Bible Societies, 1975) gives v. 44 a "C" rating ("a consider-

LUKE 20:9–18

Luke abbreviates the basic narrative of Mark's parable even more than Matthew does, both in the number of incidents and in the total word count. The basic narrative of the parable of Mark (from v. 1b to the end of v. 8, prior to Jesus' double question) includes 114 Greek words. The same narrative in Luke 20:9b–15a includes one hundred Greek words, despite some additions by Luke.[15] Both abbreviations and redactional changes can be seen in most of the five stages of the parable:

1. *Setup*. The setup is abbreviated in the extreme, so that only "a man planted a vineyard" is left, without the clear allusion to Isa 5:2 seen in Mark 12:1.[16] At the same time, Luke adds to the end of the setup by noting that the man went away on a journey "for a long time," perhaps in an attempt to make the subsequent events more plausible.

2. *Sending Slaves to Collect the Fruit*. There are three sendings of a single slave. The first time, the slave is beaten and sent back empty-handed. The second sending ends the same way, with the addition of the slave being treated shamefully. The third sending results in the slave being wounded and "thrown out."

3. *Sending the Son*. Engaging in a typical Lukan interior monologue introduced by a deliberative question ("What shall I do?" cf. Luke 12:17; 16:3), the "lord of the vineyard" decides: "I will send my son, the beloved. *Perhaps* [ἴσως] they will respect him."

---

able degree of doubt") and encloses the verse in double brackets ("passages which are regarded as later additions to the text"). However, in the 4th edition of *The Greek New Testament*, v. 44 is placed in single brackets ("presence or position in the text is regarded as disputed"). Bruce M. Metzger (*TCGNT*, 47) explains that while the editorial committee considered v. 44 "an accretion to the text," the verse was retained in the text "because of the antiquity of the reading and its importance in the textual tradition." Snodgrass (*Stories with Intent*, 286) leans toward accepting v. 44 as original in Matthew, but admits that "certainty is not possible."

15. Of course, one must make allowances for possible variations in counting due to different text-critical decisions.

16. One might argue that ἐφύτευσεν ἀμπελῶνα ("he planted a vineyard") in Luke 20:9 still points to ἐφύτευσα ἄμπελον ("I planted a vineyard") in Isa 5:2 LXX. However, since both the act of planting and a vineyard are common metaphors in the OT and the intertestamental literature, Isa 5:2 can hardly claim to have a monopoly on the phrase "to plant a vineyard." The same Greek phrase is found, e.g., in LXX Gen 9:20; Deut 28:30, 39; Amos 5:11.

4. *Killing the Son.* Like Matthew, Luke reverses Mark's order of killing and casting out the son to mirror better the order of Jesus' passion and death.[17]

5. *Double Conclusion.* Like Matthew, here Luke expands Jesus' remarks:

a^1 Jesus' first rhetorical question and

a^2 Jesus' first answer, both repeating Mark almost word for word.

b^1 Jesus' second rhetorical question ("What then is this that is written?")

b^2 Jesus' second rhetorical answer, made up of (a) *only* verse 22 of Ps 117 LXX, to which is appended (b) a loose allusion to Dan 2:34–35, 44–45 LXX ("Everyone who falls on that stone shall be broken")

In sum, we see an intriguing pattern as we move from Mark to Matthew and then to Luke. We find a progressive abbreviation of the basic narrative of the parable (up to the killing of the son), balanced by redactional additions here and there by both Matthew and Luke. The additions are especially notable in the expansion of Jesus' second answer at the end of the parable, though even here Luke abbreviates the citation of Ps 117 LXX, citing only verse 22: "The stone that the builders rejected, this became the cornerstone." There is also the tendency, barely visible in Matthew but clearer in Luke, to make the story more plausible. For example, in Luke no slave is killed before the sending of the son, and "perhaps" (ἴσως) is added to the owner's inner deliberation about sending his son.

What is telling in all this is that, as we shall soon see, the same general tendencies are found in Thomas's version of the parable. In Thomas the word count of the basic narrative is reduced to 66 words—though the actual reduction is not as severe as mere numbers might indicate, since Coptic is a highly agglutinative language, employing a single compound word for two or more Greek words. Despite the overall reduction of the narrative, a few clauses are added, most of which are in line with Thomas's redactional tendencies, including his tendency to make the story more plausible. In other words, Thomas pushes to their logical conclusions the

---

17. This is a prime example of the type of "minor agreement" of Matthew and Luke against Mark that arises spontaneously and coincidentally when two later Evangelists, both better Greek stylists and more systematic thinkers, rework a Christian text from one generation earlier. Such minor agreements are not so remarkable when balanced against the far more numerous times when Matthew and Luke go their separate ways in rewriting Mark.

redactional tendencies already present in Matthew and especially Luke's reworking of Mark.

COPTIC GOSPEL OF THOMAS 65–66

The Gospel of Thomas displays the same tendencies to abbreviate, to make more plausible, and to add redactional perspectives:

1. *Setup.* The setting of the stage is brief: "A usurious [or good?]¹⁸ man had a vineyard, and he gave it to some farmers so that they might work it and that he might receive his fruit from them." In many ways, this introduction reflects Luke, who, like Thomas, omits the clear allusion to Isa 5:2. Also in keeping with his tendency to abbreviate, Thomas moves the reference to "receiving fruit from them" into the setup, perhaps because he omits the reference to the owner going on a journey. Interestingly, Thomas's wording of "in order that he might receive his fruit from them" conflates phrases from all three Synoptics: the ἵνα (Coptic ϢΙΝΑ) purpose clause and reference to taking the fruit *from* the farmers in Mark 12:2 (repeated by Luke), the singular "fruit" (καρπός) in Luke 20:10 (contrast Mark and Matthew), and the curious possessive "*his* fruit," found only in Matt 21:34.¹⁹

---

18. The Coptic text is uncertain at this point because of a small but important lacuna within the word ⲚⲬⲢⲎ[ⲤⲦⲎ]Ⲥ. The incomplete word is certainly Greek, but it could be either χρηστός ("good," "benevolent") or χρήστης ("usurious," or simply "a creditor"—though the Greek word can also mean "prophet" or "debtor"). While χρηστός is well attested in Coptic texts, χρήστης is not. However, χρήστης may make better sense in the context of the fraught relations between the owner and the tenants as well as in the larger context of Thomas, i.e., the preceding negative statements made about a rich man (logion 63) and merchants and traders (logion 64). Nevertheless, granted the range of meanings of χρήστης in Greek, it is unwise to construct a whole interpretation of Thomas's version of the parable on a dubious reading of a Greek adjective. On this see Plisch, *Gospel of Thomas*, 160–61. Interestingly, Nordsieck (*Thomas-Evangelium*, 253) argues against χρήστης as the original reading because the word never occurs again either in Thomas or in the rest of the Nag Hammadi codices. But this would not be the only case of a Greek word occurring in a single logion of Thomas and nowhere else in the whole of the Nag Hammadi writings. Another example, ⲌⲒⲌⲀⲚⲒⲞⲚ (a Greek word with a Semitic origin), occurs in Gos. Thom. 57 (four times in the one parable) and nowhere else in the whole Nag Hammadi corpus.

19. Theoretically, one might translate the pronoun αὐτοῦ at the end of Matt 21:34 as "its [the vineyard's] fruit," since the masculine form αὐτοῦ could refer to the masculine noun ἀμπελών ("vineyard") in v. 33 instead of ἄνθρωπος ... οἰκοδεσπότης ("a

Please check all the Coptic carefully, since it has been rekeyed.

2. *Sending the Slaves to Collect the Fruit.* Here Thomas conflates Matthew and Luke in line with his tendency to slim down the narrative and perhaps to make the story more plausible as well. Thomas follows Luke (1) in having only one slave sent each time and (2) in having each slave only beaten, not killed—thus increasing the plausibility of the owner sending his son. On the other hand, following Matthew, Thomas reduces the sending of the slaves to two instances, thus shortening the narrative. The precise wording of Thomas's first sending again reflects his tendency to conflate. Only one slave is sent (as in Mark and Luke), but the slave is qualified by the possessive pronoun ("*his* slave"), echoing Matthew's "*his* slaves" (21:34) in the first sending. While Thomas has moved up one type of purpose clause into the setup ("that [ϢΙΝΑ] he might receive his fruit from them," conflating all three Synoptics), he retains another type of purpose clause in the first sending: "that [ΧΕΚΑΑC] the farmers might give him the fruit of the vineyard." This repeats almost word for word Luke's rewriting of Mark's purpose clause in Luke 20:10: "so that they [the farmers] might give him [some] of the fruit of the vineyard." Instead of Mark's "that he might receive [some] of the fruits of the vineyard from the farmers" (represented in part in Thomas's first purpose clause [ϢΙΝΑ] in the setup), Luke writes "that they [the farmers] might give him [some] of the *fruit* of the vineyard"—Luke alone writing "fruit" (καρπός) in the singular, while Mark and Matthew use the plural "fruits" (καρποί). This is a clear sign of Thomas's knowing and copying Luke's redactional change to Mark; Thomas even takes over the Greek word καρπός, using the singular definite article to make clear that the noun is to be understood in the singular. That Luke's ἀπὸ τοῦ καρποῦ ... δώσουσιν ("that they might give ... [some] of the

---

man ... householder"), also in v. 33. Indeed, some form of the pronoun αὐτός occurs three times in v. 33, each time referring to the vineyard. However, the larger context and flow of thought in vv. 33–34 argue for αὐτοῦ in v. 34 referring to the householder, since he is the (understood) subject of every finite verb in the parable throughout vv. 33–34, with the exception of ὅτε δὲ ἤγγισεν ὁ καιρὸς ("but when the time drew near"). Hence, in the main clause in v. 34 that clearly has the householder as the understood subject ("he sent his slave to the farmers to receive ... fruits"), the natural sense of αὐτοῦ is "his," thus emphasizing the right of the householder to what he demands from the farmers. Not surprisingly, therefore, "his" is the translation used by the RSV, NRSV, and the revised NT of the NAB. Even if one took αὐτοῦ as referring to the vineyard, the basic point of my argument would remain the same: this redactional intervention of Matthew is reflected in Thomas's version since the phrase rendering "vineyard" (ΜΑ Ν̄ΕΛΟΟΛΕ) is likewise masculine.

fruit") is indeed a unique redactional touch of Luke's can be seen from the fact that nowhere else in the New Testament does καρπός (here in the partitive construction ἀπὸ τοῦ καρποῦ, with "some" understood) occur as the object of the simple verb δίδωμι ("to give") when human beings are the subject.[20] The only time this construction occurs is here, in Luke's redactional alteration of Mark in Luke 20:10, which is closely followed by Thomas:

Luke 20:10: ἵνα ἀπὸ τοῦ καρποῦ τοῦ ἀμπελῶνος δώσουσιν αὐτῷ
Gos. Thom. 65: ⲆⲈⲔⲀⲀⲤ ⲈⲚⲞⲨⲞⲈⲓⲈ ⲚⲀϯ ⲚⲀϤ ⲘⲠⲔⲀⲢⲠⲞⲤ
ⲘⲠⲘⲀ ⲚⲈⲖⲞⲞⲖⲈ

This is not the result of stray memories or alternate oral performances. Along with the other traces of Luke's redaction (see below), it furnishes a strong argument that Thomas knew Luke's version of the parable.

To proceed with the sending of the slaves: the farmers "seize" the slave (similarly Mark and Matthew). To be precise, the express mention of the slave(s) as the object of the act of seizing follows Matthew, as does the possessive "his." The farmers proceed to "beat" him, as they do in all three Synoptics. Following Mark and Luke, Thomas has no killing in the first sending of the slave. Actually, this is necessitated by the logic of having only a single servant sent. If he were killed, there would be no one to report to the owner the farmer's refusal to render their due. Having a number of servants sent on a single mission allows Matthew to have one beaten, another killed, and still another stoned. The killing in Matthew's version is conflated with the mere beating in Mark and Luke by Thomas's additional comment that "a little more and they would have killed him."

The return of the beaten slave poses a problem for Thomas, who seems at pains to create a more plausible story. Luke had already coped with the problem of plausibility by having an inner monologue in which the owner

---

20. By way of contrast, note that in Mark 4:8 (the parable of the Sower), the construction ἐδίδου καρπόν has "the seed" as its understood subject (likewise in the Matthean form of the same parable, 13:8). In Heb 12:11 "discipline" (παιδεία) is the subject of the compound verb ἀποδίδωσιν, which has καρπόν as its object. Finally, in Rev 22:2 the tree of life is the subject of ἀποδιδοῦν + καρπόν. Thus in the entire New Testament the only time the simple verb δίδωμι is used with humans (the farmers) as the subject and fruit as the object (granted, in a partitive construction) is in Luke's redactional change of Mark in Luke 20:10, followed closely by Thomas.

weighs possibilities after the second sending (Luke 20:13: "Perhaps…"). As part of the attempt to increase plausibility, Thomas not only takes over this inner monologue of deliberation but anticipates it here—he will still use it again after the second sending—to justify the sending of a second slave after the first has been beaten. However, the owners' deliberation at this point in Thomas is anything but clear. From the first modern publication of Thomas to the present day, commentators have found the owner's deliberation as he prepares to send the second slave unintelligible. In the Coptic text as it stands, the owner thinks, "Perhaps he did not know [= recognize] them"—the "he" referring to the first slave and the "them" referring to the farmers. Does the owner think that the servant mistakenly went to the wrong farmers, who vented their annoyance at what seemed an unjust demand for a share of their crops? This seems so contrived that other commentators suggest emending what they judge a corrupted text by writing, "Perhaps they [the farmers] did not recognize him [as my duly sent slave]." Alternately, one might hypothesize that Thomas is introducing in a clumsy way the gnostic theme of the ignorance of the Creator God and/or his minions (but then shouldn't the ignorance of the owner be stressed?).[21] In the end, one must admit that none of these solutions is completely satisfying. In any event, what is clear is that Thomas takes Luke's deliberating soliloquy ("perhaps") and moves it forward, apparently in an attempt to make the owner's action more plausible. Placed after the first sending, the deliberation makes the second sending slightly more intelligible—if no less fruitless. The two separate deliberations introduced by "perhaps" also provide an added structural element to this schematic story.[22]

3. *Sending the Son.* Again we find conflation. Thomas follows Matthew (1) in making the independent statement "he sent his son" the first main clause in this section (the Greek ἀπέστειλεν … τὸν υἱὸν αὐτου corresponding exactly to the Coptic ϪΟΟΥ ⲘⲠⲈⲨϢⲎⲢⲈ), and (2) in omitting the adjec-

---

21. For the suggestion that the "slaves of the vineyard owner are either sinners or archons who keep the free men in subjection," see Quarles, "*Gospel of Thomas,*" 530–31. He points to a possibly parallel idea in the Coptic Gospel of Philip (see, e.g., 52:5–15).

22. In Thomas's copying of Luke's "perhaps" and using it twice within his narrative, Simon Gathercole ("Luke in the *Gospel of Thomas,*" NTS 57 [2011]: 114–44, esp. 121) sees an editorial tendency of Thomas, namely, to extend further a redactional feature he finds in Luke. For the full extent of Luke's influence on Thomas in this parable, see 127–31. Gathercole (129–31) also counters the various arguments of Kloppenborg (*Tenants in the Vineyard,* 173–277) in favor of Thomas's independence in this parable.

tive "beloved" (ἀγαπητός), present in Mark and Luke. Like Luke (contrary to Mark and Matthew), Thomas makes the master's deliberative soliloquy a main clause. Into the "lord of the vineyard's" deliberation Luke pointedly inserts an adverb encountered nowhere else in the New Testament: "*Perhaps* [ἴσως] they will respect him [i.e., my son]." Thomas parallels this with his own adverb ΜΕϢΑΚ ("*Perhaps* they will respect him, my son"). Interestingly, ΜΕϢΑΚ occurs nowhere in Thomas except in logion 65, in the two Lukan-like deliberations of the owner. In addition, besides reflecting Coptic grammar,[23] the dual object ("him"/"my son") in the Coptic text manages to conflate Luke's "him" and Matthew and Mark's "my son."

4. *Killing the Son.* The climax is cut to the bare bones for maximum shock value and mystery: "Those farmers, since they knew that he was the heir of the vineyard, seized him [and] killed him." The Coptic for "those farmers" (ΑΝΟΥΟΕΙΕ ΕΤΜΜΑΥ) repeats Mark's ἐκεῖνοι δὲ οἱ γεωργοί. Only Mark and Thomas use both the "far-demonstrative" ("those") plus the definite article with "farmers," and neither (unlike Matthew and Luke) notes that the farmers see the son. Pointedly, only Thomas uses the verb "know" of the farmers, purposely contrasting the "knowing" (gnostic?) farmers with the "not-knowing" slave who was sent first. Thus it may be that Thomas has intentionally redacted the Synoptic parable to turn it into an allegory of the ignorant slaves of the owner (= the demiurge, the blind and tyrannical Creator God?) versus the rebellious free agents who have knowledge. None of the three Synoptics has the theme of not-knowing/knowing at the two points where Thomas enunciates the theme. The terse "they seized him [and] killed him" of Thomas reflects the equally terse "seizing they killed him" of Mark, at which point Thomas abruptly ends the parable. The sudden ending with no further elaboration, commentary, or scriptural reference fits in perfectly with the hidden meaning of Jesus' words that Thomas has inculcated from the prologue and first two logia of the work. The explanatory comments of Jesus or the Evangelists found in the Synoptics, as well as any citation of the Old Testament, to

---

23. The Coptic grammar of the particular verb used for "to respect" (ϢΙΠΕ) demands first the use of the pronoun with a preposition (ϨΗΤϤ) and then the noun as object (ΜΠΑϢΗΡΕ). It is intriguing to note that Thomas's version of this parable contains two purpose clauses in the earlier part of the parable and two deliberations in the middle part, as well as the (grammatically necessary) double object of the verb "respect." The redactional hand of a single person who favors balance and doublets seems to be at work here, rather than stray memories and multiple oral performances.

which Thomas shows itself hostile, are systematically removed throughout Thomas. So here as well. In keeping with this (gnostic?) program, the Synoptic elaborations and commentary are replaced with Thomas's frequent refrain, calling on the possessor of true knowledge (a gnostic?) to seek and find (cf. logion 2) the hidden message (cf. prologue): "Let him who has ears hear."[24]

5. *Double Conclusion*. From what has just been said, it is obvious that Thomas would omit the double conclusion. After all, the first conclusion has Jesus prophesying the destruction of Jerusalem, implicitly fitting the whole parable into the larger story of Jesus' ministry to his own people (seen as the culmination of the multiple sending of rejected prophets to Israel), his rejection by their leaders, and their subsequent punishment via the destruction of their ancient capital and temple. The sweep of a collective, people-oriented salvation history, understood as a pattern of prophecy and fulfillment and climaxing in the ministry and death of the earthly Jesus, is not a congenial theme to Thomas, a work dedicated to secret, saving, and timeless truths revealed only to the solitary initiate. The second conclusion would be even more unpalatable: an explicit citation of the Old Testament as prophecy, proclaiming clearly the ultimate denouement of the story: the death and resurrection of Jesus.

In the end, though, one might claim that Thomas's suppression of the double ending does not entirely succeed. On the one hand, the very core of this parable already carries within itself echoes of the Old Testament and the theme of prophecy. No Jewish-Palestinian audience of Jesus' time, listening to a well-known prophet and teacher as he addressed the religious leaders in the Jerusalem temple, could hardly miss the scriptural allusions inherent in symbols like the vineyard, the owner of the vineyard sending his servants to make claims on those working in his vineyard, and the rejection of those servants by the workers. One would have to be ignorant not only of individual scriptural texts but also of the master narrative governing the Jewish Scriptures to miss the references. For all his abbreviations, even Thomas does not succeed in suppressing the Old Testament allusions entirely.

On the other hand, the "ghost" of the double conclusion haunts Thomas's reductive redaction. In a sense, we still find two endings, however

---

24. Thomas's beloved tag is found as well in logia 8, 21, 63, 96. So intent is Thomas on a terse ending in logion 65 that he chooses the shorter form of the tag; the longer version can be found at the end of logia 8 and 21: "Let him who has ears *to hear*, hear."

much disguised. The first conclusion, the riddling "Let him who has ears hear," replaces the clarifying conclusion that prophesies the destruction of Jerusalem. The second conclusion remains hidden in plain sight, despite its transformation into a separate saying of Jesus, a transformation that obliterates the opening rhetorical question with its citation formula ("Or have you not read this scripture?").[25] As is his tendency here as elsewhere, Thomas follows Luke, who takes over from Mark only verse 22 from Ps 117:22–23 LXX. Of course, for Thomas there can be no question of the fulfillment of Old Testament prophecy, let alone Jesus citing Old Testament prophecy to show that it is fulfilled in his own life and fate. Such a prophecy-fulfillment pattern is explicitly rejected by the Thomasine Jesus in logion 52.[26] Instead, Thomas creates a separate logion, introduced by the formulaic ΠΕϪΕ ΙC ("Jesus said").[27] The prophecy becomes a riddling challenge of Jesus: "Show me the stone that the builders rejected; it is the cornerstone." All sense that Jesus is citing an Old Testament text is lost—intentionally.[28]

---

25. For all of its use of Greek loanwords, Thomas never employs γραφή (scripture); likewise, it never has Jesus cite an OT text explicitly and verbatim; cf. Plisch, *Gospel of Thomas*, 32.

26. Plisch (*Gospel of Thomas*, 133–35) grasps the import of logion 52 better than does DeConick (*Original Gospel of Thomas*, 184–85) or Marvin Meyer (*The Gospel of Thomas: The Hidden Sayings of Jesus* [San Francisco: HarperSanFrancisco, 1992], 103). A mere piling up of parallels from the church fathers and apocryphal works does not aid understanding if careful attention is not paid to the context of the parallel and to the intent of the individual author. Perhaps the two most relevant parallels for logion 52 are the Nag Hammadi tractate Ap. Jas. 6:22–7:1 and Origen's *Commentary on John* 2.34 (Greek text in A. E. Brooke, ed., *The Commentary of Origen on S. John's Gospel* [2 vols.; Cambridge: Cambridge University Press, 1896], 2:100–101); on this issue see Plisch, *Gospel of Thomas*, 133–34. Interestingly, in the end, neither Plisch nor DeConick thinks that logion 52 goes back to the historical Jesus.

27. On the question of whether one should translate ΠΕϪΕ as "said" or "says" in these formulaic introductions of the logia in Thomas, see Plisch, *Gospel of Thomas*, 24–25. I stick to the traditional translation in the past tense, which is used by the vast majority of translators. Plisch varies his translation according to context.

28. Contrary to the suggestion of John Dominic Crossan (*In Parables: The Challenge of the Historical Jesus* [San Francisco: Harper & Row, 1973], 93), Ps 117:22 LXX hardly represents the earliest stage in the allegorizing of the parable of the Wicked Tenants, an allegorizing that is then developed by the Synoptics. Much more likely, the addition of Ps 117:22 LXX represents form-critically a second stage in the parable's expansion, in that it provides a positive conclusion to the parable via the son's

CONCLUSION

In sum, far from being an independent and primitive form of the parable of the Wicked Tenants, Thomas represents the logical conclusion of tendencies already visible in Matthew and Luke's redaction of Mark. On the large scale, the parable's core narrative is increasingly abbreviated (from Matthew to Luke to Thomas), and yet each abbreviator adds a few redactional touches of his own along the way. On the level of verse-by-verse redaction, Thomas shows a consistent tendency to conflate the three Synoptic versions as he severely abbreviates the basic story. While traces of both Matthew and Mark can be detected, it is Luke's redactional changes that are most clearly mirrored in Thomas. They include: (1) Luke 20:9: the abrupt beginning of the story without the clear allusion to Isa 5:2; (2) Luke 20:10: the phrase "in order that *they might give to him* [some of] the fruit of the vineyard"; (3) the omission of the killing of any slave (in keeping with the sending of only one slave each time); (4) the inclusion of "perhaps" (Luke's ἴσως, Thomas's ΜΕϢΑΚ) in the owner's soliloquy, expressing hope that the farmers will respect his son. This point is especially telling since ἴσως never appears anywhere else in the New Testament, just as Thomas never uses ΜΕϢΑΚ outside logion 65. Luke pointedly inserts the adverb to make the owner's decision slightly more plausible. Thomas follows Luke both in wording and intention. To try to escape the obvious conclusion of Thomas's dependence on Luke by conjuring up a separate primitive version of the parable used by both Luke and Thomas is to create a deus ex machina while at the same time cutting oneself with Ockham's razor.[29] Thomas's overall redactional intent is seen (1) in his abbreviations and complete omissions, thus rendering the parable's meaning completely "hidden" (cf. Thomas's prologue), and (2) in his insertion of the (gnostic?) theme of not-knowing/knowing—all to the end of inviting the (gnostic?) reader to divine the meaning behind the story, now rendered allegorical in an esoteric (gnostic?) rather than a Synoptic sense. In the end, what we have in Gos. Thom. 65–66, as I would claim we have in the rest of the Synoptic parallels in Thomas, is an intriguing example of the *Rezeptionsgeschichte* of the Synoptic Gospels in the second century C.E. Contrary

---

vindication, thus balancing and overcoming the first conclusion's negative theme of destruction.

29. Yet this is precisely what Nordsieck (*Thomas-Evangelium*, 254–60), following many others, does.

to the claims of Nicholas Perrin, I do not think that Thomas follows after and is dependent on Tatian's Diatessaron.[30] Rather, along with the cases of conflation and abbreviation we find in the Didache, Polycarp, Justin Martyr, and other second-century Christian writers, Thomas lies on the arc of meshing, digesting, and harmonizing that moves from the Synoptic Gospels to the Diatessaron. Hence Thomas is indeed important within the overall history of the composition and reception of the Synoptics, but not for the reason proffered by its most passionate champions.

---

30. The hypothesis that Thomas was originally composed in Syriac and shows dependence on the Diatessaron has been championed in recent years by Nicholas Perrin in *Thomas and Tatian: The Relationship between the Gospel of Thomas and the Diatessaron* (AcBib 5; Leiden: Brill; Atlanta: Society of Biblical Literature, 2002). He repeats his thesis in more popular form in *Thomas, the Other Gospel* (Louisville: Westminster John Knox, 2007). See also his continued defense of Syriac as the original language of Thomas in "The Aramaic Origins of the *Gospel of Thomas*—Revisited," in Frey et al., *Thomasevangelium*, 50–59.

Unity and Diversity in Paul

From the Acts of the Apostles to Paul: Shaking off the Muffled Majesty of Impersonal Authorship

Matt Whitlock

When considering the unity of the New Testament, how can one build a bridge between the Acts of the Apostles and the uncontested Pauline letters? Scholars have long sought to bridge these works through theological or historical methods, either comparing the theology of the Pauline speeches in Acts with the theology of the Pauline letters, or comparing the Paul in Acts with the historical Paul in the letters. Theological methods have produced debatable and tenuous connections at best.[1] Historical methods have failed to agree on a common ground. Indeed, the latter has produced two distinct terrains, leading Thomas Phillips to discuss the "brackish waters" of "Paul's split personality within contemporary scholarship" between the character Paul in Acts and the historical Paul in the letters.[2] So while historical and theological methods have affirmed the diversity between Acts and the Pauline letters, they have yet to build a bridge with sustainable unity, shape, or legacy. Leander Keck's conclusion twenty

---

1. The majority of scholars still side with Phillip Vielhauer's conclusion that there are few theological connections between Acts and Paul's letters. Vielhauer examines both through four theological lenses, setting the foundation for the modern debate: (1) Christology, (2) natural theology, (3) law, and (4) eschatology. See Phillip Vielhauer, "On the 'Paulinism' of Acts" (trans. Wm. C. Robinson Jr. and Victor P. Furnish), in *Studies in Luke–Acts: Essays Presented in Honor of Paul Schubert* (ed. Leander E. Keck and J. Louis Martyn; Nashville: Abingdon, 1966), 33–50. For a rebuttal of Vielhauer's position, see Stanley E. Porter, *Paul in Acts* (Peabody, Mass.: Hendrickson, 2001), 199–205.

2. Thomas E. Phillips, *Paul, His Letters, and Acts* (Peabody, Mass: Hendrickson, 2009), 1, 3.

years ago, therefore, still stands: "The Paul who emerges from the letters and Acts is a richly diverse figure, about whom no easy conclusion can be reached concerning his *historical* shape or *theological* legacy."[3]

Is it possible, however, that the bridge between Acts and Paul has been constructed of the wrong framework, one that does not use the materials from Acts and the Pauline letters? Given that neither impersonal theological propositions nor precise historical accounts make up the frameworks of Acts or Paul's letters, I argue that Acts is composed of a narrative arrangement that builds the context for reading Paul's letters. According to Frank Matera, Acts erects a narrative bridge connecting "the story of the church to the apostolic writings of the New Testament by offering readers of the New Testament *a narrative context* for reading the letters of Paul, Peter, James, and John."[4] Following Matera's lead, I will further develop this context in relation to Paul.

What is this narrative context, how is it constructed, and how does it create a framework for bridging Acts and Paul's letters? In this essay, I argue that Acts creates a narrative context involving an arrangement of multiple interpretive voices. Luke, in other words, artistically arranges multiple voices to interpret situations in his narrative, some voices interrogating, some misunderstanding, and others transforming situations into God events, that is, events involving God's actions.[5] Once this narrative context is set up in Acts and the interpretive voices are realized, they become personalized in the New Testament, especially in the letters of Paul, whose voice interprets the diverse situations of his communities as God events.

---

3. Leander E. Keck, "Images of Paul in the New Testament," *Int* 43 (1989): 341 (emphasis added). In his conclusion, Phillips (*Paul, His Letters, and Acts*, 190) quotes these lines from Keck and asserts that the majority of scholars still agree with Vielhauer's assertion. Phillips then offers his own thesis, arguing that Luke embellishes his portrait of Paul in order to rehabilitate the image of "the Paul of the letters," making Paul more acceptable for the post-Pauline churches.

4. Frank J. Matera, *New Testament Theology: Exploring Diversity and Unity* (Louisville: Westminster John Knox, 2007), 96–97 (emphasis added). Matera claims that the narrative of Acts "enables readers to inscribe Paul into a larger theological narrative that has its origins in Israel's history" (97). In this essay I focus on one element of this larger theological narrative: the interpretation of God events.

5. The terms *situations* and *events* are derived from the philosophy of Alain Badiou and are explained in depth in section 3 below.

Indeed, akin to what Henry James describes as shaking off "the muffled majesty of authorship," I am suggesting that Luke shakes off his narrator's interpretive powers and assembles a cast of characters, from Peter to Paul, to interpret situations in his narrative so that they become transformed into God events. James, commenting on his own writing in *The Golden Bowl*, states:

> It's not that the muffled majesty of authorship doesn't here *ostensibly* reign; but I catch myself again shaking it off and disavowing the pretence of it while I get down into the arena and do my best to live and breathe and rub shoulders and converse with the persons engaged in the struggle that provides for the others in the circling tiers the entertainment of the great game.[6]

James's words are useful for describing the arrangement of Acts and how it serves as a bridge to Paul's letters. It becomes possible to see how Luke's shaking off "the muffled majesty of authorship" serves as a pathway to Paul's personal, epistolary voice, which interprets the situations of his communities as God events. Luke, therefore, is akin to what James aspires to be, an author who searches for points of view through which to interpret action, through which to see his story, an author who lives and breathes and rubs shoulders and converses with his characters, "with the persons engaged in the struggle." Luke provides impressions and interpretations of the characters themselves, enabling the readers of the New Testament "in the circling tiers" to also rub shoulders with these characters, to be engaged in "the entertainment of the great game." Luke serves as a Jamesian author not only in his narrative but also in connection with the letters that follow it, albeit unintentionally. From a canonical perspective, Acts sets up the context for Paul himself to live, breathe, rub shoulders, and converse with his communities, allowing the readers of the New Testament to be engaged in the process of interpreting God events.

In what follows, (1) I describe the narrative context of Acts, focusing primarily on its interpretive arrangement, (2) provide an example of this context by examining Paul's discourse in Acts, particularly his Lystra speech (Acts 14:8–18), (3) describe Paul's interpretive voice in his uncontested letters against the backdrop of the narrative context of Acts, and (4)

---

6. Henry James, *The Art of the Novel: Critical Prefaces* (New York: Scribner's, 1947), 328.

provide an example of Paul's interpretive voice in his opening words to the Thessalonians (1 Thess 1:1–10). By doing so, I aim to construct a bridge between the diverse interpretive voices of Acts and the interpretive voice of Paul in his uncontested letters. I conclude by discussing how Acts and Paul inform us about interpretation today.

1. The Narrative Context of Acts: Shaking off the Muffled Majesty

The narrative arrangement in Acts—which sets up the narrative context for Paul's letters—is best understood by applying the literary theory of Mikhail Bakhtin, a theorist comparable to Henry James.[7] Bakhtin's literary approach captures the form of Acts. Bakhtin describes a novel as "a diversity of social speech types (sometimes even diversity of languages) and a diversity of individual voices, artistically organized."[8] In novels, diverse voices are artistically arranged around specific objects or situations, often interpreting them. Although Bakhtin classifies the novel as a modern genre, he uncovers its roots in ancient literature, especially in works that are rife with dialogue. Acts typifies this kind of literature, which Bakhtin categorizes under the "prehistory of the novel." When discussing this prehistory, Bakhtin briefly states that key dialogic elements that are in novels are also in the Gospels and Acts.[9]

Acts is rife with speech-acts. It presents a diversity of social speech types and individual voices that are artistically organized around situa-

---

7. For similarities between Bakhtin and James, see José Antonio Álvarez Amorós, "Henry James and Mikhail Bakhtin on the Art of Fiction," in *Proceedings of the 24th International Conference of the Spanish Association for English and American Studies* (ed. Ángel Mateos-Aparicio and Silvia Molina Plaza; Ciudad Real: University of Castilla-La Mancha, 2002), 1–35. Both James and Bakhtin are interested in how diverse characters are positioned around objects or situations, providing diverse perspectives or voices.

8. Mikhail Bakhtin, "Discourse in the Novel," in *The Dialogic Imagination: Four Essays by M. M. Bakhtin* (ed. M. Holquist; trans. C. Emerson and M. Holquist; Austin: University of Texas Press, 1992), 262.

9. Mikhail M. Bakhtin, *Problems of Dostoevsky's Poetics* (ed. and trans. V. W. McGee; Austin: University of Texas Press, 1986), 111, 135. Bakhtin finds "dialogic syncrises" and "anacrises" in the Gospels and Acts, defining *syncrisis* as "the juxtaposition of various points of view on a specific object," and *anacrisis* as "provocation through discourse."

tions described by the narrator. Some voices are interrogators, who do not recognize the full significance of these situations or who do not understand them. Others are interpreters, who speak about God's activity in these situations, transforming them into God events.

In Acts 2:1–41, for example, individual voices are artistically organized around a situation first depicted by the narrator (vv. 1–4). The narrator describes the community in a house at Pentecost (vv. 1–2) when a sound from the sky "like a rushing violent wind" fills the house. Tongues like fire rest upon each of the community members (v. 3) as they speak in a diversity of tongues (v. 4a). Up to this point in the narration (vv. 1–4a), the narrator uses the active voice to describe the actions of a sound (ἦχος … ἐπλήρωσεν in v. 2) and of tongues like fire (γλῶσσαι ὡσεὶ πυρὸς … ἐκάθισεν in v. 3). The narrator also uses the passive voice to depict the appearing of tongues like fire (ὤφθησαν in v. 3) and the filling of the Spirit (ἐπλήσθησαν in v. 4a), as well as two passive participles (φερομένης in v. 2; διαμεριζόμεναι in v. 3) depicting the driving wind and distribution of the tongues. The narrator then assigns the agency behind some of these acts: it is the Holy Spirit that gives (ἐδίδου) the community the ability to speak in these diverse tongues (v. 4b). But a gap remains: where did the Spirit come from? God's ultimate agency and involvement are not depicted by the narrator here. Instead, the narrator chooses to see this situation through the lenses of his characters, whose voices are artistically arranged around the situation (vv. 5–36).

After the narrator depicts the community speaking in a diversity of tongues (vv. 1–4), he describes a diverse multitude of Judeans and converts to Judaism from "every nation under heaven" (v. 5). They observe this situation and comment. They ask questions and misunderstand (vv. 5–13). The narrator describes their reactions as "confused" (v. 6), "astounded" and "amazed" (v. 7), and "amazed and perplexed" (v. 12). The multitude speaks, asking three questions (vv. 7, 8, and 12), making a first-person plural observation (vv. 9–11), and misunderstanding the cause of the situation (v. 13). In verse 7 they ask: "Are not all these people who are speaking Galileans?" In verse 8 they ask: "How does each of us hear in his or her native language?" In verses 9–11 they say what they hear: the community is worshipping God in diverse tongues. In verse 13 they claim that the community has had too much wine. So Luke, shaking off the muffled majesty of his narrator, chooses to see through the eyes, hear through the ears, and speak through the voices of his characters. As a result, Luke's narrative now begs for another explanation, an interpretation, another layer, which is reflected in the question in verse 12: "What does this mean?"

In answer to the question, Peter himself comments on the meaning of the situation (vv. 14–36). What stands out in Peter's explanation is God's agency behind what the onlookers observed, questioned, and misunderstood. Through Peter's discourse, the situation depicted by the narrator (vv. 1–4) and viewed and questioned by the onlookers (vv. 5–13) becomes a God event (vv. 14–36). God is the source of the outpouring of the Spirit (vv. 17–19). Indeed, God acts sixteen times in Peter's discourse: God says (v. 17), pours out (two times in vv. 17 and 18), gives wonders and signs (v. 19), works deeds, wonders, and signs (v. 22), raises from the dead (v. 24), does not abandon (v. 27), does not give over to corruption (v. 27), makes known and fills (v. 28), swears an oath and seats (v. 30), raises (v. 32), says (v. 34), places enemies as a footstool (v. 35), and appoints the Lord and Messiah (v. 36). With this layer of interpretation, Peter transforms the Pentecost scene into a God event, an event in which God is the ultimate agent, who raised Jesus from the dead (v. 32) and now caused this event at Pentecost (vv. 17–19).

In short, Acts 2:1–41 includes a variety of social speech types, a diversity of voices. Luke centers voices on a situation that is transformed into a God event by an interpretation. By doing so, Luke shakes off the muffled majesty of his narrator's voice and introduces an orchestra of other voices, of diverse speech types, ranging from sounds, to tongues, to questions, to misunderstandings, to observations, to interpretations, and ultimately to responses (vv. 37–41).[10]

Luke continues to use this arrangement throughout the early parts of Acts. After the God event at Pentecost, a crippled man is healed (Acts 3:1–8); other characters observe and are baffled by this situation (vv. 9–11); and Peter then interprets the situation as a God event (vv. 12–26).[11]

---

10. For a similar articulation of this pattern in Lukan pericopae, especially in Acts, see Linda M. Maloney, "*All That God Had Done with Them*": *The Narration of the Works of God in the Early Christian Community as Described in the Acts of the Apostles* (New York: Lang, 1991). Maloney detects a pattern of transition, arrival, assembly, report, and response.

11. "The God of Abraham, of Isaac, and of Jacob, the God of our ancestors has glorified God's servant Jesus" (v. 12); "God raised him [Jesus] from the dead" (v. 16a); "God has brought to fulfillment what God had announced through the mouth of all the prophets" (v. 18); "the Lord may grant you times of refreshment" (v. 20); "times of universal restoration about which God spoke through the mouth of his holy prophets" (v. 21); "a prophet like me [Moses] the Lord … will raise up" (v. 22); "the covenant that God made with your ancestors when God said to Abraham" (v. 25); "God raised up

Next, some of the religious leaders in Jerusalem become annoyed, mainly over the apostles' teaching (4:1–2), and question the power behind the healing of the crippled man (v. 7). Peter again interprets the situation as a God event (vv. 8–12).[12] This scene is then followed by further dialogue among the leaders (vv. 15–17) and between the leaders and the apostles (vv. 18–21). After the community is commanded to no longer speak, the community declares that it is better to obey God than human beings (v. 19) and prays together as one (vv. 23–31), attributing all major events thus far in the narrative, including Jesus' death (v. 28), to God's activity.

Up to the point of Paul's conversion (Acts 9:1–18), the arrangement of narration, interrogation and misunderstanding, and interpretation continues, with God's activity playing a central role in all interpretations.[13] Given this arrangement, Joseph Fitzmyer suggests a more appropriate title for Acts: "the Acts of God through the Apostles."[14] Even more, I suggest: "the Acts of God as Interpreted by the Apostles," which best reflects the narrative, which centers not only on the acts of God but how the acts of God are made manifest by interpretation. For God does not directly act in the narration.[15] But God's actions are spoken about by characters. God does not explicitly appear as an active agent in the narration.[16] But other characters lay explicit claim to God's presence and involvement in its situations.

God's servant and sent him to bless you" (v. 26). Note that God's agency in Jesus' resurrection gives Jesus' name power, power by which the crippled man is healed (v. 16b).

12. Peter speaks about Jesus "whom God raised from the dead" (v. 10). God's agency in resurrecting Jesus enacts power in Jesus' name, which causes the healing.

13. Of particular importance are Gamaliel's words before the Sanhedrin (Acts 5:34–39). Gamaliel, a Pharisee and Paul's preconversion teacher, tells his fellow Sanhedrin members that their chief concern ought to be whether God is involved in the acts of the apostles. If their work is of human agency, then their movement will fade away; if their work is of God's agency, then their movement cannot be opposed.

14. Joseph A. Fitzmyer, *The Acts of the Apostles: A New Translation with Introduction and Commentary* (AB 31; New York: Doubleday, 1998), 48.

15. See John A. Darr, *On Building Character: The Reader and the Rhetoric of Characterization in Luke–Acts* (Louisville: Westminster John Knox, 1992), 51–53; William H. Shepherd Jr., *The Narrative Function of the Holy Spirit as a Character in Luke–Acts* (SBLDS 147; Atlanta: Scholars Press, 1994), 255. Both Darr and Shepherd note that God remains "offstage" in the narrative.

16. The nominative θεός occurs 63 times in Acts. In every instance but one (19:11), the nominative appears in either direct or indirect discourse of characters.

2. The Narrative Context of Acts: Paul's Interpretive Voice

Narrations, interrogations and misunderstandings, and interpretations of God events continue as Luke's story moves into Gentile territory. Both the meeting of Peter and Cornelius (10:1–11:18) and the commissioning of Paul and Barnabas (13:1–3) mark the beginning of the expansion of God events into Gentile territory. In the former, the Jerusalem community, affirming God's actions among the Gentiles, interprets what has occurred with Peter and Cornelius: "God has therefore granted to the Gentiles repentance unto life" (11:18). In the latter, Paul, the chief interpreter for the rest of the narrative, is commissioned. There are numerous examples of Paul's interpretive voice after his commissioning, some of which have been well analyzed by scholars who pay particular attention to God's agency.[17] Here I will focus on one: Paul's Lystra speech in 14:8–18, which exemplifies how Luke continues to use his narrative arrangement: narration, interrogation and misunderstanding, and interpretation.

The narrator first sets up the situation at Lystra, which involves the healing of a man (vv. 8–10). In verse 8 the narrator describes a man with crippled feet (i.e., the feet are literally powerless [ἀδύνατος]), sitting (ἐκάθητο), lame from birth, having never walked (οὐδέποτε περιεπάτησεν). In verse 9 this man listens (ἤκουσεν) to Paul as Paul is speaking (λαλοῦντος), and then Paul fixes his eye on him (ἀτενίσας), seeing (ἰδών) that he has (ἔχει) the faith to be made whole (σωθῆναι). In verse 10 Pall then calls out (εἶπεν) in a loud voice for this man to stand up (ἀνάστηθι), and, as a result, the man springs up (ἥλατο) and walks (περιεπάτει). An analysis of the verbs in this narration is revealing. The scene moves from inaction to action. The incapacitated man listens to Paul speaking. Paul sees, recognizes, and commands the man to walk. The man walks and leaps. The actions depicted by the narrator are of human agency. In verse 9 two gaps, however, are left and call for an interpretation. First, who or what does the man have faith in? Second, who or what has made him whole (σωθῆναι)?

---

17. For example, on the Areopagus speech (17:22–31), see C. Kavin Rowe, *World Upside Down: Reading Acts in the Greco-Roman Age* (Oxford: Oxford University Press, 2009), 27–41. On all the Pauline speeches in Acts, see Marion L. Soards, *The Speeches in Acts: Their Content, Context, and Concerns* (Louisville: Westminster John Knox, 1994), 184–89. Soards's work on the speeches in Acts underscores the presence of divine agency in character discourse.

As noted above, gaps in situations call for interpretation. Bystanders then step in with questions (interrogation) or their own versions of the situation (misunderstanding). This episode chiefly involves misunderstanding.[18] After the man is healed, the narrator shifts to the point of view of the crowd (οἵ τε ὄχλοι ἰδόντες), which attributes agency to Paul (ὃ ἐποίησεν). The crowd then responds by claiming, "The gods have come down to us in human form" (v. 11). Divine agency is claimed in their discourse (οἱ θεοὶ ... κατέβησαν), but divinity is misunderstood. Barnabas is identified as Zeus, who is the ruler of the heavens, and Paul as Hermes, who is the messenger of the gods in the Greek pantheon. The crowd responds by trying to offer sacrifice to them (v. 13), but Paul and Barnabas respond by tearing their clothes because of this misunderstanding (v. 14). This misunderstanding now calls for an interpretation.

Paul is recognized as chief spokesperson by the crowd (v. 12), as a messenger of the gods. For it was Paul's discourse, to which the man was listening, that had sparked the man's faith (v. 9). Paul's discourse (albeit indirect) originally sparked the situation that will now be interpreted as a God event. Paul starts by claiming that they (he and Barnabas) are human, thereby denying their agency in the event: "we are the same nature as you, human beings" (v. 15a). Next, Paul denies the agency of the cults of Zeus and Hermes, interpreting them as empty: "you should turn from these empty things" (v. 15b). Finally, Paul invites them to turn to a living God (v. 15b), who is the true divine agent in the event. Paul grounds this agency by affirming God's actions in the past (vv. 15b–17): God "made [ἐποίησεν] heaven and the earth and the sea and all that is in them" (v. 15b, quoting Ps 146:6 LXX); God "in the past permitted [εἴασεν] the Gentiles to go their own ways" (v. 16); God "did not leave [ἀφῆκεν] Godself without a witness" (v. 17a); God, "doing good [ἀγαθουργῶν], giving [διδούς] you from heaven rains and fruitful seasons, filling [ἐμπιπλῶν] your hearts with food and gladness" (v. 17b). Whereas the narrator's discourse is filled with human actions (eight active verbs noted above), Paul's is filled with God's actions (six active verbs). Robert Wall sums up well the effect of this grounding:

---

18. See William S. Kurz, S.J., *Reading Luke–Acts: Dynamics of Biblical Narrative* (Louisville: Westminster John Knox, 1993), 149–55. Kurz highlights and outlines the misunderstanding motif in Acts: accusations of a drunk community at Pentecost (Acts 2:13, 15); Simon the Magician trying to gain access to power (8:18–24); the Lystra scene depicted above (14:11–13); and Paul as a curse and then as a god at Malta (28:4–6).

"God's prior witness to the nations consists of nature's good works; but the Creator's divine goodness is now climaxed in a mission that brings the good news of salvation (= healing) to them."[19] God has acted in the past and is acting now, which is affirmed in the epithet "a living God," a living God to which Paul calls the crowd.

Pauline interpretations of God events will continue to Rome, but the interpretations will not simply progress spatially. At least four new elements are added after this point in the narrative. First, instead of following multiple interpreters, the narrative generally follows one, Paul.[20] He is chief spokesperson (ὁ ἡγούμενος τοῦ λόγου), as recognized by those at Lystra (14:12) and has become chief interpreter in the narrative. From this point forward, interpretations of God events are reserved mainly for the voice of Paul, with the exception of Peter and James (Acts 15:1–21), the risen Jesus (18:9–10; 23:11), and Agabus (21:11).[21] This role as interpreter of God events will serve as a stable bridge between Acts and Paul's letters.

Second, although Luke shakes off the majesty of his narrator's voice and now tempers the voices of multiple interpreters, thereby highlighting Paul's own, Luke is careful to place Paul's voice in the context of dialogue. Paul's voice is not monologic; rather, it is dialogic, placed in context of other voices, whether explicit or implicit voices. For example, at the Jerusalem church (Acts 15:1–21), after Paul and Barnabas report "what God had done with them" (v. 4), Peter and James respond in dialogue by interpreting and affirming God's activity (vv. 7–11, 13–21).[22] Likewise, Luke introduces Paul's voice in the context of dialogue. Mark Given points out

---

19. Robert Wall, "The Acts of the Apostles," in *NIB*, 10:199.

20. The list of multiple interpreters prior to Paul's commissioning includes: Jesus (1:7–8; 9:4–6, 10–16), angels (1:11; 5:20; 8:26; 10:3–6; 12:7–10), Peter (1:16–22; 2:14–36; 3:11–26; 4:8–12; 5:3–4, 8–9; 5:29–32; 8:20–23; 10:34–43; 11:5–17; 12:11), Peter and John (4:19–20), the Jerusalem community (4:23–31; 11:18), Gamaliel (5:35–39), the Twelve (6:2–4), Stephen (7:2–60), Phillip (8:30–35), Ananias (9:17), a voice from heaven (10:13, 15), the Spirit (10:19–20), and Cornelius (10:30–33). Angels will not interpret events after Paul's commissioning.

21. One instance of Jesus' discourse is embedded in Paul's discourse (22:17–21); Ananias's discourse also appears in Paul's discourse (22:13–16).

22. The importance of interpreting God events is evident in this scene. At issue for the Jerusalem church is what God is doing among the Gentiles. In Peter's discourse alone, God "made choice" (v. 7), "bore witness by granting" (v. 8), "made no distinction," and "purified" (v. 9). See Luke Timothy Johnson ( ) and Maloney (*"All That God Had Done with Them"*) for how God events are interpreted in Acts 15:1–21.

that of the thirteen instances the verb διαλέγομαι in the New Testament, ten are in Acts.[23] Moreover, these ten instances refer to Paul (17:2, 17; 18:4, 19; 19:8, 9; 20:7, 9; 24:12, 25).[24] Given appropriately labels Luke's Paul as "a master dialectician" and "a new-fangled apocalyptic Socrates."[25] So while Paul is the chief interpreter, he is one in the midst of dialogue.

Third, Paul's interpretive voice becomes more personal, mainly due to his defense speeches in Acts 22–26. Paul often expresses his own agency in these speeches because he is defending his own actions.[26] However, as part of his defense, Paul does connect his actions to God (e.g., 22:3, 14; 24:14–16). This personalization, coupled with God's involvement, opens the door to the epistles, where Paul's defenses of his ministry are woven together with his personal experiences and interpretations of God's agency (e.g., Gal 1:15–17).

Fourth, Luke's narrator has remained self-effacing up to this point, but now brings forth a personal voice, speaking in the third-person plural in the so-called "we" sections (16:10–17; 20:5–15; 21:1–18; 27:1–28:16). This voice is anonymous. It does not interpret situations as God events; rather, it describes situations, remaining consistent with the narrator's pattern thus far. What, then, is the narrative purpose of these "we" passages? William Kurz and Susan Marie Praeder offer a concise explanation. Kurz, quoting and commenting on Praeder's earlier literary approach to the "we" sections, asserts: " 'The *anonymity* of the first-person narrator' indicates a self-effacing narrator who draws attention not to his own identity but simply to his presence in the participation of events. The priority is not on the narrator as a historical witness, but on drawing the intended readers into a vivid presentation of the episodes."[27] Luke, indeed, shakes off his

---

23. Mark D. Given, *Paul's True Rhetoric: Ambiguity, Cunning, and Deception in Greece and Rome* (Harrisburg, Pa.: Trinity Press International), 60–61.

24. Ibid. Given also points out the diversity of those with whom Paul dialogues: Judeans (17:2, 17; 18:4, 19; 19:8); philosophers and those at the Athenian agora (17:17–18); those in the hall of Tyrannus (19:9); fellow workers (20:7, 9); and Felix, a Roman governor (24:25).

25. Ibid., 60, 67.

26. For example, compare Stephen's defense before the Sanhedrin (7:1–60) and Paul's defense in Jerusalem (22:1–22). On the one hand, Stephen refers to his actions in the first person once, as he sees the risen Jesus (7:56); on the other hand, Paul refers to his own actions in the first person throughout.

27. Kurz, *Reading Luke–Acts*, 123 (emphasis original). See Susan Marie Praeder, "The Problem of First Person Narration in Acts," *NovT* 29 (1987): 214.

muffled majesty and embraces a first-person voice, allowing his audience, in James's words, "to live and breathe and rub shoulders and converse with the persons engaged in the struggle." He does this just enough not to overwhelm other voices.[28] This feature in Acts provides a bridge to an even closer look at the interpretive and personal voice of Paul in the seven uncontested letters. In sum, Luke has employed an arrangement of diverse voices. He has shaken off his muffled majesty to allow his characters to interpret in his narrative. He ends Acts with an up-close view of Paul as the chief interpreter, which unbeknown to him, serves as a unifying bridge to the epistolary voice of Paul. In the next two sections, I will describe Paul's epistolary voice within the narrative context of Acts.

3. The Epistolary Voice of Paul in the Narrative Context of Acts

Like the interpretive voices in Acts, Paul's epistolary voice captures the situations that he and his communities face and transforms them into God events. The recent work of Alain Badiou sheds light on Paul as an interpreter and helps connect his interpretive role in his letters with Acts. Badiou's primary interest is Paul as an interpreter of the event, focusing on *the how* of Paul, not *the what*.[29] Badiou describes Paul as "a poet-thinker of the event," that is, one who recognizes what is not seen in a situation and brings it to the fore by poetically naming it as an event.[30] According to

---

28. One of the criticisms of a literary approach to the "we" sections involves asking why Luke did not use it as a literary device more often (see Fitzmyer, *Acts*, 100). But in shaking off the muffled majesty, Luke tempers his use of the first person in association with the narrator.

29. Alain Badiou, *Saint Paul: The Foundation of Universalism* (Cultural Memory in the Present; Stanford, Calif.: Stanford University Press, 2003), 1. Badiou says that he cares "nothing for the Good News [Paul] declares." He does not read Paul "to bear witness to any sort of faith, or even antifaith." For a summary of Badiou's work on the event, see Henry Krips, "The Politics of Badiou: From Absolute Singularity to Objet-a" (paper presented at the plenary session in the Bradshaw Lecture Series "Event and Process," Claremont, Claremont Graduate University, December 2007). For a summary of Badiou's work on Paul, see Alain Gignac, "Taubes, Badiou, Agamben: Receptions of Paul by Non-Christian Philosophers," in *Reading Romans with Contemporary Philosophers and Theologians* (ed. David Odell-Scott; New York: T&T Clark, 2007), 171–83.

30. Badiou, *Saint Paul*, 2.

Badiou, Paul recognizes and names Jesus' resurrection as the event, which is interpreted in the situation of Jesus' death.[31] Based on the narrative arrangement of Acts and Paul's own interpretive voice, however, I argue that Paul recognizes and names "God resurrecting Jesus" as the event in Jesus' death.

Badiou calls the act of naming an event an "interpretive intervention."[32] Badiou claims that there is a gap between a situation and an event. A situation involves an infinite number of components and elements (e.g., wind, voices, sounds, tongues); an event involves a singularity (e.g., God has acted).[33] This gap calls for an interpreter to intervene and name the event. In being named, the event is unified from the multiplicity of the situation, which was filtered through the event's unifying principle.[34] The event calls for future faithful interpreters to continue the interpretation of it and its effects, assuring its sustenance and renewal.[35]

---

31. Ibid., 70. Badiou calls Jesus' death "the evental site," which is "that datum that is immanent to a situation and enters into the composition of the event itself." He then says, "Resurrection alone is a given of the event, which mobilizes the site and whose operation is salvation." It is important to note that just because an event comes into awareness through interpretation and naming, it does not follow that the event itself is invented by the interpreter. Badiou himself confesses atheism; however, this by no means is due to the philosophical system he is setting up here.

32. See Alain Badiou, *Being and Event* (trans. Oliver Feltham; London: Continuum, 2005), 181. Badiou describes an interpretive intervention as declaring "that an event is presented in a situation; as the arrival in being of non-being, the arrival amidst the visible of the invisible."

33. Krips ("Politics of Badiou," 3) notes that the event is "like a secret heart" of a situation, "which lies in the midst, but separate from the disseminating field of facts and traces that the historian includes in it."

34. Badiou says, "I term *intervention* any procedure by which a multiple is recognized as an event" (*Being and Event,* 202). Badiou uses a historian's view of the French Revolution as a negative example. He bemoans the historian who takes inventory of all the elements, traces, and facts involved at that time, thereby undoing "the one of the event" to become "the forever infinite numbering of the gestures, things and words that co-existed with it" (180). See also Krips, "Politics of Badiou," 1–3.

35. Krips underscores Badiou's insistence of the event being renewed through continual interpretation by faithful subjects ("Politics of Badiou," 5–6; Badiou, *Being and Event,* 341–42). Krips says that this fidelity is not a matter of "sticking to formulaic instructions." This fidelity includes "resisting any attempt to 'absolutize' the Event" in the face of new contingencies. Krips, in reference to Badiou, goes on to argue that an Event "must always and already be reconstituted/renewed through continual acts of interpretation that extend it into the unknown."

A problem, however, persists in considering only the epistolary voice of Paul for claiming him as Badiou's "poetic interpreter of the event." Neither the situation nor its multiple elements exist apart from Paul's uncontested letters. That is, all that remains is the interpretive voice of Paul that has already transformed the situation into an event under the unifying principle in God's actions in Jesus. Acts, alternatively, provides a narrative context in which an interpretive process is depicted, starting with narration, moving to interrogation or misunderstanding, and ending in interpretation.[36] It depicts gaps between the narration (situation) and its meaning (event). It depicts characters, including Paul, intervening in the gap by declaring each situation a God event in Jesus. Without this narrative context of Acts, there would be no accounting for how situations call for an interpretation of a God event. Acts, in other words, underscores the importance of interpretive acts in the Pauline epistles, which, through fidelity, continue the interpretive process, a process that is necessary for the vitality, continuance, and renewal of the event, the event of God resurrecting Jesus from the dead. In short, it shows the reader what to look for in Paul's letters, in Paul's interpretive process.

4. Paul's Interpretive Voice in 1 Thessalonians 1:1–10

Given that Paul's interpretive voice is set up by Acts, what are its features in the uncontested letters? In this section, I use 1 Thess 1:1–10 to describe Paul's interpretive voice through which he recognizes God events in the situations of his communities. There are four characteristics of Paul's interpretive voice: (1) his personal voice and (2) his voice of shared situations. These first two characteristics mark the situations he intimately shares with his communities. The next two characteristics are (3) his God-centered voice and (4) his expansive voice. These characteristics mark the interpretations that he shares and expands with his communities.

Like the character Paul in Acts, the epistolary Paul interprets situations often in response to interrogations and misunderstandings. Although these interrogations, misunderstandings, and situations cannot be viewed apart from Paul's interpretive voice, they can be reconstructed by working back from Paul's interpretations. In the case of 1 Thessalonians, it is clear

---

36. Voices of interrogation (1 Cor 15:35) and misunderstanding (e.g., 1 Cor 6:12–13; 7:1–5; 8:1; 14:22–23) are embedded in Paul's interpretations.

that Paul, being orphaned from the community (1 Thess 2:17), is initially worried. He wonders whether the situations he experienced with the community would take root (3:5). As a result, he sends Timothy to the community (3:2), who in turn returns to Paul to report good news. What they had originally shared with the community had taken root (3:6). Timothy also brings back some questions from the community, misunderstandings about life after death (4:13). In the meantime, Paul also seems to have received good news from others (1:8–9). It is within this situation that Paul interprets God events and writes a letter of thanksgiving and instruction to the Thessalonians.

First, Paul's personal voice resounds throughout 1 Thess 1:1–10. Paul unites this personal voice with Silvanus and Timothy, expressed in the first-person plural (e.g., εὐχαριστοῦμεν and προσευχῶν ἡμῶν in v. 2; τὸ εὐαγγέλιον ἡμῶν and ἐγενήθημεν in v. 5; μιμηταὶ ἡμῶν in v. 6; μὴ χρείαν ἔχειν ἡμᾶς λαλεῖν in v. 8; περὶ ἡμῶν and ἔσχομεν in v. 9). Paul is not the lone interpreter of situations here. He is accompanied by coworkers in the interpretive task, coworkers who are intimately involved in the situations being interpreted.[37] In Acts, collective interpretations of God events occur (e.g., Acts 4:23–31; 11:18). At Lystra, it is both Barnabas and Paul who interpret the God event (14:14), while Paul is the one recognized as the chief spokesperson (14:12). Likewise, in 1 Thessalonians Paul is the chief spokesperson.[38] His name is listed first in the greeting (1:1). Three times in the letter he singles himself out with the first-person singular (2:18; 3:5; 5:27). These instances are significant for highlighting Paul's personal voice. Raymond Collins points out that Paul's use of the first-person singular not only confirms Paul as the author, but "the depth of his affect for the Thessalonians," emphatically expressing his ongoing desire to visit the Thessalonians after being orphaned from them (2:18), and ultimately explaining his decision to send Timothy to find out about their state (3:5).[39] This

---

37. See Sean A. Adams, "Paul's Letter Opening and Greek Epistolography," in *Paul and the Ancient Letter Form* (ed. Stanley E. Porter and Sean A. Adams; Leiden: Brill, 2010), 43–44. Adams asserts that incorporation of co-senders in Paul's letters is due chiefly to the co-senders' involvement with each community. Paul's co-senders are listed by name in four other uncontested letters: Sosthenes (1 Cor 1:1) and Timothy (2 Cor 1:1; Phil 1:1; Phlm 1).

38. See Raymond F. Collins, *The Birth of the New Testament: The Origin and Development of the First Christian Generation* (New York: Crossroad, 1993), 128.

39. Ibid., 126; quotation, 128.

depth of desire underscores Paul's personal longing for the community (cf. 1 Thess 2:8).

Furthermore, this longing for reconnection expresses Paul's personal attachment not only to the Thessalonians but to the situations he is interpreting for them, the situations that had bonded them together (i.e., "for our gospel did not come to you in word alone," 1:5). For Badiou, a key component of an interpretive process involves the inseparable connection between the interpreter and the situation that is being named as an event. Interpretations of events do not happen from afar, but within the field of the situation itself, with personal involvement.[40] So the first component of Paul's interpretive voice is the personal connection that he and his coworkers have with the situation and those involved in it. They are living and breathing and rubbing shoulders and conversing with the persons engaged in the struggle.

Second, Paul's personal voice shares in the situations of his audience. In 1 Thess 1:1–10 Paul's voice is shared in two ways: (1) his use of terms of remembrance, and (2) his use of second- and third-person plural personal pronouns. In the opening, Paul uses four verbs of remembrance and knowing (μνείαν ποιούμενοι in v. 2; μνημονεύοντες in v. 3; εἰδότες in v. 4; οἴδατε in v. 5), two of the verbs having a present, continuous aspect.[41] Paul and his coworkers remember and continue to remember the situations involving the Thessalonians. The subjects of remembrance are Paul, his coworkers, and the audience. In the first three instances, the subjects of the verb are Paul and his coworkers. In the fourth instance, the subject is the audience, "just as you know" (v. 5). In this instance, Paul invites his audience to envision the situations he is interpreting, shifting to their point of view, asking them to focus on what he wants to interpret, but through their own lenses.[42] The interpretive process, therefore, is shared.

---

40. On this point, Krips sums up Badiou well: "the process of discerning a new pattern that precipitates the emergence of the Event is not merely a matter of an academic historian years later discovering what existed all along but was hidden. Instead the process of discerning is contemporaneous with the Event—an action by the participants themselves, which, rather than cognitive in nature, is a militant commitment to see things differently" ("Politics of Badiou," 4).

41. For others instances of μνείαν ποιοῦμαι, see Rom 1:9; Phil 1:3; and Phlm 4.

42. "You know" is repeated throughout 1 Thessalonians (2:1, 5, 11; 3:3, 4; 4:2; 5:2). See Collins, Birth of the New Testament, 129.

The objects of remembrance and knowing include the audience (v. 2); the audience's work of faith, labor of love, and steadfastness of hope (v. 3); the audience's election by God (v. 4); and the actions of Paul and his coworkers, which did not come in word alone but in power (v. 5). The remembrances are focused on past, shared situations (vv. 2–3, 5), which are used as grounds for interpreting them as God events: "knowing, brothers and sisters loved by God [ὑπὸ θεοῦ], you are chosen" (v. 4). Unlike Luke's narrative genre, Paul's epistolary genre does not allow for multiple layers of voices, but terms such as *remembering* and *knowing* at least function as markers of shared situations, which have now been interpreted as God events.

Paul's extensive use of second-person pronouns in the opening of 1 Thessalonians likewise establishes the interaction between Paul and his audience over their shared situations (ὑμῖν in vv. 1 and 5; ὑμῶν in vv. 2, 3, 4, 8a, and 8b; ὑμᾶς in vv. 5a, 5b, 7, and 9). It reveals, as Collins points out, "the dialogic nature of Paul's letter."[43] What is more, there is not only "we" and "you" dialogic interaction in 1 Thessalonians, but also first-person plural instances that encompass both "the senders and addresses in a single group" (κυρίου ἡμῶν Ἰησοῦ Χριστοῦ ἔμπροσθεν τοῦ θεοῦ καὶ πατρὸς ἡμῶν in v. 3; Ἰησοῦν τὸν ῥυόμενον ἡμᾶς ἐκ τῆς ὀργῆς τῆς ἐρχομένης in v. 10).[44] Thus Paul at times is inclusive of the whole group, of himself, his coworkers, and his community, all bound together in the first-person plural. Collins focuses primarily on verse 10 as an instance of "the single 'us,'" where Jesus rescues "not only Paul and his companions but also the Thessalonian Christians, now formed into a single community of faith with Paul and those who accompanied him."[45] But in verse 3 Paul describes the community's hope in Jesus "our Lord" before "our God." God and Jesus unify Paul, his coworkers, and the Thessalonians together as "our," as one. In verse 10 it is also God's action in raising Jesus from the dead that allows for the rescuing of "us." So both instances center on a shared event in God and Jesus, more specifically, on what God has done in Jesus (v. 10) and will be in relation to Jesus (v. 3).[46] So the letter is personal and dialogic,

---

43. Ibid., 128–29.

44. Ibid.

45. Ibid.

46. Giving thanks for past and future God events is unique in comparison with Hellenistic letters. See Raymond E. Collins, "A Significant Decade: The Trajectory of the Hellenistic Epistolary Thanksgiving," in Porter and Adams, *Paul and Ancient*

placing Paul, his coworkers, and his audience around shared situations. At the same time, it is interpretive, bringing all together around events, God events in Jesus, which are interpreted by Paul and his coworkers. In both ways Paul's interpretive process is similar to Acts.

Third, Paul's voice is God-centered.[47] Just as in Acts, God-centered discourse is the connective force through which situations become events. This God-centeredness is especially the case in the openings of his letters.[48] In comparison with the thanksgiving sections in Hellenistic papyrus letters, Paul's openings uniquely focus on God and God's activity, establishing the community's connection with God.[49] Paul immediately connects God to the Thessalonians' situation. Paul utilizes a full range of cases to speak about God, which in rhetoric is a way of establishing the subject of a discourse.[50] Paul strings together his opening words with references to God: "by God," "to God," "before God," "by God," "toward God"; and he ends by depicting the act of God raising Jesus from the dead.

Letter Form, 181. Collins notes: "the author's memory comes into play more often in Paul's thanksgiving than it does in the papyri letters.... In addition, the future—especially the eschatological future—perspective with which Paul's later thanksgivings culminate is absent from the epistolary thanksgivings of the papyri letters."

47. See Raymond F. Collins, "God in the First Letter to the Thessalonians: Paul's Earliest Written Appreciation of ho theos," LS 16 (1991): 137–39. Collins points out that θεός is by far the most common noun in 1 Thessalonians (36 times), "occurring 50% more often than the next most common noun, 'Kurios (Lord)'" (139). Collins provides the following data on θεός in the uncontested letters: 153 times in Romans, 106 in 1 Corinthians, 79 in 2 Corinthians, 31 in Galatians, 23 in Philippians, 2 in Philemon.

48. Rom 1:1, 4, 7a, 7b, 8, 9, 10; 1 Cor 1:1, 2, 3, 4a, 4b, 9; 2 Cor 1:1a, 1b, 2, 3a, 3b, 4, 9; Gal 1:1, 3, 4; Phil 1:2, 3, 8, 11; Phlm 3, 4.

49. See David W. Pao, "Gospel within the Constraints of an Epistolary Form: Pauline Introductory Thanksgivings and Paul's Theology of Thanksgiving," in Porter and Adams, Paul and Ancient Letter Form, 120–22.

50. 1 Thess 1:1, 2, 9 (dative); 1:3, 4 (genitive); 1:8, 9 (accusative); ἤγειρεν in 1:10 (nominative implicit). See Mikeal C. Parsons, "Luke and the Progymnasmata: A Preliminary Investigation into the Preliminary Exercises," in Contextualizing Acts: Lukan Narrative and Greco-Roman Discourse (ed. Todd C. Penner and Caroline Vander Stichele; SBLSymS 20; Atlanta: Society of Biblical Literature, 2003), 56–58. In rhetoric textbooks from Paul's era, a writer is encouraged to establish the subject or topic by referring to it in a variety cases. See Aelius Theon of Alexandria, Progymnasmata, 74.24–35; cf. Quintilian, Inst. 9.1.34; 9.3.27–28, 67 (Latin).

The Thessalonian community is united "by God the Father," ἐν θεῷ πατρί (v. 1); that is, in the instrumental sense, they are brought into existence as a community by God.[51] Thus, from the start of the letter, Paul assigns agency to God (along with Jesus) in the birth of the community. It follows, therefore, that Paul, Silvanus, and Timothy direct their thanks "to God," τῷ θεῷ (v. 2), who has not only birthed the community but also now sustains it, which is the reason why they are thankful and continue to be thankful in the present, continuous aspect (εὐχαριστοῦμεν). The entirety of the thanksgiving (vv. 2–10) is directed to one being, God. In verse 3 the object of the community's hope is "our Lord Jesus Christ before our God and Father [ἔμπροσθεν τοῦ θεοῦ καὶ πατρὸς ἡμῶν]."[52] And the community's faith is directed "toward God," πρὸς τὸν θεόν (v. 8). Thus all the major subjects in Paul's opening are connected to God: Paul and his coworkers (v. 2), Jesus (v. 3), and the community (vv. 1, 8). God is the connective force in Paul's discourse.

Like Acts, the crux of 1 Thess 1:1–10 is God's activity. As noted above, the community has been formed by God. What is more, the community is loved "by God," ἠγαπημένοι ὑπὸ θεοῦ (v. 4), leading Paul to interpret their election (τὴν ἐκλογὴν ὑμῶν), which implies God's activity as well.[53] Throughout the opening, aside from these implicit and passive constructions, Paul, his coworkers, and the community have been doing the direct action (e.g., giving thanks, calling to mind). But in verse 10, at the climax of the opening, God's direct action is depicted by Paul. He depicts God's chief act in Jesus: "whom God raised from the dead" (ὃν ἤγειρεν ἐκ [τῶν] νεκρῶν).[54] It is from God's agency in this event that everything flows: the Thessalonians initial faith, their current standing, and their future resur-

---

51. The instrumental use of ἐν is also in 1 Thess 2:2. For this reading see Abraham J. Malherbe, *The Letters to the Thessalonians* (AB 32B; New York: Doubleday, 2000), 99. Malherbe paraphrases v. 1 as follows: "the assembly of the Thessalonians brought into being by God the Father and the Lord Jesus Christ."

52. There is a question concerning what ἔμπροσθεν τοῦ θεοῦ modifies. Are Paul and his coworkers giving thanks and remembering before God? Or does the community hope for Jesus in the presence of God? The former is awkward, especially since Paul has already directed thanks to God in v. 2. The latter is consistent with Paul's depiction of the future hope in other places (1 Thess 2:19; 3:13; 2 Cor 5:10; Phil 3:13) and the crux of his interpretation in the opening (1 Thess 1:10).

53. Collins ("God in 1 Thessalonians," 152) notes the perfect tense here. God continues to love the community.

54. Ibid., 148. Collins notes: "Half of the times that Paul makes explicit reference

rection and deliverance from judgment, to which later in the letter Paul attributes God's agency (1 Thess 4:14–16).[55]

The crux of 1 Thess 1:1–10 not only involves God's act in raising Jesus and its effects, but also the community's response to God: turning from idols to serve the living and true God (v. 9). Paul's interpretation of their response sheds light on a key question about God's role: why is God the connective force? Why, in other words, is it important for Paul that situations are interpreted as God events? For Paul's Gentile audience, the turning involves movement from many to one. The community moves from multiplicity (idols) to a singular, definitive, and living truth (God).[56] The same occurs in Luke's depiction of Paul and Barnabas in Lystra (14:15–16). In Paul's discourse there, Gentiles are described as going their own ways (v. 16). But he then invites them to turn from dead idols to the living God (v. 15). They are invited to move from multiplicity (ways and idols) to singularity (living God). Interpreting situations as God events (and not just as important events) is crucial to Paul and Luke because God is the unifying principle, the one, true, and living God (θεῷ ζῶντι καὶ ἀληθινῷ). Interpretations involving God are what fill the gaps between situations and important events, both for Paul and Luke. God is the connective force.

Fourth, Paul's voice is expansive. Paul paradoxically speaks about shaking off his own voice. He is similar to Luke here, but in his own way and within his own genre. The gospel did not come to the community "in word alone" but in power (1 Thess 1:5). And now "the word of the Lord" has sounded forth from the Thessalonians (v. 8a), but not from Paul. The majesty of his voice has been shaken off, but the word that he originally sounded forth in Thessalonica has now, through others, rested upon Paul's own ears in other places, Macedonia and Achaia (v. 8). The Thessalonians' faith in God has gone forth in every place (ἐν παντὶ τόπῳ), in such a way that Paul and his coworkers need not say anything (v. 8b). Paul's voice need not speak because other voices are now speaking about God events, about the community's faith in God. Paul's gospel, Paul's interpretation of God

---

to God in 1 Thessalonians, he links the mention of God with a reference to Jesus." See 1 Thess 1:3, 9–10; 2:14–15 (2x); 3:2, 11, 13; 4:1, 14; 5:9, 18, 23.

55. Ibid. Collins points out that for Paul the last day is "the day in whose scenario God is the initiator and chief actor."

56. Ibid., 140. Collins recognizes the significance here: "God is singular, the idols are plural. There is one God, but many idols."

events, has become universalized, going forth everywhere through people other than himself.[57]

In sum, Paul, Silvanus, and Timothy initially shared a powerful situation with the Thessalonian community. Having to depart quickly, they were then orphaned from the community and wondered whether what had occurred took root. After sending Timothy and receiving good news from him and many other people about the state of the community and God's actions in it, Paul personally interprets the entire shared situation, past, present and future, as a God event, clothing it in references to God. This interpretation assures the community that they are chosen by God. It assures them that they will indeed be raised together from the dead by God, tempering their concerns and misunderstandings about life after death. First Thessalonians is Paul's earliest uncontested letter. From this point forward, Paul will continue to share situations with diverse communities, uniquely marking each as a God event, just as the interpreters in Acts moved from Jerusalem to Rome, marking the situations as God events.

CONCLUSION

What unifies the Acts of the Apostles and Paul's uncontested letters is not simply *content*, but *the act* of interpretation, personal interpretation of God events, more specifically, God's event in Jesus. This act of interpretation, however, is not exclusive, concentrating only on one God event in the past (i.e., God resurrecting Jesus), but inclusive to all the events that precede it (e.g., creation in Acts 14:8–18) and all effects that follow (1 Thess 1:1–10), effects that continue to be interpreted as God events. This ongoing interpretation is presented in both Acts and in the Pauline epistles. As demonstrated above, both Acts and 1 Thessalonians focus on God's actions in Jesus not as a past event but as present effects interpreted as God events, from Jerusalem to Rome in Acts, and from Thessalonica to Macedonia and Achaia in 1 Thessalonians. On the one hand, this interpretation of God events is the *unifying* principle between Acts and Paul, moving from multiplicity to one God. On the other hand, the continuing interpretation of the effects of this event is the *diversifying* principle between Acts and Paul's uncontested letters, as situations are interpreted in diverse settings.

---

57. In moving from situations to an event, Paul creates an expansive and universal message and a growing and evolving fidelity to it. This quality is what draws Badiou's philosophy to Paul. See Badiou, *Saint Paul*, 108–11.

Declaring the coexistence of unity and diversity in the New Testament remains part of the legacy of Frank Matera. Matera advocates an approach that affirms the coexistence of unity and diversity, as demonstrated in his *New Testament Ethics*, *New Testament Christology*, and *New Testament Theology*.[58] Matera has built frameworks from the New Testament onto which diverse voices attach and unify. His students remain committed to this coexistence, though they articulate it in diverse ways. What is more, Matera's commitment to unity and diversity does not end with New Testament texts. Matera's passion for placing the voices of the New Testament in modern contexts is apparent in his *Strategies for Preaching Paul*.[59] It is, therefore, appropriate to end by discussing how the interpretive patterns in Acts and Paul inform us today.

Both Acts and Paul invite interpreters not only to look *in* and *toward* the text, interpreting God events and rubbing shoulders alongside Luke's characters and Paul's communities, but also to look *out* and *beyond* the text, onto current situations. The interpretive patterns of Acts and of Paul's uncontested letters suggest the need to continue dialogue, interpreting situations that are potentially God events. *What* Paul said in Acts and in the letters has challenged interpreters over the centuries; but *how* Paul interprets events in Acts and in the letters challenges interpreters to look outward, onto a modern scene, to transform the most challenging and mundane situations into God events. In his *Strategies for Preaching Paul*, Matera confesses: "As I often tell my students, while I believe in Christ, my passion is for Paul. In reading his letters, I encounter someone who has understood how the proclamation of the gospel illumines the human situation and solves the most mundane problems."[60] Matera then speaks about Paul being "deeply pastoral" and challenges his students to "understand Paul's pastoral technique" and Paul's insight into the human situation. Matera challenges his students to ask: "How can I respond to the needs of my congregation in light of what God has done in Christ?"[61]

---

58. Frank J. Matera, *New Testament Ethics: The Legacies of Jesus and Paul* (Louisville: Westminster John Knox, 1996), 1–10, 248–55; *New Testament Christology* (Louisville: Westminster John Knox, 1999), 243–56; *New Testament Theology*, 423–80.

59. Idem, *Strategies for Preaching Paul* (Collegeville, Minn.: Liturgical Press, 2001), 1–3.

60. Ibid., 2.

61. Ibid., 179.

Luke also models this interpretive technique in his own way, shaking off the muffled majesty of authorship and allowing diverse voices to interpret situations as God events. New situations produce vibrancy in interpretation, challenging us to interpret God events in new ways, just as the voices in Luke's narrative do, just as the epistolary Paul does. Luke's technique, therefore, leaves us not with an answer but with an interpretive question to ponder, one crafted by Luke Timothy Johnson: "How can we understand the actions of God that go beyond our previous grasp of the way God acts?"[62]

---

62. Johnson, *Scripture and Discernment*, 106.

CRUCIFORMITY ACCORDING TO JESUS AND PAUL

Michael J. Gorman

The subtitle of Frank Matera's important book on New Testament ethics serves as a fitting summary of the New Testament: "The Legacies of Jesus and Paul."[1] A natural question arising from this characterization is whether and how these two figures and their legacies are in sympathy or in conflict. Interest in the connection between Jesus and Paul, and between the Gospels and Paul—two related but not synonymous topics—has been experiencing a revival.[2] This may be partly driven by concern in some quarters that while Jesus preached and practiced a radical and inclusive reign of God, Paul altered and restricted that message.[3] One significant area of interest in this discussion, then, is the topic of the freedoms and demands associated with the soteriological offer—that is, ethics.

In this essay I will not attempt to determine whether Paul was more or less "liberal" than Jesus on inclusivity or other contemporary issues. Rather, I will to go back to a more fundamental moral/spiritual question: the basic nature of discipleship in both Jesus and Paul as cruciformity, or cross-shaped discipleship. The significance of this congruence should not be underestimated, for in dealing with the story of the cross and resurrec-

---

1. Frank J. Matera, *New Testament Ethics: The Legacies of Jesus and Paul* (Louisville: Westminster John Knox, 1996). I offer this small project in gratitude for the many large contributions of Frank Matera to New Testament theology and ethics.

2. See, e.g., Todd D. Still, ed., *Jesus and Paul Reconnected: Fresh Pathways into an Old Debate* (Grand Rapids: Eerdmans, 2007); James D. G. Dunn, *Jesus, Paul, and the Gospels* (Grand Rapids: Eerdmans, 2011); Michael F. Bird and Joel Willitts, eds., *Paul and the Gospels: Christologies, Conflicts and Convergences* (LNTS 411; London: T&T Clark, 2011).

3. See, e.g., the more popular work by J. R. Daniel Kirk, *Jesus Have I Loved, but Paul? A Narrative Approach to the Problem of Pauline Christianity* (Grand Rapids: Baker Academic, 2012).

tion in both the Gospels and Paul, we are engaging the Christian master story and thus also the very heart of Christian ethics.

Cruciformity as a Potential Key Connection between Jesus and Paul

Despite its potential significance, the cruciform connection between Jesus and Paul has received insufficient scholarly attention, normally only mentioned briefly in discussing this or that text rather than viewed as a fundamental link. We begin, therefore, with a brief review of two hints at the significance of this connection.

A recent helpful contribution to the Jesus-Paul question comes from James Dunn.[4] He posits three major continuities between Jesus and Paul: (1) the openness of God's grace, (2) eschatological tension and the Spirit, and (3) the love command, specifically in relation to the Law.[5] While each of these has ethical implications, only the last is specifically ethical in focus. Dunn concludes that *"Paul drew his attitude to the Law from Jesus,"* that *"nowhere is the line of continuity and influence from Jesus to Paul clearer than in the love command,"* and that both Paul and Jesus "summed up the whole law" in the love command and used it "to discern the commandments that really mattered."[6]

Dunn is certainly onto something important here, but he does not tell us much about the nature, or content, of this love command. Nor, curiously, does Dunn connect this ethical theme materially to Jesus' death.[7] In the conclusion to his book on New Testament ethics, however, Frank Matera begins to make the connection that Dunn, at least here, fails to note.[8] Matera offers seven themes as a synthesis of the enduring ethical legacy of Jesus and Paul, their common "soteriological ethic."[9] The fourth theme is this: "The personal example of Jesus and Paul instructs and sus-

---

4. Dunn, *Jesus, Paul, and the Gospels.*

5. Ibid., 95–115.

6. Ibid., 114–15 (emphasis original).

7. Dunn does note that for Paul (Rom 8:4) the purpose of Christ's death was so that the Law might be fulfilled in believers (ibid., 113). He also briefly links Jesus' death to the first two continuities, but only in discussing Paul (103–4, 108)—not Jesus.

8. Matera, *New Testament Ethics,* 248–55.

9. Ibid., 249.

tains believers in the moral life."[10] At the core of this theme is not merely the *form* of imitation but its *substance*: as Jesus called the disciples to follow him, which includes following him in his manner of dying, Paul called believers to follow Jesus by "entering into the mystery of his death and resurrection,"[11] as Paul himself had done. In other words, an essential component of the material continuity between Jesus and Paul is cruciformity (my term,[12] not Matera's)—conformity to the pattern of the Christ-story told in both the Gospels and the Pauline Letters.[13]

Matera's sixth theme connecting Jesus and Paul is "love"—for God, neighbor, and enemy, meaning Godlike mercy and compassion (for Jesus), and Christlike self-sacrifice, as manifested on the cross (for Paul).[14] A bit surprisingly, Matera does not posit here a connection between cruciformity and love in Jesus, though the overall argument of the book suggests that he does actually make that connection.[15]

What I propose to do in the remainder of this essay is to develop Matera's thesis about the centrality of cruciform imitation/discipleship in both Jesus and Paul, connecting it, finally, to the love command stressed by Dunn. I will proceed primarily by demonstrating thematic connections between the mandates associated with the three synoptic passion predictions in Mark and Paul's own teaching.

We will see that discipleship for Jesus is a passion-shaped vocation, or metaphorical taking up of one's cross (Mark 8:34 par.). It consists specifically of (1) self-denial and suffering in witness to the gospel (8:31–34 par.); (2) hospitality to the weak and marginalized, represented by children (9:31–37 par.); and (3) service to others rather than domination (10:32–45 par.). At many levels the nature of this existence is paradoxical, not least in the very notion that the life of the living should take the form of dying.

So too for Paul, whose constant participation in the death of Jesus means life for himself and especially others (e.g., 2 Cor 4:8–12). Although Paul does not use the term *disciple* or *discipleship* per se, his spirituality

---

10. Ibid., 252.

11. Ibid.

12. See esp. Michael J. Gorman, *Cruciformity: Paul's Narrative Spirituality of the Cross* (Grand Rapids: Eerdmans, 2001).

13. Matera, *New Testament Ethics*, 252.

14. Ibid., 254–55.

15. For example, Matera interprets Jesus' self-giving service and ransom in Mark (Mark 10:45) as the supreme example of Jesus' compassion (ibid., 34).

of Spirit-enabled conformity to Christ crucified includes the summons to embody Jesus' threefold call: (1) bearing faithful witness even to the point of suffering; (2) identifying with the weak as an expression of God's cruciform wisdom and power; and (3) lovingly, as a servant, seeking the benefit of others rather than self. In sum, Paul's spirituality of participation in the death of Christ is congruent with—indeed fundamentally the same as—Jesus' call to cross-shaped discipleship.[16]

THE NATURE, PURPOSE, AND AUTHENTICITY OF THE "PASSION PREDICTIONS"

It has long been noted that three texts in Mark's Gospel (with parallels in Matthew and Luke) serve to convey Jesus' predictions of his own suffering, death, and resurrection. These "passion predictions," as they are usually called, are followed by misunderstanding on the part of the disciples and then corrective teaching by Jesus about discipleship in light of his own fate. This combination of passion prediction and summons to passion-shaped discipleship is so consistent (especially in Mark), and so indicative of the inseparability of Christology and discipleship for the synoptic evangelists, that two conclusions seem to follow.

The first conclusion is that each of these texts should be referred to not merely as a "passion prediction" but as a "passion prediction-summons," meaning a call to passion-shaped discipleship, or, in a word, cruciformity.[17] The key point here is the substantive correlation between the form of Jesus' death and the shape of the disciples' life, with each being paradoxical.[18]

The second conclusion, perhaps a bit more controversial in some scholarly circles, is that Mark—no matter how creative or insightful a storyteller-theologian he was—is probably portraying something inherent to the message of Jesus himself. Hence the title of this essay refers to "Jesus"

---

16. This essay expands upon a short article, "Cruciformity," *Dictionary of Scripture and Ethics* (ed. Joel B. Green et al.; Grand Rapids: Baker Academic, 2011), 197–98.

17. Although the verb "crucify" appears in Mark only in the passion narrative, it is clear from 8:34 that the means of Jesus' predicted death will be crucifixion, and this almost certainly goes back to Jesus himself (see below).

18. See especially Narry F. Santos, *Slave of All: The Paradox of Authority and Servanthood in the Gospel of Mark* (JSNTSup 237; Sheffield: Sheffield Academic Press, 2003), with a detailed discussion of our texts (145–212). Matera rightly notes that in Mark the "key to unlocking this paradoxical reasoning" about discipleship lies in adopting God's point of view about Jesus as suffering Messiah (*New Testament Ethics*, 22).

rather than to "Mark" or "the Markan Jesus." The following summary of a line of argument for this claim (which cannot be justified at any length here) will at least explain the unqualified references to Jesus.[19]

1. Diverse authors and expressions of early Christianity associated Jesus' death with the demands of discipleship (e.g., apart from the Gospels, Heb 12:1–2; 1 Pet 2:18–25; 3:17–18; 1 John 3:16; Rev 2:10, 13 [with 1:5]; and of course Paul).

2. Mark bears witness to the early Christian conviction that this association between Jesus' death and discipleship goes back to Jesus himself.

3. Matthew and Luke, who each independently took up Mark's death-and-discipleship theme, confirm the appropriateness of Mark's attributing its origin to Jesus.

4. The putative Q source may also have preserved an independent death-and-discipleship saying of Jesus in Luke 14:27// Matt 10:38.[20]

5. John also preserves the connection, linking it specifically to love (13:1, 34–35; 15:12–13).

6. By virtue of the criterion of multiple attestation, then, the origin of this connection in Jesus is quite plausible. *The remembered Jesus, or better, the narrated Jesus—who is the only Jesus about whom we have direct knowledge—is consistently the Jesus who connects his cross to that of his disciples.*

7. Moreover, it is historically quite plausible that Jesus expected his own death by crucifixion as the consequence of his being perceived by the Roman authorities as a political threat.

8. It is also quite plausible that once Jesus came to this realization, he began to summon his followers to participate in this aspect of his vocation, just as he had earlier summoned them to participate in his mission of preaching, healing, and exorcising.

---

19. Those who view the situation differently may see this study as a comparison of Mark and Paul and/or an intracanonical conversation.

20. So Joel Marcus, *Mark 8–16: A New Translation with Introduction and Commentary* (AB 27A; New Haven: Yale University Press, 2009), 616, and many interpreters, though the texts may be just restatements of Markan material or a distinct oral tradition.

9. By the time of Jesus, "taking up one's cross" was possibly already an idiom for self-consecration to the point of death.[21]

This line of argument still allows for the possibility that the early church shaped the teachings of Jesus they remembered (e.g., the addition of precise details from the passion narrative, as in Mark 10:33–34, or of interpretive glosses, such as "daily" in Luke 9:23). It also allows for the possibility that Mark creatively brought together, for his theological narrative, Jesus' passion predictions and Jesus' summons to cross-shaped discipleship. If Mark did so, however, he was almost certainly constructing a literary narrative that was faithful to the intentions of Jesus. Similarly, this argument also allows for the possibility that Paul himself had some effect on the content and structure of Mark.

In what follows, I will seek to demonstrate the congruity between the teachings of Jesus on cross-shaped discipleship and those of Paul.[22] Although I will proceed with the basic assumption that the congruity is due largely to the influence of the Jesus tradition—the remembered and narrated Jesus—on Paul (and I think my analysis of texts supports that claim), that is not my main concern or my thesis.[23]

---

21. Ibid., 617.

22. Although Marcus lists numerous important parallels between Mark and Paul (*Mark 1–8: A New Translation with Introduction and Commentary* [AB 27; New Haven: Yale University Press, 1999], 73–75), including their common stress on "Jesus' crucifixion as the apocalyptic turning point of the ages" (74), he does not mention cruciform existence.

23. There was undoubtedly movement in both directions, a reciprocity of influence, so to speak. If others think the flow is largely in reverse (i.e., Paul to Mark to the remembered/narrated Jesus), there will obviously be significant differences in historical reconstruction, but we will agree on the congruity. (We must also keep in mind, of course, that the remembered Jesus who speaks in the New Testament is also the *translated* Jesus.) For a balanced treatment of the influence of the Jesus tradition on Paul, see Michael Thompson, *Clothed with Christ: The Example and Teaching of Jesus in Romans 12.1–15:13* (JSNTSup 59; Sheffield: JSOT Press, 1991).

The First Passion Prediction-Summons and Its
Pauline Parallels: Cruciform Witness to the Gospel

Jesus

The dialogue that prompts Jesus' first passion prediction in Mark and its corollary summons to discipleship (Mark 8:31–9:1) concerns his identity and, implicitly, the identity and character of the Messiah (8:27–30). Peter's confession of Jesus as the Messiah leads Jesus to order the disciples to keep silent concerning his messianic identity before teaching them about the character of his messiahship. Although Jesus does not explicitly accept the title "Messiah," it is clear from the context that he is both accepting and redefining that role. His messiahship will be one of suffering and death before resurrection, of shame before honor, and the command to silence probably gives voice to his refusal to pursue honor.[24] The power of exorcisms, healings, and other works narrated in the first half of the Gospel will be largely transformed into the powerlessness of shame, suffering, and death anticipated and finally narrated in its second half.

It is clear, too, that the disciples' acknowledging Jesus as the Messiah will require a dramatic intellectual and personal conversion. The intellectual transformation is a conversion of their imagination about what messiahship entails for *Jesus*, while the personal transformation is a conversion of their imagination about what Jesus' messiahship entails for *them*: a conversion of their very lives. Believing in this Messiah—in this *sort* of Messiah—is no mere academic exercise but one with serious, inseparable, and unexpected existential consequences. Indeed, the narrative of this Messiah's mission will become the pattern for theirs; in a very real sense, his story will become their story. As Richard Hays has remarked, "When we embrace Mark's answer to the question, 'Who do you say that I am?' we are not just making a theological affirmation about Jesus' identity; we are choosing our own identity as well."[25]

The disciples, in other words, are called to "take up their cross and follow" Jesus in a deliberate act, or better, an intentional habit, of reliv-

---

24. See David Watson, *Honor among Christians: The Cultural Key to the Messianic Secret* (Minneapolis: Fortress, 2010).

25. Richard B. Hays, *The Moral Vision of the New Testament: Community, Cross, New Creation: A Contemporary Introduction to New Testament Ethics* (San Francisco: HarperSanFrancisco, 1996), 79.

ing his story in new ways in their own situations. The two occurrences of the verb *follow* ("If any want to become my followers, let them ... follow me"[26]) suggest that Jesus is referring to both one's initial decision and one's ongoing life.[27] The specific form of cross-shaped discipleship required in this first prediction-summons is self-denial, even self-abandonment, in witness to Jesus and the gospel, with the possibility of suffering and yet also the hope of salvation for those who embrace the shame of the Messiah's cross. The summons is not "'a counsel of perfection' addressed to a spiritual elite but the apocalyptically realistic advice that, for *everyone*, life is *only* to be found in treading the pathway of death."[28]

This call to self-denial and self-abandonment—"a living death"[29]—is offered as the antithesis of attempts at self-preservation and self-advancement that, ironically, yield just the opposite. The parallel phrases "for my sake" and "for the sake of the gospel" (v. 36), together with the mention of shame vis-à-vis the words of Jesus (v. 38), suggest a context of public testimony (of word or deed or both) that either bears glad witness to, or else denies, the teaching, ministry, and messiahship of Jesus that constitute the "good news." This denial in the interest of self-preservation may refer to active denunciation or to more passive accommodations to social pressures and norms.

The "mutual rebuking contest"[30] between Peter and Jesus suggests that a nonnegotiable dimension of faithful witness is embracing the notion, with all attendant consequences, of Jesus as *suffering* Messiah. At the same time, because there is an inseparable connection between Christology and discipleship, this portrayal of discipleship as faithful witness implies that Jesus too was a faithful witness, exemplified above all in his willingness to suffer and die.

Thus we may identify six key elements of cruciformity in the first passion prediction-summons: it has a *christological, narrative* shape with *faithfulness* and *suffering* (rather than *shame*) as its specific ethical content, and a *paradoxical* character of gaining *life through death*. All of these elements are also found in Paul's Letters.

---

26. All Scripture quotations are from the NRSV unless otherwise indicated.

27. John R. Donahue and Daniel J. Harrington, *The Gospel of Mark* (SP 2; Collegeville, Minn.: Liturgical Press, 2002), 263.

28. Marcus, *Mark 8–16*, 624.

29. Ibid., 625.

30. Hays, *Moral Vision*, 79.

PAUL

Throughout Paul's Letters, faithful witness to Jesus and the gospel, even to the point of suffering, is a prominent theme connected both to Paul himself (and other ministers of the gospel) and to Pauline communities as a whole.

Paul is well known for his references to his own suffering, whether in the form of brief, even cryptic, passing references (1 Cor 15:30–32; 2 Cor 1:8–10), so-called catalogues, or short interpretive narratives. In 2 Cor 4:7–11, for instance, we find a catalogue of sorts merged with an interpretive narrative that describes for the Corinthians the life of Paul and his companions. Paul uses a passive form of the verb παραδίδωμι to characterize their ministry: "we are always being given up [παραδιδόμεθα] to death for Jesus' sake" (4:11). As Matera and others have noted,[31] not only is this verb, especially in the passive voice, commonly used in the New Testament of Jesus' deliverance to death, but it appears precisely in the passive voice in two of the three passion predictions (παραδίδοται, Mark 9:31; παραδοθήσεται, 10:33; cf. also παραδώσουσιν in 10:33; similarly, Matthew and Luke). That is, Paul characterizes the apostolic life of suffering in the same language of deliverance to death that Jesus uses in Mark to describe his passion. The point, for the moment, is not the question of influence but simply of linguistic similarity and substantive congruence.[32]

---

31. Frank J. Matera, *II Corinthians: A Commentary* (NTL; Louisville: Westminster John Knox, 2003), 111.

32. Two additional points need to be made here. First, the absence of this passive verb from the passion prediction-summons in Mark 8, which is more specifically about the disciples' suffering than either Mark 9 or Mark 10, is not of great significance. For one thing, there are passive forms of other, related verbs in Mark 8 (be rejected, be killed, in v. 31) to show that this fate is inflicted upon Jesus. For another, and more importantly, Mark 8 is the only prediction-summons that specifically mentions Jesus' suffering (πολλὰ παθεῖν, v. 31), which becomes the focus of the summons as well as the prediction. If Paul is drawing on the Jesus tradition, he is echoing the tradition's close association of three elements (being handed over/παραδίδωμι, suffering, and death), though perhaps not the precise words that will become the text of Mark 8. Second, it is possible that Paul's use of παραδίδωμι derives not from the traditions of Jesus' teaching behind Mark 8–10 but from more generic early Christian traditions of describing Jesus' death with this verb. Paul seems to quote such traditions in Rom 4:25 (passive voice) and 8:32 (active voice, with God the Father as subject/actor), as well as Gal 2:20 (active voice plus reflexive pronoun, with Jesus as the subject/actor and object/recipient; cf. Eph 5:2 and Gal 1:4, which uses δίδωμι). This possibility still

In a brief reference to his suffering for the gospel as he writes to the Thessalonians, Paul also characterizes his team's missionary witness in language with notable similarities to Mark 8: "though we had already suffered [προπαθόντες] and been shamefully mistreated at Philippi, as you know, we had courage [ἐπαρρησιασάμεθα] in our God to declare to you the gospel [εὐαγγέλιον] of God in spite of great opposition" (1 Thess 2:2). Though the three Greek terms highlighted here are not unexpected in their context, it is worth noting that forms of the same words or words with shared roots also appear in Mark 8: "suffering" (παθεῖν, 8:31), "openly" or "courage/boldness" (παρρησίᾳ, 8:32; only here in Mark), and "gospel" (εὐαγγελίου, 8:35). That these parallels are more significant than one might initially think will become evident below in the discussion of Philippians.

If 1 Thessalonians is any indication, although Paul worries about his communities when they suffer, he does not find their suffering surprising. Indeed, such suffering is both an emblem of faithfulness to the gospel and an experience of conformity—involuntary imitation, so to speak—to the fate of Jesus, Paul, and other believers (1 Thess 1:6; 2:14–16; 3:3–4).

Paul's expectation that his communities will suffer comes to sharpest expression in Philippians.[33] Writing while in prison (1:7, 13–14), in the first chapter he weaves together his own suffering for Christ/the gospel, its effects both on the advance of the gospel and on his own spiritual condition, and the role of the Philippians as coparticipants both in spreading and in suffering for the gospel.

We have already seen that several key words of Paul's vocabulary for his own suffering echo Jesus' description of his suffering and death in Mark. Similarly, in Philippians (especially in ch. 1, but also later), several words and themes occur that appear also in passion prediction-summons texts in Mark, especially Mark 8. These words and themes refer both to Paul's suffering and to that of the Philippians. The following table illustrates these connections:

---

raises the question of the genesis of this way of describing Jesus' death. Did Jesus' teaching influence the traditions, or did the tradition shape the way Jesus' words were remembered and/or conveyed?

33. 2 Tim 3:12 also undoubtedly summarizes Paul's perspective (cf. 2 Tim 1:8, 12; 2:3, 8–9; 3:11; 4:5).

WORD, PHRASE, OR THEME	MARK	PHILIPPIANS
Christ/ Messiah	You are the Messiah [χριστός] (8:29)	"Christ" (χριστός) 37x in Philippians, 18x in ch. 1 (the highest concentration of occurrences of "Christ" in any letter and in any chapter of the Pauline corpus)
suffering	the Son of Man must undergo great suffering (8:31)	my suffering (1:17) the privilege ... of suffering for him as well (1:29) the sharing of his sufferings (3:10)
openness/ boldness[34]	He [Jesus] said all this quite openly [παρρησία]. (8:32)	dare to speak the word with greater boldness and without fear [τολμᾶν ἀφόβως] (1:14)[35] my speaking with all boldness [ἐν πάσῃ παρρησίᾳ] (1:20)
self-denial[36]	If any want to become my followers, let them deny	Do nothing from selfish ambition or conceit, but

---

34. The precise nuance of παρρησία in the two texts is debated, but the significance for our purposes is merely the presence of the same Greek word in connection to similar words in both contexts.

35. That which is signified by the phrase τολμᾶν ἀφόβως is semantically similar to παρρησία.

36. The content of Phil 2:1–4 is more closely linked to the third passion prediction-summons, about nondomination and service, but the notion of self-denial is present in the first prediction-summons, too.

taking up the cross	themselves and take up their cross and follow me. (8:34)	in humility regard others as better than yourselves. Let each of you look not to your own interests, but to the interests of others. (2:3–4)
		he humbled himself and became obedient to the point of death—even death on a cross (2:8)
		enemies of the cross of Christ (3:18)
		by becoming like him in his death (3:10)
save/gain—lose/forfeit life salvation for my [Christ's] sake for the gospel	For those who want to save their life will lose it, and those who lose their life for my sake, and for the sake of the gospel, will save it. For what will it profit them to gain [κερδῆσαι] the whole world and forfeit their life? Indeed, what can they give in return for their life? (8:35–37)	It is my eager expectation and hope that … Christ will be exalted now as always in my body, whether by life or by death. For to me, living is Christ and dying is gain [κέρδος]. (1:20–21) my imprisonment is for Christ (1:13) proclaim Christ … proclaim Christ … Christ is proclaimed (1:16–18) your sharing in the gospel from the first day until now (1:5) you share in … the

defense and confirmation
of the gospel (1:7)

what has happened to
me has actually helped to
spread the gospel (1:12)

I have been put here for
the defense of the gospel
(1:16)

Only, live your life in a
manner worthy of the
gospel of Christ ..., striving side by side with one
mind for the faith of the
gospel, and are in no way
intimidated by your oppo-
nents. For them this is
evidence of their destruction, but of your salvation.
(1:27–28)

Yet whatever gains [κέρδη]
I had, these I have come
to regard as loss [ζημίαν]
because of Christ. More
than that, I regard everything as loss [ζημίαν]
because of the surpassing
value of knowing Christ
Jesus my Lord. For his
sake I have suffered the
loss [ἐζημιώθην] of all
things, and I regard them
as rubbish, in order that I
may gain [κερδήσω] Christ
(3:7–8)

shame[37]	Those who are ashamed of me and of my words in this adulterous and sinful generation, of them the Son of Man will also be ashamed when he comes in the glory of his Father with the holy angels. (8:38)	It is my eager expectation and hope that I will not be ashamed in any way (1:20)[38]
coming		the one who began a good work among you will bring it to completion by the day of Jesus Christ (1:6)
		so that in the day of Christ you may be pure and blameless (1:10)

What are we to make of all this? It seems highly probable that these two texts are related in some way. At the very least, we must conclude that in multiple ways Paul describes his own life and that of the Philippians in language that is remarkably reminiscent of the words attributed to Jesus in Mark 8. All six of the key elements of cruciformity in Jesus' first passion prediction-summons identified above (p. 180) are emphatically present in Philippians as well. That is, Paul's narrative of both apostolic and ordinary existence in Christ focuses on the vocation of faithful, bold witness that leads to suffering with and for a suffering Messiah, without shame (cf. Rom 1:16–17; 2 Tim 1:8–12). Such faithfulness to the point of suffering will guarantee the salvation of those who practice it, even if it costs them their life; it is the ultimate gain in spite of the greatest apparent loss.

---

37. Whatever its origin in Christian circles, the theme of "no shame" echoes Isa 52:14; 53:3, 8, as Marcus rightly notes (*Mark 8–16*, 629). Craig Keener suggests that Paul's mention of shame in Rom 1:16 and elsewhere may derive from texts about eschatological shame in Isa 28:16 LXX as well as Isa 45:17; 54:4; 65:13; 66:5 (*Romans* [NCCS; Eugene, Ore.: Cascade, 2009], 26 n. 37). Jesus may have been indebted to the same texts.

38. I have altered the NRSV ("will not be put to shame"), following James P. Ware, *Paul and the Mission of the Church: Philippians in Ancient Jewish Context* (Grand Rapids: Baker Academic, 2011), 204–5.

The Second Passion Prediction-Summons and Its
Pauline Parallels: Cruciform Hospitality to the Weak

JESUS

The second passion prediction-summons (Mark 9:30–37) again has the pattern of prediction–misunderstanding–corrective teaching and call to discipleship. The prediction itself is the shortest of the three (v. 31).

The narrative intimates that Jesus' prediction of his betrayal, death, and resurrection provokes a dispute among the disciples as to their relative "greatness" (9:33–34). This sequence suggests that the disciples were fixating on Jesus' resurrection and the glory that it would mean for him and them, in a way similar to the narrative in 10:35–37. Embarrassed when confronted, they are silent about their own argumentative quest for power (9:34); so Jesus, somehow aware of the subject of their arguing, sits down to teach them the true meaning of greatness (9:35–37).

Jesus' embrace of a child is an "enacted parable,"[39] a *mashal vivant*. The child is not an example to be imitated (as in 10:13–16) but a person to be taken care of. "Jesus is not teaching a lesson about being childlike, but speaking to the issue of status."[40] Children in antiquity had little status and significance, especially outside the Jewish world.[41] Although Jews valued children as real human beings who should be cared for, in Greco-Roman culture and law children were not persons but possessions, without legal rights, and were often victims of abortion, infanticide, exposure, and other forms of mistreatment that Jews, and then Christians, condemned. Even Jews, however, did not equate children with adults but ascribed to them a subordinate status and significance. Throughout the ancient Mediterranean world children were most often seen as immature, intellectually weak, and of far less significance and status than adults.[42]

---

39. Marcus, *Mark 8–16*, 681.

40. M. Eugene Boring, *Mark: A Commentary* (NTL; Louisville: Westminster John Knox, 2006), 281.

41. On children in antiquity, see James Francis, "Children and Childhood in the New Testament," in *The Family in Theological Perspective* (ed. Stephen C. Barton; Edinburgh: T&T Clark, 1996), 65–85; Odd Magne Bakke, *When Children Became People: The Birth of Childhood in Early Christianity* (trans. Brian McNeil; Minneapolis: Fortress, 2005).

42. This is not to say that parents had no emotional bonds to their own children,

The child in Jesus' enacted parable both represents children as a group ("one such child") and serves as an icon of all the lowly: those who are weak, needy, less honored, marginalized ("Whoever wants to be first must be last of all and servant of all," 9:35b). Since the parable is Jesus' response to the argument about achieving greatness, which would mean also achieving honor and power, his "upside-down logic"[43] means that greatness, honor, and power are achieved by service to those without honor and power. In a claim that is nothing short of a theological revolution, Jesus proclaims that such hospitality to the powerless is in fact hospitality to him and, ultimately, to God the Father (9:37).

So what does this mean for Jesus' disciples? Cross-shaped discipleship has a christological, counterintuitive, and countercultural character that is marked especially by service to those without status, which implies a decisive predisposition toward the weak rather than toward the powerful. The normal path to greatness—to power and honor—is replaced by a path to "lastness," a path of downward mobility that takes one, paradoxically, both to greatness and to God.

Paul

If for Jesus the little child both represents children as a group and serves as an icon of all the weak, vulnerable, and marginalized, for Paul the "weak" are both less defined and yet more closely tied to the concrete situations that Paul addresses. For him, "weakness" ($\dot{\alpha}\sigma\theta\acute{\epsilon}\nu\epsilon\iota\alpha$) is a polyvalent term, yet he clearly affirms the predisposition toward the weak and low-in-status found in Jesus, grounding this predisposition in the salvific act of God in Christ, who displayed God's love by dying for the weak—the ungodly, the sinner (Rom 5:6–8).

This perspective appears already in Paul's earliest letter: "help the weak" (1 Thess 5:14). But we see it most fully developed in 1 Corinthians and Romans. Debate about the precise constitution of groups and/or house churches in Corinth and Rome continues, and cannot be rehearsed here. Resolving the debate, however, is not necessary to highlight Paul's fundamental, Jesus-like conviction: that communities of those who are in Christ must attend to, and even give preference to, the weak.

---

but that children's overall status and significance were deferred and utilitarian (e.g., economic promise) rather than present and inherent.

43. Marcus, *Mark 8–16*, 681.

In 1 Corinthians the exhortation is grounded in the gospel itself, indeed in the self-revealing action of God on the cross, in the Corinthian community, and in the ministry of Paul (1:18–2:5). God is revealed as the one who operates through and among the weak—the weakness of the Messiah's shameful death on a Roman cross, which is indeed "the weakness of God" (1:25); the weakness of the status-poor "nobodies" who make up the majority of the Corinthian community, who are the weak chosen by God (1:27b); and the weakness of Paul's own persona and preaching, an apostle beset by illness, unimpressive oratorical skills, and indeed an overall weakness (2:3; cf. 4:10; 2 Cor 10:10). Both weakness itself and a voluntary predisposition toward the weak are characteristic of God, Christ, and Paul. (On Paul's *choosing* weakness, see 9:22; 2 Cor 11:29.) Indeed, weakness was, paradoxically, both Paul's source of pride and his source of strength in Christ (2 Cor 11:30; 12:5, 9–10).

This taking on of weakness and its corollary preference for the weak must find expression in the Corinthian community, as Paul makes abundantly clear. He applies his practical theology of hospitable, divine, Christlike weakness to the Corinthians in three major places: his exhortation to the community about caring for the weak in conscience, in response to the controversy about eating meat offered to idols in the temple precincts (8:1–11:1);[44] his excoriation of the community for its neglect of those who are without means and come late to the supper they celebrate (11:17–34); and his discourse on the church's need to give greater attention to the weaker members—those of lesser means—of the body (ch. 12, esp. v. 22).

This Jesus-like attitude in Paul is summarized well by Rachel McRae in commenting on the apostle's response to the situation regarding the Lord's Supper at Corinth:

> In this community, the new code [of honor] embedded in the banquet reflects Jesus' ethics of service, sacrifice, and substitutionary atonement: "do not seek your own advantage, but that of the other" (1 Cor 10:24). The ritual of the Lord's Supper calls the participants to behavior based on values such as equality, rather than hierarchy; mutual servitude, rather than competition; and humility rather than the upward mobility enshrined in the power structures of the Greco-Roman world.[45]

---

44. 1 Cor 8:7–12 mentions the weak four times.

45. Rachel M. McRae, "Eating with Honor: The Corinthian Lord's Supper in Light of Voluntary Association Meal Practices," *JBL* 130 (2011): 180.

McRae is apparently alluding to all of the calls to discipleship in the Gospels that are associated with Jesus' death (especially Mark 10), but the application of these principles to the treatment of the weak (those without status), not only in 1 Cor 11:17–34 but also in chapters 8–10 and 12, is especially reminiscent of the second passion prediction-summons.

Similarly, in Romans appropriate treatment of the weak forms the subject of the lengthiest, and arguably the central, exhortation in the letter, which focuses on the mutual treatment of the weak and the strong (14:1–15:13). In that text, Paul assigns the lion's share of responsibility to the strong, who are charged with taking care of the weak (the "weak in faith" [14:1], referring to something like scrupulousness about diet and calendar), grounding his exhortation explicitly in the example of Jesus the servant (15:1–3, 8 [διάκονον]) and implicitly in the teaching of Jesus about love (13:8–10). The text contains echoes of Phil 2:6–11, which suggests that Paul's ethic of embracing the weak is ultimately grounded not only in Jesus' teaching but also in his actions, culminating at the cross, as we will see again in considering the third passion prediction-summons.

Paul, then, contends that the triune God—God the Father (1 Cor 1:18–2:5), Christ (Rom 5:6; 15:1–3, 8), and the Spirit (Rom 8:26)—has a predisposition toward the weak, a preferential option for the poor in status. The apostle constantly seeks to inculcate the same divine mind-set, with its corresponding human practices, in the communities of those "in Christ."

THE THIRD PASSION PREDICTION-SUMMONS AND ITS PAULINE PARALLELS: CRUCIFORM POWER AS LOVING SERVICE

JESUS

The third passion prediction-summons (Mark 10:32–45) contains the most detailed prediction of Jesus' death, corresponding "to a T"[46] to the passion narrative in Mark's Gospel and bearing a certain resemblance to the catalogues of suffering in Paul's Letters. The summons includes elements of the first two calls (in chs. 8 and 9) but also has a distinct focus of its own: greatness, or power, as service to others—not only to the weak, but to all. In Mark's narrative, this prediction-summons concludes a series of perico-

---

46. Marcus, *Mark 8–16*, 743.

pae on the nature of discipleship, with Peter initiating a sort of preface to the prediction-summons by reminding Jesus that he and his companions have left everything to follow him (v. 28). Jesus in turn promises present "rewards" that ironically include persecutions, prior to the ultimate reward of eternal life in the age to come (vv. 29–30). He then promises a general reward, introducing the theme of paradoxical reversal—"the last will be first"—that is the heart of the third summons itself, in verses 35–45.

There are four key aspects of this prediction-summons to note: (1) Jesus' rejection of the pursuit of glory for a practical theology of the cross, (2) the participatory nature of this practical theology, (3) the countercultural and paradoxical character of power as service rather than domination, and (4) the triple role of Jesus as the summoner, sacrifice, and exemplary servant.

1. Following the promise of eschatological reward (v. 30), James and John approach Jesus with a request that is "the equivalent of asking Jesus for a 'blank check.'"[47] When Jesus asks them to be specific, their absurd open-ended request becomes restricted to one that reflects both Jewish interest in one's place in the age to come and a broader cultural concern for honor and status (vv. 36–37). Jesus eventually says that he does not have the authority to grant such a request (v. 40), but in the meantime he raises questions that imply a different and prerequisite appointment for his disciples, a sharing in his baptism and cup, that is, his suffering and death (vv. 38–39). Here, as Eugene Boring observes, "'Theology of glory' confronts 'theology of the cross,' and not only as Christology but, as always in Mark, inseparably linked to discipleship."[48]

2. One of the most significant aspects of this passage, and a point of similarity between Jesus and Paul that has received insufficient attention, is the participatory dimension of passion-shaped existence. In the context of Mark 10, this participation would seem to refer, first of all, to the disciples' literal suffering for Jesus at some unspecified future point (cf. Mark 8). But that does not exhaust the meaning of participation in Jesus' passion; Jesus' words about participation are prompted by, and inseparably connected to, James and John's pursuit of glory and greatness (vv. 35–40). When Jesus surprises them by saying that he does not have the authority to grant the eschatological glory they desire (v. 40b), he redefines greatness

---

47. Donahue and Harrington, *Mark*, 310.
48. Boring, *Mark*, 300.

in terms of servanthood (vv. 42–45). What he offers them, in other words, is not a seat of glory but a vocation of service. This constitutes the second aspect of participating in Jesus' cup and baptism: sharing in the mind-set of greatness as service that will even suffer for others rather than "lord it over [κατακυριεύουσιν] them."

Jesus' reference to his baptism and his cup are first of all metaphors, but for Mark's audience and all subsequent audiences, there is clearly an allusion to Christian baptism and Eucharist in these words. Therefore, although the primary referents of baptism and cup are not these practices/sacraments, the images do remind Mark's readers—and us—that both entry into Christ and ongoing life in Christ mean participation in Christ's death.[49] As we will see below, this is precisely Paul's understanding of these practices/sacraments.

3. A cluster of "power" words appears in verse 42, indicating the subject at hand: ἄρχειν, κατακυριεύουσιν, μεγάλοι, κατεξουσιάζουσιν. To pursue honor at the expense of others, or in any way to dominate them in a quest for personal power, is to act like the Gentiles who do not know God, to borrow Paul's phrase (1 Thess 4:5). It is, so to speak, to "Romanize."[50] The disciples are called to share in Jesus' lordship not by acts of "lording" but by acts of self-giving serving. This, paradoxically, is the path to greatness and "firstness," as Jesus has already said (9:35; cf. 10:31).[51] Whereas in chapter 9 he had made clear that cruciform service to "all" embraces those of low and no status, even so-called nonpersons, here he makes clear that it includes absolutely everyone.

The phrase "it is not so among you" (i.e., esp. the Romans; 10:43[52]) is an indicative with imperatival force. It means that discipleship is both generally countercultural and specifically counterimperial. Better put, discipleship forms an alternative way of life to the quest for power and position, the domination and defeat of others, that characterizes "normal" human life, particularly existence in imperial mode.

4. Jesus' words preserved in Mark 10:45 summarize all three predictions and interpret them in the two images of sacrifice (ransom) and servant. Space does not permit consideration of the former, or of the contro-

---

49. See also, e.g., Donahue and Harrington, *Mark*, 311; Boring, *Mark*, 301.
50. I mean this to echo the verb "to Judaize," associated with Galatians.
51. The form of 10:43b–44 is synonymous parallelism, as in 9:35.
52. Cf. "not … like the Gentiles" (1 Thess 4:5).

verted background to the latter.[53] What is absolutely clear, however, is that Jesus sees himself as a servant and as "the best example of his own ideal of servant leadership."[54] It is likely that Mark intends us to interpret Jesus' servanthood not only as one act, his death, but as his entire ministry, culminating in his self-giving death.[55]

To summarize the third prediction, it consists of both the call to countercultural cruciform service, rather than domination, and the grounding of that call in the example of Jesus.

PAUL

In considering Paul, we are also struck by both the mandate to cruciform service itself and its basis in Jesus. As with Jesus, we find Paul rejecting the "normal" human pursuit of glory and replacing it with a practical, participatory theology of the cross in which power is exercised—counterculturally, paradoxically, and lovingly—as service rather than domination, with Jesus as exemplary servant.

Joel Marcus has constructed a helpful table of similarities between Mark 10 and Phil 2:6–11, suggesting with good reason that the similarities "reflect their common background in Isa 52:13–53:12."[56] Marcus focuses on the common elements of slavery/service, death, and subsequent exaltation. We may add that Phil 2 displays a theology remarkably consistent not only with Mark 10 and the Synoptics generally, but also with John, especially chapter 13.

Whatever we make of the historicity of the enacted parable in John 13, we have seen in Mark that Jesus implicitly refers to himself as διάκονος and δοῦλος (10:43–44). As noted above, Paul calls Jesus διάκονος in Rom 15:8, and in Phil 2:7 he characterizes Jesus as δοῦλος. Furthermore, although Paul does not use the precise verbal phrase about self-giving service (διακονῆσαι) that Mark attributes to Jesus—δοῦναι τὴν ψυχὴν αὐτου ("to give his life")—in Phil 2:7 Paul uses similar language in expressing Jesus' self-

---

53. I should note, however, that I side with those who find Isa 53 in the background.

54. Donahue and Harrington, *Mark*, 313.

55. Boring, *Mark*, 302.

56. Marcus, *Mark 8–16*, 756. Marcus does not, however, note the shared contrast, explicit in Mark and implicit in Philippians, with Roman imperial power. This sort of contrast may also be implicit in the historical context of the author of Isa 53.

giving "incarnation" with the appropriate use of a reflexive grammatical construction, ἑαυτὸν ἐκένωσεν ("emptied himself"). Similar in substance, but referring directly to Christ's death, is the sentence ἐταπείνωσεν ἑαυτὸν γενόμενος ὑπήκοος μέχρι θανάτου, θανάτου δὲ σταυροῦ in 2:8 ("he humbled himself by becoming obedient to the point of death, specifically death on a cross" [my trans.]).

The full meaning of these reflexive phrases for Paul cannot be ascertained without noting their role in the rhetorical structure of Phil 2:6–8. Here Paul uses a pattern that I have elsewhere described as "although [x] not [y] but [z]," meaning "although [status] not [selfish exploitation] but [self-giving]."[57] Paul is depicting the true meaning of Jesus' lordship as service, and in the larger context of Philippians, he is portraying Christ as the "lordly example."[58] Though not explicit, the contrast to Roman lords and others who seek to dominate or exploit others could not be more sharply drawn for an audience in a Roman colony like Philippi. Here is a lord who freely but obediently—such is the paradox expressed in the use of the reflexive constructions in combination with the word *obedient*—does not lord it over others. As a result, he is vindicated and exalted by God as Lord (Phil 2:9–11)—he is made great.

These parallels among Isaiah, Mark, and Philippians have not only christological but also ethical import. In interpreting Isaiah, both Jesus in Mark and Paul contend that both the Servant-Messiah and his disciples will be exalted by God after their voluntary-but-obedient humiliation, which Paul expresses with the reflexive constructions noted above.

On two other occasions, Paul does use a form of the verb δίδωμι ("to give") found in Mark 10:45 with a reflexive pronoun to express Christ's self-giving death: τοῦ δόντος ἑαυτὸν ὑπὲρ τῶν ἁμαρτιῶν ἡμῶν ("who gave himself for our sins"; Gal 1:4) and τοῦ ἀγαπήσαντός με καὶ παραδόντος ἑαυτὸν ὑπὲρ ἐμοῦ ("who loved me by giving himself for me" [my trans.]; Gal 2:20). Like Mark 10:45, each of these clauses from Galatians has two principal semantic parts, the act of self-giving itself and the purpose of the self-giving. They should be considered examples of synonymous parallelism, first with each other and then, together, with Mark 10:45.

---

57. See Gorman, *Cruciformity*, 91, 165–74, 186–88, 192, 197, 230–36, 243, 252, 261, 330.

58. L. W. Hurtado, "Jesus as Lordly Example in Philippians 2:5–11," in *From Jesus to Paul: Studies in Honour of Francis Wright Beare* (ed. Peter Richardson and John C. Hurd; Waterloo, Ont.: Wilfred Laurier University Press, 1984), 113–26.

That all four of these reflexive texts in Paul (Phil 2:7, 8; Gal 1:4; 2:20) are generally considered to represent pre-Pauline traditions does not diminish their theological significance for Paul. It does strongly suggest, however, that Paul is the recipient, rather than the creator, of the interpretation of Jesus' death as his utter self-donation as a servant/slave. Before the time of Paul, during his ministry, and beyond the time of the apostle, the early Christians perceived Jesus' death this way.

But does Paul see this self-giving service even to death also as an act of love? The answer would appear to be yes. Although Gal 1:4 does not mention love, Gal 2:20 does. In Phil 2 Paul does not explicitly name Christ's death on the cross as an act of love, but the immediate context ensures that Paul understands it this way, for he exhorts the Philippians to adopt the same "mind" and practices as an expression of love (2:1). Here and elsewhere, then (e.g., throughout 1 Corinthians), Paul will transfer this understanding of love to himself and to all who are in Christ. When he does so, he will transfer with it the "although [x] not [y] but [z]" pattern seen in Phil 2.

Paul's Letters indicate that he, like Jesus, saw himself as a servant/slave of others, even to the point of suffering for their salvation and edification. Moreover, in that role, Paul—again like Jesus—understood himself also as a model of servanthood for others. At the same time, Paul clearly perceived his paradigmatic servant role to be derivative: "Become imitators of me as I am an imitator of the Messiah" (1 Cor 11:1, my trans.).[59]

For our purposes, perhaps the most significant text about Paul's apostolic cruciformity is 1 Thess 2:5–9. Paul's description of the ministry that he and his colleagues offered the Thessalonians includes a clause with a form of δίδωμι and of ψυχή, as well as a form of the reflexive pronoun: εὐδοκοῦμεν μεταδοῦναι ὑμῖν οὐ μόνον τὸ εὐαγγέλιον τοῦ θεοῦ ἀλλὰ καὶ τὰς ἑαυτῶν ψυχάς (2:8; "we are determined [or 'we determined'] to share with you not only the gospel of God but also our own selves").[60] The vocabulary

---

59. For a recent argument that Paul's call to imitation is not an exercise of power but a summons to cruciform service—or "christic embodiment"—see Yung Suk Kim, *A Theological Introduction to Paul's Letters: Exploring a Threefold Theology of Paul* (Eugene, Ore.: Cascade, 2011), 109–30. He perceptively describes Paul's understanding of imitation as corporate participation in the love of God demonstrated in Christ's death and therefore as a form of "heteronomy" or "rule by others," rather than autonomy (120–21).

60. The context makes it likely that the verb refers to a past, not a present, decision. See table below.

suggests a blending of Mark 10:45 and the reflexive δίδωμι texts in Galatians. In addition, Paul and his colaborers' renunciation of the pursuit of glory (δόξαν; 2:6) echoes, and contrasts with, the desire for eschatological glory sought by Jesus' disciples (Mark 10:37). The pursuit of such "vainglory" (κενοδοξίαν, Phil 2:3 NAB; NRSV "conceit") Paul has abandoned.

Two additional aspects of this text are significant. First, Paul makes absolutely clear that this apostolic mode of service was a deliberate renunciation of power, or (better said) an exercise of power *for* others rather than power *over* them. This is expressed within a form of the "although [x] not [y] but [z]" pattern:

not [y]	we never came with words of flattery or with a pretext for greed; nor did we seek praise [δόξαν] from mortals, whether from you or from others (vv. 5–6a)
although [x]	though we might have made demands [or "thrown our weight around"] as apostles of Christ (v. 6b)
but [z]	But we were gentle among you, like a nurse tenderly caring for her own children. So deeply do we care for you that we are determined [or "we determined"] to share [μεταδοῦναι] with you not only the gospel of God but also our own selves [τὰς ἑαυτῶν ψυχάς], because you have [had] become very dear [ἀγαπητοί] to us. You remember our labor and toil, brothers and sisters; we worked night and day, so that we might not burden any of you while we proclaimed to you the gospel of God.[61] (vv. 7–9)

Second, Paul sees this apostolic cruciformity as an act of love. This is clear from the metaphor of the nurse caring for *her own* (τὰ ἑαυτῆς) children and from the actual language of love that is somewhat masked by the NRSV's "very dear to us": Greek ἀγαπητοί, "beloved." It is clear in the context that this self-giving love includes, but is not limited to, the Pauline team's voluntary renunciation of financial support from the Thessalonians and thus their engaging in manual labor (2:9).

Similar in substance is Paul's renunciation of apostolic privilege, especially the right to support, in 1 Cor 9, where he once again uses the

---

61. Brackets indicate the more likely translation, as the NAB and NIV both indicate.

"although [x] not [y] but [z]" pattern. He also specifically identifies himself as a δοῦλος, not by using the noun but by using the verb "to enslave" (δουλεύω) with a reflexive pronoun, again transferring the reflexive-pronoun christological pattern we see in the (pre-Pauline?) texts in Galatians and Philippians:

although [x]	Do we not have the right to our food and drink? Do we not have the right to be accompanied by a believing wife, as do the other apostles and the brothers of the Lord and Cephas? (vv. 4–5) For though I am free with respect to all (v. 19a)
not [y]	Nevertheless, we have not made use of this right (v. 12b) But I have made no use of any of these rights (v. 15a)
but [z]	but we endure anything rather than put an obstacle in the way of the gospel of Christ (v. 12c) I have made myself a slave to all [πᾶσιν ἐμαυτὸν ἐδούλωσα; "I have enslaved myself to all" (my trans.)], so that I might win more of them (v. 19b)

It also appears that Paul has once again blended the "although..." and the reflexive patterns with an allusion to Jesus' passion prediction-summons by indicating that his slavery is "to all" (πᾶσιν; cf. "slave of all," πάντων δοῦλος, in Mark 10:44).

As noted above, one of the most significant points of similarity between Jesus and Paul, but one that has generally been neglected, is the participatory dimension of the call to suffering and servanthood. It is commonly acknowledged that participation is at the heart of Pauline theology and spirituality, indicated by such central terms and phrases as "in Christ," κοινωνία with/in Christ and the Spirit (e.g., 1 Cor 10:16; Phil 2:1), and words beginning with the prefix συν- ("co-"). Especially important for our purposes is Paul's notion of co-crucifixion (Rom 6:6; Gal 2:19), which appears to refer both to initiation into Christ through faith as manifested in baptism and to ongoing existence in Christ. Paul's theology of baptism and its consequences may very well be not only similar to, but actually indebted to, the tradition of Jesus referring to his death as a baptism. As Dunn puts it, "Paul could speak of a *baptism* into *Christ's death*, only because he was aware of the tradition that Jesus had spoken of his *death* as a *baptism*."[62]

For Paul, as for Jesus, participation in the Messiah's suffering and death has two dimensions, literal suffering and self-giving service to God and others. We see the former in texts like Rom 8:17 (συμπάσχομεν; "co-suffer with Christ" [my trans.]) and Phil 3:10 (κοινωνίαν [τῶν] παθημάτων αὐτοῦ; "participation in his sufferings" [my trans.]), in which suffering is presented as a normal part of participation in Christ, and as the prerequisite to glory. The latter is rooted in the baptismal reality of dying with Christ as the death of the old self that makes possible (and necessary) a life of self-presentation to God that yields, in turn, self-sacrificial service to others (Rom 6; 12). Such service renounces the use of power over others, seeking their welfare rather than one's own (cf. also Rom 12:10; Phil 3:3).

At several points Paul refers to this cruciform existence implicitly or explicitly as servanthood/slavery. The parallels between Phil 2:3–4 and 2:6–8 suggest that those in Christ are to be Christlike slaves to others, while Gal 5:13 explicitly uses the verb δουλεύω: "through love become slaves to one another." Moreover, Paul's example of himself as a slave (1 Cor 9:19; 11:1) is offered in the context of the admonition to the "strong" at Corinth to adopt Paul-like slavery—forgoing rights for the good of others—in their treatment of the weak. This understanding of servanthood is consonant with the understanding of the servant practices described by Jesus in Mark 10. And Paul is exemplary to others only as an imitator of Christ the servant.

But Is It Love?

As we have seen, when Paul speaks of self-giving service/slavery, he specifically calls it love, connecting, for example, Gal 5:13 to the fulfillment of the command to love one's neighbor (Gal 5:14). Moreover, in other letters the immediate (e.g., Phil 2:1–11) or wider (e.g., 1 Corinthians) context makes the same connection implicitly. But what about Jesus, according to our primary witness in this essay—Mark?

Richard Hays contrasts Mark's ethic of "simple external obedience," whose norm is the cross, with both Matthew's focus on "the intention of

---

62. James D. G. Dunn, *Jesus Remembered* (Grand Rapids: Eerdmans, 2003), 809 (emphasis original).

the heart" and Paul's focus on the Spirit as the source of moral power and the way of the cross as the way of love.[63] Discipleship, the way of the cross, is not about love in Mark; it is "simply the way of obedience."[64] Hays grants that Jesus in Mark affirms the law's double love command (12:28–34), but only as an answer to a scribe's question, not as an instruction to his disciples.[65]

Hays's distinction seems a bit like splitting hairs; surely hearers/readers of Mark should heed all of Jesus' teaching, whatever its prompt or form. If, for Jesus, rightly understanding the essence of the law to be love of God and neighbor means being close to the kingdom of God (Mark 12:34), as Hays notes,[66] and if, as Hays rightly claims, in Mark "the secret of the kingdom of God is that Jesus must die as the crucified Messiah,"[67] then does not Mark imply a connection between the way of the cross and the way of love?

Indeed, could one not make the case that for Mark (and possibly therefore for Jesus), it is *precisely the cross that fulfills the double love command, meaning faithful obedience to God and self-giving love for others*? What else could *love* mean in Mark or in the teaching of Jesus generally? Even if love of neighbor is mentioned only once in Mark, and the content is not specified there (other than the affirmation that it is something different from offering temple sacrifices), it must have *some* content. And what better understanding of love does the Gospel of Mark offer, even if only implicitly, than self-giving servanthood after the example of Jesus?[68]

For Paul, cruciform power as service is clearly a critical dimension of his understanding of love, and he seems to think this derives from both the teaching and the example of Jesus.[69] But even Paul may have had to make

---

63. Hays, *Moral Vision*, 83–85, quotations from 83.
64. Ibid., 84–85.
65. Ibid., 84.
66. Ibid.
67. Ibid., 76.
68. Similarly, Richard A. Burridge, *Imitating Jesus: An Inclusive Approach to New Testament Ethics* (Grand Rapids: Eerdmans, 2007): Jesus is "the one who rightly interprets the law precisely because of his commitment to the love of God which seeks loving self-giving in response" (172), and Jesus' teaching about power and leadership are related in Mark to his "radicalizing principles of love and the priority of the sovereign rule of God" (185). Burridge may go too far, however, in claiming that Mark puts "the double love command at the centre of Jesus' teaching" (185).
69. See further Gorman, *Cruciformity*, 268–303. McRae ("Eating with Honor,"

explicit (in Phil 2:1–4) that which was only implicit in certain christological affirmations (Phil 2:6–11). Similarly, perhaps certain affirmations in Jesus' teaching, as preserved in Mark's Gospel, require connecting the dots to make the implicit explicit. At the same time, it is noteworthy that Jesus' words about the nature of service have a "not this but that" structure to them: not κατακυριεῦσαι or διακονηθῆναι but διακονῆσαι (Mark 10:42–45; not dominion or being served, but service). When taken together, Paul's descriptions of love have a similar structure: not ζητεῖν τὰ ἑαυτοῦ but ζητεῖν τὰ ἑτέρων and οἰκοδομεῖν ἑτέρους (not self-regard, but regard for others; see 1 Cor 8:1; 10:23; 13:5; 14:4; Phil 2:1–4).

In summary, then, although the connection between cross and love is much clearer in Paul, it is not absent from, but rather implicit in, the teachings of Jesus preserved in Mark. Perhaps it was left to Paul (and John too), as well as Mark's audiences, to make the connection between servanthood and love explicit. But doing so only makes clearer what Jesus intended.

CONCLUSION

We have seen that Jesus and Paul agree that passion-shaped discipleship, or participatory cruciformity, consists of cross-shaped (1) witness to the gospel, (2) hospitality to the weak, and (3) power as loving service.[70] Did Jesus offer these three interconnected dimensions of discipleship as something like a three-point homily or sermon on the way of the cross while he and his disciples were on the way to Jerusalem? The situation is likely more complicated than that, though Mark arranges Jesus' teaching, in some sense, as precisely that. And what about Paul? Did he think of cruciformity as having precisely these three dimensions? Again, the situation is more complex than that, but at the very least Paul agrees with Mark and with Jesus that these three dimensions are indeed crucial aspects of life for those who know Jesus as the Messiah.

Indeed, I would suggest that the entire Pauline corpus may be viewed as an interpretation of Jesus' passion predictions-summonses in a new idiom, the idiom of Spirit-enabled participation in Jesus' death and resurrection,

---

166) argues that Paul "propose[s] radical changes to the Corinthian meal ritual in order to establish new social and behavioral patterns that reflect the values of humility, mutual upbuilding, and love that Jesus taught."

70. Thompson (*Clothed with Christ*) finds all of these themes in Rom 12–15; see his summary (237–41).

an idiom with its roots in one of those passion predictions-summonses (the third). Paul may very well have even had a name for this reality: "the law of Christ" (Gal 6:2; cf. 1 Cor 9:21). At the same time, paradoxically, the Gospel of Mark, the earliest bearer of those words of Jesus in written form, "provides a profound understanding of God as the one who manifests power in the weakness and folly of the cross" and calls every community of disciples to live "after the model of the one who came to serve and give his life a ransom for many" (Matera, appropriately connecting 1 Cor 1:18–25 and Mark 10:45).[71]

71. Frank J. Matera, *New Testament Theology: Exploring Diversity and Unity* (Louisville: Westminster John Knox, 2007), 21. I wish to express gratitude to my research assistant, Kurt Pfund, for help in the final stages of preparing this essay.

Galatians 3:10:
A "Newer Perspective" on an Omitted Premise

A. Andrew Das

In Gal 3:10 Paul seizes a passage from Deuteronomy that pronounces a curse upon those who do not observe the Law. In a surprising twist the apostle concludes that those who adopt the path of the Law will *themselves* suffer its curse:

> *Premise:* Cursed is everyone who does not abide by everything that is written in this book of the Law to do them.
> *Conclusion:* As many who are of the works of the Law are under a curse.[1]

Omitted premises are a regular feature of Paul's writing.[2] The implied premise, reconstructed from the stated premise and conclusion, would literally read:

> As many who are of the works of the Law do not abide by everything that is written in this book of the Law to do them.[3]

---

1. On the translation of ἐκ, see most recently Don Garlington, "Paul's 'Partisan ἐκ' and the Question of Justification in Galatians," *JBL* 127 (2008): 567–89; with the corrective by Jan Lambrecht, "Critical Reflections on Paul's 'Partisan ἐκ' as Recently Presented by Don Garlington," *ETL* 85 (2009): 135–41.

2. E.g., John D. Moores, *Wrestling with Rationality in Paul: Romans 1–8 in a New Perspective* (Cambridge: Cambridge University Press, 1995).

3. Without the implied premise, Paul would be saying that those who obey the Law are under a curse since the Law pronounces a curse on everyone who does not obey it—a non sequitur.

Ancient rhetoricians commended as a matter of style the omission of premises in enthymemes that would have been clear or obvious.[4] Paul is assuming in Gal 3:10 that Law-observers simply do not do all that is written in the Law. Its adherents have not attained, at least from Paul's experience, the comprehensive, perfect obedience that it demands.[5]

Older commentators frequently concluded from Gal 3:10 that Paul was reminding the self-righteous of the perfect standard of Moses' Law.[6] E. P. Sanders's *Paul and Palestinian Judaism* ushered in a new paradigm. Judaism in the Second Temple and tannaitic eras, as Sanders explained, was never a pattern of religion devoid of God's grace without the merciful provision for failure.[7] Pauline interpreters are now generally skeptical of an assumed premise of the failure of perfect obedience since the Law required faithfulness, not sinless perfection.[8] Paul could hardly have assumed a contentious premise with which his rivals would have disagreed. Scholars are left searching for other ways to understand Gal 3:10.[9]

---

4. Aristotle, *Rhet.* 1.2.13 (1357a); 2.22.3 (1395b); 3.18.2, 4 (1419a); Epictetus, *Diatr.* 1.8.1–4; Quintilian, *Inst.* 5.14.24; 5.10.3; Aelius Theon, *Progymnasmata* 3.99–100. For the citation system employed for Theon, see George A. Kennedy, *Progymnasmata: Greek Textbooks of Prose Composition and Rhetoric* (SBLWGRW 10; Atlanta: Society of Biblical Literature, 2003).

5. Aristotle distinguishes logical syllogisms from rhetorical enthymemes (*Rhet.* 1.2.14–15 [1357a]). The latter's premises may only indicate what is *generally* true; see Kjell Arne Moreland, *The Rhetoric of Curse in Galatians* (Emory Studies in Early Christianity 5; Atlanta: Scholars Press, 1995), 118 n. 22, 204.

6. The implied premise was obvious; e.g., Albrecht Oepke, *Der Brief des Paulus an die Galater* (3rd ed.; THKNT; Berlin: Evangelische Verlagsanstalt, 1973), 105. Among those who see Paul confronting Jewish legalism, see Hans Hübner, *Law in Paul's Thought* (trans. James C. G. Grieg; SNTIW; Edinburgh: T&T Clark, 1984), 18; Ernest De Witt Burton, *A Critical and Exegetical Commentary on the Epistle to the Galatians* (ICC; Edinburgh: T&T Clark, 1921), 163.

7. E. P. Sanders, *Paul and Palestinian Judaism: A Comparison of Patterns of Religion* (Philadelphia: Fortress, 1977).

8. E.g., Timothy G. Gombis, "The 'Transgressor' and the 'Curse of the Law': The Logic of Paul's Argument in Galatians 2–3," *NTS* 53 (2007): 81–93, esp. 82–83.

9. "New perspective" interpreters in the mold of James D. G. Dunn or N. T. Wright offer an alternative by tracing the apostle's critique in Gal 3:10 to the "works of the Law," that is, the Law's ethnic boundary-marking features as Paul opposed a mistaken nationalism. See James D. G. Dunn, "Works of the Law and the Curse of the Law (Gal. 3.10–14)," in *Jesus, Paul, and the Law: Studies in Mark and Galatians* (Louisville: Westminster John Knox, 1990), 215–41; N. T. Wright, *The Climax of the Covenant: Christ and the Law in Pauline Theology* (Minneapolis: Fortress, 1991), 3, 150.

This widespread skepticism of an assumption that people fail to obey God's Law perfectly is unwarranted. Additional evidence from Deuteronomy and Second Temple Judaism will demonstrate that such an omitted premise would not have been contentious after all (section 1). Modern interpreters frequently point to the sacrificial system or other means of enjoying God's grace and mercy to explain why perfect obedience was attainable in Second Temple Judaism. Paul or his rivals, these interpreters contend, would never have viewed perfect or blameless obedience as difficult. Such a conclusion is premature and does not sufficiently account for the apostle's reconceptualization of God's grace and mercy in terms of Christ (section 2). The implied premise in Gal 3:10 supports Paul's apocalyptic perspective that the Law only brings about an enslaving curse: God's saving work is associated strictly with the Abrahamic promises and not Mount Sinai (section 3).

Human Inability to Avoid Sin

For Paul to assume in the midst of the conflict at Galatia that people do not perfectly obey the Law does not by any means strain credulity. Deuteronomy 27–30, the passage to which Paul alludes, offers a pessimistic appraisal of native human ability to observe the Law. Many Second Temple Jews agreed with that appraisal. Some therefore extolled the exemplary obedience of certain rare individuals who were able to do what the vast majority could not, while other Jewish authors commended a dependence upon God to provide what they were lacking in their own ability.

Deuteronomy 27–30

Timothy Gombis made Deuteronomy the starting point for interpreting Gal 3:10: "If [Paul's] argument can be made to make sense with this text [Deut 27:26] being read according to its probable meaning in its original narrative setting, then there is no reason to attempt to construe Paul as citing it in any other way, especially as quoting it *against* its meaning in its original context."[10] Unfortunately, Gombis did not devote much space in his article to that original context. The context of Deuteronomy actually

---

10. Gombis, "Transgressor," 85.

renders an omitted premise of the unlikelihood of perfect obedience quite plausible in Gal 3:10.

The wording of Paul's citation of Deut 27:26 reflects the broader context of Deut 27–30, especially in Paul's use of the phrase "the words of this Law":

Deut 27:26	τοῖς λόγοις		τοῦ νόμου τούτου
Gal 3:10	τοῖς γεγραμμένοις	ἐν τῷ βιβλίῳ	τοῦ νόμου
Deut 28:58	τὰ γεγραμμένα	ἐν τῷ βιβλίῳ	τούτῳ
Deut 28:61	τὴν μὴ γεγραμμένην	ἐν τῷ βιβλίῳ	τοῦ νόμου τούτου
Deut 29:19	αἱ γεγραμμέναι	ἐν τῷ βιβλίῳ	τοῦ νόμου τούτου
Deut 29:20	τὰς γεγραμμένας	ἐν τῷ βιβλίῳ	τοῦ νόμου τούτου

(Deut 29:20 is identical with 29:26 and 30:10)

Note Paul's use of ἐν τῷ βιβλίῳ and his alteration of λόγοις to γεγραμμένοις.[11] The apostle's citation of Deut 27:26 must be considered within the larger context of Deut 27–30.[12] Paul is not the first to treat Deut 27 within its broader context. Several Second Temple texts borrow Deut 27–32's fourfold

---

11. For a thorough discussion of the relationship between Paul's text and its OT precursors, see Christopher D. Stanley, *Paul and the Language of Scripture: Citation Technique in the Pauline Epistles and Contemporary Literature* (SNTSMS 69; Cambridge: Cambridge University Press, 1992), 238–43; François Vouga, *An die Galater* (HNT 10; Tübingen: Mohr Siebeck, 1998), 74; Guy Waters, *The End of Deuteronomy in the Epistles of Paul* (WUNT 2/221; Tübingen: Mohr Siebeck, 2006), 79–86. Paul's omission of τούτου draws attention to the entirety of the pentateuchal Law and not just Deuteronomy. E. P. Sanders (*Paul, the Law, and the Jewish People* [Minneapolis: Fortress, 1983], 22) contended that Deut 27:26 functions in Gal 3:10 solely because of its use of key words, but see the contrary position in A. Andrew Das, *Paul, the Law, and the Covenant* (Peabody, Mass.: Hendrickson, 2001), 163–67.

12. Hans-Joachim Eckstein, *Verheißung und Gesetz: Eine exegetische Untersuchung zu Galater 2,15–4,7* (WUNT 86; Tübingen: Mohr Siebeck, 1996), 124–28. Deuteronomy 27–32 is thought to be a composite text; A. D. H. Mayes, *Deuteronomy* (NCBC; London: Marshall, Morgan & Scott, 1979), 337, 343–46, 348–51, 358–59, 367–68, 371–72, 374–76, 379–82. On the secondary nature of Deut 27:26, see also Gerhard Wallis, "Der Vollbürgereid in Deuteronomium 27, 15–26," *HUCA* 45 (1974): 48.

pattern of sin, punishment, repentance (turning point), and salvation (Jub. 23; T. Mos. 2–10).[13] That Second Temple Jewish interpreters could treat Deut 27–32 as a unit renders plausible that Paul might have as well.[14]

The book of Deuteronomy offers a sober and pessimistic appraisal of Israel's future in the Mosaic covenant. The fear and failure of Israel upon the return of the spies in Deut 1:19-46 casts a dark shadow over the rest of Deuteronomy. The story of the spies' return functions as an archetype for Israel's future.[15] The alternatives of blessing and curse remain a decision for "today" (Deut 1:26).[16] The first- and second-person narration throughout 1:19–46 functions as a means of including future generations of readers with their forebears in these events.[17] Deuteronomy 1:30 can therefore speak of these past events as having taken place "before your eyes." Each generation faces the same issues the wilderness generation encountered; the sinful choices of that first generation do not bode well for Israel's future (1:35).

---

13. On this fourfold pattern based on Deut 27–32, see George W. E. Nickelsburg, *Jewish Literature between the Bible and the Mishnah* (2nd ed.; Minneapolis: Fortress, 2005), 72–73, 75–76. Jubilees 23:32 refers to Moses, and the command to write down the words is reminiscent of Deut 31:19.

14. On the variety of Second Temple appropriations of Deut 27–30, 32, see Waters, *End of Deuteronomy*, 29–77.

15. Martin Rose, *5. Mose* (ZBK 5; Zurich: Theologischer Verlag, 1994), 2:477: "um etwas 'Uranfängliches' und Fundamentales: der Ungehorsam gehört zum Wesen des Volkes Israel"; Norbert Lohfink, "Darstellungskunst und Theologie in Dtn 1,6–3,29," *Bib* 41 (1960): 118; followed by Paul A. Barker, *The Triumph of Grace in Deuteronomy: Faithless Israel, Faithful Yahweh in Deuteronomy* (Paternoster Biblical Monographs; Carlisle, U.K.: Paternoster, 2004), 25.

16. J. G. McConville and J. G. Millar, *Time and Place in Deuteronomy* (JSOTSup 179; Sheffield: Sheffield Academic Press, 1994), 42–43.

17. For first-person narration, see 1:19; Ian Cairns, *Word and Presence: A Commentary on the Book of Deuteronomy* (International Theological Commentary; Grand Rapids: Eerdmans, 1992), 32. Each generation is faced with the same situation before God as at Mount Horeb. On the second-person forms, see J. Ridderbos, *Deuteronomy* (trans. Ed M. van der Maas; Grand Rapids: Zondervan, 1984), 60: "Moses addresses the people directly … even though he is speaking to a new generation that is not directly responsible for what happened then." On the use of pronouns to include the present generation, see also McConville and Millar, *Time and Place*, 31–32. See the explicit conflation of generations in 5:3; R. Norman Whybray, *Introduction to the Pentateuch* (Grand Rapids: Eerdmans, 1995), 96: "The reader is to understand that that moment in the past and the present moment are one"; so also Brevard S. Childs, *Introduction to the Old Testament as Scripture* (Philadelphia: Fortress, 1979), 215.

The central section of Deuteronomy (11:31–26:15) consists of a legal code. This code anticipates serious failures on the part of the people: idolatry (ch. 13), murder (ch. 19), and sexual sin (ch. 22). John Goldingay commented: "The common casuistic form of the laws (e.g., 13:2–3, 7–8, 13–14 [1–2, 6–7, 12–13]) assumes that Israel will sin."[18] "Since the framework to Deuteronomy's laws so forcefully portrays Israel's sinfulness, it is not strange that the laws themselves presuppose acts and events which are less than ideal."[19]

The section immediately prior to the legal code (9:1–10:11) narrates the tragic golden calf incident (cf. Exod 32–34). The people prove to be "stubborn" and unrighteous (9:4–9, esp. v. 6; cf. 10:16). The golden calf incident represents Israel's sin as an unrighteous people par excellence.[20] Patrick D. Miller observed: "The sin of the people is not a single, rash action against the will of God but a persistent pattern of disobedience—at Horeb (v. 8), Taberah, Massah, Kibroth-hattaavah, and Kadesh-barnea (vv. 22–24)."[21] God therefore instituted the Law at a site of utter failure (9:8). Moses' intercessory prayer in the wake of the golden calf episode does not offer any virtue or merit on the part of the people but appeals instead to the patriarchal promises (9:25–29; cf. 9:5). When God commands the people in the next chapter to circumcise their hearts (10:16), that command is again grounded in God's gracious action on behalf of a chosen people and their patriarchs (10:15, 22). The contrast between Israel's disobedience and Yahweh's faithful actions recurs repeatedly throughout Deuteronomy:

> The persistent deep-seatedness of [Israel's] rebellions causes one to wonder if it is not something more than just unwillingness. The consistent grounds of hope in Deuteronomy have been Yahweh's grace and faithfulness to the patriarchal promises. This strong emphasis, and the contrast between Israel's faithlessness and Yahweh's faithfulness, suggests that Israel cannot rely on itself and its ability. Ultimately, it has to rely on Yahweh.[22]

---

18. John Goldingay, *Theological Diversity and the Authority of the Old Testament* (Grand Rapids: Eerdmans, 1987), 155.

19. Ibid.

20. Cairns, *Word and Presence*, 102, 104.

21. Patrick D. Miller, *Deuteronomy* (IBC; Louisville: John Knox, 1990), 122; also Barker, *Triumph of Grace*, 88: "[Israel's] history is not of occasional blemishes amidst an otherwise good record. Israel's sin is persistent and deep-seated."

22. Barker, *Triumph of Grace*, 106.

Deuteronomy 27–32, the section to which Paul alludes, immediately follows and, along with the golden calf incident, frames the legal code. The establishing of a stone altar on Mount Ebal, the mountain of curse, in 27:1–8 is not a hopeful sign for the people (cf. 11:29; 27:13). "All this may then be an indication that in Israel's history the curse of the law will be more prominent than the blessing (cf. 31.16–17), because the law … was not able to bring blessing (*heil*) to a sinful people."[23] Fourteen verses in chapters 27–28 outline Israel's blessings under the covenant; sixty-six verses list curses for disobedience. The preoccupation with the covenantal curses in these chapters offers a sober assessment of Israel's future. Whereas the blessings and curses appear to be open-ended possibilities dependent on Israel's obedience or disobedience in 28:1–44, in 28:45–48 declarative statements of fact replace the earlier conditional clauses: the curses come upon Israel *because* they did not obey. A dark future actuality replaces the conditionality.[24] Deuteronomy 29:3 therefore laments that "to this day the LORD has not given [Israel] a mind to understand, or eyes to see, or ears to hear."[25] Deuteronomy 29:18 (MT 17) describes an Israel vulnerable to sin as a contagion or as a root that is "sprouting poisonous and bitter growth." Indeed, Deut 29:23 (MT 22) envisions a day, after the poison has spread, when Israel will be no better than Sodom and Gomorrah. The only solution for the stubborn ways of Israel is the direct, empowering intervention of its God. Faithful to the covenant promises, God will circumcise the people's hearts, thereby rendering the commands easy (30:6, 11–14; 31:21–22). Without that divine assistance, the people *prove unable to obey and inevitably fall into sin.* In 31:16–17 the Lord predicts to Moses that the time will "soon" come after his death that the people will turn to foreign gods. The Lord will be forced to turn away from Israel and to permit trouble to fall upon the people. Moses, in his final address, bitterly chastises Israel as a stubborn and rebellious people who will surely turn away (31:27–29).

---

23. Ridderbos, *Deuteronomy*, 248–49, esp. 249.

24. Dennis T. Olson, *Deuteronomy and the Death of Moses: A Theological Reading* (OBT; Minneapolis: Fortress, 1994), 122: "Deuteronomy has transformed the blessing and curse list from a list of *possible* consequences (blessing or curse) to a declaration of *assured* future events, events leading inevitably to curse, judgment, and exile (28:45–68). … [The] human struggle for obedience and fidelity to God seems fated to end in curse, judgment, and death."

25. See the discussion of this verse in Barker, *Triumph of Grace*, 119–29; Olson, *Deuteronomy and Death of Moses*, 132.

He recognizes that apostasy would soon take place. Divine wrath against Israel's senseless disobedience dominates 32:13–33. The dark context of Deuteronomy and Israel's history of failure culminating in the Babylonian exile render plausible the thesis that Paul's omitted premise concerns the native inability to observe and obey all that is written in the Law.[26]

The obedience that Deuteronomy admonishes should be rigorous. In its composite citation, Gal 3:10 includes material from Deut 27:26. The context of that verse (27:15–26) identifies sins committed in *secret*.[27] Moving a boundary marker, misleading the blind on the road, and depriving the disenfranchised of justice are not as egregious as many other sins mentioned in Deut 27:15–26. The Law must be obeyed *in its entirety* and not just in public or heinous matters. Even secret sins jeopardize the community's relationship to God.[28] Paul includes in Gal 3:10 the word *all*. In

---

26. Israel's exile as a continuing phenomenon is a particular emphasis of N. T. Wright's "new perspective" approach (e.g., *Climax of the Covenant*, 144–48). Wright has offered a far too monochromatic portrait of an ongoing exile within the diversity of Second Temple Judaism; see the critique of Mark A. Seifrid, "Blind Alleys in the Controversy over the Paul of History," *TynBul* 45 (1994): 73–95. Paul's assumed premise in Gal 3:10 must be noncontroversial for all parties concerned. Paul may consider Israel in a state of exile, but his rivals would never assume an ongoing exile as they offered to the Galatians a far more optimistic advocacy of obedience under the Law. Wright also divorced corporate Israel's observance of the Law from the actions and responsibility of individual Israelites. Neither Galatians nor Deuteronomy makes that sort of sharp disjunction. As John M. G. Barclay (*Obeying the Truth: Paul's Ethics in Galatians* [Minneapolis: Fortress, 1988], 149–50) has shown, Gal 5:25–6:10 neatly alternates between corporate responsibility and individual accountability. Likewise, Deut 29 alternates between sections emphasizing individual accountability and sections emphasizing corporate responsibility; see Barker, *Triumph of Grace*, 137–38. The failures of individual Israelites accrue to the nation as a whole. Individuals and corporate entities are *both* responsible for sin.

27. Elizabeth Bellafontaine, "The Curses of Deuteronomy 27: Their Relationship to the Prohibitives," in *A Song of Power and the Power of Song: Essays on the Book of Deuteronomy* (ed. Duane L. Christensen; Winona Lake, Ind.: Eisenbrauns, 1993), 260–67.

28. The list of secret sins in Deut 27 places no emphasis on those sins that *distinguish* the Jewish community. Despite Dunn's emphasis against his critics that he does not limit "works of the Law" to the boundary markers of circumcision, Sabbath, and food laws, and that the phrase refers to obedience of the Law in its entirety, he nevertheless maintained in his more recent work: "In speaking of 'works of the law' Paul had in mind this boundary-marking, separating function of the law" (James D. G. Dunn, "The New Perspective: Whence, What and Whither," in *The New Perspective on Paul:*

Deut 5:32 (MT 31) God shares with the people "all" the commandments that they must be careful to obey by not turning to the right or left (5:32–33; also Deut 7:12 LXX). God commands diligent obedience of "all" the statutes and commands in Deut 6:24–25; 8:1; 11:22, 32; 13:18; 15:5; 17:19; 19:9; 24:8; 26:16; 27:10 (LXX); 28:1, 15; 31:12; 32:46. This repeated emphasis on doing "all" that God commands poses a problem for those who deny the Deuteronomic command to obey God's Law *perfectly.*

Many interpreters point to the hortatory elements in Deuteronomy's warnings as proof that Deuteronomy advocates comprehensive obedience but not perfect obedience. This is a confusion. Sanders's distinction between the strict demand of the Law and its gracious framework is helpful.[29] Deuteronomy enjoins the complete and absolute avoidance of transgression even if the framework of the people's covenant relation-

---

Collected Essays [WUNT 185; Tübingen: Mohr Siebeck, 2005], 8; cf. also 22–26, 43). The boundary markers remain *primarily* in view since they are those aspects of the entire Law that are in particular situations "contentious" (ibid., 26, also 24). Likewise Kent L. Yinger (*Paul, Judaism, and Judgment According to Deeds* [SNTSMS 105; Cambridge: Cambridge University Press, 1999], 171): "Though the meaning of ἔργα νόμου ['works of the law'] is broader than a few selected identity markers, the focus of Paul's usage is on circumcision and food laws because it was precisely this subset of religious activity which both Jews and non-Jews recognized as *the distinguishing identifiers* of Jewishness and which Paul understood to be relativized through faith in Christ." The "works of the Law" in Gal 3:10, however, most likely refers primarily to the demand for comprehensive obedience of the Law. Precisely *because* the Law demands obedience in its *entirety* (Gal 3:10), the Gentiles must be circumcised and observe the Law in the same manner as a Jew (thus the issue with the withdrawal at Antioch in Gal 2, or circumcision at Galatia). To demonstrate a concern over the boundary-marking elements of the Law in the larger context of Galatians is not of itself decisive for the interpretation of Gal 3:10, contra Dunn, Yinger, Gombis, and others. To claim that "works of the Law" (ἔργων νόμου) *always* highlights the Law's boundary-marking aspects overextends the evidence. In Rom 4:4–5 Paul uses the language of "works" for general human effort in developing the "works [of the Law]" (ἔργων [νόμου]) from 3:27; see A. Andrew Das, "Paul and Works of Obedience in Second Temple Judaism: Romans 4:4–5 as a 'New Perspective' Case Study," *CBQ* 71 (2009): 795–97, 803–12. In Rom 7:7–25 Paul posits an "I" who struggles to obey but ultimately proves unable to do what the Law commands. The ethnic, boundary-marking features are nowhere in view. This section of Romans demonstrates that Paul could indeed criticize human inability to obey God's Law. The assumed premise in Gal 3:10 that no one perfectly obeys the Law is not so outlandish after all.

29. Sanders, *Paul and Palestinian Judaism*, 235–36, 543; see also Das, *Paul, Law, and Covenant*, 12–69.

ship permits the restoration of sinners to God. The practical result of a people restored to their relationship to God in the face of sin does not mitigate Deuteronomy's repeated emphasis that *every* command should be observed without failure.

THE IDEAL OF PERFECTION AND THE REALITY OF FAILURE IN THE DEAD SEA SCROLL COMMUNITY

The pessimistic outlook of Deuteronomy was not abandoned in Second Temple Judaism. Although Dead Sea Scroll authors label themselves blameless or perfect (1QS II, 2; cf. VIII, 21; IX, 6, 8; 1QSb I, 2), the authors simultaneously exhort their members to walk in that perfect manner (CD II, 15–16; cf. 1QS I, 8; III, 9; IX, 18–19). Both aspects of the paradox are present in 1QH IX, 35–36: "Righteous men, put away iniquity! Hold fast [to the Covenant], all you perfect of way [וכול תמימי דרך]."[30] Perfect behavior remained an *ideal* toward which they were to strive. The writer of the Thanksgiving Hymns speaks of himself as "a foundation of shame and a source of impurity, an oven of iniquity and a building of sin, a spirit of error and depravity" (1QH IX, 21–22; cf. IV, 19: "the depravity of my heart"). His past is in the realm of wickedness and in continuity with the sins of his ancestors (XII, 29–35, esp. 34–35). The author of the Community Rule likewise numbers himself among "evil humankind, to the assembly of unfaithful flesh," with the same sinful tendencies as those "who walk in darkness" (1QS XI, 9–10). "The Angel of Darkness" leads astray "all the sons of justice (righteousness)" and causes them to perform unlawful and iniquitous works (1QS III, 21–23).[31] As long as the Angel of Darkness remains active in the world, community members cannot reach genuine perfection. The spirits of darkness and light both struggle for control in the heart of each individual (1QS IV, 23–24). Human beings inevitably walk in both wisdom *and* folly. Community members therefore look forward to the eschaton when they would be "cleansed" of this tendency toward

---

30. English translations and numbering, unless otherwise noted, are from Florentino García Martínez, *The Dead Sea Scrolls Translated: The Qumran Texts in English* (trans. Wilfred G. E. Watson; 2nd ed.; Leiden: Brill, 1996). This translation of 1QH IX, 35–36 is by Jacqueline C. R. de Roo, *"Works of the Law" at Qumran and in Paul* (Sheffield: Sheffield Phoenix, 2007), 27.

31. De Roo, *"Works of the Law,"* 27–29.

sin (1QS III, 21–23; IV, 18–22; XI, 14–15; 1QH XIV, 8–10; VII, 15–17).[32] In the interim, the community member must rely on God, who enables people to do what is good (1QS I, 2, 3, 11, 12, 13, 14, 17). Perfect obedience of the Law was not possible for individuals on their own. Only God could restore the transgressor to a blameless righteousness.

Exemplary Individuals: Jubilees, Abraham, and Hagiography

Second Temple Jews recognized the effectiveness of the sacrificial system and repentance for maintaining the relationship with God despite transgression.[33] They looked forward, like the author of the Qumran Community Rule, to the day when Israel would be perfectly obedient.[34] Second Temple literature upholds certain exemplary individuals in Israel's history who were rare exceptions to the rule of sin. "Abraham was perfect in all of his actions with the LORD and was pleasing through righteousness all of the days of his life" (Jub. 23:10; cf. 15:3).[35] Jacob, Leah, and Joseph were "perfect" (Jub. 27:17; 36:23; 40:8). Noah "was righteous in all of his ways just as it was commanded concerning him. And he did not transgress anything which was ordained for him" (Jub. 5:19). Philo qualifies that Noah attained a perfection relative to his generation; he was "not good absolutely" (οὐ καθάπαξ; Abr. 7 §§36–39; cf. Deus 25 §117; 26 §122; 30 §140; Abr. 6 §34; 9 §47). Philo emphasizes instead the sinlessness of Moses (Mos. 1.28 §162; 2.1 §1; 2.2 §§8–11; Leg. 3.46 §134; 47 §140; Ebr. 23 §94; Sacr. 3 §8).[36] The concession in Second Temple Jewish texts that only very rare, exceptional individuals perfectly obey God's Law renders plausible that a

---

32. Sanders, Paul and Palestinian Judaism, 279–80, 283–84, 291.

33. On the sacrificial system see, e.g., Jub. 6:14; 34:18–19; 50:10–11; Philo, Spec. 1.35 §§188–190; 42–47 §§226–256. On repentance see Jub. 1:22–23; 23:26; 41:23–27; Philo, Virt. 33–34 §§175–186; Fug. 18 §99, 105; 28 §160; Abr. 3 §19; 4 §26; Spec. 1.35 §§187–188; 43–46 §§236–253; QG.1.84; Mut. 21 §124; Somn. 1.15 §91.

34. E.g., Jub. 1:22–24; 5:12; 50:5; cf. the admonition of careful obedience of the entire Law in 23:16.

35. Translation by O. S. Wintermute, OTP, 2:100; cf. Jub. 24:11; Sir 44:20; CD III, 2–3; Pr. Man. 8; T. Ab. 10:13; Philo, Mig. 23 §§127–130; Abr. 45 §§275–276; Quis Her. 2 §§6–9; m. Qidd. 4:14.

36. See the more detailed discussion of these texts in Das, Paul, Law, and Covenant, 12–44. Dunn ("New Perspective," 57) downplayed such Second Temple texts as instances of eulogy and hagiography. Recognizing the implicit element of eulogy and hagiography does not diminish the paraenetic use of these models of sinless conduct.

Jew of this period would assume that his or her coreligionists do not obey God's Law without sin.

Such Second Temple texts—the Dead Sea Scrolls, Philo, and Jubilees— exemplify the balance between the command (and failure) to obey the Law perfectly on the one hand and God's gracious election with provision for fail- ure on the other. The nature of that balance, always present, varies from text to text and genre to genre. Some Second Temple authors define righteous- ness in a manner that is *inclusive* of provision for failure.[37] These authors express optimism with respect to Law observance in view of God's election and merciful provision. Other authors, especially in the wake of the Second Temple's destruction, devalue Israel's election and mercy in an almost exclu- sive focus on God's strict standards. Many Second Temple texts therefore distinguish between native human inability to obey God's Law perfectly and the divine empowerment of obedience with provision for failure.[38]

THE DEMAND FOR PERFECT OBEDIENCE
VERSUS PROVISION FOR FAILURE

In advocating for the "new perspective," Dunn commented on Gal 3:10: "the righteousness of the law included use of the sacrificial cult and benefit of the Day of Atonement."[39] Paul could therefore describe his Law observance

---

Sanders admitted from the Jubilees exemplars: "Perfect obedience is specified" (*Paul and Palestinian Judaism*, 381; cf. Jub. 1:23–24; 20:7).

37. E.g., Israel fell away in Pss. Sol. 9:1–2, but God also shows mercy and forgives the "righteous" transgressor who repents and calls on the Lord (3:5, 8; 9:6–7; 13:10– 12). The "righteous" nevertheless rigorously strive to avoid any sin at all (14:1–2; 3:6–7; 9:5; 14:2). The "righteous" have not avoided sin as originally commanded (e.g., 9:5; 17:8) but have availed themselves of God's provisions for mercy (13:9–10; 16:3, 11, 15). The righteous are also beneficiaries of God's election of Israel (9:8–10). For further discussion, see Sanders, *Paul and Palestinian Judaism*, 387–409; and Daniel Falk, "Psalms and Prayers," in *The Complexities of Second Temple Judaism* (vol. 1 of *Justification and Variegated Nomism*; ed. D. A. Carson, Peter T. O'Brien, and Mark A. Seifrid; Grand Rapids: Baker, 2001), 35–51.

38. On divine empowerment in Second Temple Judaism, see, e.g., 1QS XI; Wis 7:15; 12:16, 19; 15:3; Bar 3:7; Jub. 1:21–24; 5:12; 12:20; Das, "Paul and Works of Obedi- ence," 798–801.

39. James D. G. Dunn, *The Epistle to the Galatians* (BNTC; Peabody, Mass.: Hen- drickson, 1993), 171. Likewise Wright (*Climax of the Covenant*, 146): "The Torah does not envisage that all Jews will be perfect all the time, and it therefore makes provision for sin, through repentance and sacrifice, so that atonement may be made"; see also,

as "blameless" (Phil 3:6). Dunn unfortunately appealed to the gracious context of "covenantal nomism" to negate its embedded demand: "The mistake, once again, has been to read into the argument the idea that at this time the law would be satisfied with nothing less than sinlessness, unblemished obedience."[40] Norman Young exemplified the same confusion: "Judaism made no such demand" "to obey the whole law without failure."[41] Against such assertions, the Law's strict demand for obedience must be maintained with the same integrity as its merciful provision for failure.

What is really at issue is the *means* by which those who transgress may be righteous before God according to the apostle. Richard Hays called any supposed critique of a failure to obey God's Law perfectly "a ridiculous caricature of Judaism" since "the rival Missionaries could easily have refuted [Paul] by pointing out that the Law makes ample provision for forgiveness of transgressions through repentance, through the sacrificial system, and through the solemn annual celebration of the Day of Atonement."[42] "[T]ransgressions were dealt with according to the Law's provisions."[43] Paul, however, never mentions animal sacrifice as efficacious in his letters. He speaks instead of the efficacy of *Christ's* death. The covenantal curse that the Law places on those who fail to obey its commands (3:10) is resolved only by the one who became a "curse" on humanity's behalf (3:13). Jesus Christ "gave himself for our sins" (1:4).[44] The Law may "imprison" and "guard" (3:23), but it does not offer help with transgression (2:21; 3:21).[45]

In Sanders's paradigm, atoning sacrifice functioned as part of the framework of God's gracious election and covenant relationship with the people of Israel. In Gal 6:16 Paul invokes the "Israel of God." Most interpreters have identified the "Israel of God" as those Jews and Gentiles who follow Paul's rule that circumcision and uncircumcision do not count for anything in light of the cross of Christ. The "Israel of God" would therefore

---

e.g., Andrew H. Wakefield, *Where to Live: The Hermeneutical Significance of Paul's Citations from Scripture in Galatians 3:1–14* (AcBib 14; Atlanta: Society of Biblical Literature, 2003), 19, 68.

40. Dunn, *Galatians*, 171.

41. Norman H. Young, "Who's Cursed—and Why? (Galatians 3:10–14)," *JBL* 117 (1988): 83.

42. Richard B. Hays, "The Letter to the Galatians," *NIB* 11:257.

43. Ibid.; see also 312.

44. If this verse represents pre-Pauline material, then Paul could assume his rivals would agree that the only effective means for addressing sin was Jesus Christ.

45. Christ's Spirit, not the Law, counteracts the flesh in Gal 5–6.

consist of those in Christ rather than those under the Law. A minority of interpreters have proposed that Paul is speaking of two *separate* groups: those who follow his rule as well as "the Israel of God."[46] The apostle closes the letter in 6:10–16 as he opened it in 1:6–9—on a fiercely polemical note.[47] He may have coined the phrase "Israel of God" in opposition to the false "Israel" in the Galatians' midst who were promoting Gentile circumcision. In either interpretive approach, the Israel of God would recognize the irrelevance for salvation of Jewish ethnic identity. God's elect people are defined by their oneness and faith in Christ, whether Jew *or Gentile* (3:27–29). Paul therefore sees Abraham's "covenant" availing only through the one "seed," Jesus Christ (3:15–17, 29). The gracious elements in Second Temple Judaism—the election of a people, the covenant, provision for failure—are all understood by Paul in terms of Christ.[48] If the only solution for sin is in Jesus Christ (cf. 2:21; 3:21), then the Law offers no viable provision in itself for transgression. Without a useful mechanism to receive God's mercy and forgiveness, transgression of the Law would be, from Paul's standpoint, a serious problem for those "under the Law."[49] The Law's commands are sundered by Paul from their gracious and merciful context within Second Temple Judaism.[50]

ISRAEL'S LAW (SECOND TEMPLE JUDAISM)

Obedience to the Law	God's grace and mercy
	election (of Israel)
	sacrifice and repentance for sin

---

46. The crux is whether Paul employs an epexegetical καί renaming the previous group or a conjunctive καί for *separate* groups with the second group consisting of ethnic Jews or Jewish Christians; see, e.g., Hans Dieter Betz, *Galatians* (Hermeneia; Philadelphia: Fortress, 1979), 322–23.

47. Jeffrey A. D. Weima, "Gal. 6:11–18: A Hermeneutical Key to the Galatian Letter," *CTJ* 28 (1993): 90–107.

48. On the problems of the "two covenant" or *Sonderweg* theory, see A. Andrew Das, *Paul and the Jews* (Peabody, Mass.: Hendrickson, 2003), 96–106.

49. Paul therefore recognized that his "blameless" Law observance as a Jew was of little value in view of what God had done in Christ (Phil 3:3–11).

50. What many have overlooked are the implications of this reconceptualization for the "new perspective" popularized by Dunn and Wright: the "new perspective" interpreter cannot appeal to animal sacrifice, Israel's election, or any other mechanism of repentance or atonement apart from faith in Christ.

"In Christ" (Paul)

Obedience (fruit of Christ's spirit)   God's grace and mercy

election (in Christ)

Christ's death for sin

This approach does not represent a step backward into the traditional assumption of Jewish legalism but gives due recognition to the consequences of Paul's christological priorities. The following chart compares the "newer" perspective offered above with the "new perspective":

The "New Perspective"	A "Newer Perspective"
Second Temple Judaism	
The Law does not demand perfect obedience	The Law does demand perfect obedience
God's grace and mercy present	God's grace and mercy present (contra the "traditional" view)[51]
Paul	
"Works of the Law" = the entirety of the Law (contrary to certain critics)	"Works of the Law" = the entirety of the Law
"Works of the Law" is particularly focused on boundary markers	"Works of the Law" refers primarily more broadly but includes boundary markers
The Law does not demand perfect obedience	The Law does demand perfect obedience

---

51. This understanding of Second Temple Judaism does not rule out the possibility of synergistic strands of thought; see Simon J. Gathercole, *Where Is Boasting? Early Jewish Soteriology and Paul's Response in Romans 1–5* (Grand Rapids: Eerdmans, 2002); Charles H. Talbert, "Paul, Judaism, and the Revisionists," *CBQ* 63 (2001): 1–22; Timo Eskola, *Theology and Predestination in Pauline Soteriology* (WUNT 2/100; Tübingen: Mohr Siebeck, 1998); idem, "Paul, Predestination and 'Covenantal Nomism'—Reassessing Paul and Palestinian Judaism," *JSJ* 29 (1997): 390–412. Paul critiques the Law in Gal 2:21; 3:21, however, as being *itself* incapable of salvation.

| Animal sacrifice avails for for-giveness | Christ's death avails for sin; animal sacrifice does not |

This "newer perspective" corrective represents a fresh starting point for interpreting Gal 3:10. Since Paul and his rivals would have agreed that Christ's death avails for sin, what were the points of their disagreement and what role does 3:10 play in that discussion?

THE ROLE OF GALATIANS 3:10 IN THE "NEWER PERSPECTIVE" DEBATE AT GALATIA

Many interpreters have contended that Paul's *real* argument against Moses' Law is stated in 3:11–12: the Law, based on works, is simply not of faith. In 2:15–16 Paul rends asunder faith in/of Christ from the Law of Moses. The question is why there should be a contrast at all, especially when Paul's rivals would have viewed the Law and faith as *complementary*. This disjunction would have been controversial at Galatia, and so Paul explains in 3:10 *why* the Law is not a component of God's justifying activity. Galatians 3:10 therefore serves as crucial support for the contrast in 3:11–12.

Interpreters normally take δῆλον in 3:11 with the preceding ὅτι: "Now it is evident that no one is justified before God by the law; for 'The one who is righteous will live by faith'" (NRSV). In this translation the Hab 2:4 citation in Gal 3:11b offers the basis for the conclusion stated in 3:11a. Most commentators do not consider that δῆλον may be taken instead with the *following* ὅτι: "*Because* no one is justified before God by the Law, *it is clear that* 'The righteous will live by faith.'" Andrew Wakefield concluded on the basis of his *Thesaurus linguae graecae* investigation: "The evidence from Greek literature and other writings suggests [that δῆλον should be taken with the *following* ὅτι], not only because δῆλον ὅτι is more common than ὅτι … δῆλον, but even more because, in those cases when ὅτι both precedes *and* immediately follows δῆλον, Greek usage hardly ever matches the δῆλον with the ὅτι that precedes."[52] The initial ὅτι in 3:11 serves, then,

---

52. Wakefield, *Where to Live*, 164; see also 207–14 and his critique of Hermann Hanse, "ΔΗΛΟΝ (zu Gal 3[11])," *ZNW* 34 (1935): 299–303, esp. 302. On the usage of δῆλον in Greek literature, see Wakefield, *Where to Live*, 207–14: in twenty-nine instances δῆλον goes with the following ὅτι and only in three instances with the prior ὅτι. Wakefield's approach is not unprecedented (cf. *Where to Live*, 163 n. 97); see Frank

to signal that the conclusion of 3:10 forms the basis for 3:11: Since no one is justified before God by the Law (3:11a) (because those ἐξ ἔργων νόμου are under its curse [3:10]), it is clear that "the righteous will live by faith" (3:11b).[53] The problem with *doing* the Law in 3:12 is that people *do not do* the Law as required (3:10).

Paul chooses in 3:10 to speak of being "under the curse" (ὑπὸ κατάραν) for the failure to do the Law. This choice of language parallels the ὑπό-phrases elsewhere in Galatians (3:22, 23, 24–25; 4:2, 3, 4, 5, 21a; 5:18).[54] The Scripture "imprisons" "under" sin in 3:22 and "under" the Law in 3:23–25. Paul speaks of a state of slavery "under" the elements of the cosmos in 4:3. Those led by the Spirit are liberated from being "under" (the power of) the Law.[55] As Paul continues in Galatians, he clarifies that those in the flesh without Christ's Spirit *cannot* fulfill what the Law demands (4:6; 5:13–14, 16–18). Paul's commonplace observation that people do not do all that the Law commands serves as support, then, for *why* the Law is an enslaving power. Christ therefore came to liberate people from the Law's curse (3:10, 13).

Paul's Galatian rivals, however, would have agreed that Christ's death avails for sin (3:13). What, then, were the grounds for their disagreement? Galatians 3:10–12 offers a glimpse into the rivals' position. Commentators frequently note that the scriptural texts Paul employs in 3:10–12 support more naturally the rivals' Law-observant position.[56] The Deutero-

---

Thielman, *Paul and the Law* (Downers Grove, Ill.: InterVarsity Press, 1994), 127; and Charles H. Cosgrove, *The Cross and the Spirit: A Study in the Argument and Theology of Galatians* (Macon, Ga.: Mercer University Press, 1988), 54 n. 32.

53. Scriptural quotations in Paul may indeed function as the conclusion of a deductive proof; see, e.g., 1 Cor 1:31; 2 Cor 10:17; Wakefield, *Where to Live*, 166–67.

54. Some view the curse in 3:10 as a mere threat: Christopher D. Stanley, "'Under a Curse': A Fresh Reading of Galatians 3.10–14," *NTS* 36 (1990): 500–501, 508–11; Joseph P. Braswell, "'The Blessing of Abraham' versus 'The Curse of the Law': Another Look at Gal 3:10–13," *WTJ* 53 (1991): 75–77; Young, "Who's Cursed—and Why?" 86–87; and most recently, Wakefield, *Where to Live*, 177–80. Christ in 3:13 is liberating from an *actual* curse and not merely a potentiality. Wakefield (p. 181) recognized that Gal 3:13 states Christ's work soteriologically; but, in denying the corresponding soteriological plight in 3:10, Wakefield merely *asserted* that redemption from the curse is not an emphasis in 3:10–14.

55. J. Louis Martyn, *Galatians* (AB 33A; New York: Doubleday, 1997), 370–73.

56. C. K. Barrett first noticed the likelihood that Paul is responding to a body of texts in use by his opponents (*Essays on Paul* [Philadelphia: Westminster, 1982], 158–63); see also Martyn, *Galatians*, 311, 315; Das, *Paul and the Jews*, 21–23.

nomic context of the citation in 3:10 pronounces a curse on those who do not observe the Law but also a blessing on those who do. The Lev 18:5 citation in Gal 3:12 declares that the one who does the Law will *live* by them. Even Hab 2:4, as understood by the Qumran community, spoke of living by faithfulness to the Qumran Teacher's interpretation of the Law (1QpHab VII, 5–VIII, 3). Paul appears to be co-opting his rivals' proof texts and reinterpreting them in support of his own point of view. If correct, the rivals betray in their choice of proof texts an optimism that the Galatians *could* obey God's Law in a satisfactory manner.[57] Leviticus 18:5 (cited in Gal 3:12) promises life to the Law observant, and obedience of the Law avoids the curse of Deuteronomy. To avoid the curse is to enjoy the Law's promise of blessing since blessing and curse are mutually exclusive alternatives.

The rivals' optimism is understandable. They preached a Christian gospel message (1:6–9).[58] They shared common ground with Paul, according to 2:15–16, that faith in/of Jesus Christ was necessary for justification.[59] "Even we believed in Christ Jesus" (2:17). They may have

---

57. Inclusive of Christ's forgiveness for transgressions; see discussion below.

58. Mark Nanos (*The Irony of Galatians* [Minneapolis: Fortress, 2002], 288–96) contended that rivals were "non–Christ-believing" Jews; εὐαγγέλιον would not indicate a Christian message. See the rebuttal of Nanos in Das, *Paul and the Jews*, 24–29.

59. Martyn, *Galatians*, 263–75; A. Andrew Das, "Another Look at ἐὰν μή in Galatians 2:16," *JBL* 119 (2000): 529–39; Martinus C. de Boer, "Paul's Use and Interpretation of a Justification Tradition in Galatians 2.15–21," *JSNT* 28 (2005): 189–216. Debbie Hunn ("Εὰν μή in Galatians 2:16: A Look at Greek Literature," *NovT* 49 [2007]: 281–90) documented the rare Greco-Roman examples of the ἐὰν μή clause as an exception to only a portion of the main clause and of the adversative use of the ἐὰν μή clause. She conceded that an exception to the entirety of the main clause "is the rule both inside and outside the NT" (p. 283), which would result in a reading supportive of Paul's rivals in which faith in/of Christ is the exception to not being justified by the works of the Law. Although critical of my reading of these verses, Hunn inadvertently confirmed it with further evidence that 2:16a is ambiguous common ground from which Paul will then offer his own interpretation. In dissenting from 2:16a as common ground, Ian Scott conceded that 2:16a may very well be ambiguous ("Common Ground? The Role of Galatians 2.16 in Paul's Argument," *NTS* 53 [2007]: 425–35, esp. 427 n. 3). Against Scott ("Common Ground?" 434–35 n. 25), Paul does not claim in the remainder of the verse that "we Jews" *know* that one is justified by faith in Christ apart from the works of the Law. What they all "know" and affirm is expressed strictly in 2:16a. In the remainder of the verse—whatever the Galatian Jewish Christians' own understanding—Paul affirms that "we Jews" are justified apart from the Law. Paul interprets the "common

confessed with Paul a creed describing Jesus as "giving himself for sins" (1:4).[60] Where they differed from Paul was in viewing the Law and Christ in a complementary relationship.[61] They had subordinated Christ's saving work into a framework of understanding based on Moses' Law. Although the rivals would have agreed with the commonplace observation that no one perfectly obeys the Law, they would not have concluded from it that the Law pronounces only a curse. Understood as an atoning sacrifice for transgression of the Law, Christ's death would have resolved the problem of imperfect obedience and would have permitted the Law to speak with a voice of blessing.

Paul, for his part, speaks of blessing and curse too, but he divorces God's blessing from Sinai's legislation in a way his rivals had not. Blessing is now exclusively associated with the promises to Abraham (3:6), and Moses' legislation, with its cursing voice, remains severed from God's dealings with Abraham (3:10–12).[62] Moses' Law may function as a scriptural witness to the blessing of Abraham on the basis of faith/faithfulness in

---

ground" *his* way. Thus, as Scott rightly recognized, Paul must *argue* for his interpretation and is still doing so at the end of the paragraph in 2:21.

60. In favor of an early Christian tradition, see Wiard Popkes, *Christus Traditus: Eine Untersuchung zum Begriff der Dahingabe im Neuen Testament* (ATANT 49; Zurich: Zwingli, 1967), 153–295, esp. 196–97, 273–74; Klaus Wengst, *Christologische Formeln und Lieder des Urchristentums* (SNT 7; Gütersloh: Mohn, 1972), 55–77, esp. 56–57, 61; C. Breytenbach, "Versöhnung, Stellvertretung und Sühne," *NTS* 39 (1993): 67–73; François Bovon, "Une formule prépaulinienne dans l'Épître aux Galates (Gal 1.4–5)," in *Paganisme, Judaïsme, Christianisme: Influences et affrontements dans le monde antique. Mélanges offerts à Marcel Simon* (ed. A. Benoit et al.; Paris: E. de Boccard, 1978), 91–107; Martin Hengel, *The Atonement: The Origins of the Doctrine in the New Testament* (Philadelphia: Fortress, 1981), 33–39. Paul cites a pre-Pauline tradition in 1 Cor 15:3 that describes Christ work similarly to Gal 1:4. The plural "sins" in Gal 1:4 is also contrary to his preference for the singular. On the other hand, the variation in language prevents certainty. In 1 Cor 15:3 Christ did not "give himself" (τοῦ δόντος ἑαυτὸν as in Gal 1:4) but rather "died" (ἀπέθανεν). He acted κατὰ τὰς γραφάς in 1 Cor 15:3, but according to the will of God the Father in Gal 1:4. Romans 4:25 and 8:32 employ παραδίδωμι (δίδωμι in Gal 1:4). In Rom 4:25 the handing over is διὰ τά παραπτώματα ἡμῶν and in 8:32 simply ὑπὲρ ἡμῶν πάντων (not ὑπὲρ τῶν ἁμαρτιῶν as in Gal 1:4).

61. Das, "Another Look," 532–39.

62. Presumably those in Israel's history were justified, *like Abraham*, by faith in the promises. What Christ ushered in is a new era in which that faith/faithfulness finds its fulfillment in the coming of Faith (3:22). On this distinction between Abrahamic blessing and Mosaic curse, see the similar comments in Martyn, *Galatians*, 324–28.

3:6–9, but Paul abstracts the principle of faith/faithfulness from the pentateuchal testimony and juxtaposes it over against Sinai's legislative demand. Paul can therefore speak of the Law in this narrower sense as *opposed* to faith (3:12); the Law is not "of faith" but rather "of works." This contrast of the Law with faith would have been a departure from the other Jewish Christian teachers. God's gracious dealings, for Paul, bypass Sinai and proceed straight from Abraham to Christ. Christ represents the beginning of a new era in history, the dawning of a "new creation" (6:15).[63] As an interruption in history, Sinai is robbed of any gracious significance. Paul will, of course, render the interruption implied in the logic of 3:6–14 explicit in 3:15–18. Whereas the rivals maintained continuity between Christ's saving work and Moses' Law, Paul posits the discontinuity of a new age that was promised to Abraham. As an interruption in God's saving action from Abraham to Christ, Mount Sinai does not offer an effective means of atonement for sin or failure. Its legislation has been reduced, conceptually, to an empty husk of demands with no effective provision for failure. Why foist the Sinaitic Law upon the Gentiles?

Conclusion

Second Temple Jewish authors agreed with Deuteronomy that human beings are incapable of obeying God's Law apart from divine assistance. Even with that gracious empowerment, some Second Temple authors concluded that individuals who perfectly obeyed the Law were exceedingly rare and exceptional, at best. Whereas transgression of the Law could be rectified for the Jews by God's merciful provision, Paul and other adherents of the early Christian movement reconceptualized such grace and mercy in terms of Christ (Gal 3:13). In view of the apocalyptic new age dawning in Christ, Paul went further in viewing God's saving activity as having nothing to do with Sinai's legislation, a point of view that rendered problematic the strict obedience commanded by the Mosaic Law. Those who adopt the path of the Law inevitably fall under its curse for their failures to obey. Galatians 3:10 therefore offers a supporting argument for why the Law, along with its ethnic distinctions, should not be foisted upon the Gentiles. An omitted premise faulting failure to obey the Law has been

---

63. The rivals would have agreed with the apostle in 1:4 that Jesus death is ὑπὲρ τῶν ἁμαρτιῶν (note Paul's avoidance of παραπτώματα; cf. Rom 4:25; 8:32), but he also adds that Jesus thereby rescues the Galatians from "the present evil age."

far too quickly dismissed. Having moved beyond the "new perspective" impasse, a new starting point is possible for understanding Paul in relation to his Christ-believing Jewish peers.

THE BODY IN QUESTION:
THE SOCIAL COMPLEXITIES OF RESURRECTION*

Luke Timothy Johnson

In an earlier essay on 1 Corinthians, I argued on the basis of a close examination of chapter 15, as well as of Paul's language about πνεῦμα throughout the composition, that Paul sees the resurrection as more than an event of the past that involved Jesus alone.[1] Instead, he understands resurrection as a reality of the present that involves, indeed defines, the present existence of believers. The crucified Messiah Jesus has been exalted. As Lord he shares God's rule over all things. He has become not simply a living being (through resuscitation), but life-giving Spirit—that is, a source of the Spirit who gives life (1 Cor 15:45). An analysis of Paul's language about the Holy Spirit, in turn, shows that it is precisely the presence of that Holy Spirit among and in believers that enables them to confess Jesus as Lord, that gifts them with extraordinary capacities, and that makes them holy. Paul's language about the Holy Spirit is a way of speaking about the resurrection/exaltation of Jesus as a new creation that fundamentally affects human existence. I suggested, further, that this state of affairs demands of us, in turn, a mode of thinking and speaking that engages the conditions of human existence (that is, ontology) and not merely the actions of human agents (that is, history).

---

* Originally one of the Payton Lectures delivered at Fuller Theological Seminary (2010) and then at the Stone-Campbell Journal Conference at Cincinnati Christian University (2011), this essay is offered in tribute to Frank Matera in celebration of his long and fruitful life of scholarship, and in grateful acknowledgment particularly of his work in the Letters of Paul.
1. See "Life-Giving Spirit: The Ontological Implications of Resurrection," *Stone Campbell Journal* 15 (2012): 75–84.

Paul's way of thinking and speaking about Spirit (πνεῦμα), in turn, demands as well a fresh consideration of body (σῶμα).[2] Three statements in 1 Corinthians impel such reconsideration. First, when Paul responds to the question of an imagined interlocutor concerning the future resurrection, "with what sort of body do they come" (15:35), he ultimately replies that the body "is raised a spiritual body" (σῶμα πνευματικόν, 15:44). Second, in his discussion of sexual immorality, Paul rebukes the Corinthians for forgetting that "your bodies are members of Christ" (6:15). Third, he states flatly in 12:27, "You [plural, ὑμεῖς] are the body of Christ." The three statements point to three aspects of Paul's perception of the body among those who have been baptized in the Holy Spirit and profess Jesus as exalted Lord: (a) the future condition of body as totally suffused with Spirit; (b) the persistence of the empirical body (σῶμα ψυχικόν) that remains at the disposal of the individual as the medium of worldly (and spiritual) expression; (c) the communal or collective σῶμα of the community that is at once the sanctuary of the Holy Spirit (3:16–17) and the σῶμα of the Messiah. Given these three aspects, the meaning of σῶμα in any specific instance will not necessarily be perfectly clear. The presence of the resurrection πνεῦμα complicates the language of the body.

THINKING ABOUT THE BODY

A good preparation for examining Paul's language about πνεῦμα and σῶμα is to recollect how our default mode of thinking about the body—inherited from Descartes and extended by science and technology—prevents us

---

2. My claim to "freshness" here is relative rather than absolute. Certainly, Paul's language about σῶμα has received massive attention, especially by scholars interested in Paul's theological anthropology. See, e.g., John A. T. Robinson, *The Body: A Study in Pauline Theology* (London: SCM, 1952; repr., Lima, Ohio: Wyndham Hall, 1988); Rudolf Bultmann, *Theology of the New Testament* (trans. Kendrick Grobel; 2 vols.; New York: Scribner's, 1951–1953), 1:190–210; Robert H. Gundry, *Sōma in Biblical Theology, with Emphasis on Pauline Anthropology* (SNTSMS 29; Cambridge: Cambridge University Press, 1976); Robert Jewett, *Paul's Anthropological Terms: A Study of Their Use in Conflict Settings* (AGJU 10; Leiden: Brill, 1971); James D. G. Dunn, *The Theology of Paul the Apostle* (Grand Rapids: Eerdmans, 1998), 55–78. Such analyses, however, have tended to be both synthetic (drawing from all the "great letters"), and lexical (focusing, e.g., on the semantic nuances of πνεῦμα, σῶμα, and σάρξ). My essay more modestly seeks only to examine the complexities of σῶμα in view of the resurrection πνεῦμα, and stays almost completely within the frame of 1 Corinthians.

from truly engaging with what Paul is saying.[3] Our tendency is to think in terms first of the individual human body. Pervasive individualism—evident above all in contemporary American culture—makes talk about a "social body" seem secondary and derivative, at best a metaphor.[4] The individual body, moreover, tends to be considered in isolation from the world and from other bodies. The sense of separate somatic existence is expressed and reinforced by the development of distinctive posture, clothing, housing, and variable zones of personal safety.[5] In pathological cases, the bodies of others—whether the "others" are animals, people, microbes, or even food—are viewed essentially in terms of threat to the integrity of the individual organism, which must maintain itself against dangerous entanglement.[6]

The individual body, furthermore, is considered in purely physical terms. Indeed, the progression in contemporary thought has been from the ghost in the machine to simply the machine, or perhaps better, the workings of brain chemistry within the machine.[7] Finally, the body is thought of in terms of problem-solving: the dramatic exchanges of blood and vital organs in medical technology is matched by the routines of exercise and diet, and more drastically, in the kind of body engineering expressed by fetal harvesting, gender changing, plastic surgery, and cloning.[8] In this

---

3. See William C. Placher, *The Domestication of Transcendence: How Modern Thinking about God Went Wrong* (Louisville: Westminster John Knox, 1996).

4. The premise of the American experiment—derived from John Locke (*Second Treatise on Government*, 1690) and other Enlightenment thinkers—is that society is formed by contract among independent individuals, who must "consent" to being governed by common rules or authority; more recently, see John Rawls, *A Theory of Justice* (Cambridge: Harvard University Press, 1971).

5. A direct symbolic line runs from the "body language" of individualism to the acquisitive use of possessions: corresponding to the *noli me tangere* of political individualism is the *keep off the grass* of gated "communities"; for a brilliant fictional rendering, see T. Coraghessan Boyle, *Tortilla Curtain* (New York: Penguin, 1996).

6. See, e.g., Nena Baker, *The Body Toxic* (New York: North Point, 2009).

7. For accessible discussions of the complex issues in the philosophy of mind, see John Heil, *Philosophy of Mind: A Contemporary Introduction* (London: Routledge, 2004); and William Jaworski, *Philosophy of Mind: A Comprehensive Introduction* (Oxford: Wiley-Blackwell, 2011).

8. One must wonder whether any sense of irony went into the efforts of James Villepigue and Hugo Rivera as they wrote *The Body Sculpting Bible for Women: The Way to Physical Perfection* (rev. ed.; Hobart, N.Y.: Hatherleigh, 2006) and the companion volume for men.

construal, the body is considered as a form of property. It is something I have. I own it and can dispose of it as I choose. I can sell my body for profit. I have rights over my body just as I have rights over my other property.[9]

The development of cultural criticism has slightly modified such a mechanistic view of the body by alerting us to the ideological interests that can be at work in the social construction of the body in diverse cultures.[10] Such analysis reminds us that different cultures have different notions of what is beautiful or admirable in human bodies—bald is not always bad and bowed legs can suggest qualities of leadership[11]—and that body-typing can and has played a role in a variety of racist and sexist political programs.[12] But the modification offered is slight, for the body is still regarded as a problem to be solved, or as an object to be manipulated, or as a property to be negotiated. And it is still the individual rather than the social body that is of primary interest.

A more fruitful way of thinking about the body is through reflection on our own bodily experience. When I reflect bodily—that is, tap my foot, wrinkle my brow, sigh deeply, ponder the itch in my left ankle, and, above all, perform the amazing mental trick of remembering the former me—I realize that every sense of my self is of my bodily self. As long as I remember me I remember my body. I cannot conceive of me absent from my body. Although my cells have sloughed off and been replaced endlessly, somehow what I call me has been borne through the years—and through entropy to ever greater corpulence—by the body. I realize, then, that whereas there is some truth to the claim to "have" my body—I can indeed dispose of it in a variety of ways—there is an equal truth to the claim that I "am" my body. I cannot dispose of body completely without also dispos-

9. The premise is foundational especially for early feminist discourse; see, e.g., *Our Bodies Ourselves: A Course by and for Women,* by the Boston Women's Health Book Collective (Boston: New England Free Press, 1971).

10. The work of Michel Foucault in this regard is of fundamental importance; see, e.g., *Discipline and Punish: The Birth of the Prison* (trans. Alan Sheridan; New York: Vintage, 1977).

11. See the instructive essay on ancient body assumptions in Abraham J. Malherbe, "A Physical Description of Paul," in *Paul and the Popular Philosophers* (Minneapolis: Fortress, 1989), 165–70.

12. Obvious examples are the propaganda posters produced in Nazi Germany depicting Jews with subhuman features and the stereotypical representations of African Americans in the United States during the era of segregation; similar are the pictorial representations of "the Hun" and the "Yellow Peril" by Allied propaganda.

ing of me. In the strict empirical sense, when my body disappears, so do I. Likewise, when I commit my body, I commit myself. This is the basis of all covenant and all witness.[13]

If this is so, and all our experience confirms that it is, then the body does not lie outside myself as a problem to be solved, as a sculpture to be carved, as a project to be engineered. If I so objectify my body, I alienate myself from my true somatic condition. As the philosopher Gabriel Marcel has instructed us, the body-self does not lie in the realm of the problematic but properly in the realm of the mysterious.[14] I cannot detach myself from my body as though it were not me. That way lies the most profound alienation. The mysterious, Marcel tells us, is that in which we are inescapably involved as persons.[15] A budget is a problem; marriage is a mystery. A broken timepiece is a problem, but a dying friend is a mystery. Making budget decisions mysterious is simply silly, but treating a marriage like a problem is tragic. Weeping over a stolen automobile shows confusion; failure to weep for a dying friend reveals alienation.

My body, furthermore, is not isolated from its physical environment.[16] The world is as much within me as outside me. The microbes, thank goodness, are not simply out there, they are in here, doing their quiet good work. I suck in and expel the world's atmosphere, in the process feeding the green things around me that also in turn feed me. I have, in fact, eaten quite a considerable part of my environment over the past sixty-five years,

---

13. For the connection between body and possessions, see Luke T. Johnson, *Sharing Possessions: What Faith Demands* (2nd ed.; Grand Rapids: Eerdmans, 2011), 1–10, 29–34; for the body as basis of witness and covenant, see idem, "The Revelatory Body: Notes Toward a Somatic Theology," in *The Phenomenology of the Body* (ed. D. J. Martino; Pittsburgh: Simon Silverman Phenomenology Center at the University of Duquesne, 2003), 69–85.

14. See esp. Gabriel Marcel, "Outline of a Phenomenology of Having," in *Being and Having* (trans. Katharine Farrer; London: Collins, 1949), 168–89.

15. See idem, *Mystery of Being* (trans. Rene Hague; 2 vols.; Chicago: Regnery, 1950), 1:242–70.

16. The intersection of theology and ecology is currently a busy one; see, among many offerings, Kyle S. Van Houtan and Michael S. Northcott, eds., *Diversity and Dominion: Dialogues in Ecology, Ethics, and Theology* (Eugene, Ore.: Wipf & Stock, 2010); Thomas Jay Oord, *Divine Grace and Emerging Creation: Wesleyan Forays in Science and Theology of Creation* (Eugene, Ore.: Pickwick, 2009); and my own small contribution, "Caring for the Earth: Why Environmentalism Needs Theology," *Commonweal* 132 (2005): 16–20.

and while retaining some of it in storage, I have also returned an astounding mountain of body-stuff for the world's cycle of regeneration. As I take, so do I gift; as I eat, so am I eaten; while I live, and assuredly when I die.[17] My body is not the exception to the world, it is the rule; it is not separate from the world, it is the world in concentrated form.

Finally, my reflection on my own experience of being and having a body suggests to me that thinking first if not always in terms of my individual body rather than in terms of the social body is also, in its way, a form of alienation. It is obvious that we are born out of the bodies of others, and in fact bear their bodies within us, just as when we give birth our bodies are carried forth by our children and their children. Just as we derive from the bodies of others so also are we dependent on other bodies. Not only at birth but also at burial, not only in first but also in second infancy, we are utterly dependent on other bodies, other selves, in all essentials.[18] These moments of entry and departure, however, only accentuate the fundamental dependence of any individual body on the bodies of others throughout human life; indeed, a life cut off from other bodies becomes less and less human. When John Donne declared that "no man is an island, entire of itself,"[19] he spoke the soberest truth.

Such reflection on the lived experience of somatic existence does not bring us all the way to Paul's perceptions, but it serves to call into question the default sense of the body peddled by radical individualism and late-capitalist commodification. When we recognize how, even when thinking of the empirical body, we can speak of being as well as having body, and can perceive that the membrane distinguishing the human body from the world is permeable with traffic moving both ways, and can acknowledge the ways in which the body of every individual person is willy-nilly implicated in the bodies of others, we are better able to consider the statements that Paul makes as he seeks to sort out the complexities of somatic existence in light of the resurrection and the empowerment of the Corinthian community through the Holy Spirit.

---

17. A point made brilliantly by Jim Crace, *Being Dead* (New York: Picador, 1999).

18. See esp. Timothy P. Jackson, "A House Divided Again: 'Sanctity' vs. 'Dignity' in the Induced Death Debate," in *In Defense of Human Dignity* (ed. Robert P. Kraynak and Glenn E. Tinder; Notre Dame, Ind.: University of Notre Dame Press, 2003), 139–63.

19. John Donne, *Meditation 17*.

It is precisely in the turn to language about πνεῦμα and σῶμα that we encounter the greatest difference between Paul's assumptions and our own. Whereas the two terms seldom touch for us,[20] for Paul they are always mutually implicated. Paul would have agreed with his contemporary James that "the body without a spirit is dead" (Jas 2:26), but he also shared the conviction of the entire prophetic tradition that spirit without a body is powerless and inarticulate. Spirit, even God's Holy Spirit, requires a body for its self-expression. We do not find in 1 Corinthians any trace of a dualism that privileges the spirit and seeks its release from the body; instead, we find spirit and body in mutual dependence. What makes the language in 1 Corinthians so complex, however, is that Paul does not have in mind only the animate (natural) body that he calls ψυχικός, but the consequences for human bodies of being animated by God's πνεῦμα. Thus Paul refers to God's breathing into the clay so that the first Adam became a living being, ψυχὴν ζῶσαν, but his concern throughout the letter is the social implications of Christ becoming "life-giving Spirit" (πνεῦμα ζῳοποιοῦν, 15:45).

The Assembly as the ΣΩΜΑ ΧΡΙΣΤΟΥ

Unlike our contemporary focus, Paul's attention is given primarily to the social rather than the individual body. As with his language of the πνεῦμα, he can speak of the individual's σῶμα in terms of self-disposition. Thus husband and wife each has ἐξουσιάζειν over the body of the other in their sexual relationship (7:4), and the unmarried woman whose concern is for the things of the Lord is holy in "body and spirit" (7:34). Paul pummels and enslaves his own body to keep himself worthy of proclaiming to others (9:27). He proposes the possibility of "handing over" his own body (13:3). But in the majority of instances, σῶμα has a collective sense.

The body is one of three metaphors that Paul uses for the Corinthian assembly as such: in 3:6–9 he tells them that they are God's "field" (γεώργιον), which Paul has planted and which Apollos has watered, but to which God gives growth. They are also God's "building" (οἰκοδομή), whose foundation of Jesus Christ Paul, as a wise builder, has established, and on that foundation others can build (3:9–15). And because the Holy Spirit

---

20. Our usage retains a vestigial element of the ancient strong conviction when we refer only to a living ("animate") human's "body" and to a dead human's "corpse."

dwells in/among them (τὸ πνεῦμα τοῦ θεοῦ οἰκεῖ ἐν ὑμῖν), they are God's "temple sanctuary" (ναός, 3:16–17). Paul's favorite metaphor for the assembly, however, is that it is the Messiah's body, which he develops fully in chapter 12, and exploits also in chapters 6 and 10. That this is Paul's favorite community metaphor is indicated by his use of it throughout 1 Corinthians, and with some frequency elsewhere in his letters.[21] The metaphor is not a passing figure that Paul seizes on to make a single point, but rather represents a fixed conviction concerning the character of the assembly. The fact that Paul uses it so widely and in such differing contexts, plus the fact that he develops it so extensively in 1 Corinthians, raises the question whether σῶμα Χριστοῦ is only a metaphor, or is it, for Paul, perhaps something more?

We are able to ask this question more responsibly in 1 Cor 12 because, as most commentators observe, the use of "body" as a metaphor for the city-state was common among ancient rhetoricians.[22] Especially when the topic was one of political harmony addressed to city-states in conditions of discord and strife, the metaphor was frequently and usefully deployed. Members of a society should think of themselves as analogous to a human body, all of whose parts work together peacefully for the common good. It would be foolish to deny that Paul's language about the body in 1 Cor 12 bears precisely the same sort of force and points in the same direction. This is a community, after all, whose fleshly, all-too-human condition is described in terms of rivalry and competition and strife and schism (3:1–4), and it is incontestable that Paul seeks among them harmony and cooperation rather than division (1:10). Paul's emphasis in 12:14–26 on unity within diversity, and on the mutually useful functions of the parts of the body, makes the political point in a fairly conventional fashion.

Several aspects of Paul's discussion, however, suggest that something more than a political metaphor is at work.[23] We note at once that as he dis-

---

21. See Rom 12:4–5; Eph 4:4–16; 5:30; Col 1:18, 24; 3:15.

22. See Margaret M. Mitchell, *Paul and the Rhetoric of Reconciliation: An Exegetical Investigation of the Language and Composition of 1 Corinthians* (Louisville: Westminster John Knox, 1991), 157–64; also Dale B. Martin, *The Corinthian Body* (New Haven: Yale University Press, 1995), 38–46.

23. While impressed by the wealth of comparative material and etic analysis brought to bear on the question of the body in 1 Corinthians by Martin (*Corinthian Body*, 87–103) and Jerome H. Neyrey (*Paul, in Other Words: A Cultural Reading of His Letters* [Louisville: Westminster John Knox, 1990], 102–46), I find their approach less satisfactory than a more traditional emic appreciation. It is noteworthy that neither

cusses the mutual functions of the members, he twice states that it is God who has placed the members as they are and has arranged the social body the way it is (12:18, 24). While an appeal to divine order would not in the least be out of place in a Greco-Roman discourse on harmony,[24] there is a directness and concreteness to Paul's statements that is exceptional. When we look at how Paul sets up this discussion, moreover, we see that he has prepared his hearers for God's direct involvement in the social body.

Paul says in 12:3 that no one can declare "Jesus is Lord, except in the Holy Spirit." This statement is followed by a series of affirmations concerning the Spirit. In 12:4–7 Paul attributes the diversity of gifts, the diversity of ministries, and the diversity of powerful deeds, respectively, to "the same spirit, the same Lord, the same God," concluding, "It is the same God who works τὰ πάντα ἐν πᾶσιν ['all things in everyone']," a phrase that provocatively anticipates Paul's later description of the eschatological telos as ὁ θεὸς τὰ πάντα ἐν πᾶσιν ("God will be all things in all things," 15:28). The specific presence of the Spirit within all the community's activities is repeated several times in the verses that follow: gifts are given "through the Spirit" and "according to the Spirit" (12:8), "in the same Spirit" and "in the one Spirit" (12:9). Paul concludes, "all these the same Spirit energizes, distributing specific [gifts] as it chooses" (12:11). To summarize: the Holy Spirit not only enables the confession of Jesus as Lord, but the Spirit is the power (ἐνεργεῖν) at work in every activity of the assembly.

When Paul subsequently states in 12:12 that, just as bodies have many members but are nevertheless one body, "so also [is] the Christ," he requires us to think in terms other than of simple comparison. The "Christ" in this context cannot be the empirical Jesus who ministered in Palestine some twenty years earlier and then was crucified. It can refer only to the present social body that is the assembly, which Paul daringly terms "the Christ." Paul means, I think, that the Corinthian assembly *is*, in a very real (that is, in an ontological and not merely moral) sense, a bodily expression of the risen Jesus who has become life-giving spirit (1 Cor 15:45). Certainly, it is not yet the σῶμα πνευματικόν of the eschatological resurrection. But it is definitely an anticipation of that spiritual body. If Paul were asked, "Where is the body of the resurrected Jesus now?" he has given his response in 1 Cor 12: "The body of the resurrected Christ is this assembly (12:27)—

---

study pays sufficient attention to the ways in which πνεῦμα and σῶμα interpenetrate in 1 Corinthians.

24. See, e.g., Dio Chrysostom, *Or.* 38.9, 11, 18, 20, 51; 39.8; 40.5, 15, 35; 41.10.

together with all those who call on the name of the Lord in every place, theirs and ours" (1:2).

Such is the conclusion I would draw from Paul's statement in 12:13, "For in one Spirit we have all been baptized [ἐβαπτίσθημεν] into one body—whether Jew or Hellene, whether slave or free—and we have all been given to drink [ἐποτίσθημεν] one Spirit."[25] The Spirit stands instrumentally at the beginning and end of this statement. The ritual of baptism into the community is also, by means of the Spirit, a baptism "into the body" that is Christ; such baptism is, says Paul, also a matter of this body "drinking the one Spirit." In light of Paul's later declaration in 15:45 that the eschatological Adam became "life-giving spirit," as well as Paul's alignment of Spirit-Lord-God in 12:4–7, I have no doubt that Paul regards the Corinthian community as the bodily expression of the resurrected one, living through the Spirit that comes from him. Thus, he concludes in 12:27, "You [plural] are Christ's body, and individually members [of it]." This is more than metaphor for Paul. Perhaps a better term would be *symbol*, in the strong sense of a sign that participates in that which it signifies.[26]

Taking Paul's language so seriously makes more intelligible two further features of his language concerning the community. In his discussion of eating foods offered to idols in 8:1–13, Paul makes a distinction between a knowledge that puffs up the individual and a love that builds up the other (8:1). When Corinthians convinced of the rightness of their position concerning idols act without consideration for the effect their actions might have on others, they are puffed up but do not build up: "the weak person is destroyed by your knowledge, the brother for whom Christ died" (8:11). Paul here uses a fragment of the Jesus story to provide a norm for behavior that "builds up," namely, living (and dying) for the sake of others as Christ did for them.[27] In contrast, the one acting obliviously to the effect on others does not build up but tears down. But this is not a mere matter of imitation

---

25. The balanced passive verbs perhaps suggest the ritual actions of initiation into the community: being plunged into water (by others) and being given to drink (by others). Compare the similar constructions in Gal 3:27 ("you were baptized into Christ, you were clothed [ἐνεδύσασθε] with Christ").

26. See Jorg Splett, "Symbol," *Encyclopedia of Theology: The Concise Sacramentum Mundi* (ed. Karl Rahner; New York: Seabury, 1975), 1654–57.

27. Here the reference to the Jesus story is an allusion; in 11:24 ("this is my body for you") it takes the form of a direct citation of the words of Jesus. The implication in both instances is the same: the pattern of Jesus' self-donation is to be the pattern of their own. For Paul's subtle use of the Jesus story, see esp. Richard B. Hays, *The Faith*

(act toward others as Christ acted for them); it is more a matter of identifi-cation. Paul adds, "Thus, by sinning against the brothers and by pummel-ing their conscience while it is weak,[28] you are sinning against Christ [εἰς Χριστὸν ἁμαρτάνετε]" (8:12). The phrase "sinning against Christ" assumes the strongest sort of connection between each member of the community (or the community as a whole) and the resurrected Lord.[29]

The second aspect of Paul's language that gains greater intelligibility in light of his understanding of the church as the body of Christ is his striking use of the phrase "mind of Christ" (νόος Χριστοῦ) in 1 Cor 2:16. The phrase occurs at the conclusion of Paul's discussion of the wisdom that has been given to the Corinthians through the Holy Spirit. They have received, he says, not the spirit from the world but the Spirit that is from God, so that "we might know the gifts that have been given to us by God" (2:12). Rather than the Spirit as the power of extraordinary performance (as in tongues, healing, and prophecy), Paul here stresses the Spirit as the means of elevat-ing and shaping human thinking. The context of this passage makes clear that the most important Spirit-guided perception is the recognition that the crucifixion of Jesus has reversed ordinary human status markers. The cross that appears to the world as weak and foolish is God's strength and God's wisdom (1:18–31). Paul wants them to measure themselves by this paradoxical, cruciform, norm. Thus they also were among the weak and foolish, among the things that are not, which God has brought into being (1:26–29).

But having "the mind of Christ" pushes the perception given by the Spirit even more. As Paul's use of the Jesus story in 8:11 ("the brother for whom Christ died") makes clear, the Spirit is to lead the community to perceive and act in imitation of Jesus. Having "the mind of Christ" enables the members of the body to act in harmony, to seek the good of the whole rather than the good of the individual alone, to build up the body of Christ

---

of Jesus Christ: The Narrative Substructure of Gal 3:1–4:11 (2nd ed.; Grand Rapids: Eerdmans, 2002).

28. For the translation of τύπτοντες, see Anthony C. Thiselton, The First Epistle to the Corinthians (NIGTC; Grand Rapids: Eerdmans, 2000), 654–55.

29. It is clearly impossible for a member of the Corinthian assembly to "sin against" the human Jesus; commentators are correct to see in this passage an assump-tion concerning the identification of Christ and the church implied by Acts 9:5, "I am Jesus, whom you are persecuting." Something more than a moral "identifying with the weak" is meant here. See Alfred Wikenhauser, Pauline Mysticism: Christ in the Mystical Teaching of Saint Paul (Freiburg: Herder, 1960).

through love. If the Corinthian community is for Paul the body of Christ, then the mind that guides this body's behavior should be Christ's own mind.[30] Growing progressively into such maturity through mutual love and service is the sort of moral activity that transforms Christians according to the image of Christ in anticipation of full participation in God's life that is future resurrection.

Sexual Involvement

The two behavioral issues most preoccupying Paul's readers in Corinth involve sex and food. Paul's perception of the community as the body of the Messiah, enlivened and empowered by the Holy Spirit, profoundly affects his treatment of each subject. Almost all of 1 Cor 5–7 deals in one way or another with sexuality.[31] I will comment briefly on Paul's discussion of marriage in 7:1–40 and on his instruction for excommunication in 5:1–12, before concentrating on his puzzling statements in 6:12–20.

Readers familiar only with the stereotype of Paul as misogynistic and against sex are surprised to discover not only the most liberated ancient discussion of sexuality (Paul addresses both genders equally in terms of power, and refuses to define females in terms of marriage and progeny),[32] but also one of the most robust and positive treatments of sexual activity

---

30. On this see Luke T. Johnson, "Transformation of the Mind and Moral Discernment in Paul," in *Early Christianity and Classical Culture: Comparative Studies in Honor of Abraham J. Malherbe* (ed. John T. Fitzgerald, Thomas H. Olbricht, and L. Michael White; NovTSup 110; Leiden: Brill, 2003), 215–36.

31. Helpful guidance is found in Will Deming, *Paul on Marriage and Celibacy: The Hellenistic Background of 1 Cor 7* (SNTSMS 83; Cambridge: Cambridge University Press, 1995); O. Larry Yarbrough, *Not Like the Gentiles: Marriage Rules in the Letters of Paul* (SBLDS 80; Atlanta: Scholars Press, 1985); and, most recently, Robert H. Von Thaden, "The Wisdom of Fleeing *Porneia*: Conceptual Blending in 1 Corinthians 6:12–7:7" (PhD diss., Emory University, 2007).

32. In sharp contrast to a standard treatment of οἰκονομία (such as Xenophon's), Paul does not address men as householders with young wives whom they must instruct, but begins his discussion in 7:2–3 by addressing both female (γυνή) and male (ἀνήρ) with regard to their reciprocal sexual rights and responsibilities, and continues with the same reciprocity through 7:10–16. Similarly, Paul's discussion of the unmarried in 7:32–40 makes clear that the value of women is not totally defined by their role in the household. In this respect, Paul is more "liberated" than the closest parallel in Greco-Roman philosophy; see Roy Bowen Ward, "Musonius and Paul on Marriage," *NTS* 36 (1990): 281–89.

anywhere.[33] Let us grant that Paul prefers celibacy in the present circumstances as a way of dedicating oneself to the Lord without anxiety (7:1, 7,
32–34); let us grant as well that Paul regards marriage as a means of avoiding sexual immorality (πορνεία) and disordered passion (7:2, 9). But when
Paul speaks of sexual activity within the covenant relationship of marriage,
he is entirely positive, and his discussion reveals, indirectly, some of his
basic assumptions about spirit and body.

Husbands and wives have authority (ἐξουσιάζειν) over each other's
bodies—that is, each can expect the other to engage sexually. They are to
"give what is owed" (τὴν ὀφειλὴν ἀποδιδότω) to each other. Indeed, so seriously does Paul take this that he forbids withdrawing from sexual activity
except by mutual consent, and then only for a time, and then only in order
to pray. After a short time, they are to "come together again" (ἐπὶ τὸ αὐτὸ,
7:3–5). More prolonged sexual abstinence in marriage allows Satan to test
the couple through their lack of self-control (ἀκρασία, 7:5). Even more
striking is Paul's statement concerning the spiritual effect of married sex.
He considers that, although such is not always the case (7:16), it is possible
that an unbelieving man in a mixed marriage is "made holy" (ἁγιάζειν)
through the (believing) woman and the unbelieving woman is "made holy"
through the (believing) man. He is convinced of this, it seems, from the
belief that the children of such a relationship are also made "holy" (ἅγιά,
7:14). His language almost suggests that holiness is a kind of infection that
can be sexually transmitted.[34] I pause over this point because it shows us
how Paul thinks of "body" not in mechanical but in relational terms, so
that the body sexually engaged with another has spiritual implications.[35]

This same potentially "infecting" power of sexual activity—now opposite the "holiness" that is communicated through sex within marriage—lies
behind Paul's command to the Corinthians in 5:1–12 that they excommu-
nicate a member whose πορνεία (sexual immorality) is grotesquely incom-
patible with a holy community. Paul shows himself concerned more with

---

33. A failure to seriously engage Paul is a notable deficiency in Michel Foucault's
History of Sexuality (trans. Robert Hurley; 3 vols.; New York: Vintage, 1980); for a cre-
ative effort at engaging Paul and Foucault, see V. Nicolet-Anderson, "Constructing the
Self: Thinking with Paul and Michel Foucault" (PhD diss., Emory University, 2010).

34. Both Neyrey (*Paul, in Other Words*) and Martin (*Corinthian Body*) are helpful
in providing anthropological perspectives on such language.

35. Note in 7:34 that Paul states "being holy both in body and spirit [καὶ τῷ σώματι
καὶ τῷ πνεύματι]" as the goal.

the integrity of the body of the church than the body of the man living in (at least legal) incest (5:1).[36] He draws the comparison to yeast that infects a whole lump of dough—so can such immoral sexual activity infect the common body of the church (5:6). Paul expects the members to gather together and "expel from your midst the one who has acted this way" (5:2). They are not to "mingle" (συναναμίγνυσθαι) or to "eat with" (συνεσθίειν) such a one (5:11).[37]

Two aspects of this intriguing passage are of special interest to our topic. The first is the way Paul speaks of the man being handed over to Satan "for the destruction of the flesh, so that the spirit might be saved in the day of the Lord" (5:5). The image of Satan as an inimical power on the fringes of the community is found elsewhere in Paul,[38] and anticipates the statement we have just seen in Paul's discussion of marriage (7:5). That the individual man's fleshly (i.e., merely human) body is affected by such excommunication is clear.[39] But whose πνεῦμα is being saved? Is it his, or is it the Holy Spirit of the community? If we avoid harmonizing this passage with the more clearly pedagogical intention expressed by the parallel in 1 Tim 1:20, excommunication in the 1 Corinthians passage seems entirely for the purpose of protecting the holiness of the corporate body of the church.[40]

The second aspect is the way Paul describes the communal act of expulsion. Paul is absent in body, he says, but is present in spirit, and has

---

36. See the discussion with ancient references in Thistleton, *First Epistle to the Corinthians*, 382–88; also Gordon D. Fee, *The First Epistle to the Corinthians* (NICNT; Grand Rapids: Eerdmans, 1987), 194–228.

37. The command here is directly contrary to the advice in 7:5, where temporary separation is to be followed by being ἐπὶ τὸ αὐτό; in both cases, however, the premise is the same: somatic contact bears pneumatic implications.

38. See 2 Cor 2:11; 11:14; 12:7; 1 Thess 2:18; 2 Thess 2:9; 1 Tim 1:20; 5:15.

39. But not without ambiguity: the noun ὄλεθρος ("destruction") is clear enough (see 1 Thess 5:3; 2 Thess 1:9; 1 Tim 6:9); but given the semantic range of σάρξ in Paul's correspondence, the destruction could be to the "fleshly body" itself, or to the "fleshly dispositions" leading to immorality (cf. Gal 5:13, 16–17, 19). See Anthony C. Thistelton, "The Meaning of σάρξ in 1 Cor 5:5: A Fresh Approach in the Light of Logical and Semantic Factors," *SJT* 26 (1973): 204–28.

40. See Luke T. Johnson, "The Social Dimensions of *Sōtēria* in Luke-Acts and Paul," in *The Society of Biblical Literature 1993 Seminar Papers* (SBLSP 32; Atlanta: Scholars Press, 1993), 520–36. Paul's express wish in 1:7–9 is that the community be prepared for the day of the Lord.

already made his judgment on the case (5:3). Now, the entire assembly is to come together in the name of the Lord (ἐν τῷ ὀνόματι τοῦ κυρίου ἡμῶν Ἰησοῦ), with Paul's and their spirit gathered together (συναχθέντων ὑμῶν καὶ τοῦ ἐμοῦ πνεύματος) with the power of the Lord Jesus (σὺν τῇ δυνάμει τοῦ κυρίου ἡμῶν Ἰησοῦ, 5:4). The assembly is not merely a gathering of individuals that votes on membership. It is the body of Christ that acts in the power of the Holy Spirit. In the way Paul expresses the corporate action of the community in the act of excommunication, we detect the premises for his later explicit designation of the church as the σῶμα Χριστοῦ.

The final passage concerning sexual activity is both the most important for appreciating Paul's extraordinarily strong view of the body as redefined by the resurrection of Christ, and, alas, also the most difficult. It is difficult above all because Paul's language about the body shifts between the singular and the plural. In 6:12–14 he speaks of the individual bodies of the Corinthians. He begins by citing (or crafting) the slogan "food for the belly, the belly for food," whose implication is that sex is a closed physical transaction with no further meaning.[41] Paul clearly rejects this position, not only for sex but, as we shall see in a moment, for food as well. He redirects the Corinthians' perception by insisting that the σῶμα is not for sexual immorality, but "for the Lord," and, reciprocally, "the Lord is for the body" (6:13). The singular term "body" (σῶμα) here still seems to mean the individual, but stated without qualification, it points the way toward the collective meaning.

What does Paul mean by stating that the body is for the Lord and the Lord is for the body? He asserts the impact of the resurrection on the understanding of the human body: "God both raised the Lord and will raise us by his power" (6:14). At the very least, Paul here establishes the connection between the (past) raising of Jesus and the (future) resurrection of believers. The implications Paul draws from his statement, however, indicate that, for him, the reality of the resurrection is not merely either past or future; it is above all a present reality. The power of the Lord is already present and active in the somatic existence of the all-too-empirical Corinthians to whom Paul writes. He therefore reminds them

---

41. Determining whether Paul is citing slogans of the Corinthian assembly (perhaps deriving ultimately from his own preaching) or is setting up straw positions of fictive interlocutors is difficult; among responsible discussions, see John C. Hurd, *The Origin of 1 Corinthians* (2nd ed.; Macon, Ga.: Mercer University Press, 1983); and Mitchell, *Paul and Rhetoric of Reconciliation*, 65–99.

of this reality of which they should have been aware: "do you not know that your bodies [both terms plural, τὰ σώματα ὑμῶν] are members [τὰ μέλη] of Christ?" (6:15).[42] The moral inconsistency of having sex with a prostitute—Paul uses the expression μὴ γένοιτο[43]—derives from the fact that believers' individual bodies also form the body of the resurrected one: "Shall I take the members of Christ and make them members of a prostitute?"[44]

As in chapter 7, Paul's understanding of sexual intimacy bears ontological implications. Paul implicitly rebukes the Corinthians (οὐκ οἴδατε, "do you not know") for their failure to recognize the meaning of Gen 2:24, which he quotes, "the two shall become one flesh,"[45] when he affirms, "the one who clings to a prostitute becomes one body [with her]" (6:16). Using the same participle (κολλώμενος), he adds, "but the one who clings to the Lord is one spirit [πνεῦμα] with him" (6:17). Everything we have seen in the discussion of the body of Christ in 1 Cor 12 we find also in this discussion of sexuality: the individual members are, because of the resurrection of Jesus, intimately joined to his Spirit, and by that means also become the bodily expression of the life-giving spirit in the world. Their actions involve not simply their own private bodies and spirits; they implicate the body of Christ and the Holy Spirit.

Once more, in 6:19, Paul reminds them of what they already should know: their (plural) body (singular) is the sanctuary of the Holy Spirit that

---

42. Paul concentrates his use of the implied rebuke, οὐκ οἴδατε ("do you not know"), in this discussion of sexual behavior (5:6; 6:2, 3, 9, 15, 16, 19). The statement that they are members of Christ's body clearly anticipates 12:27.

43. See Abraham J. Malherbe, "*Mē Genoito* in the Diatribe and Paul," in *Paul and the Popular Philosophers* (Minneapolis: Fortress, 1989), 25–34.

44. "The members" (τὰ μέλη), respectively, "of Christ" (τοῦ Χριστοῦ) and "of a prostitute" (πόρνης) might refer to the bodily parts of the individual Christian engaged in sex with a prostitute (the body parts that belong to Christ should not be made the property of a prostitute; compare the τὰ μέλη in Rom 6:13, 19; 7:5, 23), or to the community members who are μέλη τοῦ Χριστοῦ and are entangled sexually with the body parts of prostitutes.

45. In 1 Cor 15:45 Paul also cites Gen 2 when he refers to the first Adam becoming "a living being" (εἰς ψυχὴν ζῶσαν, Gen 2:7), in contrast to the eschatological Adam who is σῶμα πνευματικόν. The use of Gen 2 in the present passage testifies to the in-between state of the Corinthian bodies: they are possessed by the Spirit, but are still empirically involved, and not yet at the stage of being "spiritual bodies."

they (plural) have from God that is "among/within them" (plural),[46] and they do not therefore belong to themselves. They have been bought for a price and should therefore glorify God in their (plural) body (singular, 6:20).[47] By "glorifying God" Paul means that they must recognize and live by the recognition that God is indeed present among them, both individually and corporately.[48] Only such a strong ontological sense of the unity between the Spirit of the resurrected one and the community can make intelligible Paul's command and explanation in 6:18. Flee sexual immorality, he tells them. This is the straightforward moral implication of what he has been telling them. But his explanation appears extremely odd.

Paul declares that every sin a person commits is "outside the body" (ἐκτὸς τοῦ σώματος), but the one who commits sexual immorality "sins against his own body" (εἰς τὸ ἴδιον σῶμα ἁμαρτάνει). But surely this is wrong if we understand things in a commonsense fashion. Many sins are "inside the body" and affect one's "own body" with at least the same severity as does fornication. Drunkenness has obvious physical consequences; so do rage, gluttony, and sloth. If we think of body simply in terms of the individual, Paul is certainly mistaken. But perhaps by "his own body" (τὸ ἴδιον σῶμα) Paul does not mean the individual but the corporate body, that is, the body of Christ. We remember his statement concerning making another stumble, "by sinning against your brother for whom Christ died, you have sinned against Christ" (8:12). By implicating body and spirit sexually with the body and spirit of a prostitute, Paul thinks, harm is done to the body of Christ and the Holy Spirit in a distinctive fashion. We might still debate the proposition's truth or falsity. But it makes sense at least if Paul's intended meaning for "one's own—proper—body" is the body of Christ.

THE IMPLICATIONS OF MEALS

When we turn to the way Paul connects the Corinthian meals with the resurrection—and thereby further complicates the social meanings of "body"—we must acknowledge from the start that some of Paul's lan-

---

46. τὸ σῶμα ὑμῶν ναὸς τοῦ ἐν ὑμῖν ἁγίου πνεύματός ἐστιν οὗ ἔχετε ἀπὸ θεου.

47. ἠγοράσθητε γὰρ τιμῆς· δοξάσατε δὴ τὸν θεὸν ἐν τῷ σώματι ὑμῶν.

48. The meaning of δοξάζω here is that found in Rom 1:21: to "glorify God" is to recognize and respond to the claims of God; see Luke T. Johnson, *Reading Romans: A Literary and Theological Commentary* (Macon, Ga.: Smyth & Helwys, 2001), 32–36.

guage is strange to us not because of his distinctive theological perspective but because he shares ancient cultural convictions concerning meals that are no longer our own. In no other context is the default enlightenment understanding of the body—especially in first-world countries—revealed than with respect to eating food. Americans mostly eat apart rather than together; food is fast and take-out and devoured in the car, or, if at home, before the television.[49] We obsess about food, but mostly in terms of the technology of the body: its safety in processing, its fat and sodium content, its nutrients, how it will make us slimmer or fatter. Food is certainly not a mystery; it is a problem. As Robert Farrar Capon has astutely observed, contemporary Americans neither fast nor feast—both profoundly religious responses to reality—we diet.[50] Dieting is the supreme expression of body technology, and the triumphal expression of somatic individualism.

In contrast, ancient Greco-Roman and Jewish culture agreed with most cultures in most times and places by regarding meals as the most profound expression of human communion. Meals were magical because they both made and expressed the one social body that consisted in many individual members.[51] Meals, indeed, enabled those not joined by biological or ethnic ties to establish κοινωνία. The ancient conviction that "friendship is fellowship" (φιλία κοινωνία) meant the most profound sort of sharing at both the physical and mental levels: physical through the sharing of possessions (τοῖς φίλοις πάντα κοινά), and mental through the sharing of ideas and ideals (friends are μία ψυχή).[52] It is not an exaggeration, I think, to state that for Paul's world meals were a far more important means of expressing such unity and intimacy than was sexual activity. To eat together signified spiritual agreement, just as spiritual estrangement was expressed by inhospitality or, as we have seen in 1 Cor 5:1–12, excommunication.[53] Eating together was serious business, all agreed, because eating expressed and established spiritual bonds. Cultic meals both in Judaism

---

49. For a snapshot, see Craig Lambert, "The Way We Eat Now," *Harvard Magazine* (May–June 2004): 52–58, 98–99.

50. Robert Farrar Capon, *The Supper of the Lamb: A Culinary Reflection* (1969; repr., New York: Modern Library, 2002).

51. See Luke T. Johnson, "Meals Are Where the Magic Is," in *Religious Experience in Earliest Christianity* (Minneapolis: Fortress, 1998), 137–79.

52. For the topos on friendship, see G. Staehlin, "φίλος, κτλ.," *TDNT* 9:147–57; Gottfried Bohnenblust, *Beiträge zum Topos Peri Philias* (Berlin: Universitäts-Buchdruckerei von Gustav Shade, 1905).

53. Johnson, *Religious Experience in Earliest Christianity*, 163–79.

and in Greco-Roman religion extended this understanding by regarding meals partaken in honor of the god—and in which the god partakes through sacrificial offering—as establishing and celebrating a specific unity (vertically) between the god and worshippers and (horizontally) among the worshippers of the god.[54] Our interest, then, is how Paul's convictions concerning the presence of the resurrected Christ in the church affect such shared cultural norms.

After delicately examining the issues of conscience and community concern in his discussion of food offered to idols—he agrees with the strong that idols are not real, since "for us" there is one God and one Lord, but he rebukes the strong for their willingness to exercise their freedom without concern for those less strong in their convictions (1 Cor 8:1–13)—and after presenting himself as an apostolic example of relativizing individual rights for the sake of others (9:1–27), Paul warns his readers in 10:14–22 against participation in meals at idol shrines. Idols may not be real, but idolatry is real, and the act of eating in the presence of idols, just like sexual activity with a prostitute, affects the social body that is the church. Paul considers things offered to idols as sacrifices to demons, and eating at the table of idols as a fellowship (κοινωνία) with demons (10:20–21). He relies here on the common view of Jews, found already in the Septuagint's translation of Ps 95:5, "all the gods of the nations are demons." Participation in a common meal signifies for Paul participation in the powers present at the meal. He reminds his readers that this is the premise of Jewish sacrifice as well: "those who eat the sacrifices are sharers [κοινωνοί] in the altar" (10:18).

The most powerful backing for Paul's warning, however, comes from his readers' experience of their own common meals, which include the blessing of a cup and the breaking of a loaf of bread. Paul asks them rhetorically, "The cup of blessing that we bless, is it not a κοινωνία ['participation'] in the blood of the Messiah; the bread that we break, is it not a κοινωνία in the body of the Messiah?" (10:16). He wants them to answer resoundingly, "Of course they are!" The physical sharing of the cultic meal establishes and expresses the fullest sort of fellowship between worshippers and the one worshipped, and Paul assumes that his readers understand the matter in precisely the way he does. I need not point out, I hope,

---

54. See Jonathan Z. Smith, *Drudgery Divine: On the Comparison of Early Christianities and the Religions of Late Antiquity* (Chicago Studies in the History of Judaism; Chicago: University of Chicago Press, 1990), 116–43.

that such "fellowship" supposes the presence and power of the resurrected one among them—a presupposition running all through this letter. Paul then adds a statement that fills out the ancient understanding of fellowship: those who share in the meal are also "one body"; "all those of us who partake of the same loaf are one bread, one body" (10:17). Just as Paul will speak in chapter 12 of the ritual of baptism as a drinking of the one Spirit that makes them the body of the Messiah, so does he here understand the cultic meal in the same highly realistic terms, as an eating of a loaf that makes them partakers of the body of Christ and one body.

In 11:17–34 Paul returns to the common meals of the Corinthians by way of rebuke, for their "coming together" is not for the better but for the worse (11:17). There are parties formed among them when they "gather together" (11:18–19); indeed, when they "gather together" they do not really celebrate "the Lord's Banquet" (κυριακὸν δεῖπνον), that is, a meal of fellowship with the resurrected Lord as the body of Christ (11:20). Instead, they falsify the act of gathering into a body, because their party spirit is revealed by each one eating "his own meal," with the result that some become drunken with excess, while others go hungry (11:21). They bring into the cultic meal the individualism and competition that belongs in the world, not in the body of Christ. As a result, they show contempt for God's assembly and they shame the poor (11:22). We cannot be certain precisely what the Corinthians are doing—it is reasonable to suppose, as some studies have suggested, that the practices common to patronage may be at play.[55] More important is Paul's perception that the cultivation of the individual interest to the shaming of the poor and weak offends in a fundamental way the meaning of living according to the mind of Christ and building the Messiah's body. The Corinthians may gather at a meal as a body but their behavior fragments and weakens that body.

Paul understands the effect of this weakening quite literally. Because some eat and drink "without discerning the body," they eat and drink judgment (κρίμα) to themselves (11:29, 34);[56] and their condemnation is expressed by some of them "being weak, and without health, and not a few dying" (11:30). In the case of the excommunicated man, the immoral

---

55. See Gerd Theissen, "Social Integration and Sacramental Activity: An Analysis of 1 Cor 11:17–34," in *The Social Setting of Pauline Christianity* (Philadelphia: Fortress, 1982), 145–74.

56. For κρίμα in the sense of condemnation, see Rom 2:2–3; 3:8; 5:16; 13:2; 1 Tim 3:6; 5:12.

person was turned over to the zone of danger and destruction that Paul designates as Satan, for the destruction of the flesh and for the saving of the spirit (1 Cor 5:5). When the Lord's Banquet is corrupted by selfishness and competition, the damage to the body of Christ is expressed internally by the mortal weakness and even death of the members of that body. Paul connects such judgment with "not discerning the body" (μὴ διακρίνων τὸ σῶμα, 11:29), and with "eating the bread and drinking the cup unworthily" (ἀναξίως, 11:27).

These statements follow immediately upon, and logically refer to, Paul's citation of the words that the Lord Jesus spoke "on the night he was handed over," words that Paul received from the Lord—we know not how—and handed on to the Corinthians as the inner meaning of the meal they called the Lord's Banquet (11:23–25). Many things can be said about these words, which represent one of the clearest cases of Paul handing on specific Jesus traditions. Given the interest of the present essay, I focus on three. First, the "body, which is for you," and the "covenant in my blood" clearly interpret the bread and wine of Jesus' final meal with his disciples in terms of Jesus' death for others. Second, this is the part of the Jesus story that is most intimately associated with their celebration of the κυριακὸν δεῖπνον—in his remembrance (ἀνάμνησις), that is, in the form of ritual memory that makes actual in the present the effect of what was done in the past.[57] The words spoken at the ritual meal communicate and remind the Corinthians *in nuce* of "the mind of Christ" (2:16) that is to guide their mutual behavior. Third, it is striking that Paul quotes Jesus as telling them not to "say this," but rather "do this" (τοῦτο ποιεῖτε). The eating and drinking in the assembly in remembrance of Jesus is to enact the meaning of his death for others. The point is made clear when Paul adds that whenever they eat *this* bread and drink *this* cup they proclaim the Lord's death until he comes (11:26).

Paul means not the fact of Jesus' death, as in a historical report, but the meaning of that death, as an expression of the mind of Christ. Thus the "body given for you" must remind us, and it should have the Corinthians, of "the brother for whom Christ died" (8:11), just as their shaming the poor should have reminded them that "when you sin against your brother you sin against Christ" (8:12). So it is that when they eat and drink unwor-

---

57. See Nils A. Dahl, "Anamnesis: Memory and Commemoration in Early Christianity," in *Jesus in the Memory of the Early Church* (Minneapolis: Augsburg, 1976), 11–29.

thily—by not discerning the body of Christ that is the church—they are "liable for the body and blood of the Lord" (11:27).

Here is the perfect example of how Paul perceives the ontological transformation of the Corinthian body through the power of the Holy Spirit as demanding moral transformation as well. The mind of Christ (2:16) requires of them that they dispose of their individual bodies in service to one another for the common good (πρὸς τὸ συμφέρον, 12:7), for the building up of the common body through love (8:1; 13:1–13). Rather than threaten the health of Christ's body through a competitive eating that mirrors the "spirit of the world," the "Spirit they have received from God" (2:12) should lead them, "when they come together to eat," to "wait upon one another" (11:33), as Christ has shown them how to do through the gift of his body for them (11:24).

Conclusions

I offer a series of short conclusions in summary of what 1 Corinthians says about πνεῦμα and σῶμα.

1. Paul's understanding of the human body is complex: it is both the self and what the self can dispose in relationships with others. Sexual activities and eating meals establish and express powerful spiritual realities.

2. Paul's default understanding of the body is not the individual but the community; specifically, because of the gift of the Holy Spirit given by the exalted Lord Jesus, he perceives the community to be the body of the resurrected Christ in the world.

3. When Paul, speaking of baptism, says that believers have been given to drink of the one Spirit, and when, speaking of the Lord's Banquet, he declares that those who have eaten the one loaf are one body, his language pushes beyond metaphor to symbolism in the proper sense.

4. Because of the resurrection of Jesus and his exaltation as Lord, the primary πνεῦμα both of the individual and the community is the Lord's, and the primary loyalty must be to the Lord.

5. Paul understands both sin and holiness to have an infectious character because of the psychosomatic complex that is the individual and social body. Sexual immorality threatens the holiness of the church; covenantal sexual love makes partners and children holy. Eating with demons weakens and sickens the church; eating at the table of the Lord saves and makes holy.

6. In contrast to the forms of individualism and competition that characterize the spirit of the world, Paul demands that the Spirit from God find expression in Christ's body through a pattern of moral behavior that is directed by and conforms to "the mind of Christ": the Spirit works for the common good, the members serve each other and build each other up according to the pattern of the one who gave [his] body for them.

FAITH, CHRIST, AND PAUL'S THEOLOGY
OF SALVATION HISTORY

Sherri Brown

Of all the books in the New Testament, only the letters of Paul are referred to so directly within the Bible itself as a difficult body of teaching that readers must approach with care—with fear and trembling even (2 Pet 3:14–18). In fact, difficulties in interpreting Paul's thought and teaching arose even before the writing of 2 Peter. Paul himself had to correct the understanding of an early letter to the church in Corinth (1 Cor 5:9–13). Indeed, the history of the interpretation of Paul is a history of conflict. He is one who regularly evokes strong opinions, to say the least, with regard to both his character and his theology and teaching. We can be sure that if Paul had been everyone's favorite apostle, we would not have the depth and breadth of the writings that we have, nor would he have become the dominant voice in the New Testament.

In recent years biblical scholars have shown a renewed interest in the translation and interpretation of eight instances of the Greek phrase πίστις χριστοῦ and its near equivalents in the Pauline corpus. In the seven letters whose authorship is undisputedly attributed to Paul, the phrase "faith" + the genitive form of "Christ" (or "Jesus Christ," "Jesus," or "the Son of God") occurs seven times: Rom 3:22, 26; Gal 2:16 (twice), 20; 3:22; Phil 3:9. In addition, the phrase also occurs in Eph 3:12, the authorship of which is disputed by scholars. The context of each occurrence is Paul discussing justification: either deliberating the revelation of God's righteousness or teaching his churches how God makes people righteous (i.e., how people are brought into covenant relationship with God). Since this genitive construction is always founded in "faith," Paul thus teaches that God makes people righteous by means of faith, and this faith is connected to Jesus Christ. But how, exactly?

A great deal of scholarship has focused on πίστις χριστοῦ in Paul's theology—some of it brilliant and some of it more staid contributions to party lines and denominational factions. In the present study I do not intend to rehash the well-documented issues in detail or to uncover a thus far undiscovered exegetical nugget in this well-mined field. Rather, I hope to suggest a larger picture of the narrative of salvation history in which Paul finds himself and his readers. Since this study is part of a larger work that seeks to honor biblical scholar, teacher, mentor, and friend Frank J. Matera, I will also highlight his substantial contributions to the interpretation of Paul's letters and to my own understanding of Paul's theology and Christology. Therefore, Matera's broad-based work in Pauline theology and Christology is fundamental for this current research.[1] In that vein, Matera has noted that the foundational experience underlying Paul's Christology is the call and conversion that led him to focus his Christology on the death and resurrection of Christ. This starting point determines how Paul understands God's revelation, the human condition, and salvation. In this article I therefore explore the connection between the interpretation of the πίστις χριστοῦ texts and justification, in terms of Paul's Christology as well as his understanding of the cross and salvation history.[2]

The πίστις χριστοῦ Issue

In the occurrences of the πίστις χριστοῦ construction, some form of "Christ" always follows "faith" in the genitive case, indicating that Christ

---

1. Frank Matera's body of scholarship is immense and far-reaching. The works that are most incisive for the present study include: "Christ in the Theologies of Paul and John: A Study in the Diverse Unity of New Testament Theology," *TS* 67 (2006): 237–56; "The Culmination of Paul's Argument to the Galatians: Gal 5.1–6.17," *JSNT* 32 (1988): 79–91; *Galatians* (SP 9; Collegeville, Minn.: Liturgical Press, 2007); "Galatians and the Development of Paul's Teaching on Justification," *WW* 20 (2000): 239–48; "Galatians in Perspective: Cutting a New Path through Old Territory," *Int* 54 (2000): 233–45; *New Testament Christology* (Louisville: Westminster John Knox, 1999); *New Testament Theology: Exploring Diversity and Unity* (Louisville: Westminster John Knox, 2007); *Romans* (Paideia Commentaries on the New Testament; Grand Rapids: Baker Academic, 2010).

2. In the debate discussed below, there is significant difference of opinion among scholars about what the term *justification* means. I adopt the understanding introduced above, that justification in Paul's thought refers to how God makes people righteous, i.e., how people are brought into right, covenant relationship with God.

is in an adjectival relationship with the noun "faith." More simply put, the genitive typically shows possession. However, this genitive can be objective (with Christ as the object) or subjective (with Christ as the subject). If translated as an objective genitive, "faith in Christ," it would refer to the faith human beings have in Christ that determines their state in covenant relationship with God. With the exception of the KJV, and more recently the NET, this is how it has been translated in nearly all English translations.[3] In this light, Christians have been called to "believe in Christ to be righteous." If the phrase is translated as a subjective genitive, "Christ's faith" or "the faith of Christ," it would thus refer to the faith Christ had and has in God that makes people righteous. It could even, by metonymy, refer to the gospel narrative's climactic story of the crucifixion and obedient, saving death of Jesus Christ.[4] This would make covenant relationship with God already complete and available to all, and the call then is simply to live accordingly. These are two very different ideas, especially considering Reformation debates about the role of faith in God's plan for salvation. While these are not the only two translations possible, they are by far the most commonly discussed and debated in scholarship.[5] The objective genitive is often called the anthropological reading and the subjective genitive called the christological reading. This is not to say that one limits the work of Christ or the human response more than the other, but this terminology does highlight the respective emphases of each exegetical understanding.[6]

Traces of a debate about how to translate the πίστις χριστοῦ phrase and its variants can be found as early as the church fathers, though early translations all seem to favor the subjective genitive rendering.[7] More explicit grammatical and exegetical discussions arose in scholarship after

---

3. J. H. Moulton, *Prolegomena* (vol. 1 of J. H. Moulton, W. F. Howard, and Nigel Turner, *A Grammar of New Testament Greek*; 3 vols.; Edinburgh: T&T Clark, 1908–1963), 72.

4. Richard B. Hays, *The Faith of Jesus Christ: The Narrative Substructure of Galatians 3:1–4:11* (2nd ed.; Grand Rapids: Eerdmans, 2002), xxxi.

5. See the discussion in Paul Foster, "The First Contribution to the Πίστις Χριστοῦ Debate: A Study of Ephesians 3.12," *JSNT* 85 (2002): 75–96, esp. n. 1.

6. See the extensive discussion of these two perspectives and the state of the scholarly debate in Matthew C. Easter, "The *Pistis Christou* Debate: Main Arguments and Responses in Summary," *CBR* 9 (2010): 33–46.

7. George E. Howard, "Notes and Observations on the 'Faith of Christ,'" *HTR* 60 (1967): 461.

the Reformation, some of these discussions leading to fierce debates.[8] This conversation continued to simmer and began to boil anew among contemporary Pauline scholars in the early 1980s with the publication of a series of works. The heat was turned up in 1977, when E. P. Sanders published his now seminal work on Paul and his socioreligious context.[9] In *Paul and Palestinian Judaism*, Sanders claims that the picture of Judaism that had been generally drawn from Paul's work by scholars was historically false and certainly not in keeping with the work of Jewish scholars on rabbinic Judaism. Sanders then goes on to develop a picture of Palestinian Judaism during Paul's time that is captured in the concept of "covenantal nomism," which means that "one's place in God's plan is established on the basis of the covenant" and "obedience maintains one's place in the covenant."[10]

Sanders's work was lauded as groundbreaking and in 1983 spurred James Dunn to develop the ideas from this "new perspective" in specific exegetical insights by way of Gal 2:16. Dunn's article, "The New Perspective on Paul," carefully fleshed out the theological consequences of Paul's experience of the gospel within covenantal nomism. Indeed, "with Christ's coming God's covenant purpose had reached its intended final stage in which the more fundamental identity marker (Abraham's faith) reasserts its primacy over against the too narrowly nationalistic identity markers of circumcision, food laws and sabbath."[11] Paul's theology, then, turns on the human faith response to Christ, as those who receive the good news are called to have "faith in Christ." Dunn's work has had immense influence and put forth an argument for the objective genitive rendering of this key verse.

In the same year (1983), though quite separately, Richards Hays's pioneering dissertation, *The Faith of Jesus Christ: The Narrative Substructure of Galatians 3:1–4:11*, was published.[12] Despite its title, the book is not

---

8. See the excellent overview of the history of the discussion in Paul Pollard, "The 'Faith of Christ' in Current Discussion," *Concordia Journal* 23 (1997): 213–28.

9. E. P. Sanders, *Paul and Palestinian Judaism* (Philadelphia: Fortress, 1977).

10. Ibid., 74, 420.

11. James D. G. Dunn, "The New Perspective on Paul," *BJRL* 65 (1983): 95–122. These ideas were reprinted with more attention in *Jesus, Paul, and the Law: Studies in Mark and Galatians* (Louisville: Westminster John Knox, 1990).

12. *The Faith of Jesus Christ: The Narrative Substructure of Galatians 3:1–4:11* (SBLDS 56; Chico, Calif.: Scholars Press, 1983).

just a presentation of the πίστις χριστοῦ issue; rather the subtitle is more descriptive of Hays's area of focus. Nonetheless, his treatment of the issue in chapter 4 of the monograph, including an exegetical argument for the subjective genitive, or "faithfulness of Christ," took hold and attracted "insistent response and attention within the scholarly guild."[13] A brief presentation of Hays's central thesis in this work is best found in his own assessment by way of an extended introduction to the second edition in 2002. He provides three suggestions for the reader, the second of which has three aspects itself:[14] (1) A story about Jesus Christ is presupposed by Paul's argument in Galatians, and his theological reflection attempts to articulate the meaning of that story. This narrative substructure that Paul shares with his readers thus pervades his letters. (2) In a mysterious way, Jesus has enacted our destiny, and those who are in Christ are shaped by the pattern of his self-giving death. He is the prototype of redeemed humanity. The "faithfulness of Jesus Christ" therefore has an incorporative character, and his story transforms and absorbs the world. Paul's soteriology is thus participationist, and so Hays offers the following three logical components of this second aspect: (a) The "faithfulness of Jesus Christ" refers first of all to his gracious, self-sacrificial death on a cross; (b) Jesus Christ embodies the new creation and embraces us in his life; and (c) the cross, as Christ's saving action, is God's action of πίστις, God's demonstration of fidelity to the promise made to Abraham. These observations lead to Hays's last suggestion to the reader of his work: (3) Paul, the missionary preacher, is at least as much a poet as he is a theologian. Metaphor, allusion (especially to the story of Israel), and apocalyptic imagery are essential to the storytelling of the gospel for Paul. The exegete's task is to reconstruct this narrative framework in order to grasp Paul's intended meaning and overall frame of reference. Through these three suggestions and their components, Hays presents the underlying thread of his argument, including a potent advocacy for the subjective genitive rendering of these key phrases in Paul's work.

In the years since these publications, the πίστις Χριστοῦ issue has become a debate primarily among English-language scholars and has often been inaccurately characterized in Europe as an attack on the Lutheran interpretation of justification by faith alone. On the contrary, the debate,

---

13. As Hays points out in the 2nd ed. of *Faith of Jesus Christ*, xxiv.
14. See the discussion in ibid., xxiii–xxxiv.

as it has emerged in contemporary scholarship, has quite valuably broken
through the traditional taken-for-granted categories for interpreting Paul
and provided a forum for presenting the rich diversity of Paul's theology
and Christology.[15] The conversation has continued explicitly through
Dunn and Hays, with many other scholars weighing in as a member of one
camp or the other, or attempting to establish their own voice in the discussion.[16] Although Frank Matera has not formally entered into this debate,
he has been a strong voice in Pauline exegesis, theology, and Christology.
In his commentaries on Galatians and Romans, as well as in his sweeping
treatises on *New Testament Christology* and *New Testament Theology*, he
translates the disputed phrases with the subjective genitive and advocates
that it is the "faithfulness of Jesus Christ" that best describes Paul's understanding of God's actions in and through the Christ event.[17]

In my own study, I have been convinced by the work of Richard
Hays, Luke Timothy Johnson, Morna Hooker, and, most familiarly, Frank

---

15. James D. G. Dunn, "Foreword," in *The Faith of Jesus Christ: The Pistis Christou
Debate* (ed. Michael F. Bird and Preston M. Sprinkle; Peabody, Mass.: Hendrickson,
2009), xv–xix. Notice that the "new perspective" on Paul has taken hold across scholarship but that the same scholars (e.g., Dunn and Hays) can remain divided on the
πίστις χριστοῦ issue. Questions about both issues overlap but are not coterminus. The
division can be correlated to differing understandings of "justification" and what Paul
means by this term. Some NT scholars understand Paul's use of "justification" as primarily ecclesial, while others do not.

16. Hays continues to contribute to the discussion through larger works, including *Echoes of Scripture in the Letters of Paul* (New Haven: Yale University Press, 1989);
"ΠΙΣΤΙΣ and Pauline Christology: What Is at Stake?" in *Looking Back, Pressing On*
(vol. 4 of *Pauline Theology*; ed. E. Elizabeth Johnson and David M. Hay; SBLSymS 4;
Atlanta: Scholars Press, 1997), 35–60; and, as mentioned above, the introduction to
the 2nd edition of his *Faith of Jesus Christ*. Dunn continues to interact with Hays and
others through *Jesus, Paul and the Law* (London: SPCK, 1990); "Once More, ΠΙΣΤΙΣ
ΧΡΙΣΤΟΥ," in Johnson and Hay, *Looking Back, Pressing On*, 61–81; and, interestingly
enough, "ΕΚ ΠΙΣΤΕΩΣ: A Key to the Meaning of ΠΙΣΤΙΣ ΧΡΙΣΤΟΥ," in *The
Word Leaps the Gap: Essays on Scripture and Theology in Honor of Richard B. Hays* (ed.
J. Ross Wagner, C. Kavin Rowe, and A. Katherine Grieb; Grand Rapids: Eerdmans,
2008), 351–66. The more recent contributions include the compilation edited by Bird
and Sprinkle, *Faith of Jesus Christ*, which attempts to clarify and codify the different
positions in translation and interpretation. Likewise N. T. Wright has also weighed
in as part of an exhaustive study, *Justification: God's Plan and Paul's Vision* (Downers
Grove, Ill.: InterVarsity Press, 2009).

17. See Matera's *Galatians*, 92–104; *Romans*, 91–104; *New Testament Christology*,
102–20; *New Testament Theology*, 151–98.

Matera for the rendering of the various πίστις χριστοῦ phrases.[18] Therefore, what follows will expand upon this position without establishing a new exegetical argument for it. After brief discussions of Paul's understanding of faith and the faithfulness of Christ presented in Galatians and Romans, I will suggest what this might mean for Paul's soteriology and his story of salvation history.

FAITH AND FAITHFULNESS IN PAUL'S CHRISTOLOGY AND SOTERIOLOGY

To discuss how Paul understands faith and the role it plays in his developing theology, we must begin with who Paul was and his experience of God's activity in his life and among his people.[19] In his letters, Paul does not say where he was born, but his name would connect him with a Roman township. He does boast of his Jewish background and traces his lineage to the tribe of Benjamin. He was a "Hebrew born of Hebrews; ... as to the law a Pharisee" (Phil 3:5–6), who was "extremely zealous for the traditions" of his forebears and excelled his peers "in Judaism" (Gal 1:14). In calling himself a Hebrew he may have been indicating that he was a Greek-speaking Jew who could also speak Aramaic and could read the Scriptures in the original Hebrew. His letters reveal that he knew Greek well and addressed the Gentile churches by quoting from the Septuagint. Use of Stoic diatribe, particularly in the Letter to the Romans, also suggests that he had a Greek education. Luke also presents Paul as a "Jew" and a "Pharisee" born in Tarsus, a Hellenistic town of Cilicia (Acts 21:39; 22:3), and as a Roman citizen from birth. This information is consistent with what we glean from Paul's letters and, if correct, explains much of his background

---

18. In addition to the work of Hays and Matera already cited, Luke Timothy Johnson's article on Romans and Morna Hooker's address to the 1988 SNTS General Meeting should be added here: Luke Timothy Johnson, "Rom 3:21–26 and the Faith of Jesus," *CBQ* 44 (1982): 77–90; Morna Hooker, "Πιστις Χριστου," *NTS* 35 (1989): 321–42. See also the influential commentary by J. Louis Martyn, *Galatians: A New Translation with Introduction and Commentary* (AB 33A; New York: Doubleday, 1997).

19. For a basic introduction to the life and experience of Paul, see Joseph A. Fitzmyer, *According to Paul: Studies in the Theology of the Apostle* (New York: Paulist Press, 1993); idem, *Paul and His Theology: A Brief Sketch* (Englewood Cliffs, N.J.: Prentice-Hall, 1989). These works are the primary source for the summary that follows. For a more recent analysis of the biblical material, see Gregory Tatum, *New Chapters in the Life of Paul: The Relative Chronology of His Career* (CBQMS 41; Washington, D.C.: Catholic Biblical Association of America, 2006).

and worldview. Tarsus was a well-known center of culture, philosophy, and education; and its citizens held Roman citizenship. The reputation of its schools and cultural status is mentioned often by the political and philosophical literati of the day. Thus the Lukan Paul can boast that he is a "citizen of no mean town" (Acts 21:39), but was brought up in Jerusalem and educated at the feet of Gamaliel (22:3),[20] that is, Rabbi Gamaliel I, the Elder, whose renown in Jerusalem flourished around 20–50 C.E. This too contributes to Paul's Semitic training and mode of thought, but Paul never mentions this feature of his youth in his letters. Nonetheless, by the time of his revelatory encounter with the risen Christ, Paul must have been not merely a rabbinical disciple, but a recognized teacher with the right to make binding decisions with regard to the law. This authority is presupposed in Paul's introduction to the narrative of Acts at the stoning of Steven as well as in his going to Damascus to arrest the scattering Christian disciples (Acts 7:58–8:1; 9:1–2).

Paul wrote of the crucial turn in his life in Gal 1:11–24, following upon this career in Judaism and persecution of the church of God. After his revelation he withdrew to Arabia then returned to Damascus. Paul regarded the experience near Damascus as the turning point in his life, thus a *conversion*; but care must be taken with this term as Paul did not understand himself to be embarking upon a new religious system. Rather, he understood God bringing to culmination his promises for creation through the gospel as experienced in faith. The experience was for him an encounter with the risen Lord that was a turning point in his life and the basis for his apostolate. As a result of that revelation of Jesus Christ, Paul became a servant of Christ with a compulsion to preach the gospel. Paul's zeal for the law was transvalued to his conviction of Jesus as the Christ. Rather than being crushed by the law and thereby looking for something different, or easier to live by, he experienced a fundamental transvaluation of his beliefs.[21] Luke carefully associates Paul's conversion with his persecution of the church as he chased the scattering Christians (Acts 8–9). Thus what

---

20. The Acts of the Apostles is, of course, a secondary source for studying Paul, and Luke's reliability as an historian is also secondary to his theological agenda; but this information is generally consistent with the autobiographical information Paul provides in Gal 1–2 and Phil 3.

21. The concepts of Paul's turning point, transvaluation, and the paradigm from Torah to Christ can be found in Luke Timothy Johnson, *The Writings of the New Testament* (3rd ed.; Philadelphia: Fortress, 2010), 262–63.

he had understood to be apostasy became the truth of God's revelation. Paul began to understand Jesus as the fulfillment of all that he had previously valued—a fundamental paradigm shift.

This brief rehearsal of Paul's background and worldview aids in discussing both his use of the πίστις χριστοῦ phrases and his understanding of how God's interactions with the world shifted. As a result of his revelatory encounter with the risen Christ, his underlying story of God's covenant relationship with creation had not been superseded, but rather fulfilled and continued through a new chapter. The Greek word πίστις denotes varying nuances of belief, trust, and/or fidelity.[22] Although there are indeed cases in which one of these definitions is the emphasis, the word is also used in a general sense where all three of these aspects are intended. Paul likely allows the Greek to be ambiguous such that all three are present in the text more often than not. The modern sensibilities of many twenty-first-century exegetes may demand a specificity that is not necessarily intended by the text or its first-century author. Paul uses some form of πίστις approximately a hundred times in the letters to the Romans and Galatians alone. As a title, he uses it for the community of believers. As an action, it is the proper human response to God's covenantal activity in the world: belief, the obedience of trust, and fidelity. The categories of righteousness are the same as before Paul's revelatory encounter, but now Torah can longer be the ultimate norm—Christ is. The corporate nature of the Sinai covenant has now been transvalued for Paul into Christ and the new covenantal community formed by the Christ event.

Faith for Paul is always corporate and participatory because the gospel is active and indwelling—divine activity that is powerfully present in the members of the community and speaks in and through human creation.[23] Therefore it is not propositional but participational. In his earliest letter, 1 Thessalonians, Paul offers a prayer in closing for the perfect sanctification of the church and declares, "the one who calls you is πίστις and he will accomplish it" (5:24). God is faithful and will fulfill his promises. This is the source of Christian life. The call of God to believe is itself faithfulness, and this divine fidelity ensures that God will bring to completion what he

---

22. BDAG, 818–20, s.v. πίστις.

23. For an extensive and insightful discussion of this indwelling, or what he calls *theosis*, see Michael J. Gorman, *Inhabiting the Cruciform God: Kenosis, Justification, and Theosis in Paul's Narrative Soteriology* (Grand Rapids: Eerdmans, 2009), esp. 1–9, 161–73.

has done. This is what makes possible Christian existence and salvation. This corporate and participational essence of faith comes to the fore in Paul's Letter to the Galatians. There Paul proclaims that faithful human response is participation in Christ's faithfulness on the cross (2:16). This is how we are justified. This is followed immediately by corporate language of being crucified with Christ (2:17–21). The summons is to take on Christ's faithfulness, not to empty the cross of its power. This is all the language of participation in the incorporative body of Christ. As Jesus was not just a moral exemplar, but a gift that transformed and absorbed the world, Paul can now say that, as a member of the community of believers, "the life I now live in the flesh I live by the faithfulness of the Son of God, who loved me and gave himself for me" (Gal 2:19b–20).[24] But this is also personal and interior as faith is the summoned response of the individual to Jesus. As Matera asserts, for Paul the story of the gospel begins and ends with faith, and Jesus' death is the central moment that underlies the Christ story.[25] And participation in this incorporative faith is foundational to Paul's developing understanding of salvation in the new covenant of Christ. The discussions of the faithfulness of Christ in Paul's letters to the Galatians and Romans that follow will offer an overview of the letters, then present a few of Matera's insights on the key moments through which Paul develops this Christology and soteriology.

The Faithfulness of Christ in Galatians

The letter of Paul to the churches of Galatia is both passionate and polemical in tone, and reflects a critical moment in the early Christian movement to define its mission and identity in the larger society. Paul states several times that he founded the churches there; nonetheless he now finds his work threatened by some Jewish Christian teachers who are urging these Gentile converts to be circumcised and observe various elements of Torah. This conflict to which Paul is responding also compels him to lay out his understanding of what God has done in the world through the Christ event and the human response to this action. Paul considers the challenge of these opponents a threat to the very "truth of the gospel" (2:14).[26] The letter is thus composed as an impassioned plea to dissuade the Galatians

---

24. Hays, *Faith of Christ*, xxix.

25. Matera, *New Testament Christology*, 102; idem, *Romans*, 36.

26. For more on this issue see Matera, *New Testament Theology*, 156–59, 165–66.

from adopting such practices and thereby manifests Paul's developing theology. Again, the key issue here is his crucial decision to integrate non-Jews into the new "Israel of God," as he refers to the church (6:16), and Paul's theological foundation for pioneering this activity.

Following the address (1:1–5), the body of the letter falls into two broad sections, a doctrinal section (1:5–4:31) followed by the ethical conclusions (5:1–6:10) that result from Paul's theological instruction. This last section flows into Paul's typical concluding thoughts and final greetings (6:11–18). The address itself lays out not only the tone of the letter, but also the crux of the problem as well as Paul's criticisms (1:1–5). In his defense set forth in chapters 1–2 that the message he preached carried the authority of God, Paul develops several key themes: his vocation (1:6–24), the unity of the gospel (2:1–10), and his own union with the pillars of Jerusalem (2:11–21). He emphasizes that his call was an apocalypse—a revelation—and uses the language of the prophets to describe his call. In the second half of his doctrinal section, chapters 3–4, Paul appeals alternately to the experience of the Galatians and to the Scriptures to reinforce his introductory teaching on the oneness and sufficiency of Christ. Alluding to an underlying narrative that includes God's covenants with Abraham and Moses, Paul indicates that faith has transferred the Galatians and all believers from the realm of the flesh to that of the Spirit.[27] And it is this Spirit of God that enables humankind to share fully in the inheritance of the promise made to Abraham and fulfilled already in Christ. In chapters 5–6 Paul draws implications for Christian living from this teaching.[28] Even as he insists on freedom he always grounds this freedom in the consequences such faith has for the Christian life. Believers are called to exercise their faith in relationships with one another and focus on the care of the developing community through social responsibility. Finally, he turns back to community life, advocating the virtues of service, humility, and above all charity, before concluding with a short prayer (6:11–18).

As introduced in the discussion of faith in the previous section, the πίστις χριστοῦ question comes to the fore in Gal 2 as Paul shares his personal encounter and calling with Christ as well as his later encounters with Peter and the other disciples that serve as the foundation for his present

---

27. Matera, *New Testament Christology*, 103.

28. Matera draws out the importance of these latter chapters in understanding the implications of Paul's teaching on justification and the "truth of the gospel" in "Culmination of Paul's Argument," 79–91.

teaching on justification to the Galatians. Galatians 2:15–21 summarizes the content of the gospel, justification on the basis of faith, and, by responding to a perceived objection, confirms that this justification is achieved not "by works of the law" (ἐξ ἔργων νόμου), but "through [or 'from'] the faith of Christ" (διὰ πίστεως Ἰησοῦ Χριστοῦ; ἐκ πίστεως Χριστοῦ; 2:16).[29] Here Paul sets up an issue to which he will return in the following chapter. God sent his Son, born under the covenant of Torah, to do something the Torah could not do. Justification is therefore now possible based upon the faithfulness of Christ manifested upon the cross. The human response is likewise faith, now *in* Christ. Paul can then assert that "through the faith of Jesus Christ the promise might be given to those who believe" (3:22). Faithfulness thus embraces both the faith *of* Christ and faith *in* Christ.[30] The Letter to the Galatians develops into a rereading of Israel's story in light of the Christ event. In this letter, the "story of Christ's saving death upon the cross is the climax of the Abraham-Christ story and the hermeneutical key that unlocks the meaning of Israel's history."[31] Participation in the faithfulness of Christ, the true descendant of Abraham who gave himself up, with faith like Abraham's reckons righteousness and fulfills God's promises to Abraham's descendants of many nations who now live together in Christ as Christ lives in them.

The Faithfulness of Christ in Romans

Frank Matera suggests that studying Paul's Letter to the Romans is a "humbling and never-ending task" since it is impossible "to completely master or exhaust this remarkable text."[32] Unlike the letters to the churches Paul founded, which were situational and written in a shorthand of sorts, Romans is both "ample and magisterial."[33] As such, "it has influenced the course of Christian theology more than any other writing of the NT."[34] By the late 50s c.e., Paul had begun to wind up his work in Asia Minor and was setting his sights on the West, toward Spain. He planned to go to Jerusalem to deliver funds collected from his Gentile churches, and from there

---

29. Matera, *Galatians*, 97–98.
30. This "might well be called Christ-faith" (ibid., 102).
31. Matera, *New Testament Christology*, 105.
32. Matera, *Romans*, xiii.
33. Johnson, *Writings*, 343.
34. Matera, *Romans*, 3. See also *New Testament Theology*, 167–69.

head to Rome. Before leaving Corinth, he dictated this letter as a means of introducing himself to the churches at Rome. His secretary was Tertius (16:22), and he had Phoebe, the deacon of the church at Cenchrae who was about to leave for Rome (16:1–2), deliver it.[35] Paul had neither established nor visited the Roman churches, and he is careful throughout the letter not to assert the same role of pastoral authority as he assumed with the Galatians. Paul's purpose in writing is practical and has to do with the future of his mission, and his need to present his gospel of justification by faith compelled him to provide a fully developed account of the story of Christ.[36] In the thanksgiving, he states he had wanted to visit Rome for some time (1:10–13). At the end of the letter, he indicates that now is the time, since his mission to the east is completed. Further, he hopes to ensure that Rome will serve as his home base in his planned mission to the west (15:19–24). This will commence as soon as he delivers the collection to Jerusalem, which he deems so important. These desires frame the longest sustained theological argument found in Paul's letters.[37] This letter therefore brings to full expression Paul's interpretation of his work of evangelization and reconciliation among the Gentile churches of the east. He more fully develops his teaching on justification by faith on explicitly anthropological (1:18–3:20) and christological (3:21–5:11) bases, through which the relations between Jew and Gentile in history can be interpreted. These foundational passages detail the human condition under the power of sin as well as the possibility of justification by faith through Christ's redemptive death. In addition, they provide a basic soteriological explanation of the reconciliation of God to all humankind (1:16–17; 5:11).[38]

---

35. There is a growing consensus, especially among European NT scholars, that Rom 16 was not an original part of Paul's letter, particularly due to the textual instability of the doxology found in contemporary translations at 16:25–27. This position was suggested by T. W. Manson, who went on to claim that Romans originally consisted of fifteen chapters. See "St. Paul's Letter to the Romans—and Others," in *The Romans Debate* (ed. Karl P. Donfried; rev. and enl. ed.; Peabody, Mass.: Hendrickson, 2003), 3–15. For an argument in the same volume that advocates the integrity of Rom 1–16, see Karl P. Donfried, "A Short Note on Romans 16," 44–52. I follow Matera's claim for the integrity of Rom 1–16 as discussed in *Romans*, 327–38. He, in turn, was persuaded by Peter Stuhlmacher, *Paul's Letter to the Romans: A Commentary* (trans. Scott J. Hafemann; Louisville: John Knox, 1994).

36. Johnson, *Writings*, 343; Matera, *New Testament Christology*, 111.

37. Johnson, *Writings*, 343.

38. See also Matera, *Romans*, 3.

From a theological and thematic perspective, one can discern three sections in the doctrinal portion of the letter, the first two of which flow together and form the basis for the third, providing an overall thematic unity that follows the thesis statement in 1:16–17. In chapters 1–8 Paul first demonstrates God's way of making humans righteous. In chapters 9–11 he then shows how God's righteousness is worked out in the history of Jews and Gentiles. In chapters 12–15 Paul uses the previous argument as the basis for a model of life in the Christian community. These are the ethical conclusions of his foundational doctrine. Paul can thus wind up his letter by arguing that life in the Christian community must reflect who God is and what he has done for his people (15:1–9). The story developed in Romans is therefore "theological in the proper sense: it describes and praises the work of the one from whom, and through whom, and to whom are all things" (11:36).[39] With regard to rhetorical style, after the address (1:1–7) and thanksgiving (1:8–15), the bulk of the body of the letter (1:16–11:36) follows the form of a scholastic diatribe through which Paul lays out his fundamental theology and doctrine.[40] As with his Letter to the Galatians, Paul then follows this fundamental teaching with the ethical conclusions that flow from it, focusing on the unity of church in relation to the strife of the world (12:1–15:14). Paul then closes and offers extensive final greetings (15:14–16:27).[41]

In the structure of Paul's diatribe, he offers a restatement and elaboration of his primary thesis in 3:21–31. The πίστις χριστοῦ issue comes to the fore in this elaboration and is followed on in the exposition of 5:1–21. The universal condition of human sinfulness was described in the clearly defined section of 1:18–3:20.[42] Paul understands this condition to be the

---

39. Johnson, *Writings*, 345.

40. I continue to follow Johnson in his overall structure and how that determines meaning in Romans (ibid., 346–63). Common in Hellenistic rhetoric, the diatribe, a carefully structured argument, follows six steps. This pattern of argumentation provides the key for reading Romans as follows: (1) the thesis: justification by faith (1:16–17); (2) the antithesis: universal sin (1:18–3:20); (3) the thesis restated: universal faith (3:21–31); (4) demonstration of the thesis by example: Abraham, model of faith (4:1–25); (5) exposition of the thesis: justification given in Christ (5:1–21); (6) objections and responses to the thesis (6:1–11:36). With regard to the interpretive content that follows, Matera's work remains the primary inspiration.

41. Again, there is some debate about the integrity of Rom 16. See the brief discussion above, n. 35.

42. Matera, *New Testament Christology*, 111; idem, *New Testament Theology*, 172–79.

result of Adam's transgression and thus a part of human nature from early on (5:12).[43] In these succeeding sections, Paul argues that human efforts at self-justification and the sin that deprives all of the glory of God (3:23) are countermanded by God's expiatory act of making humans righteous through the gift of faith (3:21, 24–28; 5:18–19). Even though Torah was an intermediary gift from God that is holy, just, and good (7:12), no one will be justified by the law because no one completely fulfilled its prescriptions.[44] Therefore, God put forward Jesus as a sacrifice to establish unity between himself and humans, who are "justified by his blood" (3:25; 5:9). The gift of Jesus, however, "was not a mechanical offering, but the faithful death of a living human being: it was an act of obedience to God."[45] Thus it was an act "from faith to faith" (1:17). Matera observes: "Drawing a contrast between Adam and Christ, Paul notes that whereas Adam's singular transgression, an act of disobedience, led to a judgment and resulted in condemnation for all, Christ's righteous act of obedience led to acquittal and life for all" (see 5:15–21).[46] Paul describes this obedience most definitively in 3:21–31, where the righteousness of God is manifested in the gift and atoning sacrifice of the Son.[47] As he did in his analysis of faithfulness in Galatians, Matera once again opts for a subjective genitive rendering of the faithfulness of Christ here. He summarizes, "Christ's singular act of obedience was his death upon the cross, an act of faithfulness that manifested God's righteousness. By this faithful act of obedience of his Son, God justified humanity and dealt with sin, once and for all."[48]

Paul has come to understand that the central role he once attributed to the law now belongs to Christ. God's revelation of faithfulness and new covenant in and through the crucified Messiah Jesus takes place apart from the standard of Torah, but Torah remains a witness to God's way of

43. Matera, *New Testament Christology*, 113. See also Joseph A. Fitzmyer, *Romans: A New Translation with Introduction and Commentary* (AB 33; New York: Doubleday, 1993), 416.

44. Matera, *New Testament Christology*, 111, 114.

45. Johnson, *Writings*, 350.

46. Matera, *New Testament Christology*, 115. For more on this, see also idem, *New Testament Theology*, 179–86.

47. Matera, *New Testament Christology*, 115–16; idem, *Romans*, 96–101; idem, *New Testament Theology*, 190–93.

48. Matera, *New Testament Christology*, 116. For a fuller exegesis of the issue, see idem, *Romans*, 91–104.

making humans righteous (3:23).[49] The new life in the Spirit offered by the obedient gift to all who participate in the faith of Christ fulfills the role and purpose of Torah and is thus its telos (3:22; 8:1–2). Through the new covenant God has given Christ as the source of righteousness and salvation for the faithful, who not only participate in but fully inhabit life as a community of believers *in* Christ reconciled to God, justified by having the faithfulness *of* the obedient Christ and Son of God (3:21–26; 5:11, 21).

PAUL AND SALVATION HISTORY:
TOWARD A SOTERIOLOGY OF PARTICIPATION

One of Paul's many distinctions is that he provides our earliest record of written contemplation of God and God's work in creation from a specifically Christian viewpoint, that is, from the perspective of the Christ event. The term *Christ event* is a shorthand way of referring to "the complex of decisive moments of the earthly and risen life of Jesus Christ."[50] Paul often focuses on the passion and death of Jesus, but these moments taken together form only one component of the Christ event. Paul also often depends upon the resurrection and exaltation of Christ in re-forming his theology. Although many have noted how little interest Paul shows in Jesus' life prior to the passion,[51] I suggest that the life and teaching of Jesus are also foundational to Paul's understanding of the Christ event and therefore to the response in action he advocates to his churches. The Christ event therefore includes, at the very least, the three decisive moments of (1) the life and teaching of Jesus, (2) the passion and death of Jesus, and (3) the resurrection of Jesus the Christ.

Understanding Paul's use of the πίστις χριστοῦ construction, particularly in Gal 2 and Rom 3, from the christological perspective (thus the use of a subjective genitive) allows for a more complete understanding of how Paul understands God's action in history, through Israel, and turning on the Christ event. The difficult part of this task has always been that Paul is not a literary evangelist. He has not written a gospel that lays out his understanding in a narrative form. He is a pastor and practical theologian, and his offerings come in the form of written letters. Nonetheless, his theology and self-understanding as apostle and pastor are rooted in the

---

49. Johnson, *Writings*, 351.
50. Fitzmyer, *Paul and His Theology*, 59.
51. Ibid., 10, 59.

story of Israel and how the God of Israel has acted in consistent covenant relationship through the Christ event. But what do we mean by "theology" here? As he did not write theological treatises but letters in response to pastoral concern and congregational occasion, Paul's theology is focused on his attempts to understand who God is and how God is acting in the world. His theology is not found in carefully crafted theological concepts but in the manner in which these letters interpret what happened, is happening, and will happen in the gospel as he received it by revelation.[52] In this respect, Paul is not a systematic theologian but a concrete practical theologian who proclaims the salvation provided by Jesus Christ when he responds to, pastors, and comforts his flock.

Paul understood God's action in history as the story of the salvation of humankind, so his theology must be identified with a narrative of salvation history (Rom 11:12, 25–26; 15:7–13). Further, Paul was immersed in the Jewish writings prevalent in his time and working out of a Jewish apocalyptic worldview that focused on the revelatory activity of God in the unfolding of God's plan in and for history. Apocalypticism appears in times of persecution, rejection, and severe hardship. It arose in Judaism in the second century B.C.E. in response to an erosion of values from within and an attack on those values from without, and found its classic expression in the Jewish Scriptures during the Maccabean period in the book of Daniel. Thus it is essentially "crisis literature." Despite its elaborate symbolism, the apocalyptic worldview typically presents a rather straightforward interpretation and resulting picture of history: even when all appearances are to the contrary, God is in command of the world. Even if God's people suffer trials and tribulations, God will ultimately intervene decisively on behalf of the faithful and the oppressed and bring history to its final goal: the communion of God with humankind and all God's creation. Thus the function and emphasis are always focused on encouragement and comfort. The Jewish apocalyptic worldview understands the world to be in a cosmic battle between good and evil, but the outcome is certain, so those enduring persecution are encouraged to hold on to the end. The main objective of Jewish apocalyptic literature is to give suffering people hope and consolation in the face of affliction, but also to demand fidelity

---

52. Matera incorporates this concept of Paul telling "Christ's story" into his approach in *New Testament Christology*. He attributes his understanding of this narrative substructure to Richard Hays's work in *Faith of Jesus Christ*. See Matera, *New Testament Christology*, 84 and 270 n. 8.

and steadfastness in the face of persecution. Paul viewed creation, history, and God's action from a Jewish apocalyptic perspective.[53] Particularly in his Letter to the Galatians, Paul's theology is founded in an apocalyptic narrative about the end of the old age and the beginning of a new one.[54] Therefore, Paul's theology is best understood in terms of a narrative that provides a turning point in the revelation of salvation history coupled with a gospel that in turn reveals a participatory and indwelling soteriology in God's plan to bring creation to its goal.

Paul's Jewish apocalyptic worldview understood time linearly: history had a beginning, is ongoing, and will ultimately have an end. But this beginning and the culminating end were, and are, the same: the glory of God. Before God broke into the abyss and began to create, God's glory was all that was (2 Cor 4:6). This is likewise the goal of the world God created: to dwell with God in glory, and once the world reaches its end, the glory of God will abide. The goal of the individual is to dwell, now and forever, in the glory of God (1 Thess 2:12). Therefore, although I speak of this time as linear, its goal is to come "full circle," so to speak. Thus history should not be envisioned along a horizontal continuum, but somehow with the beginning and end in the same substantive space. Since Paul also understands the Christ event as a turning point in history, a circle is also not the most accurate pictograph. Therefore, the best way to diagram this vision of history might be the chiasm. Although the literary structure of the chiasm is an imperfect analogy that cannot be proven as the structure of Paul's story, this image of a beginning and end on the same vertical plane (i.e., in the same substantive space), with the Christ event as the crucial turning point (Rom 3:22–23) that turns creation in history back toward God and the promise of salvation in God's glory (Rom 15:7), is a helpful visual aid.

As Paul attempts to reconcile his revelatory encounter with the risen Christ and the gospel he has received with his embedded Jewish apocalyptic worldview, he looks back on history as revealed in the Scriptures and

---

53. For an introduction to apocalypticism, including Paul's apocalyptic outlook, see Greg Carey, *Ultimate Things: An Introduction to Jewish and Christian Apocalyptic Literature* (St. Louis: Chalice, 2005). The standard in introductions to this field remains John J. Collins, *The Apocalyptic Imagination: An Introduction to Jewish Apocalyptic Literature* (rev. ed.; Grand Rapids: Eerdmans, 1998). For the apocalyptic perspective in Paul's Letter to the Galatians, see J. Louis Martyn, "Apocalyptic Antinomies in Paul's Letter to the Galatians," *NTS* 31 (1985): 410–24; and his full treatment in *Galatians*.

54. Hays, *Faith of Christ*, xxxix.

develops a covenantal narrative of salvation history. God broke into space and time and acted through the word of creation; thus came the world as we know it and humankind as we know it in Adam. The character of this word is covenantal. The metaphor of covenant is the primary means by which the biblical authors in the Jewish Scriptures express the special relationship between God and God's creation in general, and God's chosen people Israel in particular. Both the texts that narrate the story of Israel and its relationship with God and the prophetic literature that communicates God's will and summons Israel to live rightly in this relationship are replete with accounts of God's covenantal activity in the world. In addition to detailed recounting of covenant-making and covenant-renewing rituals and ceremonies, this literature preserves the broader themes and symbolism of the covenant metaphor. These storytellers and prophets integrate this language into their larger works in order to share their message of life in unique relationship with God, even when the term *covenant* does not appear. At its root, a covenant is defined as "an agreement enacted between two parties in which one or both make promises under oath to perform or refrain from certain actions stipulated in advance."[55] Old Testament scholars have offered extensive historical analysis of the role and function of covenants in the Scriptures of Israel.[56] A narrative perspective on the covenant metaphor offers insight into the development of the tradition in the text of the Jewish Scriptures as a product of the lived experience of the people of Israel. This story of covenantal relationship began with the inbreaking of God, which, of course, is also Paul's story of history.

Genesis 1–3 thus recounts the invasion of God into space and time in the word of creation that suggests that the foundation of the covenantal relationship is communication. God makes an implicit covenant with Adam and all creation by way of the purpose of this creative act (1 Cor 15:45–49). God created the world, and humankind, to be in a perfect relationship of union with him. Unmediated relationship with God gave the promise of freedom to humanity in the form of obedience. Paul would say that this cosmology suggests that humankind is truly free, most fully human, when it is obedient to God (Rom 6:15–23). This covenantal relationship is marked by the dwelling place of Eden, where humankind can commune with God "in the evening breeze" (Gen 3:8). Early on, however,

---

55. George E. Mendenhall and Gary A. Herion, "Covenant," *ABD* 1:1179–1202.

56. See the discussion in D. J. McCarthy, *Old Testament Covenant: A Survey of Current Opinions* (Richmond: John Knox, 1972).

there was a breakdown for which Adam bears the burden through his act of disobedience (Rom 5:19), which leads to chaos, a fundamental disordering of the intended order of creation. Sin and death enter the world through disobedience (Rom 5:12–18; 1 Cor 15:22) and quickly spread as humankind grows (Gen 4:1–6:8). God begins to rectify this relationship with creation by offering a covenant to Noah (Gen 6–9). Noah's obedience makes possible God's covenant with creation (Gen 9:8–17). But for humankind's part, sin spread through disobedience to the covenantal relationship (Rom 11:30–32), which reaches an initial climax in the story of the tower of Babel (Gen 11:1–9). This etiological story of the origins of differing languages and the spread of humankind over the earth also provides a symbolic narrative of the scattering of humankind, which was created to be in union with God. At this point, there is a significant break in the narrative through the insertion of a genealogy (Gen 11:10–32), after which something distinctive, though still consistently covenantal, begins.[57]

God broke in and acted again through the word of covenant with humankind. This time, however, God chose to work through one man and his descendants (Gen 12:1–4). The mediator of this covenant was Abraham, and Abraham's obedience resulted in the next step in the covenantal union with God. God promises Abraham blessing, descendants, and land, as well as the extension of this covenantal relationship to Abraham's descendants not through Torah but due to Abraham's faithful obedience (Rom 4:13, 18–22). The sign of this covenantal activity is circumcision (Gen 17:1–14). Eventually, God's covenant with Abraham results in the birth of a people, the twelve tribes of Israel who, as the descendants of Abraham and marked by circumcision, are likewise the descendants of God. Abraham thus becomes Paul's go-to model for righteousness before God apart from Torah (Rom 4; Gal 3:1–4:8). However, Paul is quick to point out that although circumcision becomes the mark of this covenant, God reckoned Abraham's faith to him as righteousness prior to the command for circumcision (Gen 15:6; Rom 4:9–12). Circumcision was given as a seal of the righteousness of faith already lived (Rom 4:11). This allowed Abraham to be the ancestor to all who would believe, which would in turn allow this same righteousness to be reckoned upon them. "For this reason, those who believe are blessed with Abraham who believed" (Gal 3:6–9; see also Rom 4:16–17). This was God's plan all along, but initially God

---

57. Therefore, theologians often call Gen 1–11 the "prologue to salvation history."

worked through this one man and his descendants to provide a model for righteousness for all humankind.

In the following centuries down to the exodus, God remembers his covenant with Abraham. The exodus is a formative event in the history of Israel. The obedience of the people during the exodus and the will of God's chosen people Israel results in the formation of the Sinai covenant, as mediated by Moses and marked by the giving of the Ten Commandments (Exod 19–20). God perfected this obedience through the giving of the full Torah, the gift that guides God's people to righteousness by making transgression known (Gal 3:19). Through Torah the Israelites were able to atone for sin and attempt to reconcile themselves with God in a new way: through the discipline of the law and the act of sacrifice to God (Gal 3:24; Phil 4:18; see Exod 20:24; Lev 7; 19; 22). Paul understood this gift itself, however, as imperfect, in the sense that it reunited humankind with God, but it did not save; it did not justify (Rom 8:3; Gal 3:19–20). Nonetheless the Torah is by no means opposed to the promises of God through Abraham (Gal 3:21). Rather, the law is good and both shines a light on sin and provides a path for righteousness (Rom 7).

Eventually this chosen people of Israel formed a nation with a king. The king that epitomizes a unified Israel in union with God is David. In recognition of this, God makes a covenant with David, the mark of which is a house—a house for God in the temple and a house for David in his dynasty (2 Sam 7). The hope for a messiah and messianic expectations grew out of this covenant. Paul speaks little of the Davidic covenant in his story of the gospel and salvation history, but he does look to David as one who speaks of blessedness for all who are righteous irrespective of works of the law (Rom 4:6–8). Further, his focus on Jesus as the Christ and descended from David (Rom 1:2) bespeaks his commitment to and incorporation of this covenant into his story of God's work in the world.

And history moves forward. The kingdom divides and both nations eventually fall, leading once again to a physical scattering of the people through the Babylonian exile. The prophets are united in understanding this fall of the nation and scattering of the people to be the result of Israel's breach of covenant with God. The exile is extremely formative in the theology and literature of the people. Eventually the Israelites return and rebuild, but become a shadow of their former glory. When Roman rule takes over in the first century B.C.E., and the extreme hardship of foreign rule leads to the spread of the apocalyptic worldview, the people of Judea are ripe for a revelation, and hopes for God's promised messiah to come and bring in God's kingdom reach a fever pitch.

God responds with a new act of obedience that brings on a new creation. Paul most clearly elucidates this act in the Christ hymn of Phil 2:6–11. The story of this hymn is the story that underlies all else in Paul's gospel.[58] God breaks into space and time in a new act of covenant that is consistent with all previous covenantal activity in God's story with Israel. For Paul, fidelity on God's part in this relationship is also fundamental; therefore determining the justice of God in this story is likewise essential (Rom 9–11). However, this covenantal act is also distinctive. For Jesus is not only the human mediator of God's covenant as were Abraham, Moses, and the others before him; he is the divine Son of God who also *is* the covenant gift itself. The preexistent Christ Jesus, in the form of God, empties himself into human form, "becoming obedient to death, even death on a cross" (Phil 2:6–8). The paradox is that this scandalous death from the human perspective is in truth God's gift of expiation, an atoning sacrifice that brings about the exaltation that fulfills all God's earlier covenantal activity and puts in place a new covenant whereby justification to any and all is made possible by the faithful obedience of Christ (Rom 3:21–26; Gal 2:16, 20; 3:22; Phil 3:9). Just as right relationship with God was ruptured by the disobedience of the one man Adam, the new act of faithful obedience of the one man Jesus is the grace that brings justification (Rom 5:1–21; 1 Cor 15:20–28). As Matera asserts, "Representing humanity before God, therefore, Christ effected a 'divine interchange' whereby humanity becomes the righteousness of God (2 Cor 5:21), is freed from the curse of the law (Gal 3:13), and fulfills its just requirements in Christ (Rom 8:3)."[59] Through the life and ministry, death, and resurrection of Jesus Christ, all of God's prior covenantal activity is brought to fulfillment (1 Cor 15:3–4). Jesus is the new Adam whose faithful obedience (following the Abrahamic covenant) leads him to be the sacrifice that atones for the sin of all humankind (following the Sinai covenant), exalts him as the Christ who redeems God's people (following the Davidic covenant), and reconciles the ruptured relationship between God

---

58. Michael Gorman calls this hymn Paul's "master story" (*Inhabiting the Cruciform God*, esp. 9–39). Matera suggests that the entire story of Israel, read in light of Christ, underlies this letter and all Paul's preaching (*New Testament Christology*, 121).

59. Matera, *New Testament Christology*, 115. For the language of "divine interchange," Matera follows Morna Hooker, "Interchange in Christ," *JTS* 22 (1971): 349–61.

and humankind. Christ is indeed the climax of Israel's story.[60] But Christ is also the turning point in God's salvation history with all humankind. As the one ultimate redeeming sacrifice, the Christ event brings about an acquittal and new relationship between God and creation in a new covenantal relationship—open to all humankind.

This opening of unmediated relationship with God brings about a state whereby humankind can live in glory now, though Paul is not so naïve as to think that it is just glory now. Humankind is making its way back to the glory that is full dwelling with God. Again, this is a Jewish worldview, a rereading of a Jewish apocalyptic schema. It is the end of history that will bring God's plan to fruition. In his early letters to the Thessalonians, Paul focuses on the Parousia as this final invasion of God into creation that brings salvation in terms of life together with Christ for the faithful (1 Thess 4:13–5:11). Later, Paul focuses on the resurrection of Christ as the firstfruits of resurrected life with Christ in the glory of God (1 Cor 15:1–28; Rom 6:5–11). This understanding of salvation history is all rooted in God's ongoing covenantal relationship with creation and humankind as the apex of that creation. The Christ event, according to Paul, is the turning point of history and God's salvific work in creation with humankind. If the life and ministry of Jesus show "God's truthfulness to confirm the promises to the patriarchs" as well as God's mercy and glory to the Gentiles (Rom 15:8–9), and the crucifixion puts in place the new covenant through which Jew and Gentile alike are justified by the faith of Christ (Gal 3:24–29; Rom 3:21–31; 5:12–21), then the resurrection is for Paul the proof of the possibility of this new hope and life in the Spirit (Rom 8). Humankind still must choose to accept this gift of covenant relationship or not. The gift is free and available to all.

Participation in the gospel provides life in the new community of the faithful. This is also how Christianity makes sense in terms of its Jewish history, and how it was born and began to spread among first the Jewish people and then also to the Gentiles through the vocation of Paul and his developing theology of salvation history. The primary actor of this story is God who is Father; the agent of salvation is Jesus Christ who is Lord; and the beneficiaries are all who choose to inhabit the faithfulness of Christ in the hope of salvation in the glory of God.[61]

---

60. Matera, *New Testament Christology*, 133.
61. Ibid., 121.

From ΠΑΡΟΥΣΙΑ το ΕΠΙΦΑΝΕΙΑ: The Transformation of a Pauline Motif

Raymond F. Collins

At the beginning of his study of the Christology of the Letters to the Thessalonians, Frank Matera wrote apropos 1 Thessalonians, "Paul employs this letter to recall former teaching and exhort the Thessalonians to remain faithful to their call and election as a sanctified community that must stand blameless before the Lord on the day of his parousia (5:23). Paul also takes the occasion of this letter to provide the community with further teaching about the Lord's parousia."[1]

The ΠΑΡΟΥΣΙΑ in 1 Thessalonians 2:19

The reference to the παρουσία in 1 Thess 5:23 is, in fact, the final mention of the παρουσία in this letter, which contains three other uses of the term (cf. 2:19; 3:13; 4:15).[2] The term first occurs in 2:19, where it is appears in a two-verse description of Paul's hope to underscore his affection for the Thessalonians so as to emphasize the depth of his longing to be with the Thessalonians when circumstances prevented his being with them. To show how much he desired to be with the Thessalonians, Paul wrote, "For what is our hope or joy or crown of boasting before our Lord Jesus at his coming [ἔμπροσθεν τοῦ κυρίου ἡμῶν Ἰησοῦ ἐν τῇ αὐτοῦ παρουσίᾳ]? Is it not you? Yes, you are our glory and our joy!"[3]

---

1. Frank J. Matera, *New Testament Christology* (Louisville: Westminster John Knox, 1999), 88.

2. Paul uses the term παρουσία to refer to the eschatological coming of Christ only one other time in the extant correspondence, namely, at 1 Cor 15:23, but that passage will not be the focus of this essay.

3. Here and elsewhere the English text of the New Testament is that of the NRSV.

Paul's desire to be with the Thessalonians is an ultimate desire. Since *hope* (ἐλπίς), *joy* (χαρά,), *crown* (στέφανος), and *glory* (δόξα) are terms that Paul uses with eschatological connotations throughout his letters, commentators are in general agreement that the coming of the Lord to which Paul makes reference in 2:19 is an eschatological event that will take place on the Day of the Lord. Since their presence with him on the Day of the Lord will be his crowning joy, the Thessalonians should realize just how deeply his absence from them affects him. This would appear to be Paul's purpose in introducing the theme of the παρουσία in 2:19. Since Paul does not explain what he means by the παρουσία of the Lord Jesus, the idea must have been familiar to the Thessalonians. As such, it would have been a theme that Paul had opened up for the Thessalonians when he was with them.

PARAENESIS AND THE CHIASM OF 1 THESSALONIANS 3:11–5:23

The three other occurrences of παρουσία are to be linked together. First Thessalonians 3:13 and 5:23 are a pair of similarly phrased wish-prayers. The first reads, "And may he so strengthen your hearts in holiness that you may be blameless before our God and Father at the coming of our Lord Jesus [ἔμπροσθεν τοῦ θεοῦ καὶ πατρὸς ἡμῶν ἐν τῇ παρουσίᾳ] with all his saints" (3:13).[4] The Greek formula repeats verbatim the expression found earlier in 2:19. The second wish-prayer reads, "May the God of peace himself sanctify you entirely, and may your spirit and soul and body be kept sound and blameless at the coming of our Lord Jesus Christ [ἐν τῇ παρουσίᾳ τοῦ κυρίου ἡμῶν Ἰησοῦ Χριστοῦ]" (5:23).

In addition to their similar references to the παρουσία, both identifying Jesus by his name and the honorific "our Lord," both 3:11–13 and 5:23 contain other like vocabulary. Both speak about God (ὁ θεὸς ... τοῦ θεοῦ, ὁ θεός), sanctification (ἁγιωσύνη, ἁγιάσαι), and blamelessness (ἀμέμπτους, ἀμέμπτως). The literary formula found in these verses and the similarity of their vocabulary suggest that they form a literary inclusion around the hortatory part of the letter, 4:1–5:22, which many commentators consider to be the body of the letter. As such the intervenient section of the letter spells out in some detail what it means for the Thessalonians to be found

---

4. This verse is a purpose clause that is part of the wish-prayer in vv. 12–13. Some authors see this brace of verses as a wish-prayer juxtaposed with the wish-prayer in v. 11, while other authors take all three verses to be a single wish-prayer.

blameless at the coming of the Lord Jesus with that blamelessness for which Paul prays in the two embracing wish-prayers.[5] This section of the letter has a chiastic structure, at the heart of which is an apocalyptic diptych.

The outside elements of the chiasm, 4:1–12 (A) and 5:12–22 (A'), open with similar hortatory introductions, each of which employs kinship language in a formula of direct address. After a transitional λοιπὸν οὖν, which links the following paraenesis with the wish-prayer of 3:13, 4:1 continues with the introductory formula, "brothers and sisters, we ask and urge you in the Lord Jesus" (ἀδελφοί, ἐρωτῶμεν ὑμᾶς καὶ παρακαλοῦμεν ἐν κυρίῳ Ἰησοῦ). The hortatory 5:12–22 is introduced with "we appeal to you, brothers and sisters" (Ἐρωτῶμεν δὲ ὑμᾶς, ἀδελφοί), whose connective δέ links the hortatory material of 5:12–22 with the preceding unit on the children of the light, the children of the day (5:1–11). This opening formula echoes the language of 4:1, whose παρακαλοῦμεν recurs in 5:14.[6] For the purposes of the present essay, the similarities between units A and A' need not be pursued to the full, but the reader certainly notes that both units embody kinship language within the body of the exhortation (4:6, 10 [2x]), both highlight the importance of love (4:9 [2x]; 5:8), and both speak of the will of God for the community (4:3; 5:18).

The internal elements of the chiasm, 4:13–18 (B) and 5:1–11 (B'), constitute an apocalyptic diptych at the heart of the chiasm. The two units are similar not only by reason of their apocalyptic language but also with regard to their opening and closing formulae. The first unit (4:13–18), which uses apocalyptic language to speak of the future, begins with a disclosure formula, "But we do not want you to be uniformed, brothers and sisters, about those who have died" (Οὐ θέλομεν δὲ ὑμᾶς ἀγνοεῖν, ἀδελφοί, περὶ τῶν κοιμωμένων; 4:13). The language implies that Paul is imparting new information to his audience. The second unit (5:1–11), which uses apocalyptic language in an exhortation about present behavior, begins with a preterition, "Now concerning the times and seasons, brothers and sisters, you do not need to have anything written to you" (Περὶ δὲ τῶν χρόνων καὶ τῶν καιρῶν, ἀδελφοί, οὐ χρείαν ἔχετε ὑμῖν γράφεσθαι; 5:1). The language implies that Paul has already had something to say about this topic, but now he reintroduces the topic in such a way as to point to its importance.

---

5. See Charles A. Wanamaker, "Apocalyptic Discourse, Paraenesis and Identity Maintenance in 1 Thessalonians," *Neot* 36 (2002): 137.

6. Not to be pressed is the presence of ἐν κυρίῳ later in v. 12.

The similar hortatory conclusions of the two units, namely, "Therefore encourage one another ['Ὥστε παρακαλεῖτε ἀλλήλους] with these words" in 4:18 and "Therefore encourage one another [Διὸ παρακαλεῖτε ἀλλήλους]" in 5:11 show that both units have similar paraenetic import. In sum, the body of the letter is a hortatory piece with a chiastic structure. Were the chiasm to be envisioned more broadly so as to include the encompassing wish-prayers, we would have this structure:

A Wish-prayer (3:11-13)
 B Paraenetic recall (4:1-12)
  C Exhortation on hope (4:13-18)
  C' Exhortation on present conduct in light of the Day of the Lord (5:1-11)
 B' Paraenesis on responsibility with the community (5:12-22)
A' Wish-prayer (5:23)

In addition to 1:4-10 and 2:17-20, which feature Paul's only use of the term παρουσία outside the chiastically arranged material, James Hester identifies units A, C, C', and A' as sections of apocalyptic discourse within 1 Thessalonians.[7] First Thessalonians 3:11-5:23 is characterized by an interleaving of what Hester calls "pragmatic discourse" and apocalyptic discourse. The pragmatic discourse—paraenesis is straightforward language—functions at least partially to detail the content of righteous behavior that is expected of those who are to be found blameless at the παρουσία.[8]

A first purpose of Paul's use of παρουσία language in 1 Thessalonians is, therefore, paraenetic. Paul uses the motif of the coming of the Lord to motivate the Thessalonians to adopt patterns of behavior that will enable them to be found blameless at the coming of the Lord and be saved from the wrath that is coming (1:10). For Thessalonian believers the coming of the Lord is a salvific event, mention of which provides motivation for ethical behavior on their part. This ethical behavior does not derive unaided from the strength of their internal moral fiber. The wish-prayers of 3:11-13 and 5:23 make clear that this kind of behavior derives from a divine initiative. It is to the extent that the Thessalonians are blameless at the

---

7. James D. Hester, "Creating the Future: Apocalyptic Rhetoric in 1 Thessalonians," *R&T* 17 (2000): 199-200.
 8. Ibid., 201.

coming of the Lord that they are Paul's joy, glory, and crown of boasting at the coming of the Lord (2:19–20).

A MATTER OF IDENTITY IN 1 THESSALONIANS 4:13–18

The "further teaching about the Lord's parousia" to which Matera refers[9] is embodied within unit C of the expanded chiastic structure. On the basis of the Thessalonians' faith in the death and resurrection of Jesus (4:14)[10] and the word of the Lord (4:15),[11] Paul develops an eschatological scenario to respond to the Thessalonians' concerns about those who had fallen asleep in death (4:13). "Paul's answer" to the Thessalonians' concerns is, as Richard Ascough notes, "more than theological."[12] To a large extent, Paul's

---

9. Matera, *New Testament Christology*, 88.

10. Strikingly, the confessional formula of 4:14 does not employ an honorific in reference to Jesus. Twice the traditional formula cites the name of the human Jesus.

11. The source of the "word of the Lord" and the extent of its quotation continue to be sources of scholarly dispute. See, among other contributions to the question, Raymond F. Collins, "Tradition, Redaction and Exhortation in 1 Th 4,13–5,11," in *L'Apocalypse johannique et l'Apocalyptique dans le Nouveau Testament* (ed. Jan Lambrecht; BETL 53; Leuven: Leuven University Press, 1980), 325–43. Seyoon Kim considers that 4:16–17a is Paul's paraphrase of the word of the Lord ("The Jesus Tradition in 1 Thess 4.13–5.11," *NTS* 48 [2002]: 226–27). A recent attempt to clarify the matter has been offered by P. H. R. Van Houwelingen, "The Great Reunion: The Meaning and Significance of the 'Word of the Lord' in1 Thessalonians 4:13–18," *CTJ* 42 (2007): 313–17. Van Houwelingen finds the word of the Lord in v. 14. On the other hand, Stefan Schreiber, who also surveys the possibilities, finds the word of the Lord in vv. 15–16. See Stefan Schreiber, "Eine neue Jenseitshoffnung in Thessaloniki und ihre Probleme (1 Thess 4, 13–18)," *Bib* 88 (2007): 328–30.

12. Richard S. Ascough, "A Question of Death: Paul's Community Building Language in 1 Thessalonians 4:13–18," *JBL* 123 (2004): 520. Arguing his point that Paul's answer is more than theological, Ascough first links Paul's answer to his personal honor: "Paul links questions of faith and belief to his own status within the community.... His concern is a matter not of his credibility but of his honor as founder and (spiritual) representative of the community" (521). In a society in which honor and shame are dominant social concerns, Paul's honor is certainly a factor to be considered. Linking the παρουσία with Paul's honor may be an exegetical point to be raised with regard to the rhetorical question in 2:19 and the combined wish-prayer of 3:11–13, both of which speak of the παρουσία, but it is not immediately apparent that Paul's honor is at issue in the way he responds to the Thessalonians concern about those who had died.

answer appears to be sociological. It concerns the identity of the Christian community.

Insider-outsider language dominates much of the discourse of 1 Thessalonians. The Thessalonian community results from God's election (1:4). The church consists of those who have been called from among the Thessalonians (1:1). Thessalonian believers have turned from idols to serve the living and true God (1:9). They are saved from the wrath that is to come (1:10; 5:9). The kinship language that permeates 1 Thessalonians first appears in 1:4.[13] Kinship language is a language of belonging and identity. It also is the language of demarcation; it suggests that some do not belong to the family. This language is reinforced by the "one another" language (ἀλλήλους) of 3:12; 4:9, 18; 5:11, 15.[14]

Thessalonian believers are different from Gentiles who do not know God (4:5). They are the insiders; others are outsiders (4:12). They are expected not to grieve, unlike others who have no hope (4:13). They have knowledge that others apparently do not have, for others say "peace and security" while destruction is impending (5:1–3). The metaphorical and dualistic language of light and day, night and darkness, is set forth in an antithetical chiastic structure that affirms that the Thessalonians belong to God and they have nothing to do with the darkness that characterizes those outside the community (5:5; cf. 5:8).[15] The antithetical language suggests that there are strong boundaries that set the members of the community apart from those who do not belong to it.[16] The contrasting metaphors of being awake and falling asleep, of being sober and being drunk (5:6–7), serve the same purpose. Members of the community are destined for salvation, not for wrath (5:9).

The holiness language in the wish-prayers of 3:11–13 and 5:23, elements A and A' in the chiastic structure outlined above, is the language of being set apart. The holiness language of the wish-prayers, also found in 4:3, 4, and 7, leads to the members of the community being identified as the holy ones in 5:27 just after a holy kiss is mentioned as a sign of

---

13. See also 2:1, 9, 14, 17; 3:2, 7; 4:1, 6, 10 (2x), 13; 5:2, 4, 12, 14, 25, 26, 27.

14. Note that in 3:12 and 5:15 ἀλλήλους is contrasted with πάντας.

15. Cf. Wanamaker, "Apocalyptic Discourse," 141–42.

16. Cf. Duane F. Watson, "Paul's Appropriation of Apocalyptic Discourse: The Rhetorical Strategy of 1 Thessalonians," in *Vision and Persuasion: Rhetorical Dimensions of Apocalyptic Discourse* (ed. Greg Carey and L. Gregory Bloomquist; St. Louis: Chalice, 1999), 77.

the bonds that bind the members of the community to one another. They belong to the Lord and, in a sense, to one another as members of God's chosen and holy people.

In sum, community identity is a matter of major concern in Paul's first letter. Its paraenesis is embodied in the letter "in order to sustain the Thessalonians in their new identity and thereby inoculate them against the pressure of their fellow Thessalonians to withdraw from their new social group."[17] The aim of increasing and abounding in love expressed in the wish-prayer of 3:11–13 is a matter of social bonding as is the commendation and subsequent paraenesis on φιλαδελφία, sibling love, the love of brothers and sisters, in 4:9–10.[18]

A particularly significant piece of Paul's paraenesis is his exhortation on sexual morality in 4:4–5. The social purposes of the exhortation are apparent in Paul's urging conduct that will distinguish the behavior of the Thessalonians from that of Gentiles who do not know God and his observation that one ought not to engage in conduct that is harmful to one's sibling. The background for Paul's exhortation is his Jewish and biblical heritage in which sexual purity functions dualistically to separate believers from nonbelievers.[19]

COMMUNITY IDENTITY AND THE ΠΑΡΟΥΣΙΑ

The preservation and strengthening of identity is also of major concern in the two units of the apocalyptic diptych at the center of the chiastic structure outlined above. The exhortations that open and close 4:13–18 are elements of paraenesis that have a social function. Paul wants the Thessalonians to be different from outsiders who grieve (v. 13).[20] He urges

---

17. Wanamaker, "Apocalyptic Discourse," 136.

18. Cf. Rom 12:10.

19. See, e.g., the opening and closing verses of Lev 18. See further O. Larry Yarbrough, *Not Like the Gentiles: Marriage Rules in the Letters of Paul* (SBLDS 80; Atlanta: Scholars Press, 1985), 76–87.

20. Schreiber notes that these outsiders are "pagans" but also, albeit in different fashion, Jews. Cf. Schreiber, "Jenseitshoffnung," 327. That "pagans" had no hope does not mean that they did not have a belief in an afterlife. Goods found in ancient tombs—especially well known are the Egyptian pyramids and the tomb of Philip of Macedonia, discovered in 1977—and various epigraphic evidence suggests that belief in some form of an afterlife was fairly widespread. What the Thessalonian outsiders lacked was Christian hope, the hope of being with the Lord Jesus.

the members of the community to encourage one another in the circumstances at hand (v. 18).

The metaphors that pervade the paraenesis of 5:1–11,[21] the other part
of Paul's apocalyptic diptych, are clearly dualistic. Their function is to urge
the members of the community to preserve its identity in the face of opposition. The agonistic and Isaian[22] metaphor of military attire (5:8) certainly
implies that a battle is to be waged in the face of opposition. It is a matter
of community identity that both those who are awake and those who sleep
be with the Lord at the moment of salvation (5:9–10). The exhortation
with which 5:11 concludes, incorporating a building-up motif not found
in 4:18, urges the strengthening of the community's identity even more
strongly than does the exhortation of 4:18.

To return, then, to Ascough's affirmation that Paul's response to the
Thessalonians' concern for those who have died is not merely theological,
nor is it only paraenetic—Paul writes as he does in order that the Thessalonians not grieve (4:13–18) and urges them to encourage one another
with the words that he has written (4:18)—it is also sociological as well as
theological and paraenetic.

The individualism of contemporary Western society leads many Western readers of 4:13–18 to think that the Thessalonians' concern was that
of the fate of individuals who had died. Paul, however, writes in the plural
about those who have died. He distinguishes those who have died from
those who are alive (4:15). The concern seems to have been whether they
will be with "us" at the time of the expected παρουσία. Paul's response is that
yes, they will be with us. The first-person plural of "we will be [ἐσόμεθα]
with the Lord" in 4:17 encompasses both the "we" (ἡμεῖς) and the "them"
(αὐτοῖς) of 4:15–17. That is the message with which the Thessalonians are
to encourage one another.

The issue at hand is whether those who have died will be members of
the community at the παρουσία. Ascough suggests that the community's
grief over those who have died is a concern about belonging to the community.[23] He and others following him have likened the church to the voluntary associations, the religious, professional, and funerary associations,
of the Greco-Roman world. With regard to these associations,

---

21. Cf. Raymond F. Collins, *The Power of Images in Paul* (Collegeville, Minn.:
Liturgical Press, 2008), 31–38.

22. Cf. Isa 59:17.

23. Ascough, "Question of Death," 521.

Epigraphic and papyrological evidence suggests that within associations death was not simply a matter of "not living," nor was the primary
concern about death the personal salvation of the individual. Death was
inevitable but provided the opportunity for community definition. One
did not cease to be a member of an association at death; rather death
was the point at which the association celebrated a person's membership.
From among the many members, the deceased individual would be isolated and celebrated as a member of the community.[24]

For Thessalonian believers, the question is whether the dead belong to
the community that will meet the Lord at his coming.[25] Does their death
destroy the unity of the community that awaits the coming of the Lord? In
death, have the dead lost their Christian identity? Otherwise stated, what
is the relationship between the παρουσία and the resurrection of the dead?
For it is within this context that Paul offers further teaching about the
Lord's παρουσία, the occasion for a community meeting. The new information that Paul imparts in 4:13–18 is not about the reality of the παρουσία; it
is about the nature of the παρουσία and what it entails with regard to those
who have died.

That the παρουσία is an important feature in 3:11–5:23 is indicated
by its presence in the wish-prayers, 3:11–13 and 5:23, that function as
the bookends for the unit. That the understanding of the παρουσία was
problematic for Thessalonica's community of believers comes to the fore
in 4:13–18. The event of the παρουσία seems to be at the center of the problem.[26] The death of some believers is not the issue; people die all the time.
Nor does the idea of the resurrection of the dead seem to be the issue. The
issue seems to be that some members of the community might be left out
at the παρουσία.

Paul's response is that this will not happen because the "dead in Christ"[27]
will first be raised. Paul employs an apocalyptic scenario to "explain" how
it is possible for the entire community, both the dead and the living, to be

---

24. Ibid., 510.

25. Cf. Helmut Koester, "Imperial Ideology and Paul's Eschatology in 1 Thessalonians," in *Paul and Empire: Religion and Power in Roman Imperial Society* (ed. Richard
A. Horsley; Harrisburg, Pa.: Trinity Press International, 1997), 159. Cf. Van Houwelingen, "Great Reunion," 312.

26. Cf. Schreiber, "Jenseitshoffnung," 331, and the summary on 350.

27. Even this expression, οἱ νεκροὶ ἐν Χριστῷ, has dualistic overtones, since it
implies that, while some have died in Christ, others have not.

together at the coming of the Lord. The coming of the Lord is a salvific event. It is imperative that all members of the community be present so that they can be/live with the Lord. As Paul writes in 5:10, "whether we are awake or asleep[28] we may live with him." His σὺν αὐτῷ/κυρίῳ in 4:14, 17; and 5:10 is a cipher for salvation. "Being with the Lord" is the way that Paul speaks of salvation. For believers to be saved, to be with the Lord, he must be present. Hence the importance of the presence of the Lord, his παρουσία, as the focus of Christian hope.

Παρουσια: A Social and Political Term

Scholars have long sought the cultural background of Paul's use of παρουσία in this context. Paul uses the term in its ordinary sense of "presence" or "coming" in several of his letters (1 Cor 16:17; 2 Cor 7:6, 7; 10:10; Phil 1:26; 2:12), but he does not do so in 1 Thessalonians. This earliest of Paul's extant letters uses the language of παρουσία only with reference to the eschatological presence of the Lord Jesus. Paul uses the vocabulary with this connotation only one other time (1 Cor 15:21), but it appears with this meaning in later early Christian literature (2 Thess 2:1, 8; Matt 24:3, 27, 37, 39; Jas 5:7, 8; 2 Pet 1:16; 3:4; 1 John 2:28).

Helmut Koester correctly observes that the term παρουσία was introduced by Paul in this letter. It is a political term closely related to the status of the community.[29] Although the term παρουσία was widely used in its ordinary sense in reference to someone's arrival, Paul uses the term with a particular and specific connotation. The term had not previously been used in an apocalyptic/eschatological sense, not in the Hebrew Bible, the Septuagint, or Jewish apocalyptic literature.

With the meaning of "coming" or "arrival," the term was especially used in reference to the visit of a royal or official person or the visit of a god.[30] That the visit of a deity provided Paul with the cultural background

---

28. The phrase "awake or asleep" (εἴτε γρηγορῶμεν εἴτε καθεύδωμεν) is an antithetical metaphor used in reference to the living and the dead. Its language reprises the vocabulary of the paraenesis in 5:6–7. When Paul raises the issue of those who have died (τῶν κοιμωμένων) in 4:13, he uses another metaphorical expression. The verb κοιμάω properly means sleep, but it was a metaphor commonly used in reference to death (see, among many other examples, Homer, *Il.* 11.241; Gen 47:30; Acts 7:36).

29. Koester, "Imperial Ideology," 158.

30. Cf. LSJ, 1343, s.v. παρουσία. The lexicon gives a few examples of uses of the

for his use of the term in a specialized sense is hardly likely. Not only would Paul as a faithful Jew be loathe to borrow from this sector of Hellenistic culture, but also he does not speak of Jesus as "God."[31] Thus we are left with Hellenism's use of παρουσία in reference to royal visits as the cultural background of Paul's use of the term with its specialized meaning in 1 Thessalonians. Adolf Deissmann was so taken by usage of the term in papyri and on ostraca in the second century B.C.E.–second century C.E. period that he identified παρουσία as a "technical expression for the arrival or the visit of the emperor."[32]

Many have followed Deissmann not only in seeing the imperial visit as the background of Paul's use of the term but also in identifying παρουσία as a technical term when Paul uses it apropos the eschatological appearance of Jesus as Lord. If "technical term" is an apt designation of παρουσία in its specialized Pauline usage, it should be noted that such usage began with Paul.[33] He did not appropriate the technical term from prior Jewish apocalyptic discourse.[34] The background of Paul's use of the term is the Hellenistic custom of using this term in an almost technical sense to signify an official visit of an emperor, a king, or one of their important representatives.

Such παρουσίαι were well-known events in the world in which Paul lived. They would have been familiar to the inhabitants of all the major centers of population, including that of the free city of Thessalonica on the Aegean coast. On the παρουσία of an imperial or royal figure, he would be greeted with fanfare by the city's population.[35] The citizenry passed through the city gates to receive the visiting official, and often went some distance from the city itself to do so. The procession was organized in an order that corresponded to the dignity of the participants. The populace was dressed in festive garb and adorned with garlands. The city itself was decorated and festivities organized. Incense was burned and a major

term with regard to each type of visit. See also Albrecht Oepke, "παρουσία, πάρειμι," *TDNT* 5:858–71; and Adolf Deissmann, *Light from the Ancient East: The New Testament Illustrated by Recently Discovered Texts of the Greco-Roman World* (New York: Doran, 1927), 368–72.

31. Cf. Schreiber, "Jenseitshoffnung," 331.

32. Cf. Deissmann, *Light from the Ancient East*, 368.

33. Cf. Oepke, *TDNT* 5:865.

34. Among others, Koester ("Imperial Ideology," 158) and Udo Schnelle (*Apostle Paul: His Life and Theology* [Grand Rapids: Baker, 2003], 177 n. 19) offer similar caveats.

35. See, among others, Gene L. Green, *The Letters to the Thessalonians* (Pillar New Testament Commentary; Grand Rapids: Eerdmans, 2002), 223.

temple open, in which sacrifice could be offered.[36] Often the visitor was received as a benefactor; he would typically confer gifts, privileges, and liberties on the city's inhabitants. Sometimes the official visit and what it entailed by way of gifts was construed as the beginning of a new era for the city's population.

That this is the background against which the events surrounding the παρουσία as described in 4:5–17 are to be understood is confirmed by Paul's use of other "political" language in the pericope as well as within the context of 3:11–5:23. True, much of the imagery employed by Paul comes from his Jewish/apocalyptic background, but as a communicator, one sufficiently aware of the demands of rhetoric, Paul made use of images that spoke to his audience. He would have been aware of the way in which his audience perceived his images.[37] In Thessalonica that audience was a Hellenistic, Gentile audience, who had recently converted from among those who participated in various local cults.[38]

ADDITIONAL POLITICAL LANGUAGE

Most prominent among the political terms used by Paul was the κύριος title used apropos Christ. That κύριος is Paul's preferred christological title is well known. He uses the title twenty-four times in 1 Thessalonians alone. Within this letter it is significant that Paul always employs the κύριος title when he writes about the παρουσία; the term is always used in reference to Jesus (2:19; 3:13; 4:17; 5:23). In the context of the παρουσία, 2:19 mentions

---

36. In many cases, the imperial temple was not a place where a deified emperor was worshipped; rather it was a place where sacrifice could be offered to the gods (a god) as a prayer for an emperor. At the time of Paul, there was a temple of Caesar in Thessalonica. It had been built during the reign of Augustus Caesar. Cf. Holland Hendrix, "Thessalonicans Honor Romans" (PhD diss., Harvard Divinity School, 1984), 62.

37. Cf. Ascough, "Question of Death," 526; Raymond F. Collins, *The Birth of the New Testament: The Origin and Development of the First Christian Generation* (New York: Crossroad, 1993), 156. On the broader use of Paul's choice of images that spoke to a Hellenistic audience, see my *Power of Images*.

38. The cult of Cabirus was among the most prominent of the cults practiced in Thessalonica, but there were also cults in honor of Dionysus, Zeus, Asclepius/ Serapion, Aphrodite, and Demeter. On these cults see Karl P. Donfried, "The Cults of Thessalonica and the Thessalonian Correspondence," *NTS* 31 (1985): 336–56; repr. in idem, *Paul, Thessalonica, and Early Christianity* (Grand Rapids: Eerdmans, 2002), 21–48.

a crown (στέφανος), albeit used metaphorically, and surely political is the slogan, "There is peace and security" (εἰρήνη καὶ ἀσφάλεια, 5:3), a slogan that owes its origins to Roman imperial propaganda.[39] Less obvious to the contemporary reader may be the term εὐαγγέλιον,[40] "gospel" in the sense of good news, often used during the Hellenistic period in reference to a birth in the royal household or a victory by imperial armies but sometimes, it seems, in reference to the imperial cult.[41]

"Meeting" (ἀπάντησις), not otherwise used by Paul, is another "loaded political term."[42] Citing two papyri, five inscriptions, fourteen Greek literary sources, and four Latin sources, Erik Peterson proposed that ἀπάντησις was a technical term in the Hellenistic era in reference to the meeting of the citizens of a town going out of the town to welcome a king or his representative and lead him into the city.[43] Along with παρουσία, the term was used in that sense by Josephus (Ant. 11.327–328):

When he [Jaddus, the high priest] had gone to sleep after the sacrifice, God spoke oracularly to him in his sleep, telling him to take courage and adorn the city with wreaths and open the gates and go out to meet them [τὴν ὑπάντησιν], and that the people should be in white garments, and he himself with the priest in the robes prescribed by law.... He announced to all the revelation that had been made to him, and, after doing all the things that he had been told to do, awaited the coming [παρουσίαν] of the king [Alexander].[44]

---

39. Cf. Ernst Bammel, "Ein Beitrag zur paulinischen Staatsanschauung," TLZ 85 (1960): 837; and Koester, "Imperial Ideology," 161–62. Donfried writes about "the Pax et Securitas program of the early Principate" in "The Imperial Cults of Thessalonica and Political Conflict in 1 Thessalonians," in Horsley, Paul and Empire, 216–17, 222; and idem, "Cults and the Thessalonian Correspondence," 34. See also Neil Elliott and Mark Reasoner, eds., Documents and Images for the Study of Paul (Minneapolis: Fortress, 2011), 123–26.

40. See 1:5; 2:2, 4, 8, 9; 3:2.

41. Cf. Peter Stuhlmacher, Vorgeschichte (vol. 1 of Das paulinisch Evangelium; FRLANT 95; Göttingen: Vandenhoeck & Ruprecht, 1968), 196–206.

42. The description comes from Donfried, "Imperial Cults," 217.

43. "Die Einholung des Kyrios," ZST 7 (1930): 682–702. Cf. Peterson, "ἀπάντησις," TDNT 1:682–702.

44. Peterson cites his passage as well as J.W. 7.68–71, 100–103. The earlier passages offers a description of a παρουσία, as does the later, which uses ὑπάντησις, generally considered to be interchangeable with ἀπάντησις. Peterson offers footnoted references to J.W. 7.119.

Some have objected to the use of *terminus technicus* as appropriate language to describe the way that ἀπάντησις was employed in the Hellenistic world.[45] Just as παρουσία was used in everyday parlance for a person's arrival or presence and was sometimes used for the arrival of an imperial dignity, so too ἀπάντησις was a term used for all kinds of encounters[46] but was sometimes used specifically for the "official" welcome of a visiting dignitary by the citizenry outside the city walls. Hence there should be no difficulty in affirming that the scenario evoked by Paul in his use of ἀπάντησις evokes the idea of people meeting their κύριος outside the city.[47]

In a sense, the παρουσία of the Lord provides an occasion for the community ἀπάντησις. The resurrection of the dead, described by Paul with apocalyptic terminology,[48] makes it possible for all members of the community to participate. In this way, the παρουσία, the event itself as described by Paul, has a social connotation; it implies the gathering of the community in the presence of the Lord. The presence of Christ is the focus of the assembly of the entire community.

The imagery is political. The community meets Christ, its κύριος. This is an important issue in the social identity of the community. The παρουσία of Jesus Christ the Lord, "our" Lord, means that Jesus Christ will remain the center of the community even after the death of some of its members.

---

45. E.g., Michael R. Cosby, "Hellenistic Formal Receptions and Paul's Use of ΑΠΑΝΤΗΣΙΣ in 1 Thessalonians 4:17," *BBR* 4 (1994): 15–34; and Joseph Plevnik, "1 Thessalonians 4.17: The Bringing in of the Lord or the Bringing in of the Faithful," *Bib* 80 (1999): 537–46. In "A Brief Note on 'Hellenistic Formal Receptions and Paul's Use of ΑΠΑΝΤΗΣΙΣ in 1 Thessalonians 4:17,'" *BBR* 6 (1999): 39–41, Robert H. Gundry offered a rebuttal to Cosby's thesis. To a large extent the debate was about the meaning of Hellenistic formal reception and Paul's use of ἀπάντησις in 1 Thess 4:17. Does a term always and everywhere have to be used in a specialized way in order to be properly called a *terminus technicus*? I think not but have tried to avoid the use of this designation in the current essay. A misunderstanding of the use of metaphor, specifically Paul's use of metaphor, also enters into the discussion. Does a metaphorical use of a term require that each and every detail correspond to the details of the ordinary use of the term? Again, I think not.

46. The LXX, e.g., employs ἀπάντησις in the accusative some 129 times.

47. Cf., among others, Gundry, "Brief Note"; Randell E. Otto, "The Meeting in the Air (1 Thess 4:17)," *HBT* 29 (1997): 192–212, esp. 203; Koester, "Imperial Ideology," 160; Donfried, "Imperial Cults," 217; Green, *Thessalonians*, 226–28.

48. Not to be overlooked in the apocalyptic scenario is the "social function" of the trumpet blast (4:16). In Jewish apocalyptic the sound of the trumpet functions to enable the assembly of the community. Cf. 1QM III, 1–11; VII, 8–IX, 9.

A Critique?

The κύριος whom the believing community is to meet upon his παρουσία is their Lord, Jesus Christ, not an emperor, a victorious general, or some other visiting dignitary. This identification of Christ as κύριος would set the tight-knit community of Thessalonian believers apart from those who accepted the Roman emperor as their κύριος, perhaps engendering some hostility. The implicit attack on the Roman program of *Pax et Securitas*[49] in 5:3 would increase the political tension between believers and outsiders even more.[50] The Thessalonian believers saw themselves as a community over and against outsiders.

Karl Donfried and others have suggested that Paul's use of political language in 1 Thessalonians probably reflects the language of his preaching, which may have led Luke to describe the accusation made against Jason and other believers in the presence of the city's politarchs in this fashion: "They have all acted contrary to the decrees of the emperor [τῶν δογμάτων Καίσαρος], saying that there is another king [βασιλέα ἕτερον] named Jesus" (Acts 17:7).[51] It is unlikely that Paul, skilled orator that he was, would have been unaware of the political connotations of the terms that he used in proclaiming the gospel, in word and by letter.

It would be "natural," writes Yeo Khiok-Khng, "to assume that the Pauline theology and gospel in I Thessalonians is intentionally expressed as a critique to the ideology of the imperial cult."[52] While it may be difficult to establish that such a critique was Paul's expressed intention and that whatever critique was directed to the imperial cult and emperor worship, there can be little doubt that Paul would realize that his language would be construed as a critique of the status quo.

That there was an imperial cult in Thessalonica is clear. It developed gradually from about the time that the city became the capital of

---

49. A rather recently published inscription from Turkey cites this slogan apropos Pompey. Cf. Christoph vom Brocke, *Thessaloniki: Stadt des Kassander und Gemeinde des Paulus* (WUNT 2/125; Tübingen: Mohr Siebeck, 2001), 179 n. 67.

50. Cf. Neil Elliott, "The Apostle Paul and Empire," in *In the Shadow of Empire: Reclaiming the Bible as a History of Faithful Resistance* (ed. Richard A. Horsley; Louisville: Westminster John Knox, 2008), 105.

51. Cf. Donfried, "Cults of Thessalonica," in Horsley, *Paul, Thessalonica, and Early Christianity*, 31–38.

52. Yeo Khiok-Khng, "A Political Reading of Paul's Eschatology in I and II Thessalonians," *AJT* 12 (1998): 82–83.

the Roman province of Macedonia. To a large extent, the cult developed because the Thessalonians had a need to curry favor with their Roman benefactors. Honors were accorded to Roman benefactors along with the gods. In the course of time the goddess Roma was also acknowledged. Prior to Paul's arrival in the city, a temple of Caesar was built. As a free city, Thessalonica not only had its own politarchs but was also allowed to mint its own coins. These coins were, nonetheless, Roman coins. Coins minted in Thessalonica from about 27 B.C.E. refer to Julius Caesar as θεός, but they do not accord divinity to the reigning emperor. Even after the head of Augustus replaced that the image of Zeus on Thessalonian coins, the coins did not designate the emperor as θεοῦ υἱός.

The cult of the emperor appears to have been rather modest in the Thessalonica visited by Paul. The temple of Caesar was one among the many temples in the city. Indeed, the Thessalonians showed restraint in acknowledging the status of *divus filius*,[53] which the Romans accorded to Augustus.[54] The common *as*[55] minted in Rome bore the image of Augustus with the title *divus filius* on the face of the coin; the version minted in Thessalonica bore an image of Augustus on the reverse side of the *as* together with the name of the city.[56] There is no evidence that the reigning monarch was acknowledged as a god or even as a son of god in mid-first-century Thessalonica. Dedications involving Nero and later emperors identify neither the emperor nor his predecessors as divine. In Thessalonica, Romans were honored for what they did for the Thessalonians, whose benefactors they were, not for whom the Romans presumed them to be, sons of god.

Whatever critique of imperial status quo might have been implied by Paul's use of political language, the critique, with the exception of the citation of the imperial slogan in 5:3, did not confront the empire head-on.[57]

---

53. The title does not imply that the emperor was worshipped, not even in Rome. Cf. Elliott and Reasoner, *Documents and Images*, 141. Pages 141–45 of this work study "the imperial 'Son of God.'"

54. Cf. Holland Hendrix, "Beyond 'Imperial Cult' and 'Cults of Magistrates,'" *The Society of Biblical Literature 1986 Seminar Papers* (SBLSP 25; Atlanta: Scholars Press, 1986), 307–8.

55. A loaf of bread was worth about two *asses*.

56. On the reverse of the Roman coin was an image of Julius, identified as *divus*. On the face of the Thessalonian coin, as has been noted, there was an image of Julius identified as θεός. This would seem to be a recognition that the Romans accorded divine status to Julius, not that the Thessalonians proclaimed him to be divine.

57. Peter Oakes argues that even this slogan, which evokes the central theology

To a large extent Paul's metaphors used political language to evoke a civic occurrence that many had experienced. He wanted the Thessalonians to know that Jesus Christ was their Lord and that it was from him and God that peace was to be expected (1:1; 5:23). Their ultimate benefactor was Jesus Christ, not the Romans.

To appreciate properly the language of 1 Thessalonians, one must recall that the first verifiable imperial use of the κύριος title in Greece dates to the time of Nero,[58] that is, to a period subsequent to the writing of 1 Thessalonians. When Christ was acknowledged as κύριος in 1 Thessalonians, its audience may well have been unfamiliar with any use of that language to describe the emperor. They would, nonetheless, have been aware of imperial παρουσίαι. Paul relied on that experience to develop his image of the παρουσία of Jesus Christ, κύριος. The image was that of final and definitive community building, in addition to being a motivational factor in Paul's paraenesis. As a focus of Christian hope, the παρουσία implied not only the presence of Christ as κύριος but also the unity of the community, which included those marginalized by death. The παρουσία was, for Thessalonian believers, a major factor in the construction of their social identity. It was, as Stefan Schreiber observes, an "identity marker."[59]

In sum, Paul made use of a political-social concept that he was able to exploit for paraenetic reasons when he wrote about the παρουσία of Jesus Christ as κύριος in 1 Thessalonians. Paul's rhetorical use of the term in pursuit of his paraenetic purposes was ultimately social as well. His paraenesis was intended not so much to encourage individuals to be virtuous as to establish the social identity of the community of believers.

In Passing

After Paul's teaching about the Lord's παρουσία in 1 Thessalonians, the language of παρουσία is all but absent from the New Testament's Pauline corpus. Paul himself makes only one other reference to the παρουσία in the extant correspondence (1 Cor 15:23). The anonymous imitator who

---

of the new age introduced by Augustus, relates to Roman eschatology, a "golden age," and is not a specific attack upon the Roman Empire. Cf. Peter Oakes, "Re-mapping the Universe: Paul and the Emperor in 1 Thessalonians and Philippians," *JSNT* 27 (2005): 317–18.

58. Cf. Deissmann, *Light from the Ancient East*, 351–58.

59. Cf. Schreiber, "Jenseitshoffnung," 327.

wrote 2 Thessalonians says that he is going to provide additional information about the event, borrowing Paul's own phraseology in order to do so.
"As to the coming of our Lord Jesus Christ" (ὑπὲρ τῆς παρουσίας τοῦ κυρίου
ἡμῶν Ἰησοῦ Χριστοῦ), he writes in 2 Thess 2:1. Unfolding an apocalyptic scenario, the pseudepigrapher says that the Lord Jesus will annihilate
the lawless one "by the manifestation of his coming" (τῇ ἐπιφανείᾳ τῆς
παρουσίας αὐτοῦ, 2 Thess 2:8). Then, in a departure from Paul's specialized
use of the term παρουσία to refer to the eschatological coming of Jesus as
κύριος, the pseudepigrapher speaks of another eschatological coming, the
"coming [παρουσία] of the lawless one" (2:9). Apart from the fourfold use
of παρουσία in Thessalonians, these three passages represent the only use
of the terminology in the extant Pauline corpus.

The Appearance of Jesus Christ in the Pastoral Epistles

The study of 2 Thessalonians lies beyond the scope of the present essay, but
the pleonastic expression, "the manifestation of his coming," introduces a
term, ἐπιφάνεια, that is found nowhere else in the New Testament except
for the mini-Pauline corpus generally called the Pastoral Epistles. Each of
the three Pastorals, 1 Timothy (6:14), 2 Timothy (4:1, 8), and Titus (2:13),
uses the term in reference to the eschatological appearance of Jesus.[60]
Consequently many commentators suggest that παρουσία and ἐπιφάνεια
are basically synonymous and perhaps interchangeable.

After a long period of time in which historical-critical exegetes considered the Pastorals to be devoid of Christology or at least of an integrated
Christology,[61] the second half of the twentieth century saw an increased
recognition that ἐπιφάνεια is the integrating focus of the Christology of the
small corpus of texts.[62] Frank Matera writes:

---

60. The noun ἐπιφάνεια appears one other time within the minicorpus, in 2 Tim
1:10, where it refers to the incarnate manifestation of Jesus. The related verb ἐπιφαίνω
appears in Titus 2:11 and 3:4 with a similar point of reference. Apart from these two
appearances in Titus, the verb is used in the NT only by Luke, and only twice by
him (Luke 1:79; Acts 27:20). Along with the verb ἐπιφαίνω and the noun ἐπιφάνεια,
three other words derived from the root φαν-, "manifest," also appear in the Pastorals:
φανερόω, "make manifest" (1 Tim 3:16; 2 Tim 1:10; Titus 1:3), ἐπιφαίνω, "show forth"
(Titus 2:11; 3:4), and φανερός, "visible" (1 Tim 4:15).

61. Thus Hans Windisch, "Zur Christologie der Pastoralbriefe," ZNW 34 (1935):
213–38.

62. Cf. Elpidius Pax, ΕΠΙΦΑΝΕΙΑ: Ein religionsgeschichtlicher Beitrag zur bib-

The underlying narrative of the pastoral epistles is a story of epiphany or manifestation. Christ Jesus appeared in the realm of the flesh and gave himself to redeem all people. In doing this, he manifested the Savior God who wills the salvation of all people. Christ Jesus will appear again to judge the living and the dead, and when he does, the saving power of the Savior God will be manifested.[63]

A rigorous methodology would demand that the three epistles be studied somewhat independently of one another in order to highlight the nuances of their respective christologies.[64] For the purpose of the present essay, I beg the reader's indulgence for this quick overview of the Christology of the texts, which accords particular attention to their use of epiphanic language.

The two texts whose literary genera is that of documents of church order employ ἐπιφάνεια to speak, with a hortatory purpose, of a future manifestation of Jesus.[65] First Timothy 6:13–14 reads, "I charge you to keep the commandment without spot or blame until the manifestation of our Lord Jesus Christ [μέχρι τῆς ἐπιφανείας τοῦ κυρίου ἡμῶν Ἰησοῦ Χριστοῦ]."

The sole mention of ἐπιφάνεια in Titus occurs within a long sentence:[66]

For the grace of God has appeared [ἐπεφάνη], bringing salvation [σωτήριος] to all, training us to renounce impiety and in the present age to live lives that are self-controlled, upright, and godly, while we wait for the blessed hope and manifestation of the glory of our great God and

---

lischen Theologie (Münchener theologische Studien 1/10; Munich: Zink, 1955); idem, "Epiphanie," RAC 5 (1962): 832–909; Victor Hasler, "Epiphanie und Christologie in den Pastoralbriefen," TZ 33 (1977): 193–209; Lorenz Oberlinner, "Die 'Epiphaneia' des Heilswillens Gottes in Christus Jesus: Zur Grundstruktur der Christologie der Pastoralbriefe," ZNW 71 (1980): 192–213; and the brief resume in Raymond F. Collins, Letters That Paul Did Not Write: The Epistle to the Hebrews and the Pauline Pseudepigrapha (GNS 28; Wilmington, Del.: Glazier, 1988), 112–16. Two monographs that appeared toward the end of the twentieth century continue to emphasize the ἐπιφάνεια motif as the focus of the Christology of the Pastorals: Andrew Lau, Manifest in the Flesh: The Epiphany Christology of the Pastoral Epistles (WUNT 2/86; Tübingen: Mohr Siebeck, 1996); and Hanna Stettler, Die Christologie der Pastoralbriefe (WUNT 2/105; Tübingen: Mohr Siebeck, 1998).

63. Matera, Christology, 172.

64. Added to the importance of first studying any text in right, one must also allow for the possibility that different authors are responsible for the three epistles.

65. The term does not appear in the uncontested Pauline letters.

66. In the Greek text vv. 11–14 constitute a single sentence. This is not the case in the NRSV translation.

292   UNITY AND DIVERSITY IN THE GOSPELS AND PAUL

Savior, Jesus Christ [προσδεχόμενοι τὴν μακαρίαν ἐλπίδα καὶ ἐπιφάνειαν τῆς δόξης τοῦ μεγάλου θεοῦ καὶ σωτῆρος ἡμῶν Ἰησοῦ Χριστοῦ]. He it is who gave himself up for us that he might redeem us from all iniquity and purify for himself a people of his own who are zealous for good deeds. (Titus 2:11–14)

In both 1 Tim 6:14 and Titus 2:13 the term ἐπιφάνεια refers to a future event. That this future is an eschatological future is highlighted by the array of terms with eschatological connotations in Titus 2:13, "present age,"[67] "hope," and "glory."

In 1 Timothy the honorific, "our Lord,"[68] is attributed to Jesus, while in Titus, Jesus is called "our great God and Savior."[69] The ἐπιφάνεια motif is cited for paraenetic purposes in both texts. In 1 Tim 6:13–14 "Timothy" is urged to keep the commandment faithfully. Titus 2:13–14 urges "us," the audience to which the text is directed, to renounce impiety and live righteously.

The paraenetic import of the author's use of the term ἐπιφάνεια appears even more clearly when verse 13 is located within the chiastic structure of verses 11–13:

A The grace of God has appeared (ἐπεφάνη), a past event (v. 11a)
    B Paraenesis: Renounce impiety and live upright lives (vv. 11b–12)
A' The manifestation (ἐπιφάνειαν) of Jesus Christ, a future event (v. 13)

The chiasm is loosely linked to the preceding paraenesis (2:1–10) by an initial γάρ and leads to a mention of people who are zealous for good deeds (2:14).

---

67. In Jewish apocalyptic, the present, evil age is contrasted with the age to come.

68. "Christ" should not be cited as an honorific since it is appended to the name of Jesus in each case in which the name of Jesus appears in the Pastoral Epistles (1 Tim 1:1 [2x], 2, 12, 14, 15, 16; 2:5; 3:13; 4:6; 5:21; 6:3, 13, 14; 2 Tim 1:1 [2x], 2, 9, 10, 13; 2:1, 3, 8, 10; 3:12, 15; 4:1, 22; Titus 1:1, 4 ; 2:13; 3:6).

69. The interpretation of the words "great God and Savior" remains one of the great cruxes of New Testament interpretation. Every commentator on the epistle necessarily addresses the issue; e.g., see my *I & II Timothy and Titus* (NTL; Louisville: Westminster John Knox, 2002), 311–14. See also Delio Ruiz, "Se manifestó la gracia salvadora de Dios (Tit 2,11–14)," *RevistB* 65 (2003): 205–6. As I do, Ruiz takes the disputed phrase as a binomial expression that refers to Jesus Christ.

This future manifestation of Jesus Christ is the manifestation of one who had previously given himself for our redemption (v. 14). There is personal continuity between the future ἐπιφάνεια and the physical, redemptive presence of Jesus Christ in history. That redemptive presence was a manifestation of the grace of God (v. 11). A similar thought is expressed when the author of Titus again uses the verb ἐπιφαίνω in 3:4–5, "But when the goodness and loving kindness of God our Savior appeared [ἐπεφάνη], he saved us." The earthly and salvific-redemptive presence of Jesus is a manifestation of the goodness and loving kindness of God our Savior. Between God and Jesus there is a relationship that Delio Ruiz describes as binary, bipolar, and dialectical.[70]

In these two passages from Titus the manifestation of the grace of God in the past and the manifestation of Jesus Christ in the eschatological future are described in terms that highlight the salvific nature of these manifestations. The grace of God is saving (σωτήριος); it brings salvation to all (2:11). Jesus Christ is our great God and Savior (τοῦ μεγάλου θεοῦ καὶ σωτῆρος ἡμῶν, 2:13); God is our Savior (τοῦ σωτῆρος ἡμῶν, 3:4).

The hortatory function of the ἐπιφάνεια motif is not as apparent in the three uses of the term in 2 Timothy as it is in 1 Timothy and Titus, documents of church order. Second Timothy has a literary genre that differs from that of 1 Timothy and Titus. Motivational language belongs to the nature of documents that seek to establish a social order.

Second Timothy is an epistolary testament that reflects on the apostle Paul in a situation where he is presented as awaiting death. Its first use of ἐπιφάνεια appears in a passage that has marked similarity with the passages in which ἐπιφαν- language is used in Titus. Second Timothy 1:9–10 reads, "This grace [χάριν] was given us in Christ Jesus before the ages began, but it has now been revealed [φανερωθεῖσαν][71] through the appearing of our Savior Christ Jesus [διὰ τῆς ἐπιφανείας τοῦ σωτῆρος ἡμῶν Χριστοῦ], who abolished death and brought life and immortality to light."

Like the passages in Titus that use the verb ἐπιφαίνω in reference to the incarnate Jesus, 2 Tim 1:9–10 also refers to the appearance of the human Jesus. The presence of Jesus Christ is salvific; he is identified as our Savior. The salvific nature of this appearance is underscored by the author's reflection that it is due to the power and grace of God who saved

---

70. Ruiz, "Se manifestó," 200, 207.
71. Cf. n. 60 above.

us (θεοῦ τοῦ σώσαντος ἡμᾶς, vv. 8–9) that is made visible in the appearing of Jesus Christ.

When the author of 2 Timothy again uses the term ἐπιφάνεια, he does so in reference to the future eschatological appearance of Jesus Christ:

> In the presence of God and of Christ Jesus, who is to judge the living and the dead, and in view of his appearing [τὴν ἐπιφάνειαν αὐτοῦ] and his kingdom. (4:1)

> From now on there is reserved for me the crown of righteousness [ὁ τῆς δικαιοσύνης στέφανος], which the Lord, the righteous judge, will give me on that day, and not only to me but also to all who have longed for his appearing [τὴν ἐπιφάνειαν αὐτοῦ]. (4:8)

Each of these passages mentions only "his appearance," but there is no doubt that the "he" in question is the Lord Jesus Christ. Both passages clearly state that Jesus' appearance on the Day of the Lord, an almost ominous "that day," will be that of a righteous judge. The awarding of a crown[72] suggests an ending, underscoring the eschatological nature of the appearance as does the reference to Paul and others longingly awaiting that day, the Day of the Lord, at which time the Lord Jesus will be manifest.

A BRIEF COMPARISON

Apart from the simple fact that the term ἐπιφάνεια and its cognates do not occur in 1 Thessalonians, while the word παρουσία is not to be found within the corpus of the Pastoral Epistles, any comparison between the Pauline notion of the coming of the Lord Jesus, his παρουσία, and the Pastorals' notion of the appearing of Jesus Christ our Lord, his ἐπιφάνεια, must highlight the following points.

First, παρουσία always refers to a future eschatological event, enhanced by an apocalyptic scenario. The ἐπιφάνεια is often but not always a future eschatological event. Even when the ἐπιφάνεια refers to a future eschatological event, there is no accompanying apocalyptic scenario.

Second, a paraenetic interest is to be discerned in Paul's use of the παρουσία motif. Paraenetic interests are also apparent in the Pastorals' use

---

72. Cf. 1 Thess 2:19.

of the ἐπιφάνεια motif, especially when it refers to a future eschatological appearance of Jesus.

Third, whereas the use of παρουσία always refers to the future, the object of Christian hope, ἐπιφαν- language can also be used in reference to a past event. That event is the ἐπιφάνεια of the incarnate Jesus, characterized by its bipolar nature. The ἐπιφάνεια of the earthly Jesus is to be understood as the manifestation of the saving grace of God.

Fourth, Paul's use of the παρουσία motif has a sociopolitical function. It pertains to the identity of the community over and against outsiders. For the community of believers, the παρουσία is the coming of Jesus Christ as their κύριος. It is the culmination of their recognition of Jesus as κύριος.

Fifth, while the Pastorals recognize that it is the Lord Jesus Christ who appears in the future (1 Tim 6:14; 2 Tim 4:8), the κύριος title appears not to have a major function in the Pastorals' use of the ἐπιφάνεια motif. Indeed, the Epistle to Titus makes no use whatsoever of the κύριος title. The epithets that come to the fore in the Pastorals are those of "judge" (κριτής, 2 Tim 4:8; cf. 4:1) and especially "savior" (σωτήρ).[73] The future ἐπιφάνεια is the manifestation of Jesus Christ, our great God and Savior (Titus 2:13). Revelation came through the appearing of our Savior Jesus Christ (2 Tim 1:10). It is the grace of God who saved us (θεοῦ τοῦ σώσαντος ἡμᾶς; 2 Tim 1:9). Jesus Christ's incarnation is the manifestation of the grace and loving kindness of God our Savior (Titus 3:4). Indeed, the chiastic exposition of the future, eschatological ἐπιφάνεια in Titus 2:11–13 follows upon mention of the doctrine of God our Savior (τὴν διδασκαλίαν τὴν τοῦ σωτῆρος ἡμῶν θεοῦ, 2:10).

While both terms are used in Hellenism to refer to similar events, they are not simply interchangeable. Each has its respective connotations. This is clearly true with regard to the use of the terms in the New Testament, by Paul in 1 Thessalonians and by the anonymous author(s) who borrowed his authority to write the Pastoral Epistles.

THE CONTEXT OF THE PASTORALS' USE OF EPIPHANIC LANGUAGE

The Pastoral Epistles were written within a Hellenistic culture in which reference was often made to the ἐπιφάνεια of one or another powerful

---

73. This term appears only once in the undisputed Pauline letters, in Phil 3:20, where Paul writes, "we are expecting a Savior, the Lord Jesus Christ" (σωτῆρα ἀπεκδεχόμεθα κύριον Ἰησοῦν Χριστόν).

figure. The term goes back to Homer, who begin to use it as a technical term for the manifestations of god,[74] especially the visible manifestation of the deity. The term ἐπιφάνεια was commonly used with this meaning. Asclepius/Serapion was said to have brought about many cures through his appearances (ἐπιφάνειαι) in the temple of Epidaurus and elsewhere, while another text speaks of the appearance (ἐπιφάνεια) of the goddess Artemis to the Epirotes, and still another speaks of her appearing to them (ἐπιφαινομένης αὐτοῖς Ἀρτέμιδος).[75] Ister, a third-century B.C.E. historian, wrote a book entitled Ἀπόλλωνος ἐπιφάνειαι. These ἐπιφάνειαι were helping interventions of the deities.[76]

Because of the help that these gods and goddesses provided to individuals in times of crisis (personal crises, communal crises, and natural calamities), they were accorded the title of σωτήρ. Zeus was the σωτήρ beyond all others. Epigraphic evidence records the gratitude of grateful communities to Ζεὺς σωτήρ. People offered sacrifice to Ζεὺς σωτήρ after a safe sea voyage. Individuals and communities alike interceded with Zeus to be delivered from affliction. Zeus's daughter, Ἄρτεμις Σώτηρια, was renowned for the help that she gave to young people approaching the crisis of puberty and to women at the time of childbirth. The σωτήρ title was also accorded to other deities, both male and female, such as Apollos, Hermes, Asclepius/Serapion, and Tyche.

The linguistic usage of the word ἐπιφάνεια to speak of helpful divine interventions entered into Hellenistic Judaism. A number of texts in 2 Maccabees, a first-century B.C.E. document, describe the manifestations of God on behalf of Israel as ἐπιφάνειαι, "appearances." After a detailed study of the pertinent texts (2 Macc 2:21; 3:24–25; 12:22; 14:15; and 5:27), Andrew Lau concludes that as a work of its time 2 Maccabees "reflects the great interest in recorded divine ἐπιφάνειαι commonly found in contemporary literature and inscriptions."[77] Nonetheless, its author, the Epitomist, who has adopted Hellenistic conventions, "has unequivocally stamped the epiphanic language and allusions with his strong OT

---

74. Cf. Christine Mohrmann, "Epiphaneia," *RSPT* 37 (1953): 645.

75. See *SIG* 1169.34, 867.35, 557.5.

76. There has been a debate as to whether visibility or the function of assistance is the primary connotation of ἐπιφάνεια in the ancient texts. That discussion need not detain us for the moment, though it is obviously a piece of a fuller discussion.

77. Lau, *Manifest in the Flesh*, 222.

monotheistic understanding of God's redeeming acts and manifestations vis-à-vis the polytheistic ἐπιφάνειαι of the neighbouring religions."[78]

The apotheosis of Julius, the Roman emperor who was assassinated on the Ides of March, 44 B.C.E., led to a change in the use of epiphanic language. Julius was recognized as *divus* on Roman coins during the last three decades of the first century B.C.E. Even in the free city of Thessalonica, in deference to Rome, Julius was recognized as θεός on Thessalonian coinage during that era. Julius's son, Augustus, appears nonetheless to have been hesitant about being recognized as *divi filius*. The tendency to divinize emperors had nevertheless begun. Subsequently, various texts began to use epiphanic language to describe the births, coming into power, enthronement, imperial visits, victories, and the return home of these divinized emperors. There is evidence that epiphanic language was used in reference to the emperors Claudius, Caligula, Diocletian, and Valerian. To give but one example, Caligula's accession to the throne has been described as an ἐπιφάνεια.[79]

The threshold for offering divine honors to humans had been relatively high in the late first century B.C.E. in Thessalonica, the capital of Macedonia. At that time, the threshold was considerably lower in the territory of the Roman province of Asia,[80] whose capital was Ephesus. More than a century later, when the Pastoral Epistles were written, a number of Roman emperors had been recognized as *divi filii* and as θεοί in their own right. The σωτήρ title was used of these emperors. On some occasions the σωτήρ title was attributed to governors who acted on the emperor's behalf and in his stead.[81]

A striking example of the use of σωτήρ language in respect of a Roman emperor is an inscription found in Ephesus.[82] The inscription acknowledges Julius Caesar's divinized status and proclaims him to be the "common

---

78. Ibid., 222.
79. Cf. *Inscriptions of Cos*, 391.
80. Cf. Hendrix, "Beyond 'Imperial Cult,'" 308.
81. Cf. *OGIS* 668.3.
82. Use of this kind of language was not limited to Rome. A third-century B.C.E. papyrus proclaims Ptolemy IV Philopator as "the common savior of all" (τὸν πάντων κοινὸν σωτῆρον, *P. Enteux.* 11.6). A first-century B.C.E. papyrus letter from Platon to the inhabitants of Pathyris says, "King Soter, the very great God [τὸν μέγιστον θεόν], has arrived at Memphis" (*P. Bour.* 12). Within Hellenistic Judaism, 1 Maccabees uses the language of salvation both in reference to God (1 Macc 4:11) and to Judas Maccabee (4:19).

savior" because of his beneficence to all human beings. It describes Julius as "god made manifest, [born] of Ares and Aphrodite, the common savior of human life."[83] It is noteworthy that this inscription was found in Ephesus, the presumed "destination" of 1 and 2 Timothy (see 1 Tim 1:3).

The divinization of emperors, cults in their honor, and the use of σωτήρ and ἐπιφάνεια in their regard were common phenomena in the Hellenistic culture of the Roman Empire at the time that the Pastoral Epistles were written. They were facets of the culture within which the Pastorals were written. That their author(s) was familiar with that culture is beyond any doubt. Shortly after urging the addressees to offer prayers and thanksgiving for kings and those in positions of civic responsibility (1 Tim 2:2), the author of 1 Timothy notes that this is accord with the will of "God our Savior [τοῦ σωτῆρος ἡμῶν θεοῦ], who desires everyone to be saved," and then immediately proclaims that there is but one God (εἷς γὰρ θεός) and one mediator (εἷς καὶ μεσίτης). The salvific function of the one mediator, Christ Jesus, is then described in terms of his redemption of all (1 Tim 2:3–4). The language that proclaims the uniqueness of God our Savior and the uniqueness of Jesus Christ as mediator is a solemn and pointed rejection of the imperial cult (see 1 Tim 6:15).

Notwithstanding the rejection of the imperial cult, the Pastorals appropriated the language of that cult in order to speak about salvation and the tandem relationship between God and Jesus Christ.[84] Some polemical intent is to be seen in the Pastorals' appropriation of epiphanic and related terminology. It is terminology that would speak to the author's audience(s).[85] The visible ἐπιφάνεια of Jesus Christ in the past was the manifestation of the saving grace of the one God and Savior. An ἐπιφάνεια of Jesus Christ is awaited in the eschatological future, at which time he will exercise the divine functions of saving and judging. These affirmations cannot be properly made of Zeus, Artemis, Julius Caesar, or any other divinized emperor. They can only be made of the one God, our Savior, and of our great God and Savior, Jesus Christ.[86]

---

83. See *SIG* 760.6.

84. Stettler (*Christologie*, 146) notes that this appropriation of language does not imply a taking over of the Jewish-Hellenistic concept "lock, stock, and barrel."

85. Cf. I. Howard Marshall, "The Christology of the Pastoral Epistles," *SNTSU* 13 (1988): 169.

86. The use of σωτήρ is characteristic of the vocabulary of the Pastorals. Nonetheless, the three epistles do not use the terminology in the same way. In 1 Timothy the

A Brief Conclusion

The Pastorals' language of ἐπιφάνεια is religious and polemical. In contrast, the παρουσία language of 1 Thessalonians is social and political, with a touch of polemical intent. Among other things, the difference between the two terms derives from their respective secular socio-religio-political contexts and the purposes for which they were used by different New Testament writers, with their messages for Christian communities in different places and at different times.

σωτήρ title is used as an honorific of God (1:1; 2:3; 4:10), while in 2 Timothy the title is used in reference to Jesus Christ (1:10). Within the corpus, only Titus uses the title of both God (1:3; 2:10; 3:4) and Jesus Christ (1:4; 2:13; 3:6).

Virtue in the New Testament: The Legacies of Paul and John in Comparative Perspective[*]

Christopher W. Skinner

In the late fourth century St. Ambrose composed a commentary on the Gospel of Luke in which he referred to four cardinal virtues.[1] While attempting to reconcile Luke's four beatitudes (Luke 6:20–22) with Matthew's eight (Matt 5:3-10), Ambrose wrote, "*Hic quattuor velut virtutes amplexus est cardinales.*"[2] With these words he became the first church father to apply the term *cardinal* to those virtues that would subsequently become a cornerstone of Christian conduct. The four virtues to which he referred—prudence, justice, fortitude, and temperance—were eventually incorporated into the thought of Augustine[3] and Aquinas,[4] have been explored by modern theologians,[5] and are today officially included in the

---

[*] This essay reflects on issues related to New Testament ethics, New Testament theology, and the application of the diverse witness of the New Testament in society—three abiding interests in the scholarship of Frank Matera. Fr. Matera's scholarly contributions have been substantial and this essay is offered with appreciation for his many years of faithful teaching, advising, and scholarship.

1. The commentary was begun in 377 C.E. and likely completed in 389.

2. Ambrose's discussion of virtue takes place in book 5 of his commentary. He writes, "Now we must discover how Saint Luke manages to condense the eight Beatitudes into four. *There are, as we know, four cardinal virtues*: temperance, justice, prudence, fortitude" (*Commentary of Saint Ambrose on the Gospel according to Saint Luke* [trans. Íde M. Ní Riain; Dublin: Halcyon, 2001], 138).

3. See section 13 of Augustine's *On Free Will*.

4. Aquinas's most substantive exposition of the cardinal virtues is found in the *Secunda Secundae Partis* of his *Summa theologica* (questions 47–170). Aquinas was clearly influenced by the fourfold structure of virtue present within Greek philosophy, and specifically in the writings of Aristotle, whom Aquinas reverently called "the Philosopher." Cf. also Aristotle, *Nichomachean Ethics* 2–5.

5. See esp. Josef Pieper, *The Four Cardinal Virtues* (trans. Richard Winston, Clara

Catechism of the Roman Catholic Church.[6] Throughout church history, virtue has been an important element of the Christian conception of both character and behavior.

It is often the case that we find in the New Testament the basis for later Christian reflection and doctrinal development. This is true of foundational Christian doctrines such as the virginal conception, the divinity of Christ, and the Trinity, and applies also to teachings about Christian conduct. These issues are not always made explicit in the New Testament. Rather, with the New Testament writings as their guide, early church fathers and theologians, accompanied by a hermeneutic of belief, engaged in intense theological reflection that helped establish these doctrines as fixed entities. We have already mentioned the rise of virtue in early Christian discourse. What, if anything, does the New Testament have to say on the subject of virtue? That is the question before us in this essay. Before answering that question, though, we must narrow our field of inquiry.

Numerous traditions are reflected in the New Testament, all of which are important for Christian thought. Two traditions in particular stand out for their impact on subsequent doctrinal development. Frank Matera has observed, "The New Testament contains a number of witnesses to Jesus Christ, but it is the testimonies of Paul and John that have most influenced the history of Christian theology."[7] Without these two traditions, one can scarcely imagine a scenario in which foundational Christian doctrines could have emerged in their current forms. Were it not for the Pauline and Johannine corpora, would the church have been able to parse out the implications of a God who shares human sufferings while also overcoming death? Would it have been possible to arrive at the confessions that

---

Wintson, Lawrence E. Lynch, and Daniel F. Coogan; South Bend, Ind.: University of Notre Dame Press, 1966).

6. Beginning in section 1804, the Catechism reads: "Human virtues are firm attitudes, stable dispositions, habitual perfections of intellect and will that govern our actions, order our passions, and guide our conduct according to reason and faith. They make possible ease, self-mastery, and joy in leading a morally good life. The virtuous man is he who freely practices the good. The moral virtues are acquired by human effort. They are the fruit and seed of morally good acts; they dispose all the powers of the human being for communion with divine love. Four virtues play a pivotal role and accordingly are called 'cardinal'; all the others are grouped around them. They are: prudence, justice, fortitude, and temperance."

7. Frank J. Matera, "Christ in the Theologies of Paul and John: A Study in the Diverse Unity of New Testament Theology," TS 67 (2006): 237.

provided the basis for the Nicene Creed[8] or the Chalcedonian definition?[9] In short, the theological legacies of Paul and John are practically coterminous with the essential doctrines of the Christian faith.[10] Against that backdrop, in this essay I ask and answer three questions: (1) What do Paul and John have to say about virtue? (2) How does what they say compare with one another? (3) What implications do these findings have for modern discussions of Christian virtue? In the end this investigation will prove to be a study in what Matera has called "the diverse unity of New Testament theology."[11]

The question of Paul's relationship to John, whether historical or literary, will not detain us here, though some have suggested that the two associated historical figures (Paul of Tarsus and John, the son of Zebedee)[12] might have crossed paths in Ephesus in the mid-first century.[13] My goal

---

8. The Nicene Creed established the doctrine that Jesus was both divine and coeternal with the Father; this debate was part of a discussion occasioned by the theology of the Alexandrian presbyter Arius (ca. 250–336 C.E.).

9. Chalcedonian Christology affirmed that both divinity and humanity existed fully in the person of Jesus Christ. That understanding has been the basis for orthodox expressions of Christology since the mid-fifth century.

10. While I have profound disagreements with Rudolf Bultmann, I recognize that my emphasis on John and Paul is an approach that stands squarely within the Bultmannian approach to New Testament theology. Though Bultmann's magisterial New Testament theology covered issues related to the earliest kerygma and the rise of early church confession, he was primarily concerned with the teachings of Paul and John. Cf. parts II and III of his four-part *Theology of the New Testament* (trans. Kendrick Grobel; 2 vols.; London: SCM, 1951–1955), 1:187–352; 2:3–92, respectively.

11. This phrase appears in a number of his writings and plays a key role in his *New Testament Theology: Exploring Diversity and Unity* (Louisville: Westminster John Knox, 2007), esp. 423–80.

12. Though he was likely affiliated with the Johannine community, I do not believe that the individual known from the canonical Gospel tradition as John the son of Zebedee was responsible for the composition of the Fourth Gospel or Johannine Epistles. Throughout this essay I will use the designation "John" in keeping with the conventions of contemporary scholarly discourse. The use of this term is not meant to imply anything about the authorship of the Johannine corpus.

13. The subject of Paul's relationship to John is taken up in two essays from a recent volume devoted to the larger question of Paul's relationship to the Gospels. See Mark Harding, "Kyrios Christos: Johannine and Pauline Perspectives on the Christ Event"; and Colin G. Kruse, "Paul and John: Two Witnesses, One Gospel," in *Paul and the Gospels: Christologies, Conflicts and Convergences* (ed. Michael F. Bird and Joel Willitts; LNTS 411; London: T&T Clark, 2011), 169–96, 197–219, respectively. In his

here is to examine the writings attributed to Paul[14] and John[15] in order to pinpoint specific teachings that may have impacted subsequent discussions of Christian virtue, specifically the so-called theological virtues.

PRELIMINARY CONSIDERATIONS

At the outset of this examination several interpretive challenges arise. First, both the Pauline and Johannine writings were meant to address specific concerns and were occasioned by events within particular communities of faith. Practically, this means that neither Paul nor John wrote to provide a detailed exposition of Christian behavior. Their materials were written in the context of and in response to conflicts, controversies, and misunderstandings. It naturally follows that neither corpus provides a comprehensive or systematic exposition of Christian virtue. Thus most of what we discover will necessarily arise by implication.

Second, neither author wrote to a general Christian audience. Paul was writing to a number of different churches, most of which he founded; those churches were spread throughout Asia Minor. Most scholars agree that John's Letters, as well as the Fourth Gospel, were written for a specific group—the so-called Johannine community.[16] Therefore, not everything in these works is regarded as universally binding for the Christian reader.

Finally, John's writings have remarkably few statements about moral behavior,[17] which makes it necessary to read between the lines. On the other hand, Paul is very concerned with moral behavior, and the *Haupt-*

---

essay, Harding raises the possibility of Paul and John interacting with one another in Ephesus during Paul's ministry there. See pp. 170–71.

14. I will limit myself here to those letters that are regarded as authentically Pauline by a consensus of scholars.

15. My consideration of Johannine material will focus on the Fourth Gospel and the Johannine Epistles. Issues related to date, genre, and authorship complicate the decision to include the book of Revelation. Though it is often grouped with the Johannine writings, I will not discuss it here.

16. This idea has been met with increasing resistance in recent years. See, e.g., Richard Bauckham, ed., *The Gospel for All Christians: Rethinking the Gospel Audiences* (Grand Rapids: Eerdmans, 1998); and Edward W. Klink III, *The Sheep of the Fold: The Audience and Origin of the Gospel of John* (SNTSMS 141; Cambridge: Cambridge University Press, 2007); idem, *The Audience of the Gospels: The Origin and Function of the Gospels in Early Christianity* (LNTS 353; London: T&T Clark, 2010).

17. On this issue see Wayne A. Meeks, "The Ethics of the Fourth Evangelist," in

briefe contains several lists of vices and virtues, though no two lists are identical. An awareness of these factors both complicates our task and establishes the parameters of our method in approaching the Johannine and Pauline writings.

LOVE: THE JOHANNINE IMPERATIVE

Though not universal, there is wide agreement that the Gospel and Epistles of John were written for a community that was undergoing theological controversies and ecclesiastical conflicts. The Johannine community seems to have been dealing with internal theological disagreements related to the humanity and divinity of Jesus[18] as well as a struggle to maintain fellowship with those in the synagogue who were not followers of Jesus.[19] When reading the epistles, it is easy to get the impression that one is listening to one side of an extremely contentious debate. The opponents are denigrated as those who do not know or remain in the truth (e.g., 2 John 9–11), those who like to be first (3 John 9), or simply as "antichrists" (1 John 2:18–19). In the Gospel the opponents are a group consistently referred to as "the Jews" (οἱ Ἰουδαῖοι).[20] These conflicts form the backdrop for much of the content of the Johannine literature; and, unlike Paul, the writings attributed to John are not concerned with lawsuits, the

---

Exploring the Gospel of John: In Honor of D. Moody Smith (ed. R. Alan Culpepper and C. Clifton Black; Louisville: Westminster John Knox, 1996), 317–20.

18. Numerous indicators in 1 John point to the emergence of an incipient Docetism within the Johannine community. The letter appears to have been written, at least in part, to encourage its readers to adopt the position that Jesus actually existed in human flesh.

19. The two scholars most associated with this proposal are J. Louis Martyn (*History and Theology in the Fourth Gospel* [New York: Harper& Row, 1968]) and Raymond E. Brown (*The Community of the Beloved Disciple: The Life, Loves, and Hates of an Individual Church in New Testament Times* [New York: Paulist Press, 1979]). While many have undertaken a revision of the thesis that John's community was at odds with the synagogue leadership, the foundational assumptions remain in place among a large segment of Johannine scholars.

20. Few issues within Johannine scholarship have occasioned as much discussion or controversy as the identity of "the Jews" in the Gospel of John. Too much has been written on the topic to provide a comprehensive bibliography here. For a relatively recent treatment, see Reimund Bieringer, Didier Pollefeyt, and Frederique Vandecasteele-Vanneuville, eds., *Anti-Judaism and the Fourth Gospel* (Louisville: Westminster John Knox, 2001).

mediation of conflicts, household relationships, or sexual ethics. Neither do they provide a list of vices to avoid. For John, one virtue rises above all others—love.[21] Many who have written on the subject of Johannine ethics are curiously united in their denouncement of the Gospel and letters as repositories for a universal Christian morality.[22] The command to "love one another" is especially regarded by scholars as sectarian and exclusive.[23] Matera has summarized this concern:

> Many of the ethical debates found in the Synoptic Gospels concerning Jesus' observance or interpretation of the Mosaic law and the Sabbath, for example, are absent from John's Gospel. Moreover, the most explicitly ethical teaching of the Fourth Gospel—that Jesus' disciples should love one another as he has loved them—raises a series of questions. What is the content of this love? How do disciples exercise this love in real-life situations? Whom does this love include? Is this a universal love such as is found in the Gospel of Luke, or has love become exclusive and sectarian in the Fourth Gospel? In a word, there appears to be remarkably little

---

21. John P. Meier has commented, "Apart from the love that imitates Jesus' love for his own, John's Gospel is practically amoral. We look in vain for the equivalents of Jesus' teaching on divorce, oaths and vows, almsgiving, prayer, fasting, or the multitude of other specific moral directives strewn across the pages of Matthew's Gospel. Everything comes down to imitating Jesus' love for his disciples; what concrete and specific actions should flow from this love are largely left unspoken" ("Love in Q and John: Love of Enemies, Love of One Another," *Mid-Stream* 40 [2001]: 47–48). Similarly, Meeks notes, "Even in the Johannine Jesus' private teaching of his disciples, 'his instructions lack specificity.' The only rule is 'love one another,' and that rule is both vague in its application and narrowly circumscribed, being limited solely to those who are firmly within the Johannine circle" ("Ethics of the Fourth Evangelist," 318).

22. On the moral bankruptcy of the Johannine writings, see Mary E. Clarkson, "The Ethics of the Fourth Gospel," *AThR* 31 (1949): 112–15; Jack T. Sanders, *Ethics in the New Testament: Change and Development* (Philadelphia: Fortress, 1975), 91–100; Meeks, "Ethics of the Fourth Evangelist," 317–26.

23. But see the dissenting comments of John W. Pryor: "we ought to avoid concluding that the love command represents a narrowing of the broader neighbour love of the synoptic tradition. There is simply no evidence that this is so. It derives from the experienced love of Jesus for the community of disciples, and there is no indication that it implies a rejection of obligations to outsiders" (*John: Evangelist of the Covenant People. The Narrative and Themes of the Fourth Gospel* [Downers Grove, Ill.: InterVarsity Press, 1992], 163).

ethical content in the Gospel according to John, and its most explicit ethical teaching raises a host of questions.[24]

Similar concerns have been voiced by Ernst Käsemann,[25] J. L. Houlden,[26] and Jack T. Sanders.[27] As it relates to the subject of virtue, the Johannine emphasis on love begs for further examination.

LOVE IN THE JOHANNINE WRITINGS

Even a superficial reading of the Johannine literature reveals an abiding emphasis on love. Together, the various terms for love (ἀγάπη, ἀγαπάω, φίλος, φιλέω)[28] appear a total of 117 times in the Gospel and letters.[29] Fernando Segovia has argued that love is the key component to four rela-

---

24. Frank J. Matera, *New Testament Ethics: The Legacies of Jesus and Paul* (Louisville: Westminster John Knox, 1996), 92.

25. Ernst Käsemann, *The Testament of Jesus* (Philadelphia: Fortress, 1966), 59–70.

26. J. L. Houlden, *Ethics and the New Testament* (New York: Oxford University Press, 1973), 36.

27. Sanders, *Ethics in the New Testament*, 100; Sanders's denunciation of John's vision of love is particularly harsh: "Precisely because such [socially disinterested Christian] groups, however, now exist in sufficient abundance to be visible, perhaps the weakness and moral bankruptcy of the Johannine ethics can be seen more clearly. Here is not a Christianity that considers that loving is the same as fulfilling the law (Paul) or that the good Samaritan parable represents a demand (Luke) to stop and render even first aid to the man who has been robbed, beaten, and left there for dead. Johannine Christianity is interested only in whether he believes. 'Are you saved, brother?' the Johannine Christian asks the man bleeding to death on the side of the road. 'Are you concerned about your soul?' 'Do you believe that Jesus is the one who came down from God?' 'If you believe, you will have eternal life,' promises the Johannine Christian, while the dying man's blood stains the ground."

28. Even though the two terms have a long history of distinct and separate semantic domains in the Greek language, there can be little doubt that ἀγαπάω and φιλέω, and their respective cognate groups, are used interchangeably in the Fourth Gospel. For more on this, see Francis T. Gignac, "The Use of Verbal Variety in the Fourth Gospel," in *Transcending Boundaries: Contemporary Readings of the New Testament. Essays in Honor of Francis J. Moloney* (ed. Rekha M. Chennattu and Mary L. Coloe; Biblioteca di Scienze Religiose 187; Rome: Libreria Ateneo Salesiano, 2005), 193–95. See also the related comments in Dorothy Lee, "Friendship, Love and Abiding in the Gospel of John," pp. 57–74 of the same volume.

29. Ἀγάπη appears 7 times in the Gospel and 21 times in the epistles. The verbal form, ἀγαπάω, appears 37 times in the Gospel and 31 times in the epistles. The verb

tionships in the Johannine writings: (1) God's love for the disciples; (2) Jesus' love for the disciples; (3) the disciples' love for God; and (4) the disciples' love for one another.[30] While Segovia's observations are valid, there is little doubt that the clearest and most direct statements about love concern Johannine disciples (or believers, in the case of the epistles) and are directly related to the seemingly sectarian concern that they love one another. In this study I will concentrate on these specific statements.

Several times in the Farewell Discourse, the Johannine Jesus encourages his disciples to demonstrate a love for one another that imitates his own love for them. John 13:34–35 reads, "I give you a new commandment, that you love one another. Just as I have loved you, you also should love one another. By this everyone will know that you are my disciples, if you have love for one another." Three times in the span of these two verses, John's Jesus encourages his disciples to demonstrate love for one another. According to the Johannine vision of love, this practice is an imitation of Jesus himself and will serve as a source of broad external witness. The notion of love in the proximate context is related to *service*; one might even argue that service is the very content of the love Jesus commands.

At the beginning of this literary unit, Jesus has performed the highly symbolic task of washing his disciples' feet (cf. 13:1–17). The scandalous nature of this action astonishes the disciples, arresting their sense of social order.[31] During the footwashing, Jesus demonstrates the type of service he wants his disciples to imitate (vv. 3–5), and then attempts to explain the significance of what he has done (vv. 12–17). While Jesus notes that Peter—who likely represents the group in this context—will not understand what he has done until later (v. 7),[32] the implied reader understands

---

φιλέω appears 13 times in the Gospel; the nominal form, φίλος, appears 6 times in the Gospel and 3 times in the epistles.

30. See Fernando F. Segovia, *Love Relationships in the Johannine Tradition: Agapē/Agapan in 1 John and the Fourth Gospel* (SBLDS 58; Chico, Calif.: Scholars Press, 1982), 194.

31. It is often suggested that washing another's feet was a task reserved for servants. However, Mary L. Coloe ("Welcome into the Household of God: The Foot Washing in John 13," *CBQ* 66 [2004]: 408) asserts that, as a rule, servants merely provided a basin of water while the washing of one's feet was left up to each individual to perform; this would suggest that Jesus' actions subvert the social order even more than is usually thought.

32. This motif of "now" and "after" pervades several episodes in the Gospel and creates a tension between the time of Jesus' ministry (the "now") and the postresurrec-

that this act of service is meant to anticipate Jesus' impending death, which further associates this love with sacrifice. It is significant that this act is referred to as an "example" (ὑπόδειγμα, v. 15). On this point, R. Alan Culpepper notes:

> one of the established contexts in which [this term] was used was in accounts of exemplary deaths which served as models for others to follow. This connotation of the term *hypodeigma* further links the footwashing with Jesus' death, but more significantly the term appears in vv. 12–17, which have customarily been read as a second interpretation of the footwashing which treats it not as an interpretation of Jesus' death but as an example of humble service for others to follow.[33]

The ὑπόδειγμα Jesus displays is not solely concerned with death but with humility and servitude. Together, service and sacrifice represent the heart of what it means for Johannine believers to love one another.

As the Farewell Discourse advances, we come to John 15:12–13: "This is my commandment, that you love one another as I have loved you. No one has greater love than this, to lay down one's life for one's friends." Here Jesus reiterates what he has earlier commanded—that the disciples display a love for one another that imitates his love for them. In addition, the sacrificial element of this love is much more clearly stated than before. The assertion about laying down one's life for a friend is significant for at least two reasons. First, the allusion to sacrifice functions proleptically. The implied reader is ever aware of the looming threat of Jesus' execution. Here Jesus makes the implied element of sacrifice explicit by connecting his love command to the voluntary laying down of one's life. Though it has not yet

---

tion situation of the disciples (the "after"). Throughout the story the reader observes the disciples' lack of understanding in the "now" and is informed by the narrator of their remembrances and understanding in the "after." Richard B. Hays ("Reading Scripture in Light of the Resurrection," in *The Art of Reading Scripture* [ed. Ellen F. Davis and Richard B. Hays; Grand Rapids: Eerdmans, 2003], 224) argues that the narrator's report of these postresurrection remembrances of the disciples provides the reader with a hermeneutical lens through which to read the entire Gospel. He writes, "Thus in John 2:13–22 the story of Jesus' death and resurrection is posited as the key that unlocks the interpretation of Scripture. Retrospective reading of the Old Testament after the resurrection enables Jesus' disciples to 'believe' in a new way both the Scripture and Jesus' teaching and to see how each illuminates the other."

33. R. Alan Culpepper, "The Johannine *Hypodeigma*: A Reading of John 13," *Semeia* 53 (1991): 143.

occurred, Jesus describes his sacrifice with the phrase καθὼς ἠγάπησα ὑμᾶς ("as I have loved you"). In using an aorist verb, he seemingly announces the imminent completion of what has yet to occur.

The second reason this clause is significant is that the sacrifice Jesus describes is said to be for one's friends (ὑπὲρ τῶν φίλων αὐτοῦ). For some, this emphasis confirms the impression that John's concerns are sectarian rather than universal. I will say more about this issue at the conclusion of my examination of the Johannine literature.

In addition to these two passages from the Gospel, there are four instances in 1 John in which readers are encouraged to love another. As noted above, the Johannine community was experiencing a division over the confession that Jesus actually existed in the flesh. For John, the ortho-dox confession[34] is that Jesus Christ "came in the flesh" (cf. 1 John 4:1–3) and was also the representative and revealer of the Father to humanity (cf. John 1:1–18).[35] The epistles give the strong impression that those who rejected this confession were no longer welcome in the Johannine com-munity. Further, Christology and ethics are intertwined in the Johannine Epistles, with the result that action and confession cannot be separated in direct affirmations about ethical behavior.

In 1 John there is a strong connection between knowing Jesus, keep-ing his commands, and loving one's brother or sister (1:5–7; 2:3–11; 3:11–18; 4:7–23). There is also a subtle but ever-present subtext that connects knowing and following God with the appropriate Johannine christological confession; one cannot exist without the other. This connection is clearly seen in 2:10–11 (NRSV): "Whoever loves a brother or sister lives in the light, and in such a person there is no cause for stumbling. But whoever hates another believer is in the darkness, walks in the darkness, and does not know the way to go, because the darkness has brought on blindness." Inasmuch as "walking in the light" is John's shorthand for following Jesus, it seems clear that loving one's brother or sister as a byproduct of following

---

34. I recognize the problematic nature of the term *orthodox* as it applies to the development of early Christian doctrine. I am using the term here to refer to that which the Johannine community regarded as orthodox and not to some nebulous idea of orthodoxy within nascent expressions of Christianity.

35. Together, these two ideas provided a seedbed for later christological devel-opments within early Christianity. The formulation that identifies Jesus as both fully human and fully divine is derived from such statements and helped to lay the founda-tion for Chalcedonian Christology.

God is the essence of Johannine discipleship. We see this same emphasis in a longer passage from 3:11–18 (NRSV):

> For this is the message you have heard *from the beginning* [ἀπ᾽ ἀρχῆς], that we should love one another. We must not be like Cain who was from the evil one and murdered his brother. And why did he murder him? Because his own deeds were evil and his brother's righteous. Do not be astonished, brothers and sisters, that the world hates you. We know that we have passed from death to life because we love one another. Whoever does not love abides in death. All who hate a brother or sister are murderers, and you know that murderers do not have eternal life abiding in them. We know love by this, that he laid down his life for us—and we ought to lay down our lives for one another. How does God's love abide in anyone who has the world's goods and sees a brother or sister in need and yet refuses help? Little children, let us love, not in word or speech, but in truth and action.

All three aforementioned emphases—knowing Jesus, keeping his commands, and loving one's brother or sister—are present here, as is the earlier Gospel emphasis on sacrifice. Several other insights can be gleaned from this passage.

First, the "beginning" (ἀρχή) of verse 11 is probably not the same as the ἀρχή described in John 1:1 (ἐν ἀρχῇ ἦν ὁ λόγος). There the evangelist is harkening back to the beginning of time as depicted in Gen 1:1 LXX (ἐν ἀρχῇ ἐποίησεν ὁ θεὸς τὸν οὐρανὸν καὶ τὴν γῆν).[36] Rather, the phrase "from the beginning" (ἀπ᾽ ἀρχῆς)—which also appears in 1 John 1:1; 2:7, 13, 24; 3:8; and 2 John 5, 6—is likely meant to refer to the "person, words, and deeds of Jesus as this complexus reflects his self-revelation (which is also a revelation of his Father) to his disciples."[37] In other words, according to John, as far back as the beginning of Jesus' earthly ministry, the command to love one another has been a component of a distinctly Christian ethic.

Second, according to verse 14, this display of love within the community is an outward sign that Johannine believers have been transferred from the realm of death to the realm of life. The content of this love is not expressly communicated; but based upon other statements in 1 John, one can assume it relates to the confession that Jesus Christ "came in the flesh"

---

36. Hebrew: בְּרֵאשִׁית בָּרָא אֱלֹהִים אֵת הַשָּׁמַיִם וְאֵת הָאָרֶץ.

37. Raymond E. Brown, *The Epistles of John: A New Translation with Introduction and Commentary* (AB 30; Garden City, N.Y.: Doubleday, 1982), 158.

(1 John 4:3; 2 John 7), along with a concern to meet the needs of others within the community. This much is confirmed by 1 John 3:17–18, where the Torah ethic of caring for those who cannot care for themselves comes into sharper focus.[38] Orthodox Johannine confession is once again intimately connected to how one behaves, and vice versa.

Third, verse 16 again confirms the Johannine stress on sacrificial love as a means to imitating Jesus' love for his own. According to John, sacrificial self-giving is the necessary result of knowing God and is the basis for virtuous behavior within the community of faith.

Two final passages from 1 John 4 encourage believers to love one another. The first, 4:7–11, notes that God is the source of the commanded love (v. 7) and explicitly mentions sacrifice (v. 10), lending further credence to the notion that Johannine love is sacrificial service undertaken in the context of the appropriate (viz., orthodox Johannine) confession:

> Beloved, let us love one another, because love is from God; everyone who loves is born of God and knows God. Whoever does not love does not know God, for God is love. God's love was revealed among us in this way: God sent his only Son into the world so that we might live through him. In this is love, not that we loved God but that he loved us and sent his Son to be *the atoning sacrifice for our sins* [ἱλασμὸν περὶ τῶν ἁμαρτιῶν ἡμῶν]. Beloved, since God loved us so much, we also ought to love one another. (NRSV)

By now, John's flare for the redundant should be clear to the reader. Since God is the source of love, those who know God must necessarily demonstrate love toward others in a spirit of sacrificial self-giving. Of particular importance to our discussion is the use of ἱλασμὸν περὶ τῶν ἁμαρτιῶν ἡμῶν in verse 10. The term ἱλασμός is found only twice in the New Testament—here and 1 John 2:2. In the LXX, the ἱλασμός word group translates Hebrew כִּפֶּר (to cover over, pacify, make propitiation),[39] a term that, along with its cognates, appears in cultic contexts related to animal sacrifice (cf., e.g., Exod 30:10; Lev 7:7; Num 5:8; Ezek 43:20). The use of this term further advances the idea that John's servant love is characterized by sacrifice. Jesus gave his life as an act of propitiation for his followers. Thus they should follow his example by loving one another sacrificially.

---

38. See the similar comments in Jas 2:14–17.
39. BDB, 497, s.v. כִּפֶּר.

The final passage under consideration in this section is 1 John 4:20–21 (NRSV): "Those who say, 'I love God,' and hate their brothers or sisters, are liars; for those who do not love a brother or sister whom they have seen, cannot love God whom they have not seen. The command we have from him is this: those who love God must love their brothers and sisters also." As regards the command for believers to love one another, there is nothing new here. Those who know God have a duty to let their faith and confession produce a genuine response. These elements of Johannine discipleship necessarily go hand in hand.

LOVE AS SACRIFICIAL SELF-GIVING

This examination of love passages in the Johannine writings has shown that John's vision of love is characterized by two things: service and sacrifice. This love is said to be an imitation of Jesus' love—a sacrificial self-giving in the context of an all-encompassing orthodox confession. Johannine orthodoxy requires that confession, service, and sacrifice work in concert with one another; to omit one of these elements is to dishonor the spirit of Johannine virtue. The following propositions summarize John's understanding of love: (1) love comes from God; (2) God's love was on display to the world through the sacrificial self-giving of Jesus Christ for humanity; (3) believers (or disciples) must follow Jesus' example (ὑπόδειγμα), and their lives must be characterized by sacrificial self-giving toward others.

Before moving on to discuss Pauline virtues, I must raise one more time the important question of whether Johannine love is to be envisioned as extending beyond those who share the same confession. Is the sacrificial self-giving John commands intended only for those within the Johannine community or can this virtue be applied as broadly as the love of one's neighbor or even the love of one's enemies? I have already identified a number of critics who decry the supposedly sectarian nature of Johannine morality, but are there alternative ways to read these passages? Is it possible to understand this love as something intended for a wider group than simply those called "friends"—as in the Fourth Gospel—or those who share the same confession that Jesus has "come in the flesh"—as in 1 John?

It is true that the Johannine worldview with its attendant polarities (light vs. darkness, truth vs. lie, etc.) precludes any accommodation to the κόσμος on the part of Jesus followers. The alienation of the Johannine community from those in the synagogue (οἱ Ἰουδαῖοι) and the seceding "antichrists" (cf., e.g., 1 John 2:18–23) would suggest that this was historically true in the interpersonal dealings of its members. The radical, countercultural vision of Johannine spirituality calls believers to reject sin (however that is to be understood) and imitate Jesus' own example, though this does not demand that love be exclusive or sectarian. As discussed above, the Johannine passage most closely associated with providing an example for readers to follow is the aforementioned footwashing scene in John 13, but this is not the only place where an inclusive self-giving love can be found in the Fourth Gospel.

The most poignant example of the intended breadth of this sacrificial self-giving is Jesus' display of love and friendship toward those who continually fail him. Friends who consistently disappoint, deny, and even betray can hardly be called "friends." Yet Jesus treats his closest followers as friends despite their failings. Peter consistently misunderstands Jesus' message, mission, and identity, and when faced with the opportunity to display his loyalty to Jesus, he denies knowing him three times (18:15–26). Nevertheless, Jesus tenderly reinstates Peter with a symbolic reversal in the form of a threefold question-and-response sequence (21:15–19).[40]

Save for the Beloved Disciple, all of Jesus' closest followers abandon him and are absent from the scene of his crucifixion, yet he reveals himself to them, offering them an opportunity to continue in the unity that he and the Father share. The love Jesus displays toward his failing disciples reaches outside the bounds of what one would do for a friend, and in that way the sacrificial self-giving envisioned by the Johannine tradition is far from exclusive.

In light of everything we have considered here, I find the sectarian critique of Johannine love lacking in both nuance and interpretive imagination. It does not seem impossible for the Johannine vision of sacrificial self-giving to be applied broadly, and with benefit, to those who do not share the same confession or community ties as the Johannine believer. However, for this to happen, interpreters of the Johannine writings must approach the material with an appropriate level of caution. For those interested in the application of a genuinely *Christian* ethic, a nuanced appropriation of the Johannine command to "love one another" through sacrificial self-giving can prove beneficial. However—and this cannot be stressed

---

40. Most scholars regard John 21 as a later addition to the original Gospel. This is not problematic for my approach, however, since I am concerned with the final form of the narrative as it was used in performative and liturgical contexts by the Johannine Christians.

strongly enough—those with a concern to apply the ethical teachings of the Johannine literature must remain ever aware of and keep in balance the diverse voices operative within the New Testament as a whole; this final observation brings us to the study of Paul's understanding of virtue.

VIRTUE IN PAUL—WHERE TO START?

When we make the move from the Johannine corpus to the Pauline we are presented with at least three potential challenges. First, since John is less concerned than Paul with moral instruction, it was not necessary for us to examine the concept of virtue in great detail when approaching the Johannine literature. An exploration of the writings of Paul, however, necessitates some familiarity with basic ethical concepts, as well as a rudimentary understanding of the more specialized areas of virtue ethics[41] and Christian ethics/moral theology.[42] A second challenge is related to the sheer volume of Paul-related material that exists. Year after year sees the production of a seemingly inexhaustible supply of studies focusing on the life, letters, and theology of Paul. This creates a situation in which one must sift through a great deal of material to find insightful treatments of

---

41. Virtue ethics have played an important role in the Western philosophical tradition, from the early Greek philosophers—most notably Aristotle—to the medieval Christian period, finding their fullest Christian expression in the writings of Thomas Aquinas. The basic concept behind virtue ethics is that virtues are morally valuable character traits or dispositions firmly entrenched in a given individual. For more on this subject as it relates to New Testament studies, see Daniel J. Harrington, S.J., and James F. Keenan, S.J., *Paul and Virtue Ethics: Building Bridges between New Testament Studies and Moral Theology* (Lanham, Md.: Sheed & Ward, 2010).

42. Some regard Christian ethics and moral theology as the same enterprise with different names. It is typically said that Protestant scholars engage in the study of Christian ethics, while Roman Catholic scholars do moral theology. There is some truth to this dichotomy, though a more careful distinction should be made. Among Protestant theologians, there is no standard, widely accepted definition of Christian ethics. Stanley Hauerwas argues that "ethics is theology," and that as such it is quite naturally an enterprise of the church (see *The Peaceable Kingdom: A Primer in Christian Ethics* [Notre Dame, Ind.: University of Notre Dame Press, 1983], xv–xxvi). In Roman Catholic circles, moral theology is a subdiscipline within Catholic theology that addresses ethical issues, including those related to social justice, sexual and medical ethics, and moral virtue. For more on the history and practice of moral theology, see James F. Keenan, *History of Catholic Moral Theology in the Twentieth Century: From Confessing Sins to Liberating Consciences* (London: Continuum, 2010).

a given topic. Third, unlike John's letters, Paul's letters are infused with moral content interwoven into complex theological argumentation; there are also several vice and virtue lists in the undisputed letters,[43] and these lists differ according to the situations faced by the intended recipients of each letter. In short, Paul has a great deal to say about moral behavior, and commentators have a great deal to say about Paul. It stands to reason, then, that when we approach the subject of Paul's understanding of virtue, especially in an essay of this length, it can be difficult to identify a launching point in either contemporary scholarship or in the Pauline corpus. In light of these challenges, I will attempt to identify a helpful construct from contemporary Pauline studies and use that as my basis for exploring two passages from Paul's undisputed letters.

CRUCIFORM SPIRITUALITY AND THE PAULINE VIRTUES

In his book *Cruciformity*,[44] Michael J. Gorman explores at length Paul's understanding of the drama of salvation history that culminates in Jesus' crucifixion and resurrection, paying special attention to how this shapes Paul's vision of a spirituality that is conformed to the cross of Christ. For Gorman, Paul's "narrative spirituality" is corporate and inclusive, and helps form communities in which cross-shaped faith, hope, love, and power produce mutual commitment among believers and preclude all allegiances except to the God who was revealed in Jesus Christ. To speak of "conformity to the cross" is more than simply to assert the soteriological efficacy of Christ's sacrifice—a concern commonly emphasized by certain traditions within modern Christianity. It moves beyond an understanding of the cross as the source or means of one's salvation to a more complete understanding of a lived, cross-shaped spirituality. Gorman provides the following definition:

> Cruciformity is Paul's all-encompassing spirituality. It is the *modus operandi* of life in Christ. It is fellowship or communion with the Lord Jesus

---

43. Vice lists are found in Gal 5:19–21; 1 Cor 5:9–11, 6:9–10; 2 Cor 12:19–21; Rom 1:29–32; there are also vice lists in the disputed letters: Col 3:5–6; 1 Tim 1:9–10; 6:4–5; 2 Tim 3:2–5. Lists of virtues are found in Gal 5:22–23; Phil 4:8; and 1 Cor 13:1–13.

44. Michael J. Gorman, *Cruciformity: Paul's Narrative Spirituality of the Cross* (Grand Rapids: Eerdmans, 2001).

(1 Cor 10:16–17), sharing the "mind of Christ" (Phil 2:5; 1 Cor 2:16), and conformity to the image of God's Son (Rom 8:29; 2 Cor 3:18; cf. Phil 2:5–11), which is a process of conformity to his death (Phil 3:10). This conformity is not merely a conformity to his suffering—though it includes that (e.g., Rom 8:17; Phil 3:10)—but conformity to his cross-shaped narrative more broadly, the narrative of self-giving loyal obedience to God (faith) and self-giving love of neighbor. It is thus a life of ongoing co-crucifixion with Christ (Gal 2:19–20) that, paradoxically, is life-giving, both to those who live it and to those affected by it.[45]

Paul's cruciform spirituality, then, is about (1) communion with Christ through orthodox confession,[46] (2) self-giving obedience to God, (3) self-giving love to others, and (4) co-crucifixion with Christ. The first three of these features are consistent with the Johannine vision of sacrificial self-giving. Pauline ethics are ultimately more extensive and diverse than their Johannine counterpart, though these foundational elements of the Johannine approach are present in Paul. Here we have an example of the diverse unity of New Testament theology as it relates to the moral life of the community of faith.[47]

There is no approach to Paul that stands unmediated by multiple layers of interpretation. James D. G. Dunn has provided a detailed discussion of the difficulties involved in constructing a theology of Paul, and they are many.[48] Like any good theological construct, Gorman's cruciform spirituality synchronizes complex and diverse ideas into a mosaic that more or less represents the major movements in Pauline theology. As such, cruciformity is not perfect (what theological construct is?), though it does provide a helpful starting point for approaching Paul "from above." Now I will

---

45. Michael J. Gorman, *Reading Paul* (Cascade Companions; Eugene, Ore.: Cascade, 2008), 147. In a follow-up book to his volume on cruciformity, Gorman writes, "Christ's love, freedom, self-giving, humility, and so on become for Paul the standard for life in Christ, embodied in all of life's contingencies" (*Inhabiting the Cruciform God: Kenosis, Justification, and Theosis in Paul's Narrative Soteriology* [Grand Rapids: Eerdmans, 2009], 32).

46. Here again I want to be clear that my use of the term *orthodox* is intended as a specific reference to that which Paul would have considered orthodox, just as I earlier considered Johannine orthodoxy (cf. n. 34 above). It is conceivable that one could devote an entire monograph to a comparison of Johannine and Pauline views on what constitutes orthodoxy.

47. For more on this, see Matera, *New Testament Theology*, 458–68.

48. See *The Theology of Paul the Apostle* (Grand Rapids: Eerdmans, 1998), 1–23.

318 UNITY AND DIVERSITY IN THE GOSPELS AND PAUL

attempt to approach Paul "from below" by examining two passages concerned with moral behavior in which virtue lists also appear. My exegetical considerations will be filtered through the grid of Gorman's understanding of cruciform spirituality.

LIFE BY MEANS OF THE SPIRIT (GAL 5:16–26)

In Gal 5 Paul addresses the Galatian believers' misunderstanding of freedom in Christ (5:1–15) followed by a discussion of life by means of the Spirit (vv. 16–26).[49] For Paul it is impossible to legitimately appropriate one's freedom in Christ apart from the enabling of the Holy Spirit. He asserts that the freedom brought about by the cross of Christ is not about a new kind of legalism (v. 1)—that is, being enslaved to a new set of laws— or a license to live without moral boundaries (v. 13). Rather, freedom in Christ is the freedom to do what one ought to do, which can only be accomplished by means of the Spirit.

In verse 16 Paul establishes his thesis for this section: "Walk by means of the Spirit and you will never gratify [οὐ μὴ τελέσητε] the desires of the flesh." In Hellenistic Greek, οὐ μή combined with an aorist subjunctive— also known as emphatic negation—is the strongest way to negate something that could potentially occur in the future.[50] Even though human experience would tend to disagree with the content of Paul's thesis, the presence of this construction speaks to the intended rhetorical force of his argument. From here Paul uses the images of battle (vv. 17–18) and bearing fruit (vv. 22–23) to discuss fundamental spiritual realities.

The ongoing battle between flesh (σάρξ) and spirit (πνεῦμα) described in verses 17–18 does not depict a proto-gnostic dichotomy between the body—constructed of "evil" matter—and the "good" inner being, though it is possible that some early interpreters of Paul misunderstood his teaching on this point. Rather, σάρξ is used metonymically as a symbol for the powers of human unrighteousness that oppose the works of God, while

---

49. Paul's use of the dative in the phrase πνεύματι περιπατεῖτε is likely meant to indicate means, agency, or instrumentality. In order to make this nuance clear I have chosen to translate the term with the phrase "by means of the Spirit."

50. "οὐ μή is the most decisive way of negativing someth. in the future" (BDAG, 646, s.v. μή). See also the helpful treatment of this construction in Daniel B. Wallace, *Greek Grammar beyond the Basics: An Exegetical Syntax of the New Testament* (Grand Rapids: Zondervan, 1996), 468–69.

πνεῦμα seems to be a clear reference to the Holy Spirit. Gorman notes that a similar contrast describing human life as a choice between two avenues, life and death, has a long history within Judaism, as exemplified in Deut 30:15–20.[51]

After an initial introduction to the conflict between flesh and Spirit, Paul further describes the flesh-directed way of life by providing a list of fifteen vices: "immorality, impurity, sensuality, idolatry, sorcery, enmities, strife, jealousy, outbursts of anger, disputes, dissensions, factions, envying, drunkenness, carousing, and things like these" (vv. 19–21). The first three terms in Paul's list (πορνεία, ἀκαθαρσία, ἀσέλγεια) are related to sexual excesses or other sexually immoral behavior. The next two terms (εἰδωλολατρία, φαρμακεία) are related to the practice of false religions. These first five vices are followed by a grouping of eight terms, all of which are directly related to propriety in interpersonal relationships within the community (ἔχθραι, ἔρις, ζῆλος, θυμοί, ἐριθεῖαι, διχοστασίαι, αἱρέσεις, φθόνοι). The final two terms, "drunkenness" (μέθαι) and "carousing" (κῶμοι), are difficult to categorize and likely reflect Paul's desire to be as thorough as possible, even in light of his statement that his is not an exhaustive list (καὶ τὰ ὅμοια τούτοις, v. 21). There is no way to determine the logic behind this specific ordering of vices. It may be that the list has been crafted to address specific concerns within the Galatian community, though we know comparatively little about the moral life of the Galatian believers. From here, Paul contrasts these "deeds of the flesh" with a more universally applicable list of fruit—not fruits—of the Spirit.

The concept of bearing fruit as practicing or producing righteous deeds appears in multiple Matthean contexts (3:8–10; 7:16–19; 12:33; 21:43), but shows up only three times in Paul's undisputed letters.[52] Though ignored by earlier commentators, more recent works have suggested that Paul is drawing upon Old Testament imagery for the concept of fruit bearing.[53]

---

51. Michael J. Gorman, *Apostle of the Crucified Lord: A Theological Introduction to Paul and His Letters* (Grand Rapids: Eerdmans, 2004), 219.

52. In Gal 5:22 Paul speaks of the "fruit of the Spirit" (καρπὸς τοῦ πνεύματός); in Rom 6:22 he writes that being enslaved to God brings "fruit unto sanctification" (ἔχετε τὸν καρπὸν ὑμῶν εἰς ἁγιασμόν); in Phil 1:11 he affirms that the Philippian believers have been "filled with the fruit of righteousness" (πεπληρωμένοι καρπὸν δικαιοσύνης).

53. Siegfried Wibbing (*Die Tugend- und Lasterkataloge im Neuen Testament: Und ihre Traditionsgeschichte unter besonderer Berücksichtigung der Qumran-Texte* [BZNW 25; Berlin: Töpelmann, 1959], 83) earlier suggested that the source and order-

Among the passages listed as possible source material are portions of Lev 26; Deut 7; Isa 5; 27; 32; 37; 57; Jer 38; Ezek 17; 34; 36; Amos 9; Joel 2; and Zech 8.[54] In addition to this Old Testament material, virtue lists similar to the material in Gal 5:22–23 are also found in Pseudo-Crates (*Ep.* 15) and the Qumran document, *The Rule of the Community* (1QS III, 13–IV, 25). It is more likely that Paul is drawing from Old Testament tradition, though identifying precise intertext(s) proves to be difficult.

The list Paul provides includes love (ἀγάπη), joy (χαρά), peace (εἰρήνη), patience (μακροθυμία), kindness (χρηστότης), goodness (ἀγαθωσύνη), faithfulness (πίστις), gentleness (πραΰτης), and self-control (ἐγκράτεια). That these virtues are described as the "fruit" (καρπός) rather than "fruits" of the Spirit is significant. Matera notes that the singular noun is used because "the ethical life of the Christian is the singular fruit of the Spirit rather than the attainment of a series of virtues."[55] The virtues themselves are witness to one reality—the Spirit-directed life. Paul concludes his list by asserting that "against such things there is no law" (κατὰ τῶν τοιούτων οὐκ ἔστιν νόμος). In verse 23 νόμος is clearly used in the narrower sense of *statute*, making the statement ironic, since the Mosaic law (νόμος) and its relationship to justification has been a prominent theme to this point in the letter.

If Paul's cruciform spirituality is indeed characterized by co-crucifixion (v. 26; cf. 2:20) and conformity to God's Son, these nine virtues are rightly understood as a manifestation of the very nature of God as revealed in Christ. This does not mean that one can attain to the fruit of the Spirit through imitation or effort alone. The Johannine and Pauline approaches differ on this point. Rather, one must be empowered by the Spirit, and to

---

ing behind Pauline *vice lists* (esp. those in the Pastorals) derived primarily from the Decalogue.

54. Among others, G. Walter Hansen (*Galatians* [IVPNTC; Downers Grove, Ill.: InterVarsity Press, 1994], 178) cites Isa 32:15–17 and Joel 2:28–32; John M. G. Barclay (*Obeying the Truth: Paul's Ethics in Galatians* [Vancouver: Regent College Publishing, 2005], 121) argues for a combination of Isa 5:1–7; 27:2–6; 37:30–32; Sylvia C. Keesmaat (*Paul and His Story* [JSNTSup 181; Sheffield: Sheffield Academic Press, 1999], 207–8) cites Isa 27:6; Jer 38:12; Ezek 17:23; 34:27, 36:8; Amos 9:14; Zech 8:12. Examining this synthesized research, G. K. Beale ("The Old Testament Background of Paul's Reference to 'the Fruit of the Spirit' in Galatians 5:22," *BBR* 15 [2005]: 1–38) argues that Isa 32 and 57 are the primary sources for Paul's fruit-bearing imagery.

55. Frank J. Matera, *Galatians* (SP 9; Collegeville, Minn.: Liturgical Press, 1992), 202.

be so empowered one must belong to the realm of the Spirit. Paul does not encourage his Galatian audience to pursue these virtues; he speaks not in the imperative but in the indicative. These virtues are the natural outworking of walking by means of (v. 16) and keeping in step with (v. 25) the Spirit. As such, the various manifestations of the fruit of the Spirit are not ideals to which the Galatian believers should endeavor to attain, but rather outward signs that they have already been transformed by the faith(fulness) of Christ (cf. Gal 3:22).

A STILL MORE EXCELLENT WAY (1 COR 13:1–13)

Paul's great hymn to love is one of the better-known New Testament passages even among those outside the Christian tradition. Often read in the context of romantic love, 1 Cor 13 is more properly understood as a response to the Corinthians' abuse of spiritual gifts and disorderly, self-indulgent worship. Having discussed at length the edification of the community (chs. 8–11), Paul advances his argument by addressing unity and diversity in the use of spiritual gifts (12:1–31), the definition and exercise of love (13:1–13), and propriety in worship (14:1–40). Falling as it does in the middle of this broader discussion of worship in the Spirit-directed community, chapter 13 serves as the fulcrum of Paul's argument. Without the existence of love, the Corinthians will neither legitimately appropriate their spiritual gifts (ch. 12) nor conduct orderly worship (ch. 14). In other words, love is essential to the proper use of spiritual gifts, which is itself an integral part of worship and life in the community of faith.

Verses 1–3 address the relationship between superior spiritual ability and love. If one is able to speak in tongues (v. 1), prophesy (v. 2a), fathom mysteries (v. 2b), exercise extraordinary faith (v. 2c), and give all one possesses to others (v. 3), but does all of these things without love, such abilities are an exercise in futility (lit. "nothing"; οὐδέν, vv. 2, 3). Some commentators assume that these are the very abilities the Corinthian believers claimed to possess, though Carl Holladay suggests that Paul demonstrated each of these abilities inasmuch as they were "anchored in his own apostolic behavior."[56] If this were true, it would strengthen Paul's point in moving the application of his argument beyond the notion that love is

---

56. Carl Holladay, "1 Corinthians 13: Paul as Apostolic Paradigm," in *Greeks, Romans, and Christians: Essays in Honor of Abraham Malherbe* (ed. David L. Balch, Everett Ferguson, and Wayne A. Meeks; Minneapolis: Fortress, 1991), 89.

solely the result of Spirit-enablement (as in Gal 5). It would actually serve as an exhortation to imitate Paul, the paradigm for apostolic ministry.

Paul goes on to define love through a series of affirmations—both in the affirmative and in the negative—that essentially amount to a list of vices to avoid and virtues to pursue.[57] The list begins with two one-word affirmations: love is patient (μακροθυμεῖ) and kind (χρηστεύεται). The nominal forms of these two verbs appear fourth (μακροθυμία) and fifth (χρηστότης), respectively, in Paul's list of fruit of the Spirit. From here Paul shifts from a definition of what love *is* to a discussion of what love *is not*. The next eight descriptions are phrased in the negative: love does not envy (οὐ ζηλοῖ), the eighth word in Paul's list of deeds of the flesh (Gal 5:20); love does not boast (οὐ περπερεύεται); it is not proud (οὐ φυσιοῦται); it does not dishonor others (οὐκ ἀσχημονεῖ); it does not seek self (οὐ ζητεῖ τὰ ἑαυτῆς); it is not easily angered (οὐ παροξύνεται); it keeps no record of wrongs (οὐ λογίζεται τὸ κακόν); it does not delight in evil (οὐ χαίρει ἐπὶ τῇ ἀδικίᾳ). The list ends with six descriptions of this enduring love: it rejoices with the truth (v. 6b), always protects (v. 7a), always trusts (v. 7b), always hopes (v. 7c), always perseveres (v. 7d), and never fails (or "falls," πίπτει, v. 8a). This list is characterized by an avoidance of earlier vices and an others-oriented focus. This love seeks first and at all times to benefit the other.

In verses 8b–12 Paul returns to prophecies, tongues, and knowledge. Each of these, Paul says, will cease to exist. This stands in stark contrast to the affirmation with which he began in v. 8a: love never fails. The love Paul describes is enduring because at its most basic level it is self-giving, sacrificial, and oriented toward others. It is a love counterintuitive to the habits of the self-centered and fully amenable to those in need.

Paul closes his exposition by mentioning three abiding virtues: faith, hope, and love.[58] These three are "the enduring character marks of the Christian life in the present time, in this anomalous interval between the cross and the *parousia*."[59] The greatest of these, according to Paul, is love.

---

57. Hans Conzelmann provides several ancient parallels to the list Paul provides in this chapter. See *1 Corinthians: A Commentary on the First Epistle to the Corinthians* (trans. James W. Leitch; Hermeneia; Philadelphia: Fortress, 1975), 219–20.

58. Aquinas referred to these as the "theological virtues." See question 62 in the *Prima Secundae Partis* of his *Summa theologica*.

59. Richard B. Hays, *First Corinthians* (IBC; Louisville: Westminster John Knox, 1997), 230–31.

That love holds primacy of position in this brief list and in the list of fruit of the Spirit speaks to its importance in Paul's ethical teaching.

CONCLUSION

The foregoing considerations have yielded a number of insights into the individual presentations of John and Paul. The question of how to relate these two approaches to one another remains. Where and how do the Pauline and Johannine presentations of virtue cohere and where do they diverge?

First, it seems clear that both John and Paul (at least in these two passages) regard love as the highest virtue. In the Gospel and Letters of John, love is the only virtue worth pursuing. In the Pauline passages examined above, love appears first in the list of fruit of the Spirit (Gal 5:22–23) and is itself the subject of a lengthy, virtue-laden exposition (1 Cor 13:1–13). Though they share this common emphasis, the Johannine literature and Paul's Letter to the Galatians differ on the means by which this love is manifested. John regards love as something to be pursued as an imitation of Jesus. Johannine believers are explicitly instructed to love one another as God has loved them in the sacrificial self-giving displayed by Christ. In contrast to John, Paul's instruction to the Galatian church indicates that love is to be a natural outworking of their newfound relationship to God through the faith(fulness) of Jesus Christ. They remain unable to display this love on their own, apart from their status "in Christ," which has been established by the enabling Spirit. On the other hand, Paul's instruction to the Corinthians is not as clear-cut on this point, and he does appear to be exhorting them to pursue upright behavior, perhaps by imitating his apostolic paradigm. Similar to the exhortations in 1 Cor 13 are other instances where Paul encourages his audience to pursue righteousness and behave uprightly (e.g., Rom 6; 1 Thess 5:16–18).

Second, for Paul as for John, confession and virtuous behavior are interrelated. One cannot hope to display virtue apart from the enabling work of God and, in the case of Paul, the Holy Spirit. Each has a specific but complementary understanding of what constitutes a transformative orthodoxy. According to both traditions, virtuous behavior can be exhibited only by those who have been transferred into the realm of life through a correct confession.

Third, the concept of virtue in each corpus is related to sacrifice and service. For John, sacrificial self-giving is exemplified in the voluntary giving of one's life for another. This self-giving is an imitation of Jesus, who demonstrated his love for humanity by voluntarily laying down his own life (e.g., John 12:26–28). For Paul, the self-giving is twofold: one must engage in self-giving obedience to God and self-giving love toward others, both of which are an extension of one's co-crucifixion with Christ (Gal 2:20; 5:24).[60] This self-giving is an outworking (or fruit; 5:22–23) of the Spirit.

John and Paul together present virtue as necessary for the expression of the real transformation effected by God in Christ. For both traditions "'the indicative of salvation' (what God has done in Christ) grounds 'the moral imperative' (how believers ought to live in Christ). The community of those who have been sanctified in and through Christ ought to live in a way that corresponds to the gift they have received."[61]

---

60. For more on this, I refer back to the definition of *cruciformity* provided above.
61. Matera, *New Testament Theology*, 458.

Bibliography

Achtemeier, Paul J., ed. *Harper's Bible Dictionary*. San Francisco: Harper & Row, 1985.

Adams, Sean A. "Paul's Letter Opening and Greek Epistolography." Pages 33–56 in *Paul and the Ancient Letter Form*. Edited by Stanley E. Porter and Sean A. Adams. Leiden: Brill, 2010.

Aichele, George, and Gary A. Phillips. "Introduction: Exegesis, Eisegesis, Intergesis." *Semeia* 69/70 (1995): 9–10.

Aland, Barbara, et al., eds. *The Greek New Testament*. 4th ed. New York: United Bible Societies, 1994.

Allen, Graham. *Intertextuality*. London: Routledge, 2000.

Allison, Dale C. *The End of the Age Has Come: An Early Interpretation of the Death and Resurrection of Jesus*. Philadelphia: Fortress, 1985.

———. *The New Moses: A Matthean Typology*. Minneapolis: Fortress, 1993.

Amorós, José Antonio Álvarez. "Henry James and Mikhail Bakhtin on the Art of Fiction." Pages 1–35 in *Proceedings of the 24th International Conference of the Spanish Association for English and American Studies*. Edited by Ángel Mateos-Aparicio and Silvia Molina Plaza. Ciudad Real: University of Castilla-La Mancha, 2002.

Ascough, Richard S. "A Question of Death: Paul's Community Building Language in 1 Thessalonians 4:13–18." *JBL* 123 (2004): 509–30.

Badiou, Alain. *Being and Event*. Translated by Oliver Feltham. London: Continuum, 2005.

———. *Saint Paul: The Foundation of Universalism*. Cultural Memory in the Present. Stanford, Calif.: Stanford University Press, 2003.

Baird, William. *History of New Testament Research*. 2 vols. Minneapolis: Fortress, 1992–2004.

Baker, David L. *Tight Fists or Open Hands: Wealth and Poverty in the Old Testament*. Grand Rapids: Eerdmans, 2009.

Baker, Nena. *The Body Toxic*. New York: North Point, 2009.

Bakhtin, Mikhail. "Discourse in the Novel." Pages 259–422 in *The Dialogic Imagination: Four Essays by M. M. Bakhtin*. Edited by M. Holquist. Translated by C. Emerson and M. Holquist. Austin: University of Texas Press, 1992.

Bakke, Odd Magne. *When Children Became People: The Birth of Childhood in Early Christianity*. Translated by Brian McNeil. Minneapolis: Fortress, 2005.

Bammel, Ernst. "Ein Beitrag zur paulinischen Staatsanschauung." *TLZ* 85 (1960): 837–40.

Barclay, John M. G. *Obeying the Truth: Paul's Ethics in Galatians*. Minneapolis: Fortress, 1988. Repr., Vancouver: Regent College Publishing, 2005.

Barker, Paul A. *The Triumph of Grace in Deuteronomy: Faithless Israel, Faithful Yahweh in Deuteronomy*. Paternoster Biblical Monographs. Carlisle, U.K.: Paternoster, 2004.

Barrett, C. K. *Essays on Paul*. Philadelphia: Westminster, 1982.

Barthes, Roland. "Theory of the Text." Pages 31–47 in *Untying the Text: A Post-structuralist Reader*. Edited by Robert Young. Boston: Routledge & Kegan Paul, 1981.

Bauckham, Richard, ed. *The Gospel for All Christians: Rethinking the Gospel Audiences*. Grand Rapids: Eerdmans, 1998.

Baumgarten, A. I. "Korban and the Pharisaic *paradosis*." *Journal of the Ancient Near Eastern Society* 16–17 (1984–1985): 5–17.

Baur, F. C. *Paul the Apostle of Jesus Christ: His Life and Works, His Epistles and Teachings*. Repr., 2 vols. in 1. Peabody, Mass.: Hendrickson, 2003.

———. *Paulus, der Apostel Jesu Christi. Sein Leben und Wirken, seine Briefe und seine Lehre*. Stuttgart: Becher & Müller, 1845.

Beale, G. K. "Isaiah VI 9–13: A Retributive Taunt against Idolatry." *VT* 41 (1991): 257–78.

———. "The Old Testament Background of Paul's Reference to 'the Fruit of the Spirit' in Galatians 5:22." *BBR* 15 (2005): 1–38.

Bellafontaine, Elizabeth. "The Curses of Deuteronomy 27: Their Relationship to the Prohibitives." Pages 256–68 in *A Song of Power and the Power of Song*. Edited by Duane L. Christensen. Winona Lake, Ind.: Eisenbrauns, 1993.

Bellinger, William H., Jr., and William R. Farmer, eds. *Jesus and the Suffering Servant: Isaiah 53 and Christian Origins*. Harrisburg, Pa.: Trinity Press International, 1998.

Berlin, Adele. "Literary Exegesis of Biblical Narrative: Between Poetics and Hermeneutics." Pages 120–28 in *Not in Heaven: Coherence and Complexity in Biblical Narrative*. Edited by Jason P. Rosenblatt and Joseph C. Sitterson. Bloomington: Indiana University Press, 1991.

Berman, Joshua A. *Created Equal: How the Bible Broke with Ancient Political Thought*. New York: Oxford University Press, 2008.

Betz, Hans Dieter. *Galatians*. Hermeneia. Philadelphia: Fortress, 1979.

Bieler, Ludwig. *Theios Aner: Das Bild des "Göttlichen Menschen" in Spätantike und Frühchristentum*. 2 vols. Vienna: Höfels, 1935. Repr. in one volume, Darmstadt: Wissenschaftliche Buchgesellschaft, 1976.

Bieringer, Reimund, Didier Pollefeyt, and Frederique Vandecasteele-Vanneuville. *Anti-Judaism and the Fourth Gospel*. Louisville: Westminster John Knox, 2001.

Bird, Michael F., and Joel Willitts, eds. *Paul and the Gospels: Christologies, Conflicts and Convergences*. LNTS 411. London: T&T Clark, 2011.

Bird, Michael F., and Preston M. Sprinkle, eds. *The Faith of Jesus Christ: The Pistis Christou Debate*. Peabody, Mass.: Hendrickson, 2009.

Blass, F., A. Debrunner, and R. W. Funk, *A Greek Grammar of the New Testament and Other Early Christian Literature*. Chicago: University of Chicago Press, 1961.

Blomberg, Craig L. *Matthew*. NAC 22. Nashville: Broadman, 1992.

Bock, Darrell. "Scripture and the Realization of God's Promises." Pages 41–62 in *Witness to the Gospel: The Theology of Acts*. Edited by I. Howard Marshall and David Peterson. Grand Rapids: Eerdmans, 1998.

Bohnenblust, Gottfried. *Beiträge zum Topos Peri Philias*. Berlin: Universitäts-Buchdruckerei von Gustav Shade, 1905.

Bonnard, Pierre. *L'Évangile selon Saint Matthieu*. CNT 1. Neuchâtel: Delachaux & Niestlé, 1963.

Boring, M. Eugene. *Mark: A Commentary*. NTL. Louisville: Westminster John Knox, 2006.

Boston Women's Health Book Collective. *Our Bodies Ourselves: A Course by and for Women*. Boston: New England Free Press, 1971.

Bovon, François. "Une formule prépaulinienne dans l'Épître aux Galates (Gal 1.4–5)." Pages 91–107 in *Paganisme, Judaïsme, Christianisme: Influences et affrontements dans le monde antique. Mélanges offerts à Marcel Simon*. Edited by A. Benoit, M. Philonenko, and C. Vogel. Paris: E. de Boccard, 1978.

Boyle, T. Coraghessan. *Tortilla Curtain*. New York: Penguin, 1996.

Brandon, S. G. F. *The Fall of Jerusalem and the Christian Church: A Study of the Effects of the Jewish Overthrow of A.D. 70 on Christianity*. London: SPCK, 1951.

Braswell, Joseph P. "'The Blessing of Abraham' versus 'The Curse of the Law': Another Look at Gal 3:10–13." *WTJ* 53 (1991): 73–91.

Brawley, Robert L. *Text to Text Pours Forth Speech: Voices of Scripture in Luke–Acts*. Indiana Studies in Biblical Literature. Bloomington: Indiana University Press, 1995.

Breytenbach, C. "Versöhnung, Stellvertretung und Sühne." *NTS* 39 (1993): 59–79.

Brocke, Christoph vom. *Thessaloniki: Stadt des Kassander und Gemeinde des Paulus*. WUNT 2/125. Tübingen: Mohr Siebeck, 2001.

Brooke, A. E., ed., *The Commentary of Origen on S. John's Gospel*. 2 vols. Cambridge: Cambridge University Press, 1896.

Brown, Raymond E. *The Community of the Beloved Disciple: The Life, Loves, and Hates of an Individual Church in New Testament Times*. New York: Paulist Press, 1979.

———. *The Epistles of John: A New Translation with Introduction and Commentary*. AB 30. New York: Doubleday, 1982.

Brueggemann, Walter. *Journey to the Common Good*. Louisville: Westminster John Knox, 2010.

Bryant, Christopher. *A Preface to Mark: Notes on the Gospel in Its Literary and Cultural Setting*. New York: Oxford University Press, 1993.

Bultmann, Rudolf. *Theology of the New Testament*. Translated by Kendrick Grobel. 2 vols. London: SCM, 1951–1955.

Burridge, Richard A. *Imitating Jesus: An Inclusive Approach to New Testament Ethics*. Grand Rapids: Eerdmans, 2007.

———. *What Are the Gospels? A Comparison with Graeco-Roman Biography*. SNTSMS 70. Cambridge: Cambridge University Press, 1992.

Burton, Ernest De Witt. *A Critical and Exegetical Commentary on the Epistle to the Galatians*. ICC. Edinburgh: T&T Clark, 1921.

Cairns, Ian. *Word and Presence: A Commentary on the Book of Deuteronomy*. International Theological Commentary. Grand Rapids: Eerdmans, 1992.

Capon, Robert Farrar. *The Supper of the Lamb: A Culinary Reflection*. 1969. Repr., New York: Modern Library, 2002.

Carey, Greg. *Ultimate Things: An Introduction to Jewish and Christian Apocalyptic Literature*. St. Louis: Chalice, 2005.

Carson, D. A. *Matthew*. Vols. 1–2 of *The Expositor's Bible Commentary: With the New International Version*. Edited by Frank E. Gaebelein. Grand Rapids: Zondervan, 1995.

Carson, D. A., Peter T. O'Brien, and Mark A. Seifrid, eds. *Justification and Variegated Nomism*. 2 vols. Grand Rapids: Baker, 2001–2004.

Carter, Warren. *Matthew and the Margins: A Sociopolitical and Religious Reading*. Maryknoll, N.Y.: Orbis, 2000.

Childs, Brevard S. *Introduction to the Old Testament as Scripture*. Philadelphia: Fortress, 1979.

Clarkson, Mary E. "The Ethics of the Fourth Gospel." *AThR* 31 (1949): 112–15.

Clements, R. E., "A Light to the Nations: A Central Theme of the Book of Isaiah." Pages 57–69 in *Forming Prophetic Literature: Essays on Isaiah and the Twelve in Honor of John D. W. Watts*. Edited by James W. Watts and Paul R. House. JSOTSup 235. Sheffield: Sheffield Academic Press, 1996.

Collins, Adela Yarbro. *Mark: A Commentary*. Hermeneia. Minneapolis: Fortress, 2007.

Collins, John J. *The Apocalyptic Imagination: An Introduction to Jewish Apocalyptic Literature*. Rev. ed. Grand Rapids: Eerdmans, 1998.

Collins, Raymond F. *The Birth of the New Testament: The Origin and Development of the First Christian Generation*. New York: Crossroad, 1993.

———. *Divorce in the New Testament*. Collegeville, Minn.: Liturgical Press, 1992.

———. *I and II Timothy and Titus*. NTL. Westminster: John Knox, 2002.

———. "God in the First Letter to the Thessalonians: Paul's Earliest Written Appreciation of *ho theos*." *LS* 16 (1991): 137–54.

———. *Letters That Paul Did Not Write: The Epistle to the Hebrews and the Pauline Pseudepigrapha*. GNS 28. Wilmington, Del.: Glazier, 1988.

———. *The Power of Images in Paul*. Collegeville, Minn.: Liturgical Press, 2008.

———. "A Significant Decade: The Trajectory of the Hellenistic Epistolary Thanksgiving." Pages 159–84 in *Paul and the Ancient Letter Form*. Edited by Stanley E. Porter and Sean A. Adams. Leiden: Brill, 2010.

———. "Tradition, Redaction, and Exhortation in 1 Th 4,13–5,11." Pages 325–43 in *L'Apocalypse johannique et l'Apocalyptique dans le Nouveau Testament*. Edited by Jan Lambrecht. BETL 53. Leuven: Leuven University Press, 1980.

Coloe, Mary L. "Welcome into the Household of God: The Foot Washing in John 13." *CBQ* 66 (2004): 400–415.

Conzelmann, Hans. *1 Corinthians: A Commentary on the First Epistle to the Corinthians*. Translated by James W. Leitch. Hermeneia. Philadelphia: Fortress, 1975.

Cosby, Michael R. "Hellenistic Formal Reception and Paul's Use of ΑΠΑΝΤΗΣΙΣ in 1 Thessalonians 4:17." *BBR* 4 (1994): 15–34.

Cosgrove, Charles H. *The Cross and the Spirit: A Study in the Argument and Theology of Galatians*. Macon, Ga.: Mercer University Press, 1988.

Countryman, William. *Dirt, Greed, Sex: Sexual Ethics in the New Testament and Their Implications for Today*. Philadelphia: Fortress, 1988.

Crace, Jim. *Being Dead*. New York: Picador, 1999.

Crenshaw, James L. "Impossible Questions, Sayings, and Tasks." *Semeia* 17 (1980): 19–34.

Crossan, John Dominic. *In Parables: The Challenge of the Historical Jesus*. San Francisco: Harper & Row, 1973.

Crossley, James G. "The Damned Rich (Mark 10:17–31)." *ExpTim* 116 (2005): 397–401.

Culler, Jonathan D. *The Pursuit of Signs: Semiotics, Literature, Deconstruction*. London: Routledge & Kegan Paul, 1981.

Culpepper, R. Alan. "The Johannine *Hypodeigma*: A Reading of John 13." *Semeia* 53 (1991): 133–52.

Dahl, Nils A. "*Anamnesis*: Memory and Commemoration in Early Christianity." Pages 11–29 in *Jesus in the Memory of the Early Church*. Minneapolis: Augsburg, 1976.

Darr, John A. *On Building Character: The Reader and the Rhetoric of Characterization in Luke–Acts*. Louisville: Westminster John Knox, 1992.

Das, A. Andrew. "Another Look at ἐὰν μή in Galatians 2:16." *JBL* 119 (2000): 529–39.

———. *Paul and the Jews*. Peabody, Mass.: Hendrickson, 2003.

———. "Paul and Works of Obedience in Second Temple Judaism: Romans 4:4–5 as a 'New Perspective' Case Study." *CBQ* 71 (2009): 795–812.

———. *Paul, the Law, and the Covenant*. Peabody, Mass.: Hendrickson, 2001.

Davies, W. D. *The Setting of the Sermon on the Mount*. Cambridge: Cambridge University Press, 1963.

Davies, W. D., and Dale C. Allison. *A Critical and Exegetical Commentary on the Gospel According to Saint Matthew*. 3 vols. ICC. Edinburgh: T&T Clark, 1988–1997.

de Boer, Martinus C. "Paul's Use and Interpretation of a Justification Tradition in Galatians 2.15–21." *JSNT* 28 (2005): 189–216.

Decock, P. B. "The Understanding of Isaiah 53:7–8 in Acts 8:32–33." *Neot* 14 (1981): 111–33.

DeConick, April D. *The Original Gospel of Thomas in Translation*. LNTS 287. London: T&T Clark, 2007.

Deines, Roland. *Die Gerechtigkeit der Tora im Reich des Messias*. WUNT 177. Tübingen: Mohr Siebeck, 2004.

Deissmann, Adolf. *Light from the Ancient East: The New Testament Illustrated by Recently Discovered Texts of the Greco-Roman World*. New York: George H. Doran, 1927.

Deming, Will. *Paul on Marriage and Celibacy: The Hellenistic Background of 1 Cor 7*. SNTSMS 83. Cambridge: Cambridge University Press, 1995.

Dewey, Joanna. "Mark as Interwoven Tapestry: Forecasts and Echoes for a Listening Audience." *CBQ* 53 (1991): 221–36.

———. "Oral Methods of Structuring Narrative in Mark." *Int* 43 (1989): 32–44.

Donahue, John R., S.J. "Divorce: New Testament Perspectives." Pages 1–19 in *Marriage Studies: Reflections on Canon Law and Theology*. Edited by Thomas P. Doyle, O.P. Washington, D.C.: Canon Law Society of America, 1992.

———. "From Crucified Messiah to Risen Christ: The Trial of Jesus Revisited." Pages 93–121 in *Jews and Christians Speak of Jesus*. Edited by Arthur Zannoni. Minneapolis: Fortress, 1994.

———. "Jesus as the Parable of God in the Gospel of Mark." Pages 148–67 in *Interpreting the Gospels*. Edited by James L. Mays. Philadelphia: Fortress, 1981.

———. *The Theology and Setting of Discipleship in the Gospel of Mark*. Milwaukee: Marquette University Press, 1983.

Donahue, John R., S.J., and Daniel J. Harrington, S.J. *The Gospel of Mark*. SP 2. Collegeville, Minn.: Liturgical Press, 2002.

Donfried, Karl P. "The Cults of Thessalonica and the Thessalonian Correspondence." *NTS* 31 (1985): 336–56.

———. "The Imperial Cults of Thessalonica and Political Conflict in 1 Thessalonians." Pages 215–23 in *Paul and Empire: Religion and Power in Roman Imperial Society*. Edited by Richard A. Horsley. Harrisburg, Pa.: Trinity Press International, 1997.

———. "A Short Note on Romans 16." Pages 44–52 in *The Romans Debate*. Edited by Karl P. Donfried. Rev. and enl. ed. Peabody, Mass.: Hendrickson, 2003.

Dowd, Sharyn. *Reading Mark: A Literary and Theological Commentary on the Second Gospel*. Macon, Ga.: Smyth & Helwys, 2000.

Draisma, Sipke, ed. *Intertextuality in Biblical Writings: Essays in Honour of Bas van Iersel*. Kampen: Kok, 1989.

Dunn, James D. G. "ΕΚ ΠΙΣΤΕΩΣ: A Key to the Meaning of ΠΙΣΤΙΣ ΧΡΙΣΤΟΥ." Pages 351–66 in *The Word Leaps the Gap: Essays on Scripture and Theology in Honor of Richard B. Hays*. Edited by J. Ross Wagner, C. Kavin Rowe, and A. Katherine Grieb. Grand Rapids: Eerdmans, 2008.

———. *The Epistle to the Galatians*. BNTC. Peabody, Mass.: Hendrickson, 1993.

———. *Jesus, Paul, and the Gospels*. Grand Rapids: Eerdmans, 2011.

———. *Jesus, Paul, and the Law: Studies in Mark and Galatians*. Louisville: Westminster John Knox, 1990.

———. *Jesus Remembered*. Grand Rapids: Eerdmans, 2003.

———. "The New Perspective on Paul." *BJRL* 65 (1983): 95–122.

———. *The New Perspective on Paul: Collected Essays*. WUNT 185. Tübingen: Mohr Siebeck, 2005.

———. "Once More, Pistis Christou." Pages 61–81 in *Looking Back, Pressing On*. Vol. 4 of *Pauline Theology*. Edited by E. Elizabeth Johnson and David M. Hay. SBLSymS 4. Atlanta: Scholars Press, 1997.

———. *The Theology of Paul the Apostle*. Grand Rapids: Eerdmans, 1998.

Dupont, Jacques. *Les Béatitudes*. 3 vols. EBib. Paris: Gabalda, 1969–1973.

Easter, Matthew C. "The *Pistis Christou* Debate: Main Arguments and Responses in Summary." *CBR* 9 (2010): 33–46.

Eckstein, Hans-Joachim. *Verheißung und Gesetz: Eine exegetische Untersuchung zu Galater 2,15–4,7*. WUNT 86. Tübingen: Mohr Siebeck, 1996.

Eckstein, Lars. *Re-membering the Black Atlantic: On the Poetics and Politics of Literary Memory*. Amsterdam: Rodopi, 2006.

Edenburg, Cynthia. "Intertextuality, Literary Competence and the Question of Readership: Some Preliminary Observations." *JSOT* 35 (2010): 131–48.

Elliott, Neil. "The Apostle Paul and Empire." Pages 97–116 in *In the Shadow of Empire: Reclaiming the Bible as a History of Faithful Resistance*. Edited by Richard A. Horsley. Louisville: Westminster John Knox, 2008.

Elliott, Neil, and Mark Reasoner, eds. *Documents and Images for the Study of Paul*. Minneapolis: Fortress, 2011.

Eloff, Marvyn. "Ἀπό ... ἕως and Salvation History in Matthew's Gospel." Pages 85–107 in *Built upon the Rock: Studies in the Gospel of Matthew*. Edited by Daniel M. Gurtner and John Nolland. Grand Rapids: Eerdmans, 2008.

Eskola, Timo. "Paul, Predestination and 'Covenantal Nomism'—Re-assessing Paul and Palestinian Judaism." *JSJ* 29 (1997): 390–412.

———. *Theology and Predestination in Pauline Soteriology*. WUNT 2/100. Tübingen: Mohr Siebeck, 1998.

Evans, Craig A. "Jesus' Action in the Temple: Cleansing or Portent of Destruction?" *CBQ* 51 (1989): 237–69.

———. *Mark 8:27–16:20*. WBC 34B. Nashville: Nelson, 2001.

Evans, Craig A., and James A. Sanders, eds. *Paul and the Scriptures of Israel*. JSNTSup 83. Sheffield: JSOT Press, 1993.

Fee, Gordon D. *The First Epistle to the Corinthians*. NICNT. Grand Rapids: Eerdmans, 1987.

Fieger, Michael. *Das Thomasevangelium. Einleitung, Kommentar und Systematik*. NTAbh 22. Münster: Aschendorff, 1991.

Fitzmyer, Joseph A., S.J. *According to Paul: Studies in the Theology of the Apostle*. New York: Paulist Press, 1993.

———. *The Acts of the Apostles: A New Translation with Introduction and Commentary*. AB 31. New York: Doubleday, 1998.

———. *Paul and His Theology: A Brief Sketch*. Englewood Cliffs, N.J.: Prentice-Hall, 1989.

———. *Romans: A New Translation with Introduction and Commentary*. AB 33. New York: Doubleday, 1993.

Foster, Paul, "The Epistles of Ignatius of Antioch and the Writings that Later Formed the New Testament." Pages 159–86 in *The Reception of the New Testament in the Apostolic Fathers*. Edited by Andrew F. Gregory and Christopher M. Tuckett. Oxford: Oxford University Press, 2005.

———. "The First Contribution to the Πίστις Χριστοῦ Debate: A Study of Ephesians 3.12." *JSNT* 85 (2002): 75–96.

———. "Paul and Matthew—Two Strands of the Early Jesus Movement with Little Sign of Connection." Pages 86–114 in *Paul and the Gospels: Christologies, Conflicts and Convergences*. Edited by Michael F. Bird and Joel Willitts. LNTS 411. London: T&T Clark, 2011.

Foucault, Michel. *Discipline and Punish: The Birth of the Prison*. Translated by Alan Sheridan. New York: Vintage, 1977.

———. *History of Sexuality*. Translated by Robert Hurley. 3 vols. New York: Vintage, 1980.

France, R. T. *The Gospel of Matthew*. NICNT. Grand Rapids: Eerdmans, 2007.

———. *Matthew: Evangelist and Teacher*. Exeter: Paternoster, 1989.

Francis, James. "Children and Childhood in the New Testament." Pages 65–85 in *The Family in Theological Perspective*. Edited by Stephen C. Barton. Edinburgh: T&T Clark, 1996.

Freedman, David N., ed. *Anchor Bible Dictionary*. 6 vols. New York: Doubleday, 1992.

Frey, Jörg. "Die Lilien und das Gewand: *Ev. Thom* 36 and 37 als Paradigma für das Verhältnis des *Thomasevangeliums* zur synoptischen Überlieferung." Pages 122–80 in *Das Thomasevangelium. Entstehung—Rezeption—Theologie*. Edited by Jörg Frey, Edzard Popkes, and Jens Schröter. BZNW 157. Berlin: de Gruyter, 2008.

García Martínez, Florentino. *The Dead Sea Scrolls Translated: The Qumran Texts in English*. Translated by Wilfred G. E. Watson. 2nd ed. Leiden: BrillGarland, David E. *Reading Matthew: A Literary and Theological Commentary*. Macon, Ga.: Smyth & Helwys, 2001.

Garlington, Don. "Paul's 'Partisan ἐκ' and the Question of Justification in Galatians." *JBL* 127 (2008): 567–89.

Gathercole, Simon. "Luke in the *Gospel of Thomas*." *NTS* 57 (2011): 114–44.

———. *Where Is Boasting? Early Jewish Soteriology and Paul's Response in Romans 1–5*. Grand Rapids: Eerdmans, 2002.

Gignac, Alain. "Taubes, Badiou, Agamben: Receptions of Paul by Non-Christian Philosophers." Pages 171–83 in *Reading Romans with Contemporary Philosophers and Theologians*. Edited by David Odell-Scott. New York: T&T Clark, 2007.

Gignac, Francis T. "The Use of Verbal Variety in the Fourth Gospel." Pages 191–200 in *Transcending Boundaries: Contemporary Readings of the New Testament. Essays in Honor of Francis J. Moloney*. Edited by Rekha M. Chennattu and Mary L. Coloe. Biblioteca di Scienze Religiose 187. Rome: Libreria Ateneo Salesiano, 2005.

Given, Mark D. *Paul's True Rhetoric: Ambiguity, Cunning, and Deception in Greece and Rome*. Harrisburg, Pa.: Trinity Press International, 2001.

Gnilka, Joachim. *Das Matthäusevangelium*. 2 vols. HTKNT I.1–2. Freiburg: Herder, 1986–1988.

Goldingay, John. *Theological Diversity and the Authority of the Old Testament*. Grand Rapids: Eerdmans, 1987.

Gombis, Timothy G. "The 'Transgressor' and the 'Curse of the Law': The Logic of Paul's Argument in Galatians 2–3." *NTS* 53 (2007): 81–93.

Gorman, Michael J. *Apostle of the Crucified Lord: A Theological Introduction to Paul and His Letters*. Grand Rapids: Eerdmans, 2004.

———. "Cruciformity." Pages 197–98 in *Dictionary of Scripture and Ethics*. Edited by Joel B. Green. Grand Rapids: Baker Academic, 2011.

———. *Cruciformity: Paul's Narrative Spirituality of the Cross*. Grand Rapids: Eerdmans, 2001.

———. *Inhabiting the Cruciform God: Kenosis, Justification, and Theosis in Paul's Narrative Soteriology*. Grand Rapids: Eerdmans, 2009.

———. *Reading Paul*. Cascade Companions. Eugene, Ore.: Cascade, 2008.

Green, Gene L. *The Letters to the Thessalonians*. Pillar New Testament Commentary. Grand Rapids: Eerdmans, 2002.

Gundry, Judith. "Children in the Gospel of Mark." Pages 143–76 in *The Child in the Bible*. Edited by Marcia J. Bunge. Grand Rapids: Eerdmans, 2008.

Gundry, Robert H. "A Brief Note on 'Hellenistic Formal Receptions and Paul's Use of ΑΠΑΝΤΗΣΙΣ in 1 Thessalonians 4:17." *BBR* 6 (1999): 39–41.

———. *Matthew: A Commentary on His Literary and Theological Art*. Grand Rapids: Eerdmans, 1982.

———. *Sōma in Biblical Theology, with Emphasis on Pauline Anthropology*. SNTSMS 29. Cambridge: Cambridge University Press, 1976.

Gustafson, James F. *Can Ethics Be Christian?* Chicago: University of Chicago Press, 1975.

Hagner, Donald A. *Matthew*. 2 vols. WBC 33–33A. Dallas: Word Books, 1993–1995.

Hahn, Ferdinand. *Christologische Hoheitstitel: Ihre Geschichte im frühen Christentum*. FRLANT 83. Göttingen: Vandenhoeck & Ruprecht, 1963.

Hanse, Hermann. "ΔΗΛΟΝ (zu Gal 3¹¹)." *ZNW* 34 (1935): 299–303.

Hansen, G. Walter. *Galatians*. IVPNTC. Downers Grove, Ill.: InterVarsity Press, 1994.

Harding, Mark. "Kyrios Christos: Johannine and Pauline Perspectives on the Christ Event." Pages 169–96 in *Paul and the Gospels: Christologies, Conflicts and Convergences*. Edited by Michael F. Bird and Joel Willitts. LNTS 411. London: T&T Clark, 2011.

Hare, Douglas R. A. *The Son of Man Tradition*. Minneapolis: Fortress, 1990.

Harrington, Daniel J., S.J., and James F. Keenan, S.J. *Paul and Virtue Ethics: Building Bridges between New Testament Studies and Moral Theology*. Lanham: Sheed & Ward, 2010.

Hasler, Victor. "Epiphanie und Christologie in den Pastoralbriefen." *TZ* 33 (1977): 193–209.

Hauerwas, Stanley. *The Peaceable Kingdom: A Primer in Christian Ethics*. Notre Dame, Ind.: University of Notre Dame Press, 1983.

Hays, Richard B. *The Conversion of the Imagination: Paul as Interpreter of Israel's Scripture*. Grand Rapids: Eerdmans, 2005.

———. *Echoes of Scripture in the Letters of Paul*. New Haven: Yale University Press, 1989.

———. *The Faith of Jesus Christ: The Narrative Substructure of Galatians 3:1–4:11*. SBLDS 56. Chico, Calif.: Scholars Press, 1983. 2nd ed. Grand Rapids: Eerdmans, 2002.

———. *First Corinthians*. IBC. Louisville: Westminster John Knox, 1997.

———. "The Letter to the Galatians." Pages 181–348 in vol. 11 of *The New Interpreter's Bible*. Edited by Leander E. Keck. 12 vols. Nashville: Abingdon, 1994–2004.

———. *The Moral Vision of the New Testament: Community, Cross, New Creation: A Contemporary Introduction to New Testament Ethics*. San Francisco: HarperSanFrancisco, 1996.

———. "ΠΙΣΤΙΣ and Pauline Christology: What Is at Stake?" Pages 35–60 in *Looking Back, Pressing On*. Vol. 4 of *Pauline Theology*. Edited by E. Elizabeth Johnson and David M. Hay. SBLSymS 4. Atlanta: Scholars Press, 1997.

———. "Reading Scripture in Light of the Resurrection." Pages 216–38 in *The Art of Reading Scripture*. Edited by Ellen F. Davis and Richard B. Hays. Grand Rapids: Eerdmans, 2003.

Hays, Richard B., Stefan Alkier, and Leroy A. Huizenga, eds. *Reading the Bible Intertextually*. Waco, Tex.: Baylor University Press, 2009.

Hearon, Holly E., and Philip Ruge-Jones, eds. *The Bible in Ancient and Modern Media: Story and Performance*. Biblical Performance Criticism. Eugene, Ore.: Cascade, 2009.

Heil, John. *Philosophy of Mind: A Contemporary Introduction*. London: Routledge, 2004.

Hellerman, Joseph. "Wealth and Sacrifice in Early Christianity: Revisiting Mark's Presentation of Jesus' Encounter with the Rich Young Ruler." *TrinJ* 21 (2000): 143–64.

Hendrix, Holland. "Beyond 'Imperial Cult' and 'Cults of Magistrates.'" Pages 301–8 in *The Society of Biblical Literature 1986 Seminar Papers*. SBLSP 25. Atlanta: Scholars Press, 1986.

———. "Thessalonicans Honor Romans." PhD diss., Harvard Divinity School, 1984.

Hengel, Martin. *The Atonement: The Origins of the Doctrine in the New Testament*. Philadelphia: Fortress, 1981.

Hester, James D. "Creating the Future: Apocalyptic Rhetoric in 1 Thessalonians." *Religion and Theology* 17 (2000): 192–212.

Holladay, Carl. "1 Corinthians 13: Paul as Apostolic Paradigm." Pages 80–98 in *Greeks, Romans, and Christians: Essays in Honor of Abraham Malherbe*. Edited by David L. Balch, Everett Ferguson, and Wayne A. Meeks. Minneapolis: Fortress, 1991.

Hooker, Morna. "Interchange in Christ." *JTS* 22 (1971): 349–61.

———. "Πίστις Χριστοῦ." *NTS* 35 (1989): 321–42.

Horsley, Richard A., Jonathan A. Draper, and John Miles Foley, eds. *Performing the Gospel: Orality, Memory, and Mark*. Minneapolis: Fortress, 2006.

Houlden, J. L. *Ethics and the New Testament*. New York: Oxford University Press, 1973.

Houston, Walter J. *Contending for Justice: Ideologies and Theologies of Social Justice in the Old Testament*. LHBOTS 428. London: T&T Clark, 2006.

Howard, George E. "Notes and Observations on the 'Faith of Christ.' " *HTR* 60 (1967): 459–84.

Hübner, Hans. *Law in Paul's Thought*. Translated by James C. G. Grieg. Studies of the New Testament and Its World. Edinburgh: T&T Clark, 1984.

Hultgren, Arland J. *The Parables of Jesus: A Commentary*. Grand Rapids: Eerdmans, 2000.

Hunn, Debbie. "Ἐὰν μή in Galatians 2:16: A Look at Greek Literature." *NovT* 49 (2007): 281–90.

Hurd, John C. *The Origin of 1 Corinthians*. 2nd ed. Macon, Ga.: Mercer University Press, 1983.

Hurtado, Larry W. "Jesus as Lordly Example in Philippians 2:5–11." Pages 113–26 in *From Jesus to Paul: Studies in Honour of Francis Wright Beare*. Edited by Peter Richardson and John C. Hurd. Waterloo, Ont.: Wilfred Laurier University Press, 1984.

Ilan, Tal. *Jewish Women in Greco-Roman Palestine*. Peabody, Mass.: Hendrickson, 1996.

Jackson, Timothy P. "A House Divided Again: 'Sanctity' vs. 'Dignity' in the Induced Death Debate." Pages 139–63 in *In Defense of Human Dignity*. Edited by Robert P. Kraynak and Glenn E. Tinder. Notre Dame, Ind.: University of Notre Dame Press, 2003.

James, Henry. *The Art of the Novel: Critical Prefaces*. New York: Scribner's, 1947.

Jaworski, William. *Philosophy of Mind: A Comprehensive Introduction*. Oxford: Wiley-Blackwell, 2011.

Jensen, Joseph. *The Ethics of the Prophets*. Collegeville, Minn.: Liturgical Press, 2006.

Jewett, Robert. *Paul's Anthropological Terms: A Study of Their Use in Conflict Settings*. AGJU 10. Leiden: Brill, 1971.

Jipp, Joshua W. "Luke's Scriptural Suffering Messiah: A Search for Precedent, a Search for Identity." *CBQ* 72 (2010): 255–74.

Johnson, Luke Timothy. *The Acts of the Apostles*. SP 5. Collegeville, Minn.: Liturgical Press, 1992.

———. "Caring for the Earth: Why Environmentalism Needs Theology." *Commonweal* 132 (2005): 16–20.

———. "Life-Giving Spirit: The Ontological Implications of the Resurrection." *The Stone-Campbell Journal*. Forthcoming.

———. "Meals Are Where the Magic Is." Pages 137–79 in *Religious Experience in Earliest Christianity*. Minneapolis: Fortress, 1998.

———. *Reading Romans: A Literary and Theological Commentary*. Macon, Ga.: Smyth & Helwys, 2001.

———. "The Revelatory Body: Notes toward a Somatic Theology." Pages 69–85 in *The Phenomenology of the Body*. Edited by D. J. Martino. Pittsburgh: Simon Silverman Phenomenology Center at the University of Duquesne, 2003.

———. "Rom 3:21–26 and the Faith of Jesus." *CBQ* 44 (1982): 77–90.

———. *Scripture and Discernment: Decision Making in the Church*. Nashville: Abingdon, 1996.

———. *Septuagintal Midrash in the Speeches of Acts*. Milwaukee: Marquette University Press, 2002.

———. *Sharing Possessions: What Faith Demands*. 2nd ed. Grand Rapids: Eerdmans, 2011.

———. "The Social Dimensions of *Sōtēria* in Luke–Acts and Paul." Pages 520–36 in *The Society of Biblical Literature 1993 Seminar Papers*. SBLSP 32. Atlanta: Scholars Press, 1993.

———. "Transformation of the Mind and Moral Discernment in Paul." Pages 215–36 in *Early Christianity and Classical Culture: Comparative Studies in Honor of Abraham J. Malherbe*. Edited by John T. Fitzgerald, Thomas H. Olbricht, and L. Michael White. NovTSup 110. Leiden: Brill, 2003.

———. *The Writings of the New Testament*. 3rd ed. Philadelphia: Fortress, 2010.

Joosen, Vanessa. *Critical and Creative Perspectives on Fairy Tales: An Intertextual Dialogue between Fairy-Tale Scholarship and Postmodern Retellings*. Detroit: Wayne State University Press, 2011.

Kaminouchi, Alberto deMingo. *"But It Is Not So among You: Echoes of Power in Mark 10.32–45.* JSNTSup 249. London: T&T Clark, 2003.

Kaminsky, Joel, and Anne Stewart. "God of All the World: Universalism and Developing Monotheism in Isaiah 40–66." *HTR* 99 (2006): 139–63.

Käsemann, Ernst. *The Testament of Jesus*. Philadelphia: Fortress, 1966.

Keck, Leander E. "Images of Paul in the New Testament." *Int* 43 (1989): 341–51.

———, ed. *The New Interpreter's Bible*. 12 vols. Nashville: Abingdon, 1994–2004.

Keenan, James F. *History of Catholic Moral Theology in the Twentieth Century: From Confessing Sins to Liberating Consciences*. London: Continuum, 2010.

Keesmaat, Sylvia C. *Paul and His Story*. JSNTSup 181. Sheffield: Sheffield Academic Press, 1999.

Kennedy, George A. *Progymnasmata: Greek Textbooks of Prose Composition and Rhetoric*. SBLWGRW 10. Atlanta: Society of Biblical Literature, 2003.

Khiok-Khng, Yeo. "A Political Reading of Paul's Eschatology in I and II Thessalonians." *AJT* 12 (1998): 77–88.

Kim, Seyoon. "The Jesus Tradition in 1 Thess 4.13–5.11." *NTS* 48 (2002): 225–42.

Kim, Yung Suk. *A Theological Introduction to Paul's Letters: Exploring a Threefold Theology of Paul*. Eugene, Ore.: Cascade, 2011.

Kimball, Charles A. *Jesus' Exposition of the Old Testament in Luke's Gospel*. JSNTSup 94. Sheffield: JSOT Press, 1994.

King, William McGuire. "The Biblical Basis of the Social Gospel." Pages 59–84 in *The Bible and Social Reform*. Edited by Ernest Sandeen. Philadelphia: Fortress, 1982.

Kingsbury, Jack Dean. *The Christology of Mark's Gospel*. Philadelphia: Fortress, 1983.

Kirk, J. R. Daniel. *Jesus Have I Loved, but Paul? A Narrative Approach to the Problem of Pauline Christianity*. Grand Rapids: Baker Academic, 2012.

Kittel, Gerhard, and Gerhard Friedrich, eds. *Theological Dictionary of the New Testament*. Translated by G. W. Bromiley. 10 vols. Grand Rapids: Eerdmans, 1964–1976.

Klink, Edward W., III, ed. *The Audience of the Gospels: The Origin and Function of the Gospels in Early Christianity*. LNTS 353. London: T&T Clark, 2010.

———. *The Sheep of the Fold: The Audience and Origin of the Gospel of John*. SNTSMS 141. Cambridge: Cambridge University Press, 2007.

Kloppenborg, John S. *The Tenants in the Vineyard: Ideology, Economics, and Agrarian Conflict in Jewish Palestine*. WUNT 195. Tübingen: Mohr Siebeck, 2006.

Koehne, Mark Walter. "The Septuagintal Isaian Use of ΝΟΜΟΣ in the Lukan Presentation Narrative." PhD diss., Marquette University, 2010.

Koester, Helmut. "Imperial Ideology and Paul's Eschatology in 1 Thessalonians." Pages 158–66 in *Paul and Empire: Religion and Power in Roman Imperial Society*. Edited by Richard A. Horsley. Harrisburg, Pa.: Trinity Press International, 1997.

Köstenberger, Andreas J., and Peter T. O'Brien. *Salvation to the Ends of the Earth: A Biblical Theology of Mission*. New Studies in Biblical Theology 11. Downers Grove, Ill.: InterVarsity Press, 2001.

Krips, Henry. "The Politics of Badiou: From Absolute Singularity to Objet-a." Paper presented at the plenary session in the Bradshaw Lecture Series "Event and Process." Claremont, Claremont Graduate University, December 2007.

Kristeva, Julia. *Revolution in Poetic Language.* Translated by Margaret Waller. New York: Columbia University Press, 1984.

———. *Semeiotike: Recherches pour une sémanalyse.* Paris: Seuil, 1969.

Kruse, Colin G. "Paul and John: Two Witnesses, One Gospel." Pages 197–219 in *Paul and the Gospels: Christologies, Conflicts and Convergences.* Edited by Michael F. Bird and Joel Willitts. LNTS 411. London: T&T Clark, 2011.

Kurz, William S., S.J. "From the Servant in Isaiah to Jesus and the Apostles in Luke–Acts to Christians Today: Spirit-Filled Witness to the Ends of the Earth." Pages 175–94 in *Between Experience and Interpretation: Engaging the Writings of the New Testament.* Edited by Mary F. Foskett and O. Wesley Allen Jr. Nashville: Abingdon, 2008.

———. *Reading Luke–Acts: Dynamics of Biblical Narrative.* Louisville: Westminster John Knox, 1993.

Lagrange, Michel-Joseph. *Évangile selon Saint Matthieu.* EBib. Paris: Gabalda, 1927.

Lambert, Craig. "The Way We Eat Now." *Harvard Magazine* (May–June 2004): 52–58, 98–99.

Lambrecht, Jan. "Critical Reflections on Paul's 'Partisan ἐκ' as Recently Presented by Don Garlington." *ETL* 85 (2009): 135–41.

Lasch, Christopher. "Religious Contributions to Social Movements: Walter Rauschenbusch, the Social Gospel, and Its Critics." *JRE* 18 (1990): 7–25.

Lau, Andrew. *Manifest in the Flesh: The Epiphany Christology of the Pastoral Epistles.* WUNT 2/86. Tübingen: Mohr Siebeck, 1996.

Leclerc, Thomas. *Yahweh Is Exalted in Justice: Solidarity and Conflict in Isaiah.* Minneapolis: Fortress, 2001.

Lee, Dorothy. "Friendship, Love and Abiding in the Gospel of John." Pages 57–74 in *Transcending Boundaries: Contemporary Readings of the New Testament. Essays in Honor of Francis J. Moloney.* Edited by Rekha M. Chennattu and Mary L. Coloe. Biblioteca di Scienze Religiose 187. Rome: Libreria Ateneo Salesiano, 2005.

Lindemann, Andreas. "Paul's Influence on 'Clement' and Ignatius." Pages 9–24 in *Trajectories through the New Testament and the Apostolic Fathers.* Edited by Andrew F. Gregory and Christopher M. Tuckett. Oxford: Oxford University Press, 2005.

Litwak, Kenneth Duncan. *Echoes of Scripture in Luke–Acts: Telling the Story of God's People Intertextually.* JSNTSup 282. London: T&T Clark, 2005.

Lohfink, Norbert. "Darstellungskunst und Theologie in Dtn 1,6–3,29." *Bib* 41 (1960): 105–35.

Luz, Ulrich. "The Fulfillment of the Law in Matthew (Matt 5:17–20)." Pages 185–218 in *Studies in Matthew.* Translated by Rosemary Selle. Grand Rapids: Eerdmans, 2005.

———. "Intertexts in the Gospel of Matthew." *HTR* 97 (2004): 119–37.

———. *Matthew.* Translated by James E. Crouch. 3 vols. Hermeneia. Minneapolis: Fortress, 2001–2007.

Malherbe, Abraham J. *The Letters to the Thessalonians.* AB 32B. New York: Doubleday, 2000.

———. "*Mē Genoito* in the Diatribe and Paul." Pages 25–34 in *Paul and the Popular Philosophers.* Minneapolis: Fortress, 1989.

———. "A Physical Description of Paul." Pages 165–70 in *Paul and the Popular Philosophers*. Minneapolis: Fortress, 1989.

Malbon, Elizabeth Struthers. "Echoes and Foreshadowings in Mark 4–8: Reading and Rereading." *JBL* 112 (1993): 211–30.

———. "The Poor Widow in Mark, and Her Poor Rich Readers." *CBQ* 53 (1991): 589–604.

Malina, Bruce. "Wealth and Poverty in the New Testament and Its World." *Int* 41 (1987): 354–67.

Mallen, Peter. *The Reading and Transformation of Isaiah in Luke–Acts*. LNTS 367. New York: T&T Clark, 2008.

Maloney, Linda M. *"All That God Had Done with Them": The Narration of the Works of God in the Early Christian Community as Described in the Acts of the Apostles*. New York: Lang, 1991.

Manicardi, Ermenegildo. *Il cammino de Gesù nel Vangelo di Marco. Schema narrative e tema cristologico*. AnBib 96. Rome: Biblical Institute Press, 1986.

Manson, T. W. "St. Paul's Letter to the Romans—and Others." Pages 3–15 in *The Romans Debate*. Edited by Karl P. Donfried. Rev. and enl. ed. Peabody, Mass.: Hendrickson, 2003.

Marcel, Gabriel. *Mystery of Being*. Translated by René Hague. 2 vols. Chicago: Regnery, 1950.

———. "Outline of a Phenomenology of Having." Pages 168–89 in *Being and Having*. Translated by Katharine Farrer. London: Collins, 1949.

Marcus, Joel. "Idolatry in the New Testament." Pages 107–31 in *The Word Leaps the Gap: Essays on Scripture and Theology in Honor of Richard B. Hays*. Edited by J. Ross Wagner, C. Kavin Rowe, and A. Katherine Grieb. Grand Rapids: Eerdmans, 2008.

———. *Mark 1–8: A New Translation with Introduction and Commentary*. AB 27. New York: Doubleday, 2000.

———. *Mark 8–16: A New Translation with Introduction and Commentary*. AB 27A. New Haven: Yale University Press, 2009.

Marguerat, Daniel. *The First Christian Historian: Writing the "Acts of the Apostles."* Translated by Ken McKinney, Gregory J. Laughery, and Richard Bauckham. SNTSMS 121. Cambridge: Cambridge University Press, 2002.

———. *Le jugement dans l'Évangile de Matthieu*. Geneva: Labor et Fides, 1981.

Marshall, I. Howard. "The Christology of the Pastoral Epistles." *SNTSU* 13 (1988): 157–77.

Martin, Dale. *The Corinthian Body*. New Haven: Yale University Press, 1995.

Marty, Martin. *Righteous Empire: The Protestant Experience in the United States*. New York: Dial, 1970.

Martyn, J. Louis. "Apocalyptic Antinomies in Paul's Letter to the Galatians." *NTS* 31 (1985): 410–2

———. "The Culmination of Paul's Argument to the Galatians: Gal 5.1–6.17." *JSNT* 32 (1988): 79–91.

———. *Galatians*. AB 33A. New York: Doubleday, 1997.

———. *History and Theology in the Fourth Gospel*. New York: Harper & Row, 1968.

Matera, Frank. "Christ in the Theologies of Paul and John: A Study in the Diverse Unity of New Testament Theology." *TS* 67 (2006): 237–56.

———. *Galatians*. SP 9. Collegeville, Minn.: Liturgical Press, 1992.

———. "Galatians and the Development of Paul's Teaching on Justification." *WW* 20 (2000): 239–48.

———. "Galatians in Perspective: Cutting a New Path through Old Territory." *Int* 54 (2000): 233–45.

———. *New Testament Christology*. Louisville: Westminster John Knox, 1999.

———. *New Testament Ethics: The Legacies of Jesus and Paul*. Louisville: Westminster John Knox, 1996.

———. *New Testament Theology: Exploring Diversity in Unity*. Louisville: Westminster John Knox, 2007.

———. *Romans*. Paideia Commentaries on the New Testament. Grand Rapids: Baker Academic, 2010.

———. *II Corinthians: A Commentary*. NTL. Louisville: Westminster John Knox, 2003.

———. *Strategies for Preaching Paul*. Collegeville, Minn.: Liturgical Press, 2001.

Mayes, A. D. H. *Deuteronomy*. NCBC. London: Marshall, Morgan & Scott, 1979.

McCarthy, D. J. *Old Testament Covenant: A Survey of Current Opinions*. Richmond: John Knox, 1972.

McConville, J. G., and J. G. Millar. *Time and Place in Deuteronomy*. JSOTSup 179. Sheffield: Sheffield Academic Press, 1994.

McRae, Rachel M. "Eating with Honor: The Corinthian Lord's Supper in Light of Voluntary Association Meal Practices." *JBL* 130 (2011): 165–81.

Meeks, Wayne A. "The Ethics of the Fourth Evangelist." Pages 317–26 in *Exploring the Gospel of John: In Honor of D. Moody Smith*. Edited by R. Alan Culpepper and C. Clifton Black. Louisville: Westminster John Knox, 1996.

Meier, John P. "John the Baptist in Matthew's Gospel." *JBL* 99 (1980): 383–405.

———. *Law and History in Matthew's Gospel: A Redactional Study of Mt. 5:17–48*. AnBib 71. Rome: Biblical Institute Press, 1976.

———. "Love in Q and John: Love of Enemies, Love of One Another." *Mid-Stream* 40 (2001): 42–50.

———. *A Marginal Jew: Rethinking the Historical Jesus*. 4 vols. ABRL. New Haven: Yale University Press, 1991–2009.

Metzger, Bruce M. *A Textual Commentary on the Greek New Testament*. 2nd ed. New York: United Bible Societies, 1994.

Meyer, Marvin. *The Gospel of Thomas: The Hidden Sayings of Jesus*. San Francisco: HarperSanFrancisco, 1992.

Miller, Patrick D. *Deuteronomy*. IBC. Louisville: John Knox, 1990.

———. *The Ten Commandments*. IBC. Louisville: Westminster John Knox, 2000.

Mitchell, Margaret M. *Paul and the Rhetoric of Reconciliation: An Exegetical Investigation of the Language and Composition of 1 Corinthians*. Louisville: Westminster John Knox, 1991.

Mitchell, Matthew W. "In the Footsteps of Paul: Scriptural and Apostolic Authority in Ignatius of Antioch." *JECS* 14 (2006): 27–45.

Mohrlang, Roger. *Matthew and Paul: A Comparison of Ethical Perspectives*. SNTSMS 48. Cambridge: Cambridge University Press, 1984.

Mohrmann, Christine. "Epiphaneia." *RSPT* 37 (1953): 644–70.

Moloney, Francis J. *Beginning the Good News: A Narrative Approach*. Homebush, Austral.: St. Paul Publications, 1992.

———. *The Gospel of Mark: A Commentary*. Peabody, Mass.: Hendrickson, 2002.

Moore, Thomas S. "The Lukan Great Commission and the Isaianic Servant." *BSac* 154 (1997): 47–60.

———. "'To the End of the Earth': The Geographical and Ethnic Universalism of Acts 1:8 in Light of Isaianic Influence on Luke." *JETS* 40 (1997): 389–99.

Moores, John D. *Wrestling with Rationality in Paul: Romans 1–8 in a New Perspective*. Cambridge: Cambridge University Press, 1995.

Moreland, Kjell Arne. *The Rhetoric of Curse in Galatians*. Emory Studies in Early Christianity 5. Atlanta: Scholars Press, 1995.

Mott, Stephen. *Biblical Ethics and Social Change*. New York: Oxford University Press, 2011.

Moulton, James Hope, Wilbert Francis Howard, and Nigel Turner. *A Grammar of New Testament Greek*. 3 vols. Edinburgh: T&T Clark, 1908–1963.

Moyise, Steve. "Intertextuality and the Study of the Old Testament in the New." Pages 14–41 in *The Old Testament in the New: Essays in Honour of J. L. North*. Edited by Steve Moyise. JSNTSup 189. Sheffield: Sheffield Academic Press, 2000.

———, ed. *The Old Testament in the New Testament: Essays in Honour of J. L. North*. JSNTSup 189. Sheffield: Sheffield Academic Press, 2000.

Müller, Beate. *Parody: Dimensions and Perspectives*. Rodopi Perspectives on Modern Literature. Amsterdam: Rodopi, 1997.

Nanos, Mark. *The Irony of Galatians*. Minneapolis: Fortress, 2002.

Neyrey, Jerome H. *Paul, in Other Words: A Cultural Reading of His Letters*. Louisville: Westminster John Knox, 1990.

Nickelsburg, George W. E. *Jewish Literature between the Bible and the Mishnah*. 2nd ed. Minneapolis: Fortress, 2005.

Nicolet-Anderson, V. "Constructing the Self: Thinking with Paul and Michel Foucault." PhD diss., Emory University, 2010.

Nolland, John. *The Gospel of Matthew: A Commentary on the Greek Text*. NIGTC. Grand Rapids: Eerdmans, 2005.

Nordsieck, Reinhard. *Das Thomas-Evangelium*. Neukirchen-Vluyn: Neukirchener, 2004.

O'Toole, Robert F. "How Does Luke Portray Jesus as Servant of YHWH?" *Bib* 81 (2000): 328–46.

Oakes, Peter. "Re-mapping the Universe: Paul and the Emperor in 1 Thessalonians and Philippians." *JSNT* 27 (2005): 301–22.

Oberlinner, Lorenz. "Die 'Epiphaneia' des Heilswillens Gottes in Christus Jesus: Zur Grundstruktur der Christologie der Pastoralbriefe." *ZNW* 71 (1980): 192–213.

Oepke, Albrecht. *Der Brief des Paulus an die Galater*. 3rd ed. THKNT. Berlin: Evangelische Verlagsanstalt, 1973.

Olson, Dennis T. *Deuteronomy and the Death of Moses: A Theological Reading*. OBT. Minneapolis: Fortress, 1994.

Oord, Thomas Jay. *Divine Grace and Emerging Creation: Wesleyan Forays in Science and Theology of Creation*. Eugene, Ore.: Pickwick, 2009.

Orr, Mary. *Intertextuality: Debates and Contexts*. Cambridge: Polity, 2003.

Otto, Randell E. "The Meeting in the Air (1 Thess 4:17)." *HBT* 29 (1997): 192–212.

Palachuvattil, Mathew. *"The One Who Does the Will of the Father": Distinguishing Character of Disciples According to Matthew: An Exegetical Theological Study*. Tesi Gregoriana 154. Rome: Gregorian University Press, 2007.

Pao, David W. *Acts and the Isaianic New Exodus*. Grand Rapids: Baker Academic, 2000.

———. "Gospel within the Constraints of an Epistolary Form: Pauline Introductory Thanksgivings and Paul's Theology of Thanksgiving." Pages 101–28 in *Paul and the Ancient Letter Form*. Edited by Stanley E. Porter and Sean A. Adams. Leiden: Brill, 2010.

Parsons, Mikeal C. "Luke and the *Progymnasmata*: A Preliminary Investigation into the Preliminary Exercises." Pages 43–64 in *Contextualizing Acts: Lukan Narrative and Greco-Roman Discourse*. Edited by Todd C. Penner and Caroline Vander Stichele. SBLSymS 20. Atlanta: Society of Biblical Literature, 2003.

Pax, Elpidius. ΕΠΙΦΑΝΕΙΑ: *Ein religionsgeschichtlicher Beitrag zur biblischen Theologie*. Münchener theologische Studien 1/10. Munich: Zink, 1955.

———. "Epiphanie." *RAC* 5 (1962): 832–909.

Petersen, Norman. *Literary Criticism for New Testament Critics*. Philadelphia: Fortress, 1978.

Peterson, Erik. "Die Einholung des Kyrios." *ZST* 7 (1930): 682–702.

Pfister, Manfred. "Konzepte der Intertextualität." Pages 1–30 in *Intertextualität: Formen, Funktionen, anglistische Fallstudien*. Edited by Ulrich Broich and Manfred Pfister. Tübingen: Max Niemeyer, 1985.

Phillips, Thomas E. *Paul, His Letters, and Acts*. Peabody, Mass.: Hendrickson, 2009.

Pieper, Josef. *The Four Cardinal Virtues*. Translated by Richard Winston, Clara Wintson, Lawrence E. Lynch, and Daniel F. Coogan. South Bend, Ind.: University of Notre Dame Press, 1966.

Pietersma, Albert, and Benjamin G. Wright, eds. *A New English Translation of the Septuagint and the Other Greek Translations Traditionally Included under That Title*. New York: Oxford University Press, 2007.

Placher, William C. *The Domestication of Transcendence: How Modern Thinking about God Went Wrong*. Louisville: Westminster John Knox, 1996.

Pleins, J. David. *The Social Visions of the Hebrew Bible: A Theological Introduction*. Louisville: Westminster John Knox, 2001.

Plevnik, Joseph. "1 Thessalonians 4.17: The Bringing in of the Lord or the Bringing in of the Faithful." *Bib* 80 (1999): 537–46.

Plisch, Uwe-Karsten. *The Gospel of Thomas*. Stuttgart: Deutsche Bibelgesellschaft, 2008.

Pollard, Paul. "The 'Faith of Christ' in Current Discussion." *Concordia Journal* 23 (1997): 213–28.

Popkes, Wiard. *Christus Traditus: Eine Untersuchung zum Begriff der Dahingabe im Neuen Testament.* ATANT 49. Zurich: Zwingli, 1967.

Porter, Stanley E. *Paul in Acts.* Peabody, Mass.: Hendrickson, 2001.

——. "The Use of the Old Testament in the New Testament: A Brief Comment on Method and Terminology." Pages 79–97 in *Early Christian Interpretation of the Scriptures of Israel.* Edited by Stanley E. Porter and James A. Sanders. JSNTSup 148. Sheffield: Sheffield Academic Press, 1997.

Praeder, Susan Marie. "The Problem of First Person Narration in Acts." *NovT* 29 (1987): 193–218.

Pryor, John W. *John: Evangelist of the Covenant People. The Narrative and Themes of the Fourth Gospel.* Downers Grove, Ill.: InterVarsity Press, 1992.

Przbylski, Benno. *Righteousness in Matthew and His World of Thought.* SNTSMS 41. Cambridge: Cambridge University Press, 1980.

Quarles, Charles L. "The Use of the *Gospel of Thomas* in the Research on the Historical Jesus of John Dominic Crossan." *CBQ* 69 (2007): 517–36.

Rakel, Claudia. "'I Will Sing a New Song to My God': Some Remarks on the Intertextuality of Judith 16.1–17." Pages 27–47 in *Judges.* Edited by Athalya Brenner. FCB 2/4. Sheffield: Sheffield Academic Press, 1999.

Rawls, John. *A Theory of Justice.* Cambridge: Harvard University Press, 1971.

Rhoads, David. "Losing Life for Others: Mark's Standard of Judgment." *Int* 47 (1993): 358–69.

Rhoads, David, Joanna Dewey, and Donald Michie. *Mark as Story: An Introduction to the Narrative of a Gospel.* 2nd ed. Minneapolis: Fortress, 1999.

Ridderbos, J. *Deuteronomy.* Translated by Ed M. van der Maas. Grand Rapids: Zondervan, 1984.

Robillard, Valerie. "In Pursuit of Ekphrasis (An Intertextual Approach)." Pages 53–72 in *Pictures into Words: Theoretical and Descriptive Approaches to Ekphrasis.* Edited by Valerie Robillard and Else Jongeneel. Amsterdam: VU University Press, 1998.

Robinson, John A. T. *The Body: A Study in Pauline Theology.* London: SCM, 1952. Repr., Lima, Ohio: Wyndham Hall, 1988.

Robinson, Bernard. "Peter and His Successors: Tradition and Redaction in Matthew 16.17–19." *JSNT* 21 (1984): 85–104.

Rose, Martin. *5. Mose.* ZBK 5. Zürich: Theologischer, 1994.

Rosner, Brian S. *Greed and Idolatry: The Origin and Meaning of a Pauline Metaphor.* Grand Rapids: Eerdmans, 2007.

Rowe, C. Kavin. "The Book of Acts and the Cultural Explication of the Identity of God." Pages 244–66 in *The Word Leaps the Gap: Essays on Scripture and Theology in Honor of Richard B. Hays.* Edited by J. Ross Wagner, C. Kavin Rowe, and A. Katherine Grieb. Grand Rapids: Eerdmans, 2008.

——. *World Upside Down: Reading Acts in the Greco-Roman Age.* Oxford: Oxford University Press, 2009.

Ruiz, Delio. "Se manifestó la gracia salvadora de Dios (Tit 2,11–14)." *RevistB* 65 (2003): 199–214.

Sanders, E. P. *Jesus and Judaism.* Philadelphia: Fortress, 1985.

———. *Paul and Palestinian Judaism: A Comparison of Patterns of Religion*. Philadelphia: Fortress, 1977.

———. *Paul, the Law, and the Jewish People*. Minneapolis: Fortress, 1983.

Sanders, Jack T. *Ethics in the New Testament: Change and Development*. Philadelphia: Fortress, 1975.

Sandmel, Samuel. "Parallelomania." *JBL* 81 (1962): 1–13.

Santos, Narry F. *Slave of All: The Paradox of Authority and Servanthood in the Gospel of Mark*. JSNTSup 237. Sheffield: Sheffield Academic Press, 2003.

Schnelle, Udo. *Apostle Paul: His Life and Theology*. Grand Rapids: Baker, 2003.

Schoedel, William R. *Ignatius of Antioch: A Commentary on the Letters of Ignatius of Antioch*. Hermeneia. Philadelphia: Fortress, 1985.

Schrage, Wolfgang. *Das Verhätnis des Thomas-Evangeliums zur synoptischen Tradition und zu den koptischen Evangelienübersetzungen*. BZNW 29. Berlin: Töpelman, 1964.

Schreiber, Stefan. "Eine neue Jenseitshoffnung in Thessaloniki und ihre Probleme (1 Thess 4, 13–18)." *Bib* 88 (2007): 326–50.

Schulze-Engler, Frank. "Cross-Cultural Criticism and the Limits of Intertextuality." Pages 3–19 in *Across the Lines: Intertextuality and the Transcultural Communication in the New Literatures in English*. Edited by Wolfgang Klooss. Amsterdam: Rodopi, 1998.

Schüssler Fiorenza, Elisabeth. *In Memory of Her: A Feminist Theological Reconstruction of Christian Origins*. New York: Crossroad, 1983.

Schweizer, Eduard. *The Good News according to Matthew*. Translated by David E. Green. London: SPCK, 1976.

Scott, Ian W. "Common Ground? The Role of Galatians 2.16 in Paul's Argument." *NTS* 53 (2007): 425–35.

Segovia, Fernando F. *Love Relationships in the Johannine Tradition: Agapē/Agapan in 1 John and the Fourth Gospel*. SBLDS 58. Chico, Calif.: Scholars Press, 1982.

Seifrid, Mark A. "Blind Alleys in the Controversy over the Paul of History." *TynBul* 45 (1994): 73–95.

Senior, Donald. "The Death of Jesus and the Resurrection of the Holy Ones (Matthew 27:51–53)." *CBQ* 38 (1976): 312–29.

———. *Matthew*. ANTC. Nashville: Abingdon, 1998.

Shepherd, William H., Jr. *The Narrative Function of the Holy Spirit as a Character in Luke–Acts*. SBLDS 147. Atlanta: Scholars Press, 1994.

Sicker, Martin. *The Idea of Justice in Judaism*. Lincoln, Nebr.: iUniverse, 2006.

Sim, David C. *Apocalyptic Eschatology in the Gospel of Matthew*. SNTSMS 88. Cambridge: Cambridge University Press, 1996.

———. "Christianity and Ethnicity in the Gospel of Matthew." Pages 171–95 in *Ethnicity and the Bible*. Edited by Mark G. Brett. Leiden: Brill, 1996.

———. *The Gospel of Matthew and Christian Judaism: The History and Social Setting of the Matthean Community*. SNTIW. Edinburgh: T&T Clark, 1998.

———. "Matthew 7.21–23: Further Evidence of its Anti-Pauline Perspective." *NTS* 53 (2007): 325–43.

———. "Matthew and the Pauline Corpus: A Preliminary Intertextual Study." *JSNT* 31.4 (2009): 401–22.

———. "Matthew, Paul and the Origin and Nature of the Gentile Mission: The Great Commission in Matthew 28:16–20 as an Anti-Pauline Tradition." *HvTSt* 64 (2008): 377–92.

———. "Matthew's Anti-Paulinism: A Neglected Feature of Matthean Studies." *HvTSt* 58 (2002): 767–83.

Smith, Jonathan Z. *Drudgery Divine: On the Comparison of Early Christianities and the Religions of Late Antiquity*. Chicago Studies in the History of Judaism. Chicago: University of Chicago Press, 1990.

Smith, Justin Marc. "About Friends, by Friends, for Others: Author–Subject Relationships in Contemporary Greco–Roman Biographies." Pages 49–67 in *The Audience of the Gosepls: The Origin and Function of the Gospels in Early Christianity*. Edited by Edward W. Klink III. LNTS 353. London: T&T Clark, 2009.

Smith, Mark S. *The Origins of Biblical Monotheism: Israel's Polytheistic Background and the Ugaritic Texts*. Oxford: Oxford University Press, 2001.

Snodgrass, Klyne R. *The Parable of the Wicked Tenants: An Inquiry into Parable Interpretation*. WUNT 27. Tübingen: Mohr Siebeck, 1983.

———. *Stories with Intent*. Grand Rapids: Eerdmans, 2008.

Soards, Marion L. *The Speeches in Acts: Their Content, Context, and Concerns*. Louisville: Westminster John Knox, 1994.

Splett, Jorg. "Symbol." Pages 1654–57 in *Encyclopedia of Theology: The Concise Sacramentum Mundi*. Edited by Karl Rahner. New York: Seabury, 1975.

Stanley, Christopher D. *Paul and the Language of Scripture: Citation Technique in the Pauline Epistles and Contemporary Literature*. SNTSMS 69. Cambridge: Cambridge University Press, 1992.

———. " 'Under a Curse': A Fresh Reading of Galatians 3.10–14." *NTS* 36 (1990): 481–511.

Stanton, Graham. *A Gospel for a New People: Studies in Matthew*. Louisville: Westminster John Knox 1993.

Sternberg, Robert J. *Cognitive Psychology*. Belmont, Calif.: Wadsworth, 2009.

Stettler, Hanna. *Die Christologie der Pastoralbriefe*. WUNT 2/105. Tübingen: Mohr Siebeck, 1998.

Stewart, Roy. "The Parable Form in the Old Testament and the Rabbinic Literature." *EvQ* 36 (1964): 133–47.

Still, Todd D., ed. *Jesus and Paul Reconnected: Fresh Pathways into an Old Debate*. Grand Rapids: Eerdmans, 2007.

Strauss, Mark L. *The Davidic Messiah in Luke–Acts: The Promise and its Fulfillment in Lukan Christology*. JSNTSup 110. Sheffield: Sheffield Academic Press, 1995.

Strecker, Georg. *The Sermon on the Mount: An Exegetical Commentary*. Translated by O. C. Dean, Jr. Edinburgh: T&T Clark, 1988.

———. *Der Weg der Gerechtigkeit*. 3rd ed. Göttingen: Vandenhoeck & Ruprecht, 1971.

Stuhlmacher, Peter. *Vorgeschichte*. Vol. 1 of *Das paulinisch Evangelium*. FRLANT 95. Göttingen: Vandenhoeck & Ruprecht, 1968.

———. *Paul's Letter to the Romans: A Commentary*. Translated by Scott J. Hafemann. Louisville: John Knox, 1994.

Talbert, Charles H. "Paul, Judaism, and the Revisionists." *CBQ* 63 (2001): 1–22.

Tatum, Gregory. *New Chapters in the Life of Paul: The Relative Chronology of His Career*. CBQMS 41. Washington, D.C.: Catholic Biblical Association of America, 2006.

Thaden, Robert H. von. "The Wisdom of Fleeing *Porneia*: Conceptual Blending in 1 Corinthians 6:12–7:7." PhD diss., Emory University, 2007.

Theissen, Gerd. "Social Integration and Sacramental Activity: An Analysis of 1 Cor 11:17–34." Pages 145–74 in *The Social Setting of Pauline Christianity*. Philadelphia: Fortress, 1982.

Thielman, Frank. *Paul and the Law*. Downers Grove, Ill.: InterVarsity Press, 1994.

Thiselton, Anthony C. *The First Epistle to the Corinthians*. NIGTC. Grand Rapids: Eerdmans, 2000.

———. "The Meaning of σάρξ in 1 Cor 5:5: A Fresh Approach in the Light of Logical and Semantic Factors." *SJT* 26 (1973): 204–28.

Thompson, Michael. *Clothed with Christ: The Example and Teaching of Jesus in Romans 12.1–15:13*. JSNTSup 59. Sheffield: JSOT Press, 1991.

Tiede, David L. *Prophecy and History in Luke–Acts*. Philadelphia: Fortress, 1980.

Tolbert, Mary Ann. *Sowing the Gospel: Mark's World in Literary-Historical Perspective*. Minneapolis: Fortress, 1989.

Trilling, Wolfgang. *Das Wahre Israel. Studien zur Theologie des Matthäus-Evangelium*. 3rd ed. Munich: Kösel, 1964.

Tull, Patricia. "Intertextuality and the Hebrew Scriptures." *CurBS* 8 (2000): 59–90.

Upsensky, Boris. *A Poetics of Composition: The Structure of the Artistic Text and Typology of a Compositional Form*. Berkeley: University of California Press, 1973.

Van Houtan, Kyle S., and Michael S. Northcott, eds. *Diversity and Dominion: Dialogues in Ecology, Ethics, and Theology*. Eugene, Ore.: Wipf & Stock, 2010.

Van Houwelingen, P. H. R. "The Great Reunion: The Meaning and Significance of the 'Word of the Lord' in1 Thessalonians 4:13–18." *CTJ* 42 (2007): 308–24.

Verhey, Allen. *Remembering Jesus: Christian Community, Scripture and the Moral Life*. Grand Rapids: Eerdmans, 2002.

Vielhauer, Phillip. "On the 'Paulinism' of Acts." Translated by Wm. C. Robinson Jr. and Victor Paul Furnish. Pages 33–50 in *Studies in Luke–Acts: Essays Presented in Honor of Paul Schubert*. Edited by Leander E. Keck and J. Louis Martyn. Nashville: Abingdon, 1966.

Villepigue, James, and Hugo Rivera. *The Body Sculpting Bible for Women: The Way to Physical Perfection*. Rev. ed. Lima, Ohio: Hatherleigh, 2006.

Vouga, François. *An die Galater*. HNT 10. Tübingen: Mohr Siebeck, 1998.

Wakefield, Andrew H. *Where to Live: The Hermeneutical Significance of Paul's Citations from Scripture in Galatians 3:1–14*. AcBib 14. Atlanta: Society of Biblical Literature, 2003.

Wallace, Daniel B. *Greek Grammar beyond the Basics: An Exegetical Syntax of the New Testament*. Grand Rapids: Zondervan, 1996.

Wallis, Gerhard. "Der Vollbürgereid in Deuteronomium 27, 15–26." *HUCA* 45 (1974): 47–63.

Wanamaker, Charles A. "Apocalyptic Discourse, Paraenesis and Identity Maintenance in 1 Thessalonians." *Neot* 36 (2002): 131–44.

Ward, Roy Bowen. "Paul and Musonius on Marriage." *NTS* 36 (1990): 281–89.

Ware, James P. *Paul and the Mission of the Church: Philippians in Ancient Jewish Context.* Grand Rapids: Baker Academic, 2011Waters, Guy. *The End of Deuteronomy in the Epistles of Paul.* WUNT 2/221. Tübingen: Mohr Siebeck, 2006.

Watson, David. *Honor Among Christians: The Cultural Key to the Messianic Secret.* Minneapolis: Fortress, 2010.

Watson, Duane. F. "Paul's Appropriation of Apocalyptic Discourse: The Rhetorical Strategy of 1 Thessalonians." Pages 61–80 in *Vision and Persuasion: Rhetorical Dimensions of Apocalyptic Discourse.* Edited by Greg Carey and L. Gregory Bloomquist. St. Louis: Chalice, 1999.

Weima, Jeffrey A. D. "Gal. 6:11–18: A Hermeneutical Key to the Galatian Letter." *CTJ* 28 (1993): 90–107.

Weinfeld, Moshe. *Social Justice in Ancient Israel and in the Ancient Near East.* Minneapolis: Fortress, 1985.

Weissenrieder, Annette, and Robert B. Coote, eds. *The Interface of Orality and Writing: Speaking, Seeing, Writing in the Shaping of New Genres.* Tübingen: Mohr Siebeck, 2010.

Wengst, Klaus. *Christologische Formeln und Lieder des Urchristentums.* SNT 7. Gütersloh: Mohn, 1972.

Wenham, David. *Paul: Follower of Jesus or Founder of Christianity?* Grand Rapids: Eerdmans, 1995.

Whybray, R. Norman. *Introduction to the Pentateuch.* Grand Rapids: Eerdmans, 1995.

Wibbing, Siegfried. *Die Tugend- und Lasterkataloge im Neuen Testament: Und ihre Traditionsgeschichte unter besonderer Berücksichtigung der Qumran-Texte.* BZNW 25. Berlin: Töpelmann, 1959.

Wikenhauser, Alfred. *Pauline Mysticism: Christ in the Mystical Teaching of Saint Paul.* Freiburg: Herder, 1960.

Willitts, Joel. "Paul and Matthew: A Descriptive Approach from a Post-New Perspective Interpretive Framework." Pages 62–85 in *Paul and the Gospels: Christologies, Conflicts and Convergences.* Edited by Michael F. Bird and Joel Willitts. LNTS 411. London: T&T Clark, 2011.

Windisch, Hans. "Zur Christologie der Pastoralbriefe." *ZNW* 34 (1935): 213–38.

Wolde, Ellen van. "Trendy Intertextuality?" Pages 43–49 in *Intertextuality in Biblical Writings: Essays in Honour of Bas van Iersel.* Edited by Sipke Draisma. Kampen: Kok, 1989.

Wright, A. G. "The Widow's Mites: Praise or Lament." *CBQ* 44 (1982): 256–65.

Wright, N. T. *The Climax of the Covenant: Christ and the Law in Pauline Theology.* Minneapolis: Fortress, 1991.

———. *Justification: God's Plan and Paul's Vision.* Downers Grove, Ill.: InterVarsity Press, 2009.

Wüthrich, Serge. "Naître de mourir: la mort de Jésus dans l'Évangile de Matthieu (Mt 27.51–56)." *NTS* 56 (2010): 313–25.

Yarbrough, O. Larry. *Not like the Gentiles: Marriage Rules in the Letters of Paul.* SBLDS 80. Atlanta: Scholars Press, 1985.

Yinger, Kent L. *Paul, Judaism, and Judgment According to Deeds.* SNTSMS 105. Cambridge: Cambridge University Press, 1999.

Young, Norman H. "Who's Cursed—and Why? (Galatians 3:10–14)." *JBL* 117 (1988): 79–92.

Ziegler, Joseph, ed. *Isaias.* Vol. 14 of *Septuaginta: Vetus Testamentum Graecum, Auctoritate Academiae Scientiarum Gottingensis editum.* 3rd ed. Göttingen: Vandenhoeck & Ruprecht, 1983.

CONTRIBUTORS

Paul J. Achtemeier (ThD, Union Theological Seminary, New York) is the Herbert Worth and Anne H. Jackson Professor Emeritus of Biblical Interpretation at Union Theological Seminary in Richmond, Virginia (now Union Presbyterian Seminary). He is the author or coauthor of fourteen books, including major commentaries on Romans (Interpretation, 1985) and 1 Peter (Hermeneia, 1996). He is also former editor of the quarterly journal *Interpretation* and the New Testament editor of the series Interpretation: A Bible Commentary for Teaching and Preaching. Professor Achtemeier has also served as president of both the Society of Biblical Literature and the Catholic Biblical Association of America.

Sherri Brown is Assistant Professor of Religious Studies at Niagara University outside Niagara Falls, New York. She earned her PhD in Biblical Studies from The Catholic University of America in 2008. Her doctoral research on the Gospel of John was later published as a monograph entitled *Gift upon Gift: Covenant through Word in the Gospel of John* (Pickwick, 2010). She has since contributed to several compendia on the literary characteristics of the Fourth Gospel, and her future research will continue to focus primarily on the Johannine literature and other biblical narratives, with a special interest in the literary fabric of the story of God's covenant with Israel therein. In this volume she returns to her early research and publication areas in the letters and theology of the apostle Paul.

Raymond F. Collins (STD, Katholieke Universiteit Leuven) is currently a visiting scholar in the Department of Religious Studies at Brown University. In 2006 he retired from The Catholic University of America, where he served as dean of the School of Religious Studies (1993–1999) and as professor of New Testament (1993–2006). Prior to his appointment to Catholic University, he had been a member of the faculty of theology at the Katholieke Universiteit Leuven (1970–1993), where he was chair of the

Programs in English, long-time editor of *Louvain Studies*, and rector of the American College (1971–1978). He is the author of several books on the New Testament including an *Introduction to the New Testament* (Doubleday, 1983) and major commentaries on *First Corinthians* (Sacra Pagina, 1999), *1 and 2 Timothy and Titus* (New Testament Library, 2002), and *Second Corinthians* (Paideia, 2012). He currently serves as associate editor of the *Catholic Biblical Quarterly* and has contributed to *The Encyclopedia of Religion, New Jerome Biblical Commentary, Encyclopedia of Catholicism, Anchor Bible Dictionary*, and *New Interpreter's Dictionary of the Bible*.

A. Andrew Das is the Donald W. and Betty J. Buik Professor at Elmhurst College in Elmhurst, Illinois. He has written a number of scholarly monographs, including *Solving the Romans Debate* (Fortress, 2007), *Paul and the Jews* (Hendrickson, 2003), and *Paul, the Law, and the Covenant* (Hendrickson, 2001). His articles have appeared in the *Journal of Biblical Literature, Journal for the Study of the New Testament, New Testament Studies*, and *Catholic Biblical Quarterly*, as well as in edited volumes. He is currently under contract to complete a major academic commentary on Paul's Letter to the Galatians (forthcoming, 2014) and is also working on the Pauline texts on women's leadership. He is a member of numerous learned societies, including the Society of Biblical Literature, the Catholic Biblical Association of America, the Evangelical Theological Society, and the prestigious international Studiorum Novi Testamenti Societas. He is a graduate of Yale University and received his PhD at Union Theological Seminary in Virginia (1999).

John R. Donahue, S.J., received his PhD in New Testament from the University of Chicago (1972) and has taught at Vanderbilt University (1973–1980), the Jesuit School of Theology in Berkeley, California (1980–2001), and at St. Mary's University and Seminary, Baltimore (2001–2004), where he is the Raymond E. Brown Distinguished Professor of New Testament Studies (Emeritus). His numerous publications include *Life in Abundance: Studies of John's Gospel in Tribute to Raymond E. Brown* (Liturgical Press, 2005); the Sacra Pagina commentary, *The Gospel of Mark* (with Daniel J. Harrington; Liturgical Press, 2002), and *The Gospel in Parable: Metaphor, Narrative and Theology in the Synoptic Gospels* (Fortress, 1988). He is currently preparing a volume on resources and reflections on the use of the Bible for issues of social justice. Presently he is in residence at Loyola University, Maryland.

Francis T. Gignac, S.J., is Ordinary Professor and Area Director of Biblical Studies in the School of Theology and Religious Studies at The Catholic University of America, where he has taught since 1974. He has also served on the faculty of Loyola University (Chicago) and Fordham University. Professor Gignac was awarded the PhD from Oxford University (UK) in 1964 with a dissertation entitled, "The Language of the Post-Christian Greek Papyri: Phonology and Accidence." Specializing in Biblical Greek, the language of the nonliterary papyri, and issues of bilingual interference in New Testament Greek, Fr. Gignac has published a number of scholarly articles and monographs, including two volumes of a projected three-volume work, *A Grammar of the Greek Papyri of the Roman and Byzantine Periods* (Instituto Editoriale Cisalpino, 1976, 1981). He is currently preparing the third volume of his grammar.

Michael J. Gorman holds the Raymond E. Brown Chair in Biblical Studies and Theology at St. Mary's Seminary & University in Baltimore, where he has taught since 1991, and where he was dean of the Ecumenical Institute of Theology for eighteen years. He earned his PhD in 1989 from Princeton Theological Seminary. His books include *Cruciformity: Paul's Narrative Spirituality of the Cross* (Eerdmans, 2001); *Apostle of the Crucified Lord: A Theological Introduction to Paul and His Letters* (Eerdmans, 2004); *Reading Paul* (Cascade, 2008); *Inhabiting the Cruciform God: Kenosis, Justification, and Theosis in Paul's Narrative Soteriology* (Eerdmans, 2009); *Reading Revelation Responsibly* (Cascade, 2011); and two books on Christian ethics. His current projects include a book on Paul, participation, and mission, and a commentary on 2 Corinthians. He is an active member of the Society of Biblical Literature, for which he chairs the steering committee of the Theological Interpretation of Scripture unit, and he is on the editorial board of *Interpretation* and of the *Journal for the Study of Paul and His Letters.*

Kelly R. Iverson received his PhD from The Catholic University of America (Washington, D.C.) and is Associate Professor of New Testament at Baylor University in Waco, Texas. His research interests include Jesus and the Gospels (especially Mark and Matthew), ancient media, performance criticism, and the Catholic Epistles. His articles have appeared in the *Journal of Biblical Literature, Catholic Biblical Quarterly*, and *Biblical Interpretation*. He is the author of *Gentiles in the Gospel of Mark: "Even the Dogs under the Table Eat the Children's Crumbs"* (T&T Clark, 2007), and the coeditor of *Mark as Story: Retrospect and Prospect* (Society of Biblical Literature, 2011).

Luke Timothy Johnson (PhD, Yale University) is the R. W. Woodruff Professor of New Testament and Christian Origins at Candler School of Theology and a Senior Fellow at the Center for the Study of Law and Religion at Emory University. His research interests include the literary, moral, and religious dimensions of the New Testament, especially the Jewish and Greco-Roman contexts of early Christianity, Luke–Acts, the Pastoral Letters, and the Letter of James. A prolific author, Professor Johnson has authored numerous scholarly articles and more than twenty-five books. His 1986 book, *The Writings of the New Testament: An Interpretation*, now in its third edition, is widely used in seminaries and departments of religion throughout the world.

Jack Dean Kingsbury (PhD, University of Basel) is the Aubrey Lee Brooks Professor Emeritus of Biblical Theology, Union Theological Seminary in Virginia (now Union Presbyterian Seminary). Specializing in the Synoptics Gospels and literary criticism, Professor Kingsbury is the author of numerous articles and scholarly monographs including *The Christology of Mark's Gospel* (Fortress, 1983), *Matthew as Story* (Fortress, 1986), *Conflict in Mark: Jesus, Authorities, Disciples* (Fortress, 1989), and *Conflict in Luke: Jesus, Authorities, Disciples* (Fortress, 1991).

William S. Kurz, S.J. (PhD, Yale University), is Professor of New Testament at Marquette University in Milwaukee, Wisconsin. He specializes in Luke–Acts, Johannine writings, narrative and rhetorical criticism, biblical intertextuality, and theological interpretation. During his 2004–2005 sabbatical he studied patristic writers for how to interpret Scripture theologically as God's Word. This led to his seventh book, *Reading the Bible as God's Own Story: A Catholic Approach for Bringing Scripture to Life* (Word among Us Press, 2007). The manuscript of his theological commentary on Acts (Catholic Commentary on Sacred Scripture) is being edited for 2012 publication by Baker Academic. His 2009 Marquette Wade Chair Lecture was keynote for Marquette's Scripture Project's interdisciplinary symposium on theological interpretation of Scripture: "Jesus and His Spirit-Filled Disciples, Especially Paul, as the Isaian Servant of the Lord in Acts." He is the author of over forty scholarly articles in professional journals and books. The most recent of his six previous books include *Reading*

Luke–Acts: Dynamics of Biblical Narrative (Westminster John Knox, 1993); *The Future of Catholic Biblical Scholarship: A Constructive Conversation* (coauthor with Luke Timothy Johnson; Eerdmans, 2002); and *What Does the Bible Say about the End Times? A Catholic View* (Servant Books, 2004; first place award in Scripture by Catholic Press Association in 2005, translated into Polish in 2007).

John P. Meier holds the William K. Warren Foundation Chair in the Department of Theology at the University of Notre Dame in South Bend, Indiana. He received his Doctorate in Sacred Scripture at the Pontifical Biblical Institute in Rome, summa cum laude, with the papal gold medal awarded. His doctoral dissertation, *Law and History in Matthew's Gospel*, was published in the Analecta biblica series (1976). He is the author of over sixty articles in various learned journals. His subsequent books include *The Vision of Matthew* (Crossroad, 1991); the New Testament Message series commentary on Matthew (Liturgical Press, 1980); and with Raymond E. Brown, *Antioch and Rome* (Paulist Press, 1983). His major work is a five-volume series on the historical Jesus, *A Marginal Jew: Rethinking the Historical Jesus* (Doubleday, 1999–2009). Four volumes have been published; the fifth is in preparation.

Francis J. Moloney, S.D.B., was awarded a PhD at Oxford University (UK) in 1976 for his study of the use of the expression "the Son of Man" in the Gospel of John. He is currently a Senior Professorial Fellow at Australian Catholic University (Melbourne, Australia), and Emeritus Professor at The Catholic University of America, Washington, D.C., and Australian Catholic University. He holds honorary doctorates from St Mary's University and Seminary, Baltimore, and Australian Catholic University. For six years he was the Provincial Superior of the Salesians of Don Bosco in Australia and the Pacific. He is the author of many books and articles, most significantly his commentaries on the Gospel of John (Sacra Pagina, 1998) and the Gospel of Mark (Hendrickson, 2003). A collection of his major essays on the Gospel of John was published in 2005 (*The Gospel of John: Text and Context* [Brill, 2005]) and the second edition of his dissertation, *Johannine Son of Man*, was reprinted in 2007 (Wipf & Stock). His current interests are the development of synchronic readings of gospel narratives, the theological nature of early Christian literature, and the Gospel of Matthew.

Christopher W. Skinner (PhD, The Catholic University of America) is Assistant Professor of Religion at Mount Olive College in North Carolina. His primary areas of scholarly interest are narrative hermeneutics, the canonical Gospels (especially John and Mark), the Gospel of Thomas, and ancient media studies. He has published numerous articles in books and scholarly journals, and is the author of *John and Thomas: Gospels in Conflict?* (Wipf & Stock, 2009), *What Are They Saying about the Gospel of Thomas?* (Paulist Press, 2012), and along with Kelly R. Iverson, coeditor of *Mark as Story: Retrospect and Prospect* (Society of Biblical Literature, 2011). He is currently editing a volume on characterization in the Fourth Gospel (T&T Clark, forthcoming 2012) and writing an undergraduate-level textbook entitled *Reading John* (Cascade, forthcoming 2013).

Matthew G. Whitlock (PhD, The Catholic University of America) is Assistant Professor of New Testament at Seattle University. He wrote both his doctoral dissertation ("Unity in Conflict: A Study of Acts 4:23–31," 2008) and his master's thesis ("God as a Character in the Acts of the Apostles: A Study of Acts 5:17–39," 2005) under the direction of Frank Matera. His current research involves reading Luke-Acts with an eye on its aesthetic value, especially concerning its poetic tensions. He is also researching the character of Paul in the Acts of the Apostles and the historical Paul of the letters in light of modern literary theory and philosophy.

AUTHOR INDEX

CPSIA information can be obtained at www.ICGtesting.com
Printed in the USA
LVOW060257280712

291929LV00002B/32/P